The Trad Wife

Carrie Hughes lives in West Sussex, where she is a copywriter and guest lecturer in creative writing. She can often be found dreaming up stories, communing with dogs and visiting the dark side. She loves creating female characters who are stronger than they appear and forcing them into difficult situations.

Also by Carrie Hughes

The Woman From Bookclub
The Trad Wife

THE TRAD WIFE

CARRIE HUGHES

canelo
HERA

First published in the United Kingdom in 2026 by

Hera Books, an imprint of
Canelo Digital Publishing Limited,
20 Vauxhall Bridge Road,
London SW1V 2SA
United Kingdom

A Penguin Random House Company
The authorised representative in the EEA is Dorling Kindersley Verlag GmbH.
Arnulfstr. 124, 80636 Munich, Germany

Copyright © Carrie Hughes 2026

The moral right of Carrie Hughes to be identified as the creator of this work has been asserted in accordance with the Copyright, Designs and Patents Act, 1988.
All rights reserved. No part of this publication may be reproduced or transmitted in any form or by any means, electronic or mechanical, including photocopy, recording, or any information storage and retrieval system, without permission in writing from the publisher.
No part of this book may be used or reproduced in any manner for the purpose of training artificial intelligence technologies or systems. In accordance with Article 4(3) of the DSM Directive 2019/790, Canelo expressly reserves this work from the text and data mining exception.

A CIP catalogue record for this book is available from the British Library.

ISBN 9 781 83598 354 6

This book is a work of fiction. Names, characters, businesses, organizations, places and events are either the product of the author's imagination or are used fictitiously. Any resemblance to actual persons, living or dead, events or locales is entirely coincidental.

Cover design by Head Design

Cover images © Shutterstock.com

Printed and bound in Great Britain by Clays Ltd, Elcograf S.p.A.

Look for more great books at
www.herabooks.com | www.dk.com

For Claudia Cavanagh

with love

Prologue

I'm locked in the cellar of a trad wife, and I am mad as hell. This was my scoop, but I've become the twist in someone else's true crime podcast. When I came round just now, I was lying crooked and splayed like a body at a crime scene. It *is* a crime scene, if only the police would show up. Welcome to my TED Talk on why I should have trusted my instincts.

My head's pulsating like crazy. My fingers find an egg-shaped lump, and pain screams inside my skull. When it settles back to a throb, I gingerly push myself up, rubbing away the grit coating my parched lips. I am so screwed.

Faith Eversen has a lot to answer for. Faith, the hashtag wholesome influencer, loved for her authenticity and vintage charm. *It's quite the turnaround, Faith. Like when a puppy turns into an axe murderer. Cheers for the peek behind the scenes though, even if it's gloomy. Can I suggest some mood lighting?* Sounds like I have a screw loose. Maybe I do. I don't know any more.

Can't see a bloody thing. I haul my protesting body to standing and my knees give out. I stumble and crash against the wall like a drunk. My head spins and dizziness hits, then I wince at a sharp pain in my ribs. Are they cracked? I don't touch my ribcage in case I make it worse. My heart's going too fast, but once I've steadied myself, I shuffle along the wall until I reach the door and try the handle. It's locked. If only I could channel my red-hot fury and blast my way out of here. Just need my strength back first.

'Hello?' I call out in a raspy voice. I place both palms on the door. 'Let me out!' The words scratch my throat and reverberate through my skull. This can't be happening. I have to find Willow. A tremor in my chest sends shock waves through my body at what they'll do to her.

She's ours now. The parting threat is a knife to my heart. The words echo in my head along with a pounding in my ears. I try to swallow the lump in my throat, but it stays put. I'd die for her, but that would play into their hands, and her own nightmare would only just begin.

'Willow?' I croak, my throat dried out. I push away the dread, but my chest seizes up and my world collapses. This is the worst day of my life. What if it's my last?

Chapter One

Ten weeks earlier

Faith's latest video has dropped. She appears on-screen in her beautifully rustic kitchen. You could fit my entire cramped apartment inside that kitchen. Twice. 'Today, I'm making raspberry preserve. My children love it on fresh baked bread.' The soft cadence of her voice calms me.

Her peachy skin is make-up free. Her golden hair tumbles down in loose Pre-Raphaelite ringlets. I bet it smells of fresh apples. I glance out of my small kitchen window at pink sky above the high-rises. Morning traffic builds outside our apartment, and Willow sleeps while I make her school lunch. Faith scoops something into a copper jug.

'You pour the wheat berries into the grinder to mill the wheat.' She gives us a shy smile. 'It's easy.' She nods encouragement. Faith bakes her own bread. Of course she does. I've never heard of wheat berries, but I can make Willow's lunch sarnie in under a minute. Faith spends that time manually grinding wheat. She turns the metal lever in big circles and says it's a great upper-body workout.

I check a message on my phone and go to the fridge. By the time I return, the dough has risen and she's scoring the top with a lavender sprig design. I snicker. As if hungry kids care about bread artistry. I'd think it a wind-up if I hadn't seen her other reels and videos, but she lacks the arch eye contact with the camera, tongue firmly in cheek at the lunacy of a mother of six decorating their daily bread.

Faith slides the baked loaf from the Aga, and in a final touch, she adds daisy flower heads and a lavender sprig from her own lavender fields.

'Mmm.' She inhales. 'The aroma's so calming.'

This is no ordinary sandwich. This is a trad wife sandwich. Hard to believe that some women choose to live like this. It's part of my fascination. I eye my own sandwich effort with shame. I thought I was making a nutritious lunch that Willow would like to eat, but in the trad wife universe, store-bought is the devil's work.

A little girl wanders into shot wearing a sweet cotton smock that could be home-made or could have cost a fortune. She wants to help. Faith's forever composed, never losing her shit even though she's knee-deep in kids. She's like a Victoria's Secret model dressed as a pioneer from the nineteenth century. She's stepped back in time, wearing a blue chambray dress and white cotton apron, evoking a rose-tinted yesteryear. Her content isn't relatable, but it's oddly compelling. It's her niche and she's the best in the business.

Faith stands apart from the crop of super-successful mumfluencers who are overdone in a high-maintenance way. Just the word 'mumfluencer' makes me shudder. I don't want a plastic woman 'influencing' me. Most online trad wives have a manic mum energy, desperately seeking MumTok gold, mining everything for content. But Faith's life is a soothing art form.

It's like dropping in on a friend for a cup of wheat berries – ha! I kid – and then you chat while she knocks out a batch of scones. Lavender-themed scones in her case, since she often tends to her lavender farm in a soft-focus way. She talks to camera like she's FaceTiming you while whisking, chopping and stirring, with an occasional smile or inquisitive look to check you're following along. She always starts by propping up her phone to film herself in whatever insane homespun activity is on the agenda. But I know different. You don't get videos that slick from an amateur effort. She's smart, a marketer's dream, and she's reaping the rewards.

While other influencers peddle their lifestyle with fake smiles, Faith simply shows us her life as if it's perfectly normal, like a mum of six young children would grind her own wheat. *Oh, you're hangry? Would you like a cookie? Hang on, screaming toddler, while I harvest the wheat crop.*

I admire her fortitude as I wonder why she does it. Seriously, why make life difficult for yourself? Her lifestyle is both nuts and aspirational with a nostalgic allure. That potent mix is behind her standout quality.

Faith is queen of the trad wives in a peach of a role. Her videos cast a spell, but I'm a sceptic who's familiar with high-performing influencers. I've even worked with a few. She floats above the trad wife trend, and the fandom loves her. It's not just the gorgeous content, it's her air of mystery. I'm endlessly speculating on her life beyond the screen.

I slap a slice of white bread on top of the cheese and ham and cut the sandwich in quarters. A quick scan of the bread ingredients shows an abundance of additives and weird stuff, but least her lunch isn't from a vending machine. My gaze returns to Faith, a picture of contentment as she slices the loaf through the middle and adds home-made raspberry jam like it's a Victoria sponge.

Faith's riding the backlash from the girl-boss era. Millennials like me bought into a myth, but no matter how hard we work, a decent rental in the city is a distant, unrealistic dream. I do my job at full tilt, then outside of work I rush through everything else. The only thing standing still is my bank balance. As I grab a handful of cherry tomatoes, red grapes and a mini muffin for Willow's lunchbox, my eyes scan over the comments.

> Beautiful!
>
> You slay!
>
> This is insane… she grinds her own wheat? Has she literally not heard of store-bought?
>
> Apparently breadfluencing is a thing.
>
> I love this so much! You truly are an inspiration.
>
> That designer dress is like 750 bucks.
>
> I bet she hasn't had store-bought bread since she got married.
>
> Trad wives are brainwashed by alt-right men. F**k the patriarchy.
>
> God bless you, Faith! You and your family are so beautiful!!!
>
> Shit like this puts the women's movement back 200 years.

I smile at 'You slay!' since olde-worlde Faith might not know that's a compliment.

Time to wake Willow. I pause the time-warp video and so begins the daily rush to get her to school and me to the creative agency on time.

Half an hour later, we crash out of the apartment just as Beverley next door is inching through her front door past a towering stack of magazines, a bag of rubbish in her hand.

'Morning!' I call. 'Shall I take your trash?' I reach out a hand for it. Willow crouches to pet Germaine, who hobbles out, her fang-like lower teeth always on display.

'Oh, thank you, Melissa,' Beverley croons in her husky voice. She's wearing her dark magenta wig and oversized glasses.

'Can we take Germaine to the park on Saturday?' Willow asks.

'Please do. You two are my angels. You have a great day.' She blows Willow a kiss.

'You have a great day too.' Willow beams and bounces off down the stairs while I dispose of the rubbish down the trash chute. Out on the street, a car horn blasts. 'Dog poop!' she calls out cheerily, dodging it on the pavement. I'm English born and bred, while my child is a native New Yorker. Her accent is softer than if we were in the Bronx or Queens, but her speech is rapid-fire with British words like 'telly' thrown in. She calls me 'Mom' which sounds like 'Mawm' in her sweet little voice.

I take her hand, and we race to the bus stop. It's not called the school run for nothing. Faith's daughter from the video is a similar age. She's always in a prairie dress, wavy hair flying out behind her when she runs free across lavender fields. I marvel over the vast difference in their lives. No TV or devices for Faith's six kids, and no picky little eaters. They enjoy home-cooked meals and roam around the ranch. Seeing their connected family life, I wonder how to improve things for Willow and me.

Chapter Two

On the bus to Willow's school, she taps the window as we pass a woman wheeling a pushchair with an older girl skipping alongside. 'Can I have a brother or sister?'

She finds our dark little apartment lonely, but no, she's not having a brother or sister. Faith's six children are so close in age that they play together and look out for each other, a self-sufficient, happy gang. Willow and I keep occupied outside as much as our budget and the weather allows, hanging out in the play park where she'll befriend random kids. She stays close to me, while I make mental notes on podcast ideas and plan them in my mind. We sometimes do a teddy bears' picnic in Central Park with mum friends.

We can't afford Broadway shows, but on the last stormy Sunday, we acted out the entire *Lion King*, singing all the songs with toys as supporting cast. Another time, we lay a kilim throw on the floor and sat cross-legged, swaying and singing our hearts out to 'A Whole New World' while our magic carpet flew us to Arabia. We do a decent job of harmonising. Then Willow was content to sprawl out and play with her toys, after murmuring that I'm 'the best momma'.

'You're the best girl,' I said, kissing her hair. I might not make lavender soap, and we're a little too fond of $3 hot dogs from Billy's Hot Dog stand, and don't get me started on all the ice cream Willow eats, but I try to be a good mum in my own way.

After drop-off, I race back in the opposite direction and squeeze on to a downtown train. Today is my office day, but I work from home three days a week so I can rush out and pick her up in the afternoon without looks from my child-free colleagues. Crammed on the train, I slip in my AirPods and zone out fellow commuters who are too close for comfort. I watch another of Faith's videos. It's not cyberstalking. It's research. For my job. Kind of.

I'm a seasoned content creator, but Faith's reels invoke a rare sense of wonder. I don't just watch her output, I *study* it. Success leaves clues. In my work, I decode virality, getting to the heart of what makes an online video achieve millions of views. I analyse viral trends and study performance drivers like pace and hooks. She uses no tricks of the trade, her simple lifestyle is mesmerising enough. She's an anomaly. I suspect it's a ruse, which fascinates me even more.

There's Faith, milking the cow against a backdrop of mountains. Then she comes indoors to check her sourdough rolls have risen enough for her to score each child's initial in calligraphy on their respective roll. I snigger at the madness. When she slides the finished rolls from the cream-coloured Aga, I swear I catch a waft of fresh-baked aroma instead of sweat and aftershave from commuters pressing in on me. She does it effortlessly, like feeding these works of art to a family of eight isn't a massive chore.

A calm descends when I tune in to her life. Her movements are graceful, her voice warm. She's living the dream, her version of it, which is also a dream for others, given her massive following. I'm 'trad curious' but not taken in. Her socials are highly curated, the reels beautifully shot. That doesn't happen by accident. Her sincerity is coupled with a hint of knowingness, like she understands influencing is silly, that's why she's just sharing her recipes.

I power-walk to the office, admiring the golden leaves of Central Park in fall. Having grown up in England, I think in British English, but 'fall' suits me better than autumn. Not long until we're trick-or-treating, then it's Friendsgiving in November as we don't have family here, whereas Thanksgiving on Faith's homestead is as trad as it comes.

Faith's created her own bubble of faux-nostalgia, inspiring awe from those who wonder how she does it, rather than why. She gives the impression that she doesn't work, but what she's doing *is* work. I calculate she earns six figures a month from views alone, posting her idyllic life online. She's not really even a trad wife, since she out-earns her husband. She's the marketing superstar, the face of Lavender Field Ranch, which her husband, Marty, runs behind the scenes.

In the lift to my office I see Faith's posted a new picture of Cowboy Marty and his young son on horseback. Marty's sharp cheekbones and chiselled features are softened by his tousled wheat-coloured hair. I scroll through her feed for more images of the beefcake rancher and family man. One shows him in silhouette with a smaller boy on his shoulders, looking out on a vast orange sunrise. In another he holds his little girl's hand while carrying a baby in the crook of his arm. He's imposing, with a big chest and abs from whatever guys do on ranches. In one of Faith's Insta photos, he hugs her into his plaid shirt, strong cowboy arms wrapped around her, steel-blue eyes fixed on the camera. A frisson of unease travels through me.

> Faith and Marty are a real-life cowboy romance.
>
> You are GOALS! I want to be you!
>
> Click the link for my Faith and Marty fanfic!!! You know you want it.

The moment I walk in the office, Alexandra leaps up. Back to reality.

'Hey, Melissa, how are you?' She trundles her wheeled chair towards my desk. I'm a few minutes early and I'd intended to grab a coffee to rev me up for today's pressing deadlines.

'Great, thanks.' I mirror her smile. 'What can I help you with?'

'Let's brainstorm angles for the Maysara Wealth account.' Her lips are plumped, her make-up immaculate as always, a little too much in person but stunning on camera. Her jet-black hair is pulled into her signature high ponytail.

'Angles?' I dump my coat and bag on my desk and rake my fingers through my messier hair. 'Have you read the proposal that won us the account?' Authored by me, with a few tweaks by Eric, our boss.

'Yeah, but I feel we should wow him with fresh angles.'

I swivel my chair to face her. Eric asked me to help her settle in, so I won't stifle her rookie enthusiasm. 'What angles are you thinking about?'

'Um…' She flashes me a ditsy look that works better on Eric than me.

I wait a few beats in which she looks expectantly at me. The first time I helped her out, she leaned in and placed her hand on my arm, telling me she loves it when women raise up other women. When I was her age, I moved to New York from England after uni, so I get that graduates need a helping hand.

'Focus on the *why*,' I say. 'Why is Asim posting content?'

She squints at me. 'For money?'

'That's a given, but what's his passion that he's trying to communicate?'

'Um...' The moment stretches out.

'Since he was a kid, he was fascinated by the money markets. His grandparents gave him a hundred bucks towards his college fund, and he used it to play the market. He ended up paying his way through college with his investments. It's an origin story that highlights his passion and success.'

She nods with enthusiasm.

'How about a competition to find the next Asim?'

'Like how?'

'Like, his goal is expansion, but right now the business is just him. He's holding off taking on staff until he has more kudos to attract good talent. What if we create upfront kudos by running a competition on his socials for him to find a new recruit to mentor?'

'Yes. Yes, I love that.' She sits up straighter.

I could elaborate but she's talking about what a great angle it is. It's enough to keep her occupied so I can get shit done. Drafting a proposal for the V For Vegan upscale bakery is a bigger priority than Asim, who hasn't paid his first month's retainer yet. Alexandra returns to her desk, hair swishing side to side like a show pony.

As I log on, my mind returns to Lavender Field Ranch as an escape to simpler times. Faith cosplays a pioneer fantasy, rocking the nostalgia, although those times were tough. It's a façade of old-time living when she needs tech to create and upload content for mass consumption. She's made a career from pretending she has no career, when I know the work involved in producing a steady flow of content that goes viral. The contradiction nags at my consciousness, along with Faith herself. I want to unravel the mystery of her.

Chapter Three

The day rushes past as I power through my to-do list. I started here as a copywriter, and now I'm a social media manager and copywriter. I get to work with film-makers and animators who create their own form of art, and I'm always looking for the secret sauce that makes content go viral. Some of our clients are influencers, and I know it's nonsense, but it's escapism and we all need a bit of that.

Eric comes and perches on the side of my desk when I'm getting ready to leave. My heart sinks at the threat of an impromptu meeting when I'm about to launch into the school run.

'Listen.' He grimaces and leans towards me confidentially. 'I had some feedback that you're being a little… unfriendly.'

'Unfriendly?' I give him a salty look. 'Who says I'm unfriendly?' My eyes flick around the office. Angelo, our graphic designer, is wearing headphones, throwing M&Ms in the air to catch in his mouth. He tosses one too high and flinches as it bounces off his cheek. Alexandra is out filming somewhere.

Eric rubs a hand over his bald head. 'That's not important.'

'I need context. Was it Angelo?'

'Nope.'

Of course not. Angelo isn't the office stirrer. 'So, Alexandra has a problem with me?'

'We need a coherent team.'

'Sure.' I force a smile. That viper took my idea of a competition too literally. I switch into damage limitation mode. 'I thought we got along fine. We were brainstorming first thing at her request.'

He picks up my Calma Llama stress toy to squeeze. 'You can be a little abrupt.'

'*Abrupt?*' I say too abruptly. Abrupt is when you go around barking orders. Abrupt is hard and unapproachable. That's not me.

He stares at Calma Llama cupped in his hands and doesn't elaborate.

'Eric, you know I do the best work I can, balanced with mentoring the newer team members. If you want to allocate time for me to nurture Alexandra some more—'

'That's not what I'm saying. It doesn't take time to be friendly to your co-workers.'

'I *am* friendly.' And I am fuming. I tread carefully though. 'You know us Brits don't always have the same level of exuberance. It doesn't mean we don't care about people.' I inject the right level of hurt into my voice and place one palm on my chest for emphasis. If that fakery works for Alexandra, I'll make it work for me.

His mouth downturns and he gives Calma Llama little squeezes. 'Alexandra's a really great person if you give her a chance.'

Yeah, a great back-stabber. I should give her more chance to shaft me.

He stands and rocks on his heels. 'I've also had a concern shared that you aren't committed to the Maysara Wealth account.'

'A concern?' I arch an eyebrow. 'From Asim?'

'No.' He purses his lips.

No. Because the client and I get along fine. Does Alexandra have a hold over Eric? I can't picture an affair – *ew*. The job isn't worth sex with an older guy giving off dad vibes. At best, she's set up a weird dynamic with her as teacher's pet and me as 'escape goat', as Willow would say.

'In the current climate, we do everything we can for our clients.'

I nod vigorously and lean forward in a show of commitment, since jobs are lost in the current climate. 'What exactly is the concern?'

He stands and drops the squeezy llama on my desk. 'I just need you to be on top of things and… you know…' He swishes his arm around. 'Watch your attitude. We have to consider our co-workers' mental health.'

I pull back. He strides off, pretending to take a call on his mobile. *Watch my attitude*? No way is that airhead framing me as the bad guy. I'm almost as annoyed with myself for blaming my half-Britishness when a deep understanding of US culture is vital to the job. It's a line I navigate as my English accent is often a talking point with new clients along the lines of *oh, you're British! I love London*, and then we get to bond.

I've always felt 'other' from my upbringing, and I don't mean my dual nationality. From a young age, I covered up my family's beliefs. But being unfriendly is a strike against me. *I'm bloody well not unfriendly*, I want to shout for him to hear on his fake phone call. Spineless git. Why should I facilitate the world revolving around Alexandra? I save the ego-managing bullshit for clients.

I can't believe that traitor shafted me when I gave her a helping hand, unaware she'd chew it off and spit it out. I'm still seething on the subway to collect Willow. A manspreader butts his leg against my knee. I shove my tote bag between us and keep hitting my knee against it to annoy him right back.

In need of a dopamine fix, I slip into Faith's social media. Ahhh, there she is, lifting an apple pie from the Aga, the pie crust decorated with an apple tree design. Her voice is soothing honey, her home a sanctuary from the outside world. When everyone is rushing, she slows it down with mesmerising effect.

It captivates me. Me and millions of others, not that I buy into her lifestyle. The next video loads to show Faith collecting eggs in her chiffony rose-print dress. The wind ruffles her hair, natural as ever. It's not some bouncy salon blowout, since how would she find time with six kids under twelve and no childcare?

I self-soothe my way through her grid, cooing over every image. What she represents is antifeminist, but we all need vices and this is my drug of choice. My guilty pleasure. Just as I know it's not ideal to keep swigging wine, sometimes I can't help myself.

There she is, nuzzling a horse and cradling her newborn. In a sun-dappled shot, she walks dreamily through the lavender field with her small daughters, like a tribe of ethereal wood nymphs. They're wearing off-white Victoriana nightdresses. If I went out dressed like that, I'd look like an asylum escapee. I scan the comments.

So calming!

$40 for two lavender sleep pouches?? Who needs them when the videos send you to sleep.

Lol she's having a laugh!

I study it all as research for my podcast. That's what I tell myself. In a new photo, she's smiling widely, holding a home-made chocolate sponge with candles burning bright on top. The candles cast her flushed face in a golden glow. Eyes shining, her batch of blond kids gather around the cake, the girls in vintage cotton smocks, the boys in plaid shirts. It's sad that Willow doesn't get to blow out her birthday candles with siblings in a light-filled home. Not that I want more children.

A podcast episode forms in my mind on how to be more Faith. What can a working single mum on a budget take from her lifestyle? Tongue in cheek, of course, since I'm not endorsing a throwback life. But I can't deny she has it figured out, making big money from her online content while spending her days baking and roaming the farm with her kids.

My podcast is *Moms' Real Tea* about the reality of single parenthood while trying to give your child the best start. I'd like Willow to breathe clean air and not be constrained by our badly lit shoebox of an apartment. Money doesn't just buy you a spacious kitchen flooded with natural light. It buys you time to make good food and ramble in nature. It would be easy to do a snarky hit piece on Faith, but that's not the right vibe for what I have in mind. I'll identify practical takeaways for working mums, and examine why we're hooked on the idealised fantasy. Because it is a fantasy, and doesn't reflect my values.

Some fans say Faith's evoking sweet memories of childhood, but she's implanting a false vision of the past. She cherry-picks the best bits, baking pies and making lavender pouches with her kids. She's not cleaning grime from a soot-covered home with no central heating. She's not hanging wet laundry on a freezing day before dying from typhoid.

The professional in me admires her online talent, the mum in me yearns for her free-range life, while the cynic in me wants a handle on what's really going on. Because she's not for real. Surely she keeps a stash of dried pasta and store-bought cheese for when she lacks energy to make mac and cheese from scratch. And how is that even practical with all those kids?

In the videos I've watched, she's never harried. She's not delousing them or cutting gum from their matted hair. The toddler isn't headbutting her leg and demanding a snack, and why aren't the kids scribbling on the walls and breaking the TV? Oh, I forgot. They don't have TV. She must lull them into submission like she does to me. The woman has superpowers, but doesn't she feel compromised by the domestic duty? Apparently not. We all keep parts of ourselves hidden behind our public persona. I slip into bullshit mode as much as the next person when my job depends on it, but Faith's at ease with her role. Or is she?

She's either mad or savvy or somehow authentic, but I've no idea what kind of game she has going on. She's a natural on camera, yet something is off. I micro-analyse it and decide it's a barely detectable look in her eyes, an occasional clue to deeper elements at play. I want to see behind her social media curtain. What's going on at Lavender Field Ranch is more complex than she has us believe. There's another side to this story.

Chapter Four

> OMG the baby has a knife!
>
> Someone report her to Child Protection Services.

I watch a reel of Faith making burgers from scratch while her second youngest clumsily chops celery with a huge knife. Faith's oblivious. When the kids are around, she transcends the cute chaos, while I'm distracted by the toddler wielding a knife. I wince at those irreplaceable chubby little fingers. The comments light up with even more incredulity than usual. One fan says:

> Chill. She shows the babies how to chop safely.

When Willow's asleep, I set up my podcast. I love turning ideas into something real. A creative job can crush your creativity, what with daily pressure and a dickhead boss who fancies your colleague. But the podcast is all mine. Nobody at work knows I do it. The pod lays bare the part of me that's striving for more, which might be incompatible with dedication to the job. Can't have that, when I'm already *unfriendly*.

'Hey there,' I say into the mic. 'Thanks for tuning in to this episode titled, "The guilty working mum". I'm talking about the comparisons I make when I see Faith Eversen online, cooking with food from her farm.' I inject a playful hint of irony to avoid sounding snippy. I have a reason for playing nice. 'While you grab coffee, she grinds wheat. While you have daycare, her little angels entertain themselves. Must try harder! But so what if her meals are farm to table? Calling out for pizza supports local producers too.'

I take a breath and smile.

'I kid, but us working mums don't have time for this top-tier dedication. Even so, I've been looking at how to be more Faith,' I say, mock serious, to avoid sounding like a superfan. 'Most of us work, and that's a good thing. It's not throwing shade at Faith since she brings in more than me from her influencer career. So how can the rest of us feed our kids without losing our minds? Instead of life hacks, here are my trad wife hacks.'

I run through the tips in a light-hearted way, then I move on to a photo I took in Central Park.

'Here's my child and me after our weekend baking. We took banana bread to the park, laid out a rug and pretended we'd hiked in the wilds, then stopped for a picnic. We talked about swimming in an icy river and riding our horses through the imaginary valley.'

I'll add the photo tomorrow night. It only shows our feet in socks, trainers kicked off, sitting on the picnic rug.

'The photo doesn't show that the banana bread sank in the middle. We know the reality can be different to what's presented to us online. As for my baking fails, I frame them as a learning experience and tell my daughter it's character-building. We often marvel over our great characters.

'Here's the thing: my baking always starts out promising, but the end result never measures up to Faith's. I wonder if it's because my head's crammed full of endless to-do lists: *remember to sign that permission slip, must email my boss, who can I split childcare with over the winter break?*

'Would my banana bread improve if I ditched the working-mum brain clutter? It would free me to approach baking as a religious experience. Faith shows reverence to the dough in her mixing bowl. She's in tune with its immaculate conception, from grinding the wheat to churning the butter. It's a pared-back life, without the pressure of rushing to and from work, stressing about drop-offs and pickups and everything in between. It's no wonder we're enchanted by her videos. Who doesn't want to trade the hassle for slow living?'

I also pin blame on the knackered old cooker in my rental, but I don't have $15,000 spare for an Aga. I don't even have space for a bread maker. Then I finish with a final note that parenting is hard.

'Faith's in the wilds of Utah, but us city mums have survival skills too. We're all doing our imperfect best because there is no perfect, not even for a trad wife. So if the kids are fed and we keep our sense of worth from work, we're on the path of righteousness.'

There's more I could say about Faith. I suspect Lavender Field Ranch is a con. It's as if she and Marty are playing roles. She's so invested in the illusion, even if she wanted to stop, I bet she couldn't.

On Monday night, I finish editing the pod before it goes live. I should start planning the next one, but instead I write a letter. Faith's an old-fashioned person, so I write her an old-fashioned letter.

Dear Faith,

I host the 'Moms' Real Tea' podcast, and I'm fascinated by how you've arranged your lifestyle to work for you. I'm drawn to stories of women making a success of working flexibly when they have young children.

I would love to explore that on my podcast through a conversation with you. I work as a content creator and the podcast is my own passion project. If you're open to joining me for an episode, I would be delighted to have a conversation with you.

Best wishes,

Melissa

PS I know you're busy, but here's a quick intro to the latest episode.

I add a link to the promo reel, a sixty-second video that pushes viewers to click the podcast link. Despite her throwback ways, Faith has embraced the digital age and will get loads of email requests for interviews. So I hope my handwritten request stands out. Not that I've any chance when she never engages with followers and limits herself to the occasional stage-managed puff piece.

I haven't helped my cause with the biblical references in the podcast. It goes with the trad territory, but she only mentions church in passing. Anyway, she won't have time to tune in. But I'm curious. Is she happy? Brainwashed? Controlled by her cowboy husband? I want to know if she wears leggings and an old hoodie stained with baby puke when she's not filming. But my curiosity goes way beyond that.

I dive deep into her socials and find a wedding photo of her in a traditional white dress, the teen bride gazing adoringly at Marty in a tux. She gives off mad Cinderella vibes from the princess dress coupled with her humble toiling in the kitchen.

Did she choose that life, or was she sucked in? A rural mum in Utah has less choice, same as a single mum on a budget in Manhattan. Yet she's the homemaker who's winning at life, making good money from cute videos. In another photo, she and Marty stand beside a horse. She makes doe eyes at her square-jawed cowboy who's textbook handsome. Their fans go wild for this sort of content, but my skin crawls. His appeal is lost on me, since I'm biased. Other people see a family man, while I see a darker truth. His charmed life infuriates me. It's time Marty Eversen's past caught up with him, and I have a plan to make it happen.

Chapter Five

'When the days turn colder, I love baking wholesome comfort food,' Faith says in her melodic voice. She turns to the Aga and takes out a batch of cookies. Two of her daughters watch with rapt interest, faces pink. 'I made these oatmeal cookies from spelt, an ancient grain that's perfect for sweet things.'

We're on the bus, but I'm also in Faith's kitchen. I try not to escape online when I'm with Willow, but she's engrossed in a book, so I indulge an elaborate fantasy of living off-grid in the countryside. Not that it's off-grid when your Wi-Fi is good enough to upload videos of your off-grid life.

The content creator in me sees my own fantasy life in a YouTube video with high production values. Here I am milking the cow and it's not gross at all. I'm in a loose floral dress, my sun-kissed face tilting skyward with a dreamy expression. If only I had Faith's reach and an Insta-worthy home. She's making millions a year from views alone, paid by the social media companies. Then there's tasteful low-key endorsements and her online shop range.

I return to reality, since it's nearly our stop. 'Put your book away, sweetheart.' I brush a stray lock of hair behind Willow's ear. Her face is paler than usual, her expression pinched.

'You okay?' I ask, once we reach the school gates. I crouch down to see her.

She gives me a solemn nod. She's smaller than most kids her age. It's a vulnerability that tugs at my heart, along with the determined set of her little face. She's always been small and I've always been worried, from when she was newborn and her skinny frog's legs poked out of her nappy like I'd birthed Kermit in human form. We hug goodbye and she goes through the gates, clutching the straps of her Hello Kitty backpack.

I arrive at work with ten minutes to spare, but the rest of the team are already in a meeting. The three of them cluster around Eric's desk, his office separated with glass partitions from our workstations. He beckons me in. I suspect Eric's wife doesn't listen to him, so he calls work meetings that force us to listen instead. *Bro, start a podcast.*

'Did I miss something?' I pull up the remaining chair that's lower than the others, because another disadvantage is just what I need. 'I didn't see a meeting notification.'

'We're hitting the ground running.' Eric shuffles papers and doesn't look at me, the team leper.

Alexandra nods intently. I grab my work notebook and pen from my backpack. But why have a team meeting before my start time?

'Right then, Alexandra will be heading up the Maysara Wealth account,' Eric says.

I inhale sharply. Her gaze meets mine and I look away, composing myself. Why give her the account? She's fresh out of college, and I 'headed up' the pitching process. We won the account mainly from my efforts.

'Thank you for giving me this unique experience.' She holds a hand to her heart. 'I'm so humbled to be working with you guys,' she says in her acceptance speech. 'And I love being of service to others.'

Do your job then.

Angelo's congratulations are effusive. My colleagues are all-American and world-class at sincerity. I sound fake when I'm forced into spur-of-the-moment gushing, so the best I can manage is to smile and nod.

Eric's wearing a sweatshirt with a mad skateboarding pug on the front. It's from our doggy daycare account, and doesn't suit him. 'Us two dinosaurs need to step back and let the new kids take charge,' he says to me. 'Cos dinosaurs dino-snore.'

I cringe inwardly at the dad joke.

'Funny!' Alexandra says.

Eric thinks Gen Z has the edge over us because their brains are wired for TikTok. But consuming content and creating content are two different things. The latter is a skill you learn.

'It's time to go big to get results,' Alexandra says. 'Old-fashioned thinking holds us back.' She shoots a glance at me. 'We need to pivot you guys into the new paradigm.'

You need to pivot the fuck away from me.

'I had this great idea,' she says. 'I thought we could run a competition on the Maysara socials to create a buzz.'

Wow. Okay. I look at her pointedly while she acts oblivious.

'Asim said he wants to take on a new employee,' she says. 'So, what if we run a competition to find his apprentice?'

She really has no shame. If I say it's my idea does that count as 'unfriendly'? What if I strangle her with her ponytail?

'We can post videos of the process to show Asim as an expert guiding the novice.'

'Boom! It's viral.' Angelo does an explosion hand mime and accidentally elbows her in the head. Nice one, Angelo.

'I like it.' Eric looks interested.

'Right!' She rubs her elbowed head and nods her approval at Eric like a pug dog she's training with praise. 'We can do it like *The Apprentice* and set it up with a nod to the opening credits. That was my favourite show in school.'

Is she nuts? *The Apprentice* won't win over Asim's coveted high-value client base. Eric's nods are slowing, a troubled look clouds his face. *Good luck with fixing that, you dickhead.* But he doesn't curtail his favourite employee. His attractive young employee who laughs at his jokes.

'Good work, Alexandra,' he says.

Good work, idea thief, for spouting crap. I keep my pleasant smile fixed in place and feel the beginning of a headache. Not my circus, I tell myself, not until the monkeys screw up and blame me.

'Draft a proposal and let's see where we go with it.'

Once I'm released from the meeting, I plunge into work, quietly fuming. I expect Eric to swing past my desk and explain that he gave her the account to build up her experience, which is fair, although he could have told me before the meeting. But nothing. I skip lunch, working through as always so I can leave early. Then Alexandra comes over.

'Melissa, hi,' she says, her voice sugary-sweet. 'Can we get together and discuss next steps for the hydrotherapy account?'

'Sure.' I smile. 'I'm back on Thursday.'

'Let's do it before then.'

'We can Zoom tomorrow.'

'How about now?' She stands over me and opens her blue leather notebook embossed in silver with 'Wonder Woman'.

I nearly say no. I've promised Eric a content management report by this evening, so it'll be a late night. 'I'm on a deadline. Can we make it quick?' I paste on a smile and match her sweet tones, lest I'm *unfriendly*, but I know where I'd like to shove her 'next steps'.

She settles beside me in her cute outfit of a hot pink cashmere cropped jumper and perfectly fitting cargo pants. My office attire is all black so nobody notices my clothes. My 'uniform' includes black combat boots with attitude. I work in an image-conscious industry and following fashion trends costs time and money. Blending in isn't ideal in a standing-out industry, but I tell myself less is more. Before Willow, I rode the wave, lived in the moment and sought thrills. The turnaround surprised some people, especially me.

I waste twenty minutes with Alexandra that could have been a Zoom call tomorrow. All smiles, I race us through it. Eric glances over now and then. *Look how friendly I am!* So friendly, my jaw aches from smiling.

When we wrap it up, she goes to stand but thinks better of it and smooths out the fabric of her cargo pants. 'That video you did for Juice n Go? I ran your copy through AI to improve it. I'll email you the results. I think you'll be impressed.'

She fed my words into a plagiarism app? 'I don't use AI for copywriting. It sounds fake and generic.'

'Actually, I think AI does a better job.'

That's because you're an idiot.

'It's a powerful tool, Melissa. We should incorporate it into our workflow.'

I bristle at the patronising tone.

'Maybe it's an age thing?' She cocks her head, and I want to slap her.

I'm thirty. Thirty! But she's struck a nerve: content creator years are like dog years. I could remind her that workplace ageism is illegal, but I stick with the main issue. 'AI is useful for analytics and repetitive tasks, but we're creators. If we hand that over to AI it loses authenticity because it's regurgitated. We bring our own energy, not robot vibes.'

'It's best we're not closed off,' she says. 'We can use it to our advantage.'

Only if you're too lazy to write engaging copy. Only if you can't create content that sparks curiosity in the target market. But what do I know, since I'm old? If she's putting my work into AI, I might as well be redundant. Is that her aim? To plagiarise creatives, then elbow me out?

'You can redo the voiceover with the improved script. Report back when you've read my email.'

The cheek of her. I'll report back with a chainsaw.

'Do you follow?'

Seriously, who does she think she is?

'Great leadership energy,' I say with my biggest smile yet.

'You're welcome,' she snaps.

'And you're welcome to bugger off and do your own job,' I mutter as she sweeps off to tell her lapdog I've displeased her. She's playing us both and making me obsolete. I can deal with increasing workloads and sky-high expectations. But if I have to keep working with those two morons, my brain will explode. I'd better come up with a plan B for work, since I can't take much more of this. We all have our breaking point and mine is dangerously close.

Chapter Six

'Breaking in a horse is about building trust. I talk to them with my reins.' Marty smirks at the camera, channelling his big dick energy. I hate-watch every video he's in. If I weren't at the school gates, I'd give him a sarcastic round of applause. But I'm waiting for Willow to appear while Faith and *the cowboy* hang out beside the stables. A lot of followers love his throwback charm. I prefer a man who can load the dishwasher. Faith's a picture of serenity, contented baby on hip, while her husband blathers on. Neither notice their youngest boy, who toddles over, aims a toy gun at the camera and mimes firing it.

> LMAO! Is that thing loaded?
>
> Look at the cute little cowboy!
>
> Who you referring to – Marty or Caleb?
>
> Kids shouldn't play with guns.
>
> It's what the founding fathers wanted. Anyone breaking into the ranch is getting shot!

Faith stays out of the discourse, as always. Who knows her opinion on gun ownership? I shove my phone in my pocket as Willow rushes to me, a plaster above one eye, her skin raised and red beneath it.

'What happened?' I say.

She buries her face in my parka. 'Some boys threw a rock at me.'

'A rock?' I pull back and look at her in horror.

The teacher's aide comes towards me and Willow reburies her face.

'Hi, she has a letter in her bag. I wasn't there. The teacher said you can call her.'

'How did a kid in school have a rock?' I ask, less kindly than I should.

'He brought it in with him. Sorry, I have to get back to the others, but call the teacher.'

'Why didn't she call me?' My voice hardens to cover my upset. Not that I should take it out on her. I hold Willow's hand and walk us to the bus stop. 'I'm sorry that happened to you.'

'Assholes,' she snarls.

I catch my breath. My sweet child has never called anyone an asshole. 'Hey, don't use that word. It's not nice. Those boys are mean, and I'm sorry they hurt you, but we don't name-call.'

Her big eyes pool with tears that spill down her face. I wipe them away with my thumbs.

'I'll speak to Mrs Rossi. We'll work it out.'

'That'll make it worse.'

I sigh. Assholes, hurting my baby.

I fight the urge to escape, if only we had somewhere to go. Later, after Willow falls asleep, I soothe myself with more Lavender Field escapism, minus her husband. The sweet balm of Faith's voice lulls me into submission. How I envy her charming bubble where she floats around, untroubled by the outside world. That's why I'm stunned when she replies to my request.

Faith Eversen. The email sender is highlighted in bold on my phone. I gasp and rush to open it, heart somersaulting while telling myself it'll be an assistant brushing me off.

> Dear Melissa,
>
> Thank you for your letter and kind words. I love how you've taken inspiration from Lavender Field Ranch and applied it to your own life in the city. I adore NYC!
>
> I only have time for a small number of interviews a year, but I'd like to make space in my schedule for your podcast interview. Please send me a list of questions in advance.
>
> Kind regards,
>
> Faith

I can't believe I've scored an interview with the mega-influencer. She'll prefer to do it online, but I want to meet her, spend an hour with her in person. Is it possible to fly to and from Utah in a day? I can call in a favour from a mum friend who'll have Willow.

Another email pings through from her. She's realised it's a mistake. Of course it's a mistake. She mistook me for someone with better online reach. I hold my breath and click on it.

> I forgot to say, could you and your daughter come here for the interview? She can spend time with my kids while we're recording. These are my available dates…

My head swims. An invitation to Lavender Field Ranch for an actual interview. Sweet of her to invite Willow. The first available date is when her school is closed.

> Dear Faith,
>
> Thank you so much. Willow and I would love to come to you for the interview. September 15 is most convenient. I'll send you a list of questions.
>
> Kind regards,
>
> Melissa

I nearly explode with excitement. This is my big break. It could send my podcast into the stratosphere. I can get the measure of Faith and decide whether Lavender Field Ranch is one big con. I'll push beyond her usual output to reach the real story. It's risky when she holds all the aces, but the interview is my chance to look behind the closed door of the ranch house. Most importantly, I want to meet her husband, see the whites of his eyes. It's not idle curiosity. I have an ulterior motive. You don't have to be a fan to follow them. You can be a hater.

Chapter Seven

My head buzzes as I launch straight into planning the interview. My game plan involves innocuous entry-level questions as a gateway to probing deeper. I've never known an influencer to inspire such immense speculation, since Faith conceals more than she reveals. It all comes down to how much I can extract from her. I have to come away with a standout episode. And beyond that, it could fix the other issue that's been dogging me. The one that involves her husband.

It's late when I flop out in bed and turn off the light. *Bugger.* I forgot to finish the report for Eric. I grab my phone and set my alarm for an hour earlier than usual, then fall asleep. Willow wakes me two hours later, calling from her bedroom. She's thrown up all over the bed. I clean her up, put her in her only pair of fresh PJs and take her to my bed where she falls asleep with a sick bucket beside her. I stuff the dirty laundry in a bag and knot the top, hoping the smell won't permeate the whole apartment. It's a downside of NYC that washers and dryers aren't allowed in most apartments, including ours.

I fall back exhausted into bed. It only feels like minutes later when Willow wakes me, whimpering in her sleep. She's burning up. I peel back the covers and wake her from her nightmare.

'It's okay,' I coo, when she blinks at me in confusion. 'Just a bad dream.'

'Don't leave me,' she croaks.

'I'm not going anywhere.' I tilt her head so she can drink some water.

'What if you get mugged and die?'

'I won't get mugged and die.' I hope not, anyway.

'Where will I go if you die?'

Good question. I've had sleepless nights over that one.

'I'm not going to die. I'm healthy and young.' Although not according to Alexandra. 'Try to sleep.'

When the alarm goes off, I'm still knackered and fall asleep again. Next thing I know, Willow's croaking that she wants a drink of water.

Oh Christ, it's nearly nine and I haven't done the report I promised to send Eric yesterday. I tumble out of bed, grab Willow some water and check she's doing okay. She can barely lift her head to drink. I quickly call her school to say she won't be in, and pull a jumper on over the T-shirt and shorts that I slept in. Then I log on to my work laptop. Thank God it's a working-from-home day.

Eric's emailed to ask for the report. I send an apology, saying I had a family issue and promising to send it in the next hour. Then a call comes through from the school.

'Ms Fairbrock, this is Mrs Rossi,' Willow's teacher says.

'Oh hi, I think she has some kind of virus—'

'That's not why I'm calling, although I wondered if you were keeping her off because of the incident yesterday.'

I push the living room door shut, so Willow doesn't overhear. 'When a bully threw a rock at her? No, she's ill, but I'd like to know what you're doing about those boys.'

'It was a stone, not a rock, and we're dealing with it. The child in question had an issue with making the right choices yesterday.'

I snort. 'He's a bully and you need to take her safety seriously.' I've never spoken like this. Maybe I also have an issue with making the right choices today. Willow didn't want a fuss, but I'm lacking the patience to tiptoe around.

'Of course, Ms Fairbrock.' Her voice is clipped. 'I have to go. School's starting.'

I snarl to myself and return to the report, cursing the school and cursing Alexandra for interrupting me yesterday, when I could have been closer to finishing it.

When I've completed the first draft, I grab a much-needed coffee, read through the report and ping it to Eric. In response, he sends a Zoom meeting link for a session starting in ten minutes. *Great*. Is he flagging up my dwindling work ethic? Guess I'm not employee of the month. When I log in, I'm unusually relieved to see Alexandra and Angelo on the call. But within minutes, I wish it was just Eric giving me a hard time, as his news is hard to take.

Alexandra is filling the screen. She's at home, waffling on to Angelo. Behind her, the huge windows show a glimpse of the Hudson River. How can she afford that view? But it's her business. Other people are allowed nice things, even annoying people like her.

Nobody sees the reality of my dingy apartment since I'm backed up against a white wall, my screen angled away from the mess. My cute little flea market bookcase is alongside me, my grandma's beautiful handmade vase on top. The ring light casts a more flattering hue on me and the apartment. We both need it. At least they can't smell the puke. Willow's in my bed and I'm airing her room, but there isn't enough air.

Angelo's in Eric's office, beside his empty computer chair. We all say a cheery 'hi'. Angelo and Alexandra wave at the screen, looking genuinely thrilled to be there. If Alexandra's on suck-up form, she can do the talking and I'll nod in the right places, so long as Willow doesn't start throwing up again.

Eric joins Angelo. 'Thanks for joining the call. You guys ready?'

'Born ready!' Angelo grins.

'Me too.' Alexandra leans in.

I try not to puke at their perkiness.

'I've spoken to corporate about a new role within the team,' Eric says.

My ears prick up. A promotion? A higher pay grade? As my mind races ahead, Alexandra flashes a megawatt smile.

'Alex has stepped up into account management and she's doing great.'

'Good job.' Angelo claps.

My heart sinks. Willow weakly calls out, 'Mommy?'

Be there in a minute, baby, I silently beam through the wall.

Alexandra's poised and radiant, an A-lister ready to accept her Oscar. Why's Eric suddenly calling her Alex?

'*Mom*?'

'I'm thrilled to announce that Alex is now a fully-fledged social media manager.'

I can't go to Willow now because it'll look like I'm walking out in a huff. It would make more sense to promote me to a senior role. I'm the one who gets the clients in. That airhead has only been here five minutes and knows sod all. She thinks she can kick me to the kerb, an obsolete reject. But it looks like this job had Alexandra's name on it. Or is it *Alex* now? He doesn't call me 'Mel' or Angelo 'Ange'. I'm petty and I don't care. I want to speak to Eric, but I'll sound like a jealous loser, when it's humiliating enough to be the geriatric content creator. I paste on a smile, not nearly as big as Alex's. Angelo offers his warmest congratulations, and I add mine.

'Mommy!' Willow appears in the doorway. 'Why is my poop runny?'

Their smiles turn to frozen grimaces. I slip out of my chair, reach her in two strides, crouch down and whisper, 'It's okay, baby. Go back to bed. I'll be in soon.' I steer her back out of the room. Poor thing.

I race back to my seat and hear laughter and chat through my laptop. Are they laughing at Willow?

'Sorry,' I say. 'Sick kid. But yeah, massive congratulations, Alex.' I say it without a hint of snark. *You do you, Alexandra, and I'll focus on holding it together.* I had such high hopes when I started my career, and now look at me.

I long for a fresh start. If we moved further out, Willow could go to school in a nicer area, but it would mean a change of home, school and a job with homeworking. The practicalities overwhelm me and flat hunting fills me with dread. Last time, my soul nearly curled up and died from navigating a baby buggy around shady neighbourhoods that I'd rather forget. My budget will never stretch to meet the life I want for Willow.

At least we landed up next door to Beverley. The flat sucks, but you can't put a price on good neighbours. I sometimes play 'what if?' What if we had a better home close to a good school? What if we moved out of NYC?

I keep thinking of that one. But what if I uproot her and it doesn't work out?

Willow has recovered by the weekend, and on Saturday afternoon I attempt to make sourdough bread with her and her friend Coco, who's here for a sleepover. The three of us are covered in flour and they giggle at the globs of hardened grey dough in my hair. We take photos and I'll make a podcast from it and include a teaser for my interview with Faith. I'll call it, 'How does she do it?'

How does Faith do it? She's so pristine when kneading bread. She sometimes cooks with kids squealing in the background, little ones coming in and out of shot. Everyone's clean despite living on a working farm. I can't imagine filming myself giving a cookery lesson worthy of a million views while corralling six kids.

It's fun to see Willow and Coco's faces as they watch the dough rising, but we can't believe it takes ten hours to birth a sourdough loaf. When it comes out of the oven on Sunday morning, it's as flat as my mood and nothing like Faith's, even without her loving artwork on top. The girls are excited to try it but I insist we wait the prescribed ninety long minutes to let it cool. It's brunch when we finally get to the reveal. The poxy loaf is wet and gummy inside. We all peer at it in disgust. Sourdough fail. A mental image of Faith's sunlit sourdough pushes my spirits lower.

'Aww, man,' Willow says, jabbing the damp doughiness.

'Sucks,' Coco says.

Not the effect I was aiming for. 'Who's for waffles?' I say brightly, ready to pretend it never happened.

On Sunday night, I plan the interview, adding to my list of burning questions. I want clues to who Faith really is. In an older video, she has that glazed look I've seen before, when she's not talking to camera. In another, she's doing solo yoga on a decked area, surrounded by nature. She doesn't engage with the camera until the end when she whispers conspiratorially, 'It's a lifesaver.' She winks at us, sharing the secret of this elicit pleasure, akin to necking a glass of wine before noon. Then she reaches forward to end the recording.

She's never winked before, but I sometimes see a knowingness behind her eyes, a hidden depth. She's keeping secrets. Has she created this perfect on-screen illusion to convince us that everything's peachy? If it's an attempt to keep the bad stuff at bay, what's she hiding from? I suspect that she's thrown herself into creating a prettified life as a reaction to a darker element. In one of their videos, Faith and Marty lean on a wooden fence beside a horse enclosure. While she speaks to camera, he spends the whole time inspecting his knuckles.

When the cowboy's around, she shrinks a little and dims her light. *Does that make you feel good, big man on your big ranch?* If I can expose the real Marty Eversen, it'll solve a tricky issue in my personal life. I know what he's hiding and I'm ready to take him down.

Chapter Eight

My kick-ass neighbour Beverley arrives from next door, wearing black leather trousers and a studded leather jacket in a shade to match her magenta hair. Willow shoots over to welcome Germaine as she limps in. I make risotto while the three of them line up on the sofa for a cheesy musical. Germaine sits bolt upright on Willow's lap, groaning softly as Willow grooms her with an old toothbrush.

When the food's ready, I squish in between them on the sofa. 'What are we watching?'

'*Guys and Dolls*,' Beverley says.

'There aren't any dolls in it,' Willow says, 'but we like the dancing.'

When the film ends, she goes to bed. Beverley shuffles out, then returns with a couple of Martinis in proper cocktail glasses, and we discuss my dream of a balcony with a view.

'You'll need a Park Avenue residence with a deep balcony overlooking Central Park.'

'That could work.'

'You're gonna need a man with prospects. My insurance broker's cute. I'll check if he's single.'

I'm too tired to move and the cocktail tastes divine.

'Is that your folks?' Beverley nods to the image of a young couple that appears on our digital photo frame.

'It was my dad and aunt. They're both dead.'

'All my relatives are dead.' She starts pushing herself out of the couch, saying Germaine needs a lamp post. I offer to go while she stays with Willow. When I come back I mention our overnight trip to Utah.

'Utah?' She arches an eyebrow at me. 'Why the hell would you go there?'

'I'm interviewing a trad wife influencer.'

'A trad wife? One of those religious fundamentalist MAGA idiots?'

'Bit harsh.'

'I escaped from the farmlands in sixty-nine to get away from them. It wasn't right then and it sure ain't right now.'

'Faith's not like that.'

'How well d'you know her?'

'I've researched her. No way did she vote for Trump.'

Faith floats above politics and real-world concerns. Beverley has a point though. I'm no fan of the trad wife movement, but I still find myself drawn to the high production values and soothing cookery videos. I help her out of the saggy sofa and walk her to the door.

'Watch it,' she says. 'They might turn you into one of them.'

The Monday after, I'm staring into my bathroom mirror. 'So, Faith,' I ask with gravitas. 'I'm not convinced that you love domestic servitude. Is it an elaborate act?' I cock my head. 'Do you like holding us to unattainable standards when our lives are tough enough?' I've been trying out lines of questioning that don't align with the list I sent Faith, the safe list I wrote for a foot in the door.

I can't shake the feeling that the ranch is a film set and they've created their own *Truman Show*. Maybe their kids believe it, but Faith's trapped within the confines. And now it's showtime. I check I'm presentable, then we head out to the airport.

By the time we're on the plane, Willow's bouncing with excitement. I envy her pure joy. What happened to the younger me who believed NYC overflowed with opportunities? Maybe the mountain air will revive me. It's Willow's first ever flight, so I treat take-off like a fun fairground ride in case she's scared, but her mind is blown.

'Lift off!' she squeals. When the plane soars over clouds, she looks at me saucer-eyed and whispers, 'Are we going to heaven?'

'No. We're going to Lavender Field Ranch in Utah.'

I haven't shown it to her online. She might be in awe of the kids if she's seen them 'on TV'. I'd rather she treat them like normal children, albeit ones who dress like little pioneers from yesteryear. She's wearing a red tartan dress with thick tights in case it's cold in the mountains, along with her new winter boots.

While she's cloud spotting, I go over the questions. Nerves creep up at interviewing one of the most revered influencers on the planet. There's so much riding on this. It could be everything or nothing. If I handle it right, my podcast could go viral, paving the way to a better life for Willow and me. It depends on how big a glimpse Faith allows me into her real life.

She says I'll meet Marty. I want to see what he's like in the flesh, even though I can't bear the man. There's a hidden story at the ranch. If my spidey senses are right, it's the not so Insta-worthy story of Marty's dark side, and I want to tell it. My vested interest goes beyond the podcast. The patriarchy is alive and well in Utah, and red flags are flying at the ranch. As the plane descends to the runway, I don't brace myself for landing but for navigating the task ahead.

—

I've been seeking the right person for a long time. Advertising the vacancy isn't an option for what I have in mind. She needs to be a particular type of woman to suit my purpose, and I can afford to pick and choose. Melissa Fairbrock is a promising candidate. She's on her way. I just need to meet her and Willow to confirm I'm right.

Chapter Nine

When we reach arrivals, I'm grateful Faith offered to send someone to collect us. 'I see you don't drive,' she'd said in an email. For her to know, she would have listened to my other podcasts. Two return flights are a big enough expense without airport taxis. And thanks to Faith's hospitality, we're staying overnight on the ranch. I can't quite believe all the access she's giving me, a stranger. Faith didn't reveal why she chose me when she must turn down countless requests. I'm nagged by the suspicion that she's sussed out my ulterior motive, but I'm being paranoid.

I wave at a man in aviators and a Stetson, holding a sign saying 'Melissa + Willow'. My gaze lingers on his slow smile, dimples forming.

'Welcome to Utah. I'm Joel.'

Willow cranes her neck at the tall, broad man. She stares like he's unreal. 'Are you a cowboy?'

He takes off his shades. His tawny eyes match his hair. 'Guess so.'

They've sent a hot cowboy from central casting. Is everyone at the ranch gorgeous? Maybe it's a prerequisite. He guides us to his pickup truck while I regain my composure. It's noticeably cooler here than New York, and the air is so fresh. Joel tosses his cowboy hat in the back and runs his hand through his hair. I clock his strong biceps and push down my attraction, since I already have fluttery nerves from the looming interview and can't get distracted.

'Is Marty on the ranch today?' I ask on the drive there.

'Sure, he's always in the warehouse Mondays.'

My skin prickles with trepidation, but I want to see him and Faith together off camera. What's he like with her when the filming stops? Maybe he's from the *Brokeback Mountain* cowboy division and their marriage is a cover. Maybe he's as attracted to Joel as I am, but I doubt it.

The energy is different in their shared videos compared to Faith's solo content. She's a muted version of herself. When he wangs on, Faith gazes at him like he's fascinating. Rather than express a view, she'll pose it as a mild question to him. There's an undertone to their strange dynamic. She's more alert around him, as if reading his mood.

Faith's the main attraction, so why defer to him? She's a Mormon wife, that's why. They were raised as LDS – Latter-day Saints. She's soft and feminine while adoring her husband. She's definitely on the Mormon spectrum, but she didn't mind the sly religious references in my podcast, so she can't be too devout. Her only videos that mention God and church have Marty present. Those have the fewest views. He once spoke of God's will to have children. Behind the charm of her posts lies the Mormon patriarchy. And now I'm heading into the heart of it.

'Man, this place is unreal.' Willow surveys the snow-capped mountains from the back seat. The wide-open expanse takes my breath away.

'Wait till you see the ranch,' Joel says. He smells of pine trees, or maybe Utah smells of pine trees. His big, capable hands on the steering wheel distract me from the other view outside. I notice a shell bracelet on his tanned wrist.

His fingers drum out a beat on the steering wheel in time with a song playing low on the radio. I'm transfixed by his moving fingers, imagining foreplay.

What is wrong with me? I'm a professional on an assignment and there's no room for a cowboy romance in this overnight trip. Tempting though. My shoulders tense as I return to the pressure of pulling this off. It's not just the podcast. I can handle that. It's the threat hanging over me, the proverbial gun to my head.

I turn back to Willow, who gives me a gap-toothed smile. Joel looks at me and smiles too. I bite my lip. We'll be there any minute and I can't screw this up. If I don't come away with a standout interview, I'll have nothing, but so much is out of my control. Faith is a pro at showing her perfect life. Why would she jeopardise that by giving me the inside track? God, I'm deluded. I should sort out my life in practical ways, instead of dragging Willow across the country on some ridiculous notion.

'You're an influencer too?' Joel asks.

Hardly. I barely influence my own child. 'I have a podcast and I'm interviewing Faith.'

'It's a whole load of nothing,' Willow muses. Does she mean my podcast? But her voice is infused with awe as she stares at the big landscape.

'These wide-open spaces are mind-blowing,' I say.

'Mind-blowing,' she repeats.

Joel chuckles good-naturedly. 'A whole load of nothing.'

My anticipation mounts. We pass a quaint sign saying 'Lavender Field Ranch' and turn onto a long road with fenced-off farmland. I spot the famous lavender field, the harvest finished for the year. My gaze skates around, searching for Marty out on the ranch. I hold my breath. He's here somewhere, the man I intend to take down.

'*Little House on the Prairie!*' Willow exclaims as we pass a log cabin, and then we draw up at the ranch house.

I get out, instantly warmed by the sun, so bright without high-rises and pollution blocking it. I'm dying to see the reality of the place. Is it a trad wife theme park? One big influencer photo op? I'm about to find out whether Faith is an accomplished con artist and this is one big moneymaking scam.

Willow gazes around. Does she also think we're on a film set with the dramatic mountain range and cluster of quaint pioneer-style ranch buildings nestled in the valley? I'm struck by a sense of entering a different world, a place of enchantment… or is it?

Chapter Ten

There she is, queen of the trad wives, coming out to greet us, baby balanced on her hip, three-year-old Caleb toddling behind. She's just like her online persona with her dazzling smile, vivid green eyes and all that lustrous hair ruffling in the breeze. This is too weird. For a moment, I'm awestruck at the social media superstar in all her stunning beauty. But I'm not here to fangirl her, so I pull myself together. I notice she's smaller than I imagined, petite and only a little taller than me. It puzzles me, as she's nearly as tall as the beefcake husband, who I haven't spotted yet.

Willow gazes at her in wonder, lips parted in awe.

'Welcome to Lavender Field Ranch,' Faith says in her melodic voice. 'I'm so pleased you're here.'

Willow blinks and stands motionless. I can tell she's weighing up whether Faith is a Disney character, maybe Cinders in her simple dress and white apron. I feel like whispering, 'It's okay, she's real.'

'It's nice to meet you, Willow.' Faith beams down at her and introduces the two golden-haired cherubs. 'This is Caleb and Betsy.'

Willow blinks again and recovers herself. 'Thank you for having us,' she chirps, as I've taught her.

Apart from her height, Faith is exactly as she appears online, and her skin is just as dewy. So far, so authentic.

She really is the poster girl for country living. She makes a fuss of Willow and walks us to the schoolhouse, in a converted barn. Willow's eyes widen at the kids having their very own school on the ranch.

'They're excited about you joining them today. You'll all have cookies and juice, and they'll give you a tour when school is over.'

She opens the door, and I expect chaos, given their different ages, but the four oldest children sit behind desks in a semi-circle around the teacher, a straight-backed woman with steel-grey hair. She's giving Victorian governess vibes, softened only by her pale pink broderie dress, which looks wrong on her.

They turn their collective gaze on us, four angelic mini-me kids and their teacher. I smile in recognition. I bet they've no idea how famous they are in cyberspace, given they're not allowed online. Fans post comments as if the kids read them.

> Oh, Eden, don't you look cute!

And they're not just Insta-famous. Even people who don't use social media know who they are.

'Sorry to interrupt,' Faith says. 'This is Willow, who's joining you while I meet with her mom. Kids, be sure and welcome Willow.' She nods to the teacher. 'Thank you, Zina.'

Emily, who's the same age as Willow, pulls out the empty chair beside her. I give Willow an encouraging look. 'Go ahead,' I whisper. Bless her, she does just that, walking tentatively towards the rosy-cheeked kids, who smile and say hi. With a little tug to my heartstrings, I step back, and we leave the schoolhouse. No asshole rock-throwing kids here.

'They're very well behaved.'

'Sometimes,' she says, as we walk back to the house, the infant cooing contentedly. 'Zina's good at keeping them engaged.'

'Who is she?'

'The mom of one of the ranch team. She was a teacher before having kids, and now hers are grown, we asked if she'd teach ours.'

Faith's even more of a sweetheart in person, and it's hard not to glow from the warmth of this human sunbeam. It goes beyond the homespun hospitality of countryfolk. It feels like I'm being courted, when it should be the other way around. Her voice is a little higher than her usual modulated delivery on camera. Is she nervous? Join the club, since my heart's thumping, but this is a big deal for me, whereas it's all in a day's work for her. She's studying my every move with an intensity she doesn't show online. Is something going on?

We step inside the kitchen, the hallowed ground, and it's every bit as lovely as on-screen. I breathe in the comforting fug of baking and cinnamon with top notes of zesty lemon and rosemary. One corner is cluttered with appliances that aren't shown online. That end has crumbs scattering the countertop, along with milk spills. There's even a washing-up bowl filled with dirty dishes. I feel less bad about the state of my kitchen, and bolstered by the evidence that it's not all perfection.

Caleb pushes a wooden car along the pine floor. Faith takes a jug of water with slices of cucumber and lemon from the fridge, and a tall woman walks in without knocking. She's wearing a roomy pinafore dress with a white blouse underneath, along with a triangular hairkerchief over her plaited fair hair. She looks Amish, along with the little boy holding her hand, who has a mop of silky blond hair. Blond Mormon kids are a thing around here. I clocked several at the airport, and the ranch kids are all cherubic blonds, peachy pink from country living.

'Alice, this is Melissa.'

'Hello.' I smile.

She nods, gives the faintest of smiles and avoids eye contact as she takes Betsy from Faith. She turns to go without a word and the two boys follow her out.

'Thanks, Alice,' Faith calls after her. She grabs the jug and leads me through the living area.

'Is that your nanny?' I ask. Your mute nanny, who might be hearing-impaired.

'Alice? No, she works on the mail order and has the little ones when I'm in meetings. We all help each other out. Sometimes it's all hands on deck in the big barn when there's a ton of orders to fulfil. Her mom's the teacher. They live on the ranch.'

Unlike her mum's ramrod-straight posture, Alice was hunched in on herself, her shoulders rounded.

'Sounds like the mail order business is a hit.' Faith's kitchenware is part of the curated range of Frenchified items, along with food they sell for eye-watering amounts under the Lavender Field brand. Fans can coo over her aprons and dishes, and buy a little bit of her life while she adds to her fortune.

Her entrepreneurial spirit began in her teenage years with her Made in Utah brand of demure dresses for churchy girls, which she modelled herself. I wouldn't have been seen dead in any of it, but she achieved a niche following and outsourced production with the help of her parents. She gave it up after marrying Marty to follow his dream instead of hers. After the birth of her first daughter, she switched to children's dresses, further embracing divine motherhood.

She leads us to a small room with a table, laptop and recording equipment. Unlike the kitchen, this is unfamiliar territory, since her indoor videos only show the open-plan kitchen and dining room. It smells like lavender, but there's no sign of the overpriced pouches. Maybe it's her $40 lavender room spray. I grab my laptop for the recording and check her microphones can be connected. She'd offered me the use of all her kit in the ranch's recording room, but I brought my own, maxing out my carry-on bag.

'The equipment's already set up,' Faith says.

'Thanks, but I have my laptop.' I log in.

'It's better to record it with my software.' Her voice is firm, but still with her trademark sweetness. 'It avoids compatibility glitches with the mics.'

'I'll do a soundcheck.' I slide on my headphones to avoid a tense stand-off. It's working fine but doesn't bode well that she wants control of the recording. She reluctantly concedes, and we face each other across the small table. Does she know this won't be a total love-in? More of a battle of wills. I might be obsessed, but I'm no fan.

Chapter Eleven

'Firstly, Faith,' I say, 'thanks for inviting me to your beautiful home at Lavender Field Ranch.'

'You're welcome,' she says with enthusiasm. 'I'm so happy to have you here.'

I tell her I baked sourdough bread at the weekend. 'How do you bake bread so effortlessly? I was covered head to toe in flour, and my child was picking bits of dried dough from my hair like monkey grooming. Seriously, how do you do it?'

'Practice,' she says, a smile in her voice. 'When you do something every day, it's as simple as cleaning your teeth.'

'True, but I leave for work with toothpaste down my front.'

Her sweet laugh rings out and she's transformed before me. This is the Faith I know from social media, the consummate performer. My inner gremlin wants to ask if she's ever got wasted, since Mormons don't drink. I also keep wanting to swear. I'd love to hear her swear. That would be hilarious.

'Your social media is all about living a simpler life. What's driving you to achieve it?'

'I want the best for my family and me. It fell into place when we took on the ranch. Marty wanted animals and I wanted to cook. People got a kick from seeing me churn the milk while the babies ambled round in home-made clothes.' She's on-brand, acting like her success is a happy accident. But I want the real story, which means scratching at the polished veneer.

'What made you switch from making womenswear to your children's clothing range?'

'Marty thought it would be cute to make their clothes.'

'*He* makes their clothes?'

'Ha ha! No. He wanted me to make them.'

'And what did *you* want?'

There's a tiny narrowing of her eyes, the slightest head tilt at me veering beyond the approved script. 'I wanted to show other moms that you can have an income while staying home with your kids. And I wanted to share my ways of caring for my family.'

'I'm all for mums having an income, but do you actually enjoy grinding your own wheat?'

'It tastes so much better.' There's a questioning look in her smile.

'Some people believe you glamorise domestic work and hide the dross from living on a working farm—'

'I just love our natural approach. I look for the good around us.' Her voice is melodic and upbeat for the recording, but her mouth downturns and her brow furrows so I ease back.

'Your social media is enchanting. When I watch your videos, it's like you cast a spell.'

'Thank you.' Her smile returns.

'For the record, I'm here with my daughter and it's exactly as we all see it online.' Apart from the messy kitchen counter. 'Do you think it piles on the pressure for women to cook from scratch when they already do so much?'

She looks like a puzzled kitten. 'It's my choice to live this way and if women like you find inspiration, then I'm happy. Our business is based around our home, so we can be hands-on with the kids.'

'What does your husband do that's hands-on?'

'We raise the kids together. They spend time with him out on the ranch and he's involved at home.'

'Who gets up in the night?'

'Usually me, as he has to manage the ranch. He does it really well.'

'But you have a career too.'

'If I've had a bad night, Marty will take the kids and give them breakfast. He's such a good husband and father. And he teaches them about the farm.'

'I bet you teach them a lot.'

'Not like Marty. He's the business brain. You should hear his views.'

No thanks.

'He's a dynamo.'

I force a smile. She takes her devotion way too far. 'You're a success. You don't have to dim your light for anyone else.'

'Oh, but Marty lights me up. We're all so lucky to have him.'

Okay, lost cause, have it your own way.

'I'm fascinated by your videos of baking bread. How often do you bake?'

'Every day, pretty much.' She regains her serenity.

'What if you don't feel like it?'

'It's part of my routine, but if I don't bake, we'll eat something else.'

'Doritos?'

I want to push the boundaries. I'm not here for a rehash of every interview she's ever done, but Faith's holding firm.

'Your whole life is labour-intensive. What do you do to relax?'

'Kneading bread is relaxing.'

Kneading bread is *not* relaxing. 'What about having a Balinese massage like other millionaire influencers?'

'We lead a simple life here.'

I'm trying to reach the point where listeners lean in. It comes from a real conversation, getting to the heart of it, but we're skating over the surface.

'It's a full life, considering your business and six children. You have a baby every two years, will you keep going?'

She grimaces and slumps a little. I wish she was on camera to capture this moment when her persona slips, but then she wouldn't have done it. 'If it's God's will,' she says in her lilting voice.

Let's give our uteruses to Jesus, I want to lilt back. 'If God has his way, you could have ten kids or more.'

She doesn't want more kids. It's all there in her body language, but she gives a melodic 'uh huh' of agreement. So she is a little bit fake after all.

'I'm sensing that you don't want ten kids.'

Another sweet laugh. 'We have six lovely children and that's enough for me right now.'

'I hope you set God straight, because it's you who should decide.'

She gives me a hurt look for questioning her God.

None of this is headline news. Her mask slipped at the prospect of ten children, but if I push more she'll pull back. How do I get to the real story? She wants a puff piece from an adoring fan, while I'm here to discover hidden truths. My chances to ace it are running out. Why did I think myself a match for this matchless woman who does it all so well? But what she says next shocks me into silence.

Chapter Twelve

'You're a Mormon, right?' Faith asks.

I'm blindsided. She said it to shut me down, but how does she know? I'm the opposite of a good Mormon woman. She's somehow found out about my past and that's why she invited me, thinking I'd follow a softly adoring script.

I swallow my frustration at her derailing the interview. 'I'm no Latter-day Saint.' We lock eyes. 'I'm a Latter-day Sinner.'

'So you're a lapsed Mormon?'

This is too exposing. And the focus should be on her. 'I was raised LDS, but I turned away from it as a teenager. There wasn't a big Mormon community in England, so I just drifted away.' Other Mormon kids are locked in because their entire social circle is LDS. But peer pressure went in my favour. At secondary school, religious kids were weird, so I hid my background. I had a different way of being with my friends compared to home and church. Friends won out.

'Are you in contact with your family?'

I am not going there. Not with *her*, of all people. 'Not really, no.' I don't say that my dad died years ago. My mum had opinions on me skipping church as a teenager, but getting pregnant with no decent husband in sight, or any man at all, went beyond the pale.

The strangest part is that most of us deride trad wives. *I* should be the relatable one, but she's the one who's winning, and that's her point. Faith's turned the tables, but I spin them back.

'That's why your life fascinates me. I sometimes wonder about that fork in the road. Had I stayed a Mormon, would I be married and home-based with several kids instead of a single working mum? What would you be doing if you'd had a career outside the home?'

'I'd be running my clothes business.' She looks wistful. 'For women, not just kids' clothes as a part of our range.'

'How about a collab with a women's brand?'

'I get offers, but it would mean time away from family. It's better to focus on our Made in Utah range. And you?' She looks sweetly at me. 'Your podcast is about being the best parent you can. What would be your choice?'

'I like the idea of a simpler life. Time to cook and be in nature. You've made it work for you, but are you fulfilled without designing your clothes range?'

'I've found my creative outlet through making content to share with others.'

She's not so different to me. I do the same with my podcast, in a small way, balancing out the frustrations of my day job. She must dislike aspects of her life, but she's turned it to her advantage.

'Are you living the dream?' I ask.

'In many ways. We're living here in beautiful surroundings. And for you, I think it's possible to have more freedom and be less constrained.'

She nods as she speaks, holding strong eye contact, like she's sending me a message beyond her words. There's more going on that she's not saying. Does she say it to anyone? Her husband should be someone she can bitch to about being held to impossible standards, but then he's the one holding her to those standards.

'How do you define a freer life, given the constraints of your traditional lifestyle?'

'It's breathing fresh air, riding a horse, giving my children the best start in life. It's important to do what you love. You can make it work.' Is there nothing she won't reframe as a positive?

'We touched upon the traditional roles you and Marty have in your marriage. How does he feel about the huge success of your social media?'

'He's happy to run the ranch in the background. We work in harmony, since the social media account isn't me, it's Lavender Field Ranch. It's our life together.'

'What does he think about people labelling you a trad wife and saying your marriage and religion are sexist?'

'I'm not a trad wife. Our choices work for us.' She says it all in her smiling way, which comes through in her voice, but as she speaks she swipes a pointed finger across her neck in a throat-slitting gesture, telling me to kill this line of questioning.

I like these flashes of the real her, although she's only showing me, not our audience. She's too smart to let the outside world see her true colours. We round the interview off in a gracious finale, both of us playing our part.

After my initial shock, I like the angle she pushed on me. The patron saint of Mormons goes head to head with the Latter-day Sinner. Faith handed me the hook. I'll play up the conflict between us. She's never done a contentious interview, so it shows a different side of her, batting off the questions many followers would like answered. I'll add my own sound bites to direct understanding, since

Faith's answers sounded relentlessly positive, but her body language told a different story. And that's the story I want to tell.

Faith turns off the recording equipment.

'How did you know I was Mormon?'

'Your name gave me a clue. There was a Fairbrook in my class at school, so I looked it up.'

'I'm Fair*brock*, not brook, so I'm not related.' I can't believe she's checked up on me. I try to steady the terrified racing of my heart. How much does she know? Surely not everything or she'd never have asked me here.

Chapter Thirteen

Faith acts light and breezy. 'The kids'll finish school soon, so let's get dinner started.'

I take shallow breaths while I wrestle my heart rate under control. I'm freaked out by her digging into my past, but she's playing it down so I tell myself to style it out. I pack up my kit, then join her in the kitchen that I know so well from her videos.

We make a sausage and bean casserole, and I can't believe I'm cooking with Faith. Now the interview's out of the way, I'll let her take the lead, especially given her culinary expertise. She's still exuding warmth, despite my interrogative line of questioning. No sign of her bearing a grudge, but I sense she's projecting an image. A shaft of golden light bathes her face and, up close, I see light-reflecting concealer under her eyes. It's a dewily perfect match to her skin tone. She catches me looking. What else is she concealing?

'I didn't think you wore make-up,' I say. 'That's such a flattering shade for you.'

'I shot a reel earlier. It made me camera-ready since Betsy had me up in the night, but I'm blessed to have her.'

'And your family are blessed to have you, especially Marty. Does he appreciate everything you do?'

'We appreciate each other,' she says in her light voice. If I held the paring knife to her throat, would she tell me what he's really like? How far would she go to maintain the perfect image? Would she lay down her life to stay on-brand?

She asks why I left the church. I say I wanted to be like my secular friends and alcohol was a factor. 'And obviously the thing about keeping yourself pure for marriage never stuck.' I'm not sugar-coating it. This is who I am and I'll never measure up to her. 'Being more Faith' means being more fake.

'And now?'

'Since I had Willow, my values have changed for the better, but I'm not religious.'

She smiles softly. 'You think you're not, but deep down, you know the truth.'

What does that mean?

The kids' voices carry to us from outside and Faith opens the door. We step outdoors, where the air is cool and crisp after the Aga's heat. Willow's buzzing. She loves the rural paradise, while I see a darker reality. She has a go at milking Myrtle the cow. I wince at the thought of her trampled by a hefty animal that weighs a ton. 'It's icky and smells bad,' she announces, 'but it's cool to squirt the milk.'

Still no sign of Marty. How will I react to seeing him? In the meantime, I realise I've been yearning for nature and open vistas. I adore the buzz of New York, but Manhattan loves money. We're on the outside, not invited to the party. It's easy to deride Faith, but their quality of life beats ours.

At last, Marty appears, riding towards us on horseback, Marlboro Man in his cowboy hat. I expected to hate him on sight, but it's a surreal vision. He's looking straight at me. A bolt of electricity shoots through my body. He pulls back on the reins and the horse stops a few paces away, the cowboy looming over us. I swallow hard.

Faith introduces us. His interested gaze lingers on me, the trace of a smile playing on his lips. Am I supposed to swoon? Screw that. My smile stays fixed in place. He's putting on a show, unaware that I loathe him and will never change my view. 'This here's Chester.' He leans forward to pat the horse, asking Willow if she'd like a ride.

Willow looks up at him with the wonder and reverence she usually reserves for Father Christmas. She gives a wordless, wide-eyed nod. Faith looks at me, and I lift Willow up for Marty to hoist her into the saddle with him. He shows her how to use the reins.

'The world looks better when you're on a horse,' he says.

'Sure does.' Willow grins, exposing the gaps in her teeth. I love her for embracing it, even if she thinks we've landed in a Wild West theme park filled with actors. Or is that my own suspicion? Marty's all cowboy charm, but I shudder inwardly and remind myself I'm here to do a job that goes beyond the podcast. It could help fix a situation that's been brewing for a while, but it could also land me in hot water.

They clip-clop around, and she squeals in delight.

'He has the Utah rizz,' Faith says.

'What's that?'

'Charm. It works on kids, horses, adults.'

Not me though. Minutes later, he lifts her off the horse and her face is radiant. Country life suits her. The cowboy gallops off leaving clouds of dust, and the kids show us around the quaint log cabin, which is where we'll be sleeping.

It's like stepping inside a museum with a lovingly recreated olde-worlde room, minus the grinding austerity. It's decorated simply, with bare wood and buttermilk-painted walls. The kids pile en masse onto the two shabby-chic armchairs beside a wood-burning stove. I imagine cosy nights beside the fire.

'It has stairs!' Willow clomps up them with the others to the small mezzanine floor set up as a single bedroom. They bounce on the bed that Willow will sleep in. She's never slept in an upstairs bedroom. Isiah, the oldest, shows us the chi-chi little bathroom and double bedroom. I'm struck by the golden light of late afternoon bathing the interior.

Back at the farmhouse, Willow gives Faith our thank you gift of organic chocolate truffles in a wooden gift box with a quaint watercolour on the lid of Central Park.

'We made chocolate truffles, but they looked rubbish so we ate them,' Willow says. 'Mom said they tasted of failure, but I liked them with ice cream.' It was supposed to be an easy recipe, but the grainy, lumpy chocolate ganache stuck to our hands when we tried moulding it into balls. We spent last Sunday morning sourcing a worthy alternative.

Marty joins us, kicking off his boots and hanging up his cowboy hat, revealing thick, sun-streaked hair. And... he's so short. It wasn't obvious on horseback, and I hide my surprise.

I'm no gazelle and I don't judge anyone on their height, but the optical illusion stuns me. Just like in Hollywood, he and Faith must have bigged him up with camera angles for their content. I realise that he's never in the same frame as another man, and Faith is more petite than she appears online, so he's a beefcake beside her. He's not *short* short, just not the hunk of manhood from their socials. His ten-gallon hat adds another few inches and his cowboy boots are built-up, so he's more image-conscious than I imagined. Or vain.

'How's my pretty lady?' he says to Faith.

I'd get the ick if a man said that to me, but she kisses him on the lips and nuzzles in as if he's her whole world. 'Honey?' she coos, stepping back. 'Can you please open this jar?'

The cowboy smiles and unscrews the lid on some home-made tomato sauce. She gazes adoringly at him, the way she does on camera, when he should be adoring her.

'Thanks!' she says with enthusiasm. He puffs out his chest, his smile self-satisfied. I remember this couple dynamic from my childhood in the LDS Church, but it grates that someone successful in her own right needs to act helpless to stroke her husband's ego.

The six kids sit around the table with us three adults, plus the ever-contented baby Betsy. There's been online speculation that Betsy is a prop. On camera, she could pass for one of those uncanny 'reborn' dolls that simulate breathing and baby snuffles. Faith's groupies insist that 'contented moms make contented babies', but the sad truth is that some Mormons condition their children to behave from birth.

'Let us pray,' Marty says. The kids fall silent and everyone holds hands on the tabletop. Willow's between Emily and Eden, her new besties. I give her a small smile and nod to say 'go with it'. I should have primed her about saying grace, but Faith never shows this part in their videos. She's appealing to the widest possible audience, including heathen city girls who just want cute escapism. The occasional mention of church is enough virtue signalling for the believers, but they know she's one of them.

Marty's at the head of the table and says a mercifully short grace. Everyone responds with a solemn 'amen'. Willow doesn't say anything embarrassing. I'm reminded of my brother, who'd say 'Roger that' in a booming voice at the end of prayers, much to my mum's consternation.

It's good to see colour in Willow's cheeks. She can be innocent here without attracting bullies, and she fits right in with the tribe of kids, with her honey-coloured hair and ready smile. She's always wanted siblings, and back home I go out of my way to compensate with play dates, even if it's a poor substitute.

Faith serves apple pie and ice cream, all home-made. 'Marty loves pie,' she says. Pies for the Patriarchy. When the cowboy talks, his surrendered wife gazes dreamily at him. Given their online fame, I'm still surprised they've invited me, a nosy stranger, into their lives. Before coming here, I thought I'd lucked out, but now I suspect an ulterior motive connected to my past life.

After dinner, I help clear up, then we leave. We're catching the first flight out tomorrow since those seats were the cheapest.

'We won't bother you in the morning,' I tell Faith. 'I'll order a cab to the airport.'

'No need. We have it covered,' she says cheerfully.

'Really? You're sure it's not a problem?'

Faith assures me it's not, so we say our goodbyes and Marty guides us to the log cabin, holding a lantern-style torch. 'So what do you think of our life here, Willow?' he asks.

'It's way cool. I love Myrtle and the school is, like, right there.' She points in its direction. 'You don't have to ride the bus to get there, and I even like the nothing.'

'The nothing?'

She nods emphatically.

'She means the wide-open spaces.'

'Ha. The nothing. That might catch on, ladybug. I like the nothing too.'

At the cabin, he reaches forward and opens the door. A light is already burning inside.

'You have everything you need?'

'Sure. Thank you for your hospitality.' All business, I shake his hand goodbye, relieved he's not a hugger. I try not to grimace at the handshake, but I shudder inwardly.

'Thank you for having us,' Willow says, before she turns and runs into the cabin.

He smiles after her with a wistful look, as if he'd like to hang out with us some more, which is weird when he already has a shedload of kids. Then he tips his cowboy hat and says, 'Ma'am,' before turning to stride back to the ranch house.

Willow's sagging from exhaustion after our early start. 'He called me ladybug,' she says with a grin.

'I know. Isn't it quiet here?' At that moment an animal screeches outside.

Willow jumps and clings to me. 'Are there bears?' she asks in a tremulous whisper. 'Is that a bear?'

'It's the ranch animals saying good night to each other. Nothing's getting inside.' But I'm on edge too. Willow's anxiety is understandable, when those dark fairy tales for kids often involve a little rustic cottage in the wilds. 'You want to sleep in the big bed with me?' I can't have her waking up scared in the night and tumbling down the wooden staircase.

We slide under the soft cotton sheets, scented with lavender. I'd intended to make notes on promoting the podcast, but the lavender works its sleepy magic. I don't wake up until my phone alarm beeps for our early start when it's still dark. My dreams were fractured and freaky. I let them retreat into the night.

Faith has left us a breakfast basket on the kitchen counter, with milk and yogurt in the fridge. Willow eats oatmeal, yogurt and a dollop of Good Life jam – fifteen bucks a jar – while I strip the bed. I churn over the weird conversation about my Mormon past. Why all this effort for me? And why research me so heavily? I came here to understand her motivations, but I'm even less sure now she's made it personal.

There's a knock at the door. Despite the early start, butterflies flutter in my chest at the prospect of seeing Joel, now I can relax. I open the door, expecting him in all his cowboy glory, but it's Faith.

'Good morning.' She smiles. 'I hope you slept well. I'm driving you to the airport.'

'Oh, but we've put you out enough—'

'I want to talk to you on the way.'

My breath catches. My instincts warn me to stay wary. Does she know my real reason for coming here?

Chapter Fourteen

'I want to ask you something,' Faith says on the way to the airport. Willow's zoned out with earbuds and Spotify. 'We'd like you to join us at the ranch.'

'What?' I look at her in confusion. What does she even mean?

'I want your help with online promotion. When you contacted me, I saw you had the right experience.' She stares at the road ahead.

I'm stunned. She flashes a glance at me.

'You asked me here for a job interview?'

'It was a way for us to meet and decide if we could work together with no pressure or expectations.'

It starts making sense, including the background check. 'But you could give a shout out on your socials. You'd have a whole talent pool to choose from.'

'It'll attract the wrong kind of attention, and I'd be bombarded. I had a good feeling about you even before we met. You're all about living a simpler life, and I like you.'

How can she like me when I went all out to rattle her cage in the interview?

'Your podcast is honest, and you can help me relate to busy, working women. Our different perspectives can help us grow.'

My brain is on fire from this crazy turn of events. She cheerily fills me in on the details. It's a drop in salary, but this must be a cheaper place to live.

'I'd have to check how much a rental would cost here—'

'You can live in the cabin.'

'We can?'

'Rent free.'

I'd be considerably better off and could save for the first time ever, not that I can take the job. Of course I can't… or could I?

'Willow can attend school with the other kids. She fits right in. Emily loves her.'

I twist in my seat to look at her, gazing out of the window, moving her head in time with the music.

'Is Marty okay with it?'

'Marty thinks you're the answer to our prayers.'

Or the wrecking ball he didn't see coming.

At the airport drop-off, she gives Willow a big hug goodbye and then embraces me too. 'I hope you say yes.' She pulls back and looks into my eyes. It's strangely beguiling; I do almost feel like I know her after following her online for years.

'I'll think it over.'

'Sure. Please can you hold off posting the interview podcast until you've made up your mind?'

'Oh… why?'

She's already getting into her car and waving goodbye. 'Thanks, that's great.'

But I didn't agree. I should keep in with her though, while I consider the offer.

'I don't wanna go home,' Willow says.

'You liked it there?'

'I wanna go back to school with Emily.'

'That would be cool, but what about Coco and Tamsin?' She'd miss her besties from school.

'Can we have some animals?'

'Cows and horses? I don't think so.' I steer us towards check-in.

'A kid goat!' She beams at me.

When we're strapped in for take-off, my heart soars along with the plane. I came here for a podcast episode and I've come away with a job offer. As we look down on the Utah vista, I know I'm mad to consider it. Willow loves the ranch, but it's crazily small compared to Manhattan. The cabin freaked her out after dark, and it'll be too quiet and isolated, especially in winter. What if we can't shrink ourselves to fit? But then, the landscape is vast, so that might compensate.

The younger me would jump at it. The younger me took risks and shook things up, but we'd be screwed if... *when* it doesn't work out. I can't deny the professional opportunity though. If it goes tits up – *when* it goes tits up – the job will look good on my CV. This is huge. It promises so much that I'm abuzz with anticipation while consumed with fear because it's wrong on so many levels.

Wanting to say yes is a knee-jerk reaction to my job insecurity and Willow's issues at school. It's an escape route, but it could also fix the tricky situation I'm entangled in. I'd be returning on a mission, but my real intention would stay hidden. A storm is brewing in my head. It's either a gift from God or a disaster ready to happen, and what troubles me most is Marty.

Melissa's the answer to my prayers. Soon as I set eyes on her, I knew she'd suit my requirements. I won't make the same mistakes this time. The job spec is exacting and it's down to me to manage it better. Melissa's feisty, a wild mare, but I'll break her in. She thinks she's smart, but she has no idea what's gonna hit her. By the time she works it out in her pretty little head, it'll be game over.

Chapter Fifteen

I haven't been happy for a long time. I mostly ignore my dark, pulsating urge to go away and start a different life. But I've been feeling it more and more, wondering how I've ended up here. I squash the rising tide of discontent by keeping busy. Even so, I'm wary of Faith's offer. Is it too risky? Questions circle my mind but nothing lands.

'I wanna go back to the cabin,' Willow says as we arrive home.

'Me too, baby.' The dreary apartment is even smaller. How is that possible? I think of the wooden love seat on the front porch where we could watch the sun set or she'd run free with her new friends. The hopeful images are tinged with doubt.

Am I ready to give up on NYC? In my early twenties, New York was my beating heart. The wonderful chaos of a shared apartment and a new job consumed me. I knocked back fizzy wine on Fridays and danced until dawn. Then along came Willow's dad who swept me skyward then walked away without a backward glance. I love Manhattan, but it feels like I'm failing it.

'What did you think of the people there?' I expect her to enthuse about Emily, who's closest in age to her.

'Faith is so nice. She's like a fairy princess.'

'Except her dresses are looser.'

What if she keeps on being bullied? What if she runs with the wrong crowd in high school and it impacts the rest of her life? I'm not telling her about the job until I've worked out Faith's motive. I get that it's part of a bigger plan to keep her brand fresh. She can show herself coaching a city girl on trad wifery in a *My Fair Lady* reboot. It could spin her social media in a new direction. Is that all she's playing at? Because something's going on. Beverley's warning rings in my head. *They might turn you into one of them.* But if Faith wants a transformation, she'll be disappointed.

I'm overthinking. She's a successful career woman who wants me there to do a job. When Willow's asleep, I'd like to get stuck into post-production for the podcast, if it weren't for Faith asking me to hold off. Instead, I make a list.

Pros of taking the job

Fewer expenses = more financial security.

No bad influences or assholes.

I need a radical change.

Fresh mountain air, healthy lifestyle, light-filled home.

An easy move when home and school go with the job.

No commute.

No workplace bullshit.

Every day is an Insta reel waiting to happen.

~~Joel the hot cowboy~~

Maybe I won't feel like a failure.

Cons of taking the job

Cultural wilderness.

Weird Stepford energy.

What if Willow's still spooked by the cabin at night?

What if I'm spooked?

I'll miss my friends.

No public transport and I can't drive.

They might foist Jesus on us.

Handing them too much control over our lives?

Living close to Marty could be a mistake. A big mistake.

While the pros are mostly tangible benefits, the cons look like a list of irrational fears. Despite my misgivings, I'd be mad to turn it down. I take a deep breath and type an email.

> Dear Faith,
>
> Thank you so much for your time and hospitality. Willow can't stop talking about it! I loved interviewing you for my podcast.
>
> Regarding your job offer, I am interested. Please can you outline the requirements and benefits? My résumé is attached.
>
> Kind regards,
>
> Melissa

The next morning, she emails me a job spec and benefits package. Healthcare for us both, and decent holiday entitlement. I convince her to match my current salary and upgrade the job title from assistant to social media manager. The title will look good on my CV. I scour through the contract. Then I stop short at one of the requirements.

Chapter Sixteen

I reread the offending clause in the employment contract.

> You are prohibited from posting any non-official content relating to Lavender Field Ranch, its business dealings and its inhabitants, including the Eversen family. You are prohibited from sharing any details of your employers, your work or your accommodation on the ranch on any third-party media including the internet. This includes photography, videos and recordings.

My podcast brought us together. She can insist I sign an NDA, but the podcast is my passion and she's shutting it down. I email for clarification.

My phone lights up with a call from her.

'Faith? Hi.' My voice is uncertain.

'Hi, Melissa, how are you?'

'I'm confused. I thought you liked what I was trying to achieve with my podcast—'

'I do,' she says with her trademark charm and warmth. 'If you decide to join us, we'll work together on the Lavender Field brand. We don't want background noise. So many people want a piece of me. When they catch on that you're on the team, they'll target you. It's relentless and I need our work to focus on the ranch without those distractions.'

I can argue that point, but she goes on.

'More importantly, our ethos is family first. We practise what we preach. We only post content that's beneficial to the brand and then we have space to enjoy our time away from work. That's a core value. It's for our well-being and to lead our kids by example, so we have family time not screen time.'

'But it's up to me what I do outside work.'

'Yes, but it's *downtime* not work time. We're on social media for work purposes. If you join us, I'd like you to prioritise the brand during work hours and spend your downtime *living* a simpler life rather than posting about it. That's your aim, which I fully support.'

I sense the wholesome smile in her soft voice. The baby's saying 'bababa' in the background.

'Once you're here, you'll understand. It's the secret to how I balance work and family. Online content is work. Family time – real family time outside of filming and photos – that's sacred. I only go online in work hours. I don't scroll through likes and follows from people I don't know. I only check on what posts are most popular so I can do more. There'll be so many other things to occupy you and Willow that you won't care about posting content.'

She's missing the point. We content creators are enmeshed in social media. It's like telling an athlete not to be inspired by other sportspeople. I analyse content to stay ahead of trends *for my job*. Also, I'm a grown-up and can make my own fucking choices.

'I have to feed Betsy. Melissa, I want us to start off right. Did I explain it so you understand?' Her voice is full of care and patience.

'I guess... I just...' I'm thrown, which annoys me. If this had been an email, I'd have crafted a better reply. 'I'm giving it my consideration. Thanks for calling to clarify.'

We end the call and I puff out my cheeks. I'm an adult who posts and consumes content. I like cruising the internet in spare moments, but I'm pretty sure she won't budge. I bristle over her stance, when the podcast is a creative outlet, not a second job. Am I prepared to stop it because my new employer says so? My mind had been racing through all the episodes I could produce about my journey from harried NY mum to rural earth mother. I still want the measure of Faith, and this reveals another layer. Beneath the sweetness, her message is clear: she's the star, not me.

Is it worth refusing over this one issue? Most deals involve compromise, and I know how things will pan out if we stay here. Willow's a target for bullies, while the school apologists brush it off. I'm stressed from job uncertainty as Alexandra tramples over me on her way to the top. I'm in the danger zone and losing my job would be a disaster. If Faith has good intentions, she chose me because I'm a seasoned content producer who's aligned with her brand. She doesn't see me as a problematic has-been, unlike my employer.

Maybe she has a point about drawing a line. How many times do I surreptitiously check my socials during family time? One of my fears is Willow experiencing the downside of social media when she's too young to handle it. She could be sucked in by preening influencers and the impossible demands of looking desirable. My mind crosses to the dark side of cyberbullying, boys pressuring her for naked selfies, paedos masquerading as kids online. So much to fear.

At the ranch she'll be around kids with traditional values baked in. Despite their cyber fame, they don't have online accounts. She'll keep her innocence for longer. As for my podcast, I'll keep it alive in spirit by attempting a simpler family life, giving me material for when I leave the ranch, if I can work around the NDA.

Faith limits her time online, and I can too. I'll find something to do in front of the fire. Willow can read the childhood classics and I'll do what… quilting? That won't cut it. If I'm honest, I'm addicted to social media under the guise of research. I'll go crazy during the long winter nights, an addict craving her fix. I'll agree not to create my own content, but how can Faith stop me scrolling when Willow's asleep?

Anyway, it's not forever. I'd be there to do a job, just not the one they think. My fascination with Faith and Lavender Field Ranch runs deep because of Marty. He's the riskiest element. There's a big challenge on the horizon, but whether it pays off is unknowable. I add another point to my list of cons:

> What if they find out the real reason I'm infiltrating their lives?

Chapter Seventeen

After we come home from school, Willow sits at her little desk to write about the Utah trip. It gives me a warm glow that she likes writing exercises.

As I'm finishing my work, she brings me her notepad and asks me to spell the hard words, which she laboriously corrects. I catch sight of the title. Jeez, lay it on the line.

> **The best day of my life**
>
> We went in an airplane which I never done before it was better than a fairground ride because we flew over clouds!! I saw a mountain and horses and rode a horse and we stayed in a cabin like on Little House on the Prairie and I milked a cow. Emily was nice. They have their own school!! I wish we had a cabin the cabin was awesome there might be bears I forgot to ask.

I suggest ways to expand on it and later she comes back and reads her revised writing assignment aloud. She climbs onto my lap and I inhale the sweet scent of her hair. 'If you could live here,' I ask, 'or in the cabin in Utah, what would you choose?'

'The cabin!' She twists to look at me, her face lit up. I need a dose of her enthusiasm.

'Would you miss your friends and going out in the city?'

'I guess.' She shuffles around so she's kneeling on my lap and we're almost nose to nose.

'But we could come back to visit.'

She nods.

'What if I told you Faith offered me a job, and she said we can stay in the cabin, and you can go to school there?'

Her eyes widen. 'Really?'

'Really.'

'Really, *really*?'

'Really, really.'

She grins in gap-toothed joy. 'Can we go today?'

I wish her pure delight would rub off on to me. No chance when I'm nagged with the fear of it all going wrong. On the surface, accepting the offer is a no-brainer, but it's risky. *The cabin was awesome there might be bears* sums up my quandary.

She squeals and laughs. That's it then. We're going. The first thing I do is give a month's notice on our apartment. Willow goes straight off to school and tells her teacher, so I inform them when she'll be leaving. Coming home, she rushes ahead and knocks on Beverley's door where she jumps up and down to deliver the news.

'Gawd, no.' Beverley clutches at her face. 'You've gotta be kidding me.'

Willow backs into me, silenced. Beverley's so crest-fallen that I invite her over for a drink later. Back in our apartment, I tell Willow that she prefers the city and she'll miss us.

She turns up three hours later with a cocktail shaker and two glasses. 'I've mixed our drinks.'

I pour the cocktails while Willow regales her with ranch stories. '...And the cow makes a noise like this...'

Beverley digs into the chips and dips, polite but saying little. Willow's so caught up in her reverie that she doesn't notice. After I tuck her into bed, Beverley barely waits for me to close the living room door before starting.

'You thought this through, kiddo?'

'From every angle.' Now my mind's made up, I've sidestepped my doubts to throw myself into moving.

'I can't believe I went on rallies in the Seventies to save you girls from this same old shit, and you're endorsing it.'

Fair.

'How can you go live with a bunch of wackadoodle flat-earthers? You know Utah has the highest rate of marriage in the country and the highest rate of antidepressants prescribed to women? How direct is that correlation?'

'I didn't know that.'

'It's nearly double the next state in the ranking.'

But Faith's too pure for antidepressants, and I'll be needing meds if I stay here. I call up one of her videos and press play on the final frames. Faith sets down a big plate of buttermilk pancakes in front of her kids around the table.

Beverley peers at the screen. 'No one would care less about her pancakes if she wasn't young and attractive.' She flaps her hand to the right. 'Go back a little.'

I let the video play out. Beverley's dumbstruck for a few minutes as Faith carries a pail of fresh milk to her kitchen and makes buttermilk.

'She's screwing with us, right? She can't be for real. Who the fuck wants to milk a cow? I mean, come on!' She cackles.

'It's a lifestyle choice,' I say weakly.

'You sure this ain't parody?'

'She's the real deal.'

'Nice peasant dress.' She nods towards the screen. 'Did she make it on her spindle? Does she feed it through her mangle once she's scrubbed it in the river?'

'It's calming.'

'It's dumb. So what, you gonna go churning butter when you could do something more interesting with your time? You'll smell like a barnyard animal. Just you see.'

I roll my eyes.

'Blessed be the inconvenience. I'd study *The Handmaid's Tale* if I were you. Are you enrolling Willow in Jesus Camp?' She hauls herself up and brushes crumbs from her trousers.

'Beverley...'

'I didn't think you English girls put up with that patriarchal bullshit.'

I gulp my cocktail.

'But hey, enjoy trad wife boot camp. I guess it's like conversion therapy.'

'Don't hold back.'

'I'm fucking right and you know it.'

I look away.

'I'll miss you,' she says sadly.

'And we'll miss you. If you want the truth, I'm going there on a secret mission.'

She lowers her glasses and fixes me with a beady stare. 'What secret mission?'

'You've already touched upon it, but if I told you, I'd have to kill you.'

'Stop screwing around.'

'I think you'll approve. It's classified, but you'll be the first to know when I come clean.'

Chapter Eighteen

Eric's out, so I delay my resignation and screw with Alexandra instead.

'Alexa,' I call to her. 'Can you recommend an upbeat Gen Z song?'

She glares at me. Angelo looks from her to me and sinks in his chair.

'Excuse me?' She scrunches up her face in consternation. 'I'm not Alexa.'

'Isn't that what Eric calls you now?'

'He calls me Alex.'

'Oh, silly me. I thought you were Alexa.'

'You just spoke like you were giving orders to *an* Alexa.'

She's easy to wind up. 'I need youth culture alignment,' I emulate her ditsy tones, 'and you're the expert.'

She narrows her eyes on me, unsure if I'm toying with her, but she can't resist a compliment.

'It's so inspiring to work with someone who's young.' I keep up this low-level trolling all day, interrupting her with demands for her insight.

'I'm busy,' she snaps mid-afternoon, holding up a palm to fend off my latest inane request.

'Get used to it, now you're an account manager. I mean it in a friendly way. It's good to be friendly to your co-workers.'

'I don't have time,' she enunciates, glancing towards Eric's empty office, ready to lodge another complaint.

I resign first thing the next morning, after pouncing on Eric the moment he arrives.

'You're leaving?' He's dumbfounded.

'I was headhunted by an influencer with ten million followers.'

'Which one?'

'Faith at Lavender Field Ranch.'

He should know all the online movers and shakers, but his mouth downturns and he shakes his head. 'Nope.'

I feel a lightness I haven't known in ages. Alexandra looks daggers at me through the glass partition. When I return to my desk, she jumps up and marches into his office. He pacifies her with hand motions and calls Angelo in too. When Eric presumably tells them I'm leaving she shoots a look of consternation at me. I wave cheerily. So *friendly* to my co-workers.

The office door opens and Alexandra sashays over, her cheerleader smile pasted on.

'Congrats, Melissa.' There's a hard edge to her voice, her jaw tight.

'Yeah, congratulations,' Angelo says more warmly, returning to his desk. 'Respect!'

She stands over me, her manicured fingertips resting on my desk. 'Who's your new employer?'

'Lavender Field Ranch.'

Her smile disappears, replaced with the same 'how dare you' irritation she flashed at me from Eric's office.

'As in Faith Eversen? The trad wife?'

'She's not a trad wife. She makes millions from her business.'

'She's promoting trad wife values.' Her superior look returns. There's a flinty challenge in her voice.

'She's a girlboss. Trad wives don't employ a social media manager. That's me, by the way. She's an entrepreneur, using her creative skills to promote her range.' For all I know, Faith's an anti-vaxxer and flat-earther. If so, she keeps it quiet. 'I'm psyched to be running her account.'

'Have you met her?'

'Of course. She invited me to stay over. We cooked together and had dinner, her family along with my daughter and me.'

She flicks her ponytail. 'I didn't know they were recruiting.'

Has Alexandra been cruising the job ads, despite being new?

'They weren't. She liked my work and created the role specially for me. She appreciates my experience. And friendliness. I'd love to chat, but I've things to do.' I pretend to look up a number.

'I'm pleased for you.' Her face freezes into a grimace.

I drop my smile. 'You can take some credit.'

Her face is all confusion. 'How so?'

'You made the decision easier.'

She hesitates.

'I hope you get what you deserve.' I'm all out of fucks. No fucks to give.

A whirlwind month later, we're Utah bound and, this time, it's one way. I've been on a high from saying goodbye to the bad influences, the high rent, the asshole boys. Now that it's too late to turn back, my concerns have intensified. Beverley's warning rings in my ears. *Watch it. They might turn you into one of them.* Or worse. Trepidation hums through me, a sense of impending doom. What if I'm swapping my parenting podcast for true crime, with me as the cautionary tale?

Chapter Nineteen

Joel's waiting for us at Arrivals, just like before. He's even more gorgeous and my heart flips.

'Hey, city slicker.' He fist-bumps Willow and winks at me. 'Good to have you back.'

'Thanks, man,' Willow says. 'Gonna be sweet.'

Winking's friendly, right? I try not to read anything into it. He smilingly takes both our suitcases. I act cool, as I imagine kissing him. Is that a sackable offence? Workplace relationships aren't banned in my contract, and Mormons like marrying off single folk, so they might even approve. I tell myself to knock it off.

Once we're on the road, I ask if we can stop at a grocery store. 'We need some basics to last until the weekend.'

'Sure thing.' He drives us to a Walmart, saying we can get everything in one hit. It's not the rural shopping experience I'd envisaged, but Willow and I rush in and grab what we need. When we're back on the road again, Joel tells us there's been the first snowfall in the mountains. He talks to Willow about spirit animals and they discuss her choice of unicorn as if it's a real animal. When we drive on to the ranch, my mind is blown that this is our new life.

'Bunnies!' Willow exclaims as a pair of them race across a field.

'Cottontail rabbits,' Joel says.

'Can you drop us at the cabin?' I ask. 'I'll put the cold stuff in the fridge.'

'Faith asked me to bring you straight to the homestead.'

'I'll only be a minute, then we'll walk over.'

'Ohh-kaay.' He's uncertain, as if used to following instructions to the letter.

The cabin is unlocked, like last time, and Joel brings in the suitcases while I carry the grocery bags. Then he heads off, waving away our thanks.

As I finish putting the cold stuff away, his truck pulls up again outside. I go to the door and Faith jumps out, the baby strapped to her, while Joel drives off with another wave.

'Welcome.' She smiles and comes in.

Willow is rooting through the open suitcase and beams up at Faith, before taking an armful of stuff upstairs.

'Oh.' Faith stares in disgust at the sliced bread in cellophane like it's crack cocaine.

Busted.

'We baked you some rolls to help you through the first couple of days.'

'That's so kind. This'll keep.' I shove the offending loaf back in the bag.

'We always have wheat here, Melissa.'

She disapproves of store-bought. I should've known, but I can't have Willow go hungry.

'That's a lot of processed food.' She eyes it warily.

That's a lot of judgement. 'I grabbed some things to last the week. I can't perform miracles with loaves and fishes.' Although she might.

A minute in and I'm already a disappointment. I've never been so shamed by my food choices. It's healthy by normal standards, high fibre and the only sweet treats are cereal bars with no added sugar. But the rebel in me wants to start vanilla vaping and mainlining McDonald's.

'But you know how to bake,' she says.

'We love baking,' Willow says, tramping down the wooden staircase. That's my little PR powerhouse.

'We didn't know if there were baking tins in the cabin.' It's a blatant lie. I didn't think about baking at all. My sourdough fail comes back to me. It's one thing to bake at the weekend for fun, but something else entirely to rely on homebaking for your only source of bread.

'We've equipped the place with all the essentials.' She talks in the same sweet, soft voice, but she's acting violated, like I'm polluting her airspace with processed food.

'Shall we come to the ranch house?' I ask, before she withers and dies from the proximity to additives, or I bash her over the head with a block of Walmart cheese.

She nods and we step outside. That settles the online debate about whether she lives on sliced white and Pringles off camera.

I pull the door shut behind us. 'Where's the key?' I ask.

'It's safe here. You can lock yourselves in with the bolt.'

'But it's a working ranch. Anyone could walk in when we're out.'

'It's safe.' She waves it away. 'That's the upside of here versus Manhattan.'

But anyone could steal my stuff or hide in the house until after dark. A crazed fan might come prowling around. I don't say this in front of Willow, who skips along, telling Faith she gave a presentation to her classmates about the ranch, complete with the photo of her milking Myrtle.

'That's wonderful. You can give a presentation in class about city life compared to here.'

In the ranch house, Faith pours Willow a glass of milk.

'Herbal tea?' she asks me, taking a jug of pale liquid from the fridge. Hardcore Mormons don't drink tea or coffee because of some decree about the evils of caffeinated hot drinks. I'd packed my cafetiere with a bag of ground coffee stuffed inside. She'll see it as contraband, but I don't forgo my morning coffee for anyone.

I take a sip of the tea that she hands me and – *Jesus, fuck* – I want to spray it back out. *Disgusting*. I audibly gulp it down.

'What's in it?' I try not to grimace.

'Isn't it great? It's my grandma's special recipe. Packed with antioxidants.'

Now I know how boiled socks and grass cuttings taste.

We hear kids' excited voices approaching, and the four older ones burst in. Faith pours milk and they lay into a plate of oatmeal cookies. Willow lights up as Emily comes shyly towards her with a little pair of dusky pink cowboy boots.

'A welcome gift. We guessed her size,' Faith says. The boots fit and Willow nearly detonates from joy.

'I remember watching your video for baking oatmeal cookies,' I say.

She smiles. 'Let's do one tomorrow on granola bars.'

Is this a dig about Walmart cereal bars? It's either well-disguised snark or she's tutoring me in trad ways. Regardless, I'm itching to start working with her. If I'm around her five days a week, she'll let down her guard. I want to see how much of her life is reflected in the videos and how much is for show.

There's still some daylight left, so the kids take Willow to roam around. Then by evening we're settling in the cabin, and I warm up the spicy bean soup that Faith left on the hob to have with home-made rolls spread with her butter. Willow doesn't like spicy food and only eats beans if they're mixed with more interesting things, but she finishes a bowlful because Faith made it. 'Faith's so nice, Mommy, and she has nice hair.'

I'm not thrilled about her awe for Faith, but I can't object to her eating a healthy meal. At least Willow's not spooked now she has a scattering of favourite belongings around her, and she falls asleep easily.

I go to charge my laptop and realise there's no internet. The cabin has no router, the ranch Wi-Fi doesn't reach this far and my mobile signal is weak from the mountain-shaded valley. Faith thinks I won't have time to go online anyway, what with all that bread making. Home-made bread has no preservatives, so I'd have to bake two or three times a week. Sod that. I'll buy Froot Loops and chicken nuggets just to piss off the food police.

In the rush of arranging to move, I missed that Faith sees me as a trainee earth mother as well as her employee. My last job required me to summon enthusiasm for clients' brands, but that was only during work time. Now it appears I'm living and breathing the Lavender Field ethos twenty-four-seven.

'This is an experiment, okay?' I'd said to Willow before bed. 'If we don't like it, we'll go someplace else.' But I said it for me, not her, because it's not just the baking, it's the isolation and the proximity to Marty.

―

She's here. Reeled in with the promise of a better life. This'll be fun. She thinks she's in control, but women have no control on a ranch like this. The man's in charge. It's God's will. Bitch has no idea what she's signed up for.

Chapter Twenty

The next morning, I stand with a cup of coffee and marvel at the sunrise. The cabin isn't much bigger than our old apartment, but the vast landscape framed by the windows gives a sense of space. Willow can hardly wait for lessons to start, and runs to the schoolhouse at eight thirty. Their lunch is provided by silent Alice, so I needn't commit the crime of sending her to school with Walmart bread.

Faith and I only work during school hours. I turn up at the ranch house and she's wearing a Victorian nightdress with long sleeves and a ruffled high neckline. Wise move to kill Marty's passion. I assume she didn't have time to dress before the children went to school, but we begin setting up the cereal bar shoot and it turns out the nightie is daywear. Granny chic is sometimes her thing, and she has the poise to carry off wearing a potato sack.

Faith shows me how to set up the lighting for her signature aesthetic, casting flattering light and focusing the eye. I film her with a camera on a tripod. She does her little act of leaning forward to adjust the screen, as if she's propped up her smartphone to record herself. Nice touch. She says Alice used to film her, but it was more chaotic without childcare for the younger ones. As well as the camera, I move around her to film on my iPhone from different angles, including close-ups of the food prep.

She tells the camera she bakes the granola squares the same way her grandma did. That's minus the expert lighting. A huge tub hides the mess out of shot. For the reveal, we pause the filming several times for her to remove tiny caramelised shards around the edges, then again to eliminate a stray crumb with a cloth to make it camera-ready.

I sample a finished granola square, still warm from the Aga. They're what I call flapjacks, and whenever I make them, they're either rock-hard or falling apart. 'Mmm, delicious.'

'Better than Walmart?' she asks sweetly.

Rub it in, traddie. Baking from scratch is not in my contract. But her food is definitely good enough to eat, which isn't always a given. Food photographers use all kinds of hideous synthetic sprays, gunk and artificial colours, the food overcooked to appear more appetising, but it's all natural here. I savour the chewy mouthful and long for a coffee to go with it.

Marty walks in and the relaxed air suddenly feels charged with tension. 'How are ya, ladies?'

She looks coquettishly at him, as if wanting her crush to notice her at the school dance. I turn the camera back on. He takes a chunky square, cramming the whole thing in his mouth. He nods his approval and she leans in as he munches. Her girlish routine has a retro charm in the videos, but in real life, less so. *You know you're the catch?* I want to say. *He's the lucky one.*

'Honey, can you please take out the trash?' she asks him when the shoot is complete.

'Sure.'

She acts like he's her hero while he yanks the bin liner out with enough force that the bag rips.

'It's leaking,' I say, since he's unaware of the brown sludge seeping from the tear.

He swings the bag around to see. An arc of brown liquid sprays over the cabinets and little Caleb. Is that deliberate?

'Sweetie,' she says mildly, grabbing a cloth to wipe down Caleb and the rest of the mess. He shakes the bag as if seeking evidence that the sludge is indeed coming from it, then trudges out in his muddy work boots, trailing brown drips for her to clear up. Dickhead. I expect her to at least tut and roll her eyes, but nothing.

After he leaves, she pours us some more of that godawful cold herbal concoction.

'Actually, this isn't my thing,' I say.

'No?' She widens her eyes in surprise and goes to the fridge. 'I'll add some home-made elderflower and honey cordial. That makes it super-yummy.'

I miss coffee. If it wasn't strong-smelling I'd bring it to work in my reusable coffee cup. But I'm not inviting more pushback after the sinful Walmart bread and cereal bars. She thinks the cold tea is delicious, but we might as well stick a handful of hay in tepid water for all the pleasure it brings. The cordial masks the worst of it, but without coffee, booze and drugs, what vices do these people have?

'Can I have the Wi-Fi code?' I ask.

'What for?'

Duh. 'To go online.'

'You don't need it,' she says.

'I like to stay connected. Someone might need me urgently.' I can't claim sick parents as I've already told her I'm estranged from my family.

Alice comes in with baby Betsy. Faith holds out her arms.

'Try a digital detox for your personal life,' she says kindly. 'You'll feel better for it.'

I can't even cope with a caffeine detox.

She talks to Alice. I shove the phone back in my pocket and clear up after the baking. I'm strangely calm about Faith's Wi-Fi stance. Back home, I would have turned snarly if anyone questioned my lifestyle choices or imposed restrictions, but here, I'm less worked up. It's better for my cortisol levels, despite me knowing it's not on. I wonder if all the lavender is calming my nervous system. The scent permeates the cabin and homestead from Faith's lavender soap, sachets and essential oil.

By the time the kids pile in from school, I've mostly finished putting everything away. I ask Emily where Willow is.

'She's gone to the cabin.'

'Why'd she go back on her own? Is she okay?'

She nods while drinking a glass of milk. I guess they do their own thing separately after school, when I'd expected them to run around together in a free-range way. Faith asks me to film them having milk and the about-to-go-viral snack at the table, so we shoot the final segment, which only takes a few seconds. The kids aren't asked to behave in a particular way, unlike other kidfluencers who are made to perform. She doesn't direct them, these agreeable children who take after their even-tempered mum.

It's taken all day to prep, shoot and pack up, including interruptions. Faith works with speed and precision, managing it all with humble charm. When we're done, I rush to put the filming equipment away in the little office where we did our podcast. She's occupied with the kids, so I locate the Wi-Fi router under the desk. I crouch down to take a quick photo of the password printed on it.

'What are you doing?' Faith says from the doorway.

I jump and bump my head on the desk. Caught in the act, I shoot back up, ignoring the pain while I fake being normal.

'Getting the Wi-Fi code.'

She stares at me.

'Can I finish now? Willow's not used to being home alone.'

'Take a granola bar for her.'

I take the snack she hands me in greaseproof paper. 'Thanks. She'll love it.'

We say our goodbyes and I race back. Willow never went home alone before. That would be unthinkable in Manhattan. She's in the armchair with a big illustrated book.

'Faith gave me a snack for you.' I put it on a plate and pour her a glass of milk. 'Were you okay, coming back without me?'

'I wanted to play with Emily, but Mrs Bone told me to go home.'

'Oh. Is Mrs Bone nice to you?'

'Sure.'

'Is she strict?'

'She's godly. Look at the book she gave me.' She lifts the huge hardback on her lap so I can see the cover. *Big Book of Bible Stories*.

I try not to make a face. Schooling Mormon kids will include religion, but storytelling, reading and English are good skills, so I squish up in the armchair and pull her onto my lap with the book.

'What are you reading?' I get comfy.

'Jonah and the Whale.'

I wonder if it's metaphorical enough that the religious aspect isn't rammed down her throat, but no such luck. We read it together and she can't see me curling my lip. I'll find a way to balance it out. Willow's doing a better job than me at going along with their way of life, but we needn't share their beliefs.

I pour a tiny cup of coffee to feed my addiction, knowing it'll keep me up late if I drink too much now. It's cold leftovers from my morning brew. I can't be bothered to make fresh and there's no microwave to warm it. There isn't even a kettle, so I boiled a pan of water on the stove this morning.

And yet, for some reason, I'm finding this back-to-basics approach charming instead of inconvenient. What is this weird feeling? I realise that I'm blissed out. I haven't felt this way for years. If this is the effect of country living, I should rethink my plans.

A text pings through.

> You found anything out yet?

I sigh. So much for bliss.

> Give me a break. I've only just got here.

> You got one job Mel

> Yeah, I'm a social media manager.

> You know what I mean

> Get real. You think they'll offer up their secrets to me on arrival? Doesn't work like that, so back off.

Chapter Twenty-One

Just as it took all day to film the flapjack video, it takes all the following day to edit it. Faith's a natural on camera and doesn't require multiple takes, but I still need to master the editing software and produce the video in her signature style. The small study where I'd interviewed her — while she'd also interviewed me — doubles as the editing suite. The door's propped open and she comes in and out from the kitchen to check on progress.

'It's well lit, thank the Lord.' She peers at the screen.

'And thanks to your three-point lighting.' Let's not thank Jesus for her professional set-up.

When she's on a business call, I duck under the desk in my second attempt to photograph the Wi-Fi code. But it's gone. Faith had suggested a digital detox like I'm a child who's only allowed educational screen time. Seriously... is she hiding the code from me? It's doubly perverse when she owes her success to the internet.

She won't like me installing Wi-Fi in the cabin, but I'm staying connected whether she likes it or not. How else can I keep up with online trends and developments? The signal's too weak on my phone to rely on.

Alice appears at the office door wearing a flowing cream dress embroidered with lavender. 'I'll show you how to milk Myrtle,' she says in her flat voice, then turns and walks off.

'Oh.' *Bit random.*

I take a break from editing and go after her. Her little boy is sprawled with Caleb on the living room floor, sharing wooden building blocks and a few toys. I follow Alice out the front door, as she forges ahead, skirt flapping in the breeze, wellies underneath.

'Do Jonny and Caleb play together often?' I catch up with her.

'At church and we look after each other's, say if Faith has a meeting and Marty's busy. They play together when I work with Faith.'

'Are they close in age?'

'Jonny is nine months older.' She wears a wedding ring. Faith said she lives with her mum, the teacher, in the converted barn between the homestead and my cabin. Perhaps they make a habit of moving in single mothers like we're charity cases.

'How long have you lived here?' I ask as we walk to Myrtle, parked outside her cowshed.

'About three years.'

'After Jonny was born?'

She pauses before each answer, as if weighing up what to tell me. 'I gave birth to him here.' She changes the subject. 'You're scheduled to do the milking straight after you finish work. What you milk is for you. Even if you don't need it, Myrtle still needs milking, seven days a week. Each household has their own scheduled time. Please stick to it.'

'Okay.' I want to learn more about Alice coming here as a pregnant woman, but it's all about the milking now. And I can't get my head around milking a cow as part of my duties as a social media manager.

She hands me a small aluminium bucket. 'Take it home with you when it's full and pour it into a jug. Then you rinse and return it to the peg here, every day.'

It takes a while for me to get the feel of it, the rhythm. Willow's right, it is icky, but this is the upbringing I want for her. I wish I could film it for my own socials. Faith's reel of milking Myrtle right into her big smoothie cup has seven million views. I love the novelty, but it goes deeper. As I milk the cow and gaze off at the mountains, a warm sense of well-being spreads through me, filling the spaces where knots of tension once lived. My shoulders are relaxed instead of hunching towards my ears, and I feel… serene.

After a faltering start, we end up with a pail of fresh milk. I ask Alice to take a photo of me on the low milking stool, pretending to direct the final squirt of milk. If someone told me three months ago that my work break would involve milking a cow, I would call them crazy. Beverley would call me crazy, and yes, I do smell like a barnyard animal. This place isn't perfect, what with my caffeine and Wi-Fi withdrawal symptoms, but I like the airy calmness and I'm already a more relaxed version of myself.

'Put it in your refrigerator.' Alice nods towards the pail and hands back my phone.

'Is unpasteurised milk safe?' Trolls go on about harmful bugs whenever Faith chugs raw milk on camera.

'It's as God intended.' She leaves with a swish of her long cotton skirt.

I'll google the dangers of unpasteurised milk, although the kids are bursting with vitality, so Myrtle must be blessed with good bacteria. As for Alice, I still wonder inappropriately about her immaculate conception. Is her wedding ring a cover? I don't see her as a Mormon lesbian, inseminating herself with a turkey baster. And unlike me, I bet she's not reckless enough for a night of passion that ended in pregnancy.

Back at the cabin, I add a splash of Myrtle juice to some cold coffee and chug it down. Coming back out, I spot a shirtless Joel in the distance. Caught by a tug of longing, I watch him, transfixed. No wonder Utah girls choose not to move away. He's in his Stetson and jeans, forking hay from the back of an open truck into the cattle feed. The skies are pure blue, but there's more of a chill in the air, so I won't be seeing him shirtless many more times, unless…

I love a man who's good with his hands, and I heat up from imagining those hands on me. Shame I can't film him doing manly tasks around the farm. Faith's fans would find him captivating, although I'd rather keep him to myself. #CowboyRomance

I tear myself away and head back to the homestead. A delivery van pulls up outside, and I accept the big box, addressed to Faith. Inside the house, Alice is collecting Jonny, and Faith lights up when she sees the box. 'Yay, dresses! Thank you, Melissa.' She says it as if I'm the one gifting them.

I bet I'm breathing coffee fumes over her. She hands me Betsy and rips open the package. I don't want to be nosy, but I'm stuck holding the baby, so I watch her pulling out the clothes. Alice leaves without saying goodbye. I can't work her out. Faith's her employer but she doesn't seem to like or defer to her, only showing basic courtesy. I wonder if she's any better around Marty, since she works for him more. I doubt it, since she has all the charisma of a paper bag.

Faith exclaims over the dresses, holding one up to the light.

'You'll look great in that,' I say. But she looks great in everything, even hardcore pioneer dresses. She flashes a beautiful smile at me and takes the box to her bedroom, while I get back to editing with Betsy on my lap.

I'm waiting for Faith's mask to slip. No one's this perfect. I'd love to witness her pissed-off era, since I'm petty like that. If her batter goes lumpy, will she fling it at the wall in a rage? If I forget to press 'record' when filming a perfect video segment, will she stomp on her iPhone until she smashes the screen? Or will she lay into me?

Minutes later, she comes back with a chambray dress that I recognise from her reels. 'This is for you.' She holds it out to me.

'Really?' It's beautifully made and in great condition, but not my style. Another strange thing about the ranch is the women wafting around in floaty designer dresses. I don't want to fit in with them, wearing clothes I wouldn't normally be seen dead in.

'That box of dresses are all free.' She takes a gurgling Betsy from me. 'So I'm giving one of my other dresses each to you, Alice, Zina and Hel.'

That's why Alice and the dour schoolteacher look strange in their prairie chic dresses. 'Who's Hel?'

'Helen works at the big barn while she saves for college. It's been busy, but I'll introduce you sometime.'

At Faith's urging, I join her in the daily cup of horrible tea… sorry, *herbal* tea. It's a vile blend they sell online at an inflated price. I'm tempted to slip back to the cabin at lunchtime for another caffeine fix, but we only work a seven-hour day while the kids are at school, so

I skip lunch. She has some kind of home-made yogurt and wheatgrass smoothie that powers her through. Looks disgusting and I don't ask for the recipe.

I take her through the flapjack video edit, and she suggests further cuts and enhancements. She has good instincts. When she's about to leave me to make the final tweaks, I ask if there's a bus that goes into town on Saturdays.

'We're not on a bus route. If you give Alice a list, she'll pick up your groceries with hers.'

Why would I give her my shopping list? For her to judge my choices like Faith did? I've had enough food shaming, thanks very much. Plus, it's Friday and I want to explore. I want time away from here.

'I'd like to see the town. I should have driving lessons.'

'Marty takes the older kids to town Saturday mornings. You can get a ride with him tomorrow.' She breezes out.

I don't want to be without Wi-Fi all weekend. The relaxed vibe casts a dreamy spell, but it feels weird to only have minimal internet on my phone. I didn't sign up for a throwback life. I go out to the kitchen where she's prepping dinner.

'You know you suggested a digital detox?'

'Yes.' Caution comes through in her voice.

'Have you hidden the Wi-Fi code from me?'

'You didn't need Wi-Fi today.'

Mate, I need it every day. She tried selling me the digital detox under the guise of family time, but Willow needs to stay connected too. It's a purer, healthier life here, but I don't want her left behind, a country hick who can't navigate the online world.

'It's more remote than I'm used to, and I need to stay in touch with friends back home. Willow too. We promised we'd video-call.'

'You'll get used to it,' she says in her sweet way. 'Trust me.'

I should tell her to do one, but I'd prefer not to be fired in my first week. 'We go online for fun, we listen to music, learn stuff. Content creation's my thing. Online sources inspire me, otherwise I'm working in a void.'

'Try it for three months. That's a fair compromise. I bet in three months you won't want to go back.'

'That doesn't work for me. I accepted the clause about not posting online, but this isn't an option. We've made promises to people back home, like my elderly neighbour, and Willow will lose her friends. I can still lead a simpler life with internet, same as you.' Why are we even having this conversation? I'm her employee. She doesn't get to decide what's best for me outside of work.

I'll order a portable device without telling her. My first piece of redirected mail came via her this morning though, so she might guess from the packaging. I could pick it up from the post office, but in a community like this, word could get back to her. Also, anyone can walk into the cabin for a nose around when we're out. But this is mad. It's my business, not hers.

Marty comes stomping in. Faith goes straight to him, devotion in her eyes. She kisses him with such tenderness, but I'm not fooled. When she thinks no one's looking, I can tell she's only tolerating him.

She holds on to his arm. 'Honey, Melissa is asking about Wi-Fi in the cabin. I explained how we only have internet here and at the big barn where it's needed for the business—'

'We're not installing internet in the cabin. It's the devil's web. A necessary evil for work and nothing else,' he says with finality and a patronising smile.

The devil's web. Thou shalt not covet cat memes.

'Fine. I'll get a mobile connection.' I match the firmness of his voice. I'm not caffeinated enough to pussyfoot around. 'I also need a lock on the door.'

'That's not necessary,' he says.

'I'm a mum. I don't take those kinds of risks.'

The baby is squealing, so Faith walks away and I do too, unwilling to fight the cowboy alone. They're not dictating my home life. I signed up for a job not a totalitarian regime. A chill goes through me at the thought of them controlling me.

—

She thinks she can come here and do as she pleases. Pick and choose what she likes while forcing her city ways on us. But it doesn't work like that, sweet pea, not around here. She's living on my property and I'm paying her. She signed up for total immersion. Bitch needs to get with the programme.

Chapter Twenty-Two

> What you found out so far?

My jaw clenches at the text on Friday night. I don't reply and he sends another.

> You sucking up to the rich bastards? You so fucking fake

> I told you there are no fast results.

> And I'm telling you to find shit out. What's wrong with you? You falling for Marty Eversen?

> Don't insult me.

> Don't hang around that lowlife any longer than needed. Get the job done like we agreed and make them sorry they ever trusted you

I put the phone on silent and try to sleep.

On Saturday morning, I'm dozing but dimly aware of Willow moving around. The staircase creaks and then she unbolts and opens the door. She knows not to go to the ranch house unless invited or in an emergency, so I hope she isn't out there in her PJs in search of Emily. I open the checked cotton curtains and catch sight of her coming back indoors, so I stretch and pull on my bathrobe. Then I hear a jabbering male voice.

I fling the bedroom door open. Willow is standing in the kitchen peering at a radio on the counter while a presenter talks fast on what sounds like a local station.

'Where'd that come from?' I ask.

'It was on the doorstep. I heard someone leave it just now.'

Her little fingers work out how to scroll through the channels, giving us a taste of country music, an advert for used cars and a weather update. She giggles at this retro game. I doubt a radio would capture her attention back home beyond the initial 'What is it?' and 'Didn't you have Spotify as a kid?' This is how far we've descended in a matter of days.

The lack of tech bugs her in the evenings, but nowhere near as much as me, since she's more enchanted with her new life. She misses her favourite TV shows, but she has no one here to discuss them with, so TV might release its power over her. My child will be bookish and outdoorsy instead, but with some internet thrown in if I have anything to do with it.

Should I be touched or insulted by Faith's gift? I'd mentioned that we liked music, as part of my Wi-Fi campaign. But you can't have a playlist on a crappy old radio. We dance to Shania Twain and Dolly Parton. Willow loves the novelty. I've ordered a mobile Wi-Fi gizmo. It's more expensive than a wired-in router, but we can take it with us if they kick us out.

I prop the cabin door open for fresh air. It would be unthinkable back home. *Back home.* I don't consider this place home, but Willow's settled in with ease, thrilled by her new friends, her 'upstairs bedroom' and our own milk from Myrtle. I had enough of an internet connection last night to confirm that unpasteurised milk is risky, along with instruction on how to safely heat and cool it to fix the problem. More domestic drudgery.

Fast little footsteps sound along the path. Willow goes out to greet Emily, who asks if we want to go into town. I grab my bag. Picking up groceries has taken on more significance now it's a once-a-week event. I can't believe the thrill of food shopping, when it was a humdrum chore in NY.

Marty corrals the older kids into his nine-seat people carrier that they call a minivan. Not for the first time, the practicalities of six kids hits me. And they might have several more.

Faith comes out with Isiah. 'How do you spell "agronomist"?' he asks his dad.

'Uhh...'

Faith looks away and Marty glances sidelong at me. Muppet.

I pause to stretch out his discomfort. 'A-G-R-O-N-O-M-I-S-T.'

'Dang!' Marty shouts. 'I knew I was right.'

Yeah, impressive.

'Your daddy's so smart,' Faith says. It's not even sarcasm. There's no look of complicity between us to say we're humouring him. I can't believe she's chosen to pass on his genes six times and counting.

She goes back inside and her lame-brain husband opens the front passenger door for me. *I'm a really smart guy. I have words. I use the best words.*

Willow scoots into the middle row with Emily.

'Is Faith coming?' I ask.

'She's already done the grocery shopping this week.'

Willow chats with Eden and Emily behind us, while Isiah and Martin are on the back row. Willow's talking about the kids from her last school. *Don't mention the asshole boys.*

Marty says Faith is relieved to have my help. 'She spends too much time on social media. Now she'll have more time for family.'

I glance back at the kids, their noise level rising. 'It's great they're all close in age. Are you from a big family?' I'd already tried asking him this at dinner when we first visited, but one of the kids interrupted and the conversation went in another direction.

'I'm one of six.'

'Wow. What's the age range?'

'The oldest is my brother Asher, who's eight years older than me. The youngest is Beth, who's four years younger.'

Asher. I'm showing an innocent interest, but I know about Asher. It's not idle chit-chat. I'm hoping he'll let slip something of interest. Shame that my tormentor hates me playing the long game. His texts last night urged me to find immediate answers.

The boys squabble loudly in the back. Marty whips his head around. A chill descends, the boys silenced by his glare, all of us silenced. He turns his attention back to the road ahead as we approach the centre of town.

'Did you get along with Asher when you were all at home?' I ask.

'I looked up to him, yeah. I wanted to be like him.'

'You still close?'

'He's the other side of Salt Lake and I see him in the holidays.' He pulls into a parking space.

'How long have we got?'

'An hour,' he says.

I wish I had longer to sit in a coffee shop and tap into their Wi-Fi. Frustration niggles at me that it's the weekend and I'm still fitting around my employers' schedule. My fault for not having a car. I'd expected a bus service at least, but I should have checked.

'Can Emily come to the store with us?' Willow asks Marty.

'If your mom says it's okay.'

'Sure.' So long as she doesn't rat on me for buying non-approved items. As it turns out, they don't stop talking and barely notice. It's mostly wholefoods anyway, although Faith might expect me to make my own yogurt, butter and cheese from Myrtle's milk, and my own pasta from the supply of wheat. Sod that. I'll cook wholesome food on my terms, so I've bought everything for a homebaking extravaganza tomorrow to set us up for the week. The rebel in me grabs a bottle of wine and a big bar of chocolate.

Emily takes Willow's hand outside the grocery store, and they zip along to the coffee shop for ice cream. I speed up, loaded with groceries, pulled by the promise of coffee and a quick go with the Wi-Fi. Then I spot Marty sitting in the window where he's bought ice creams for him and the kids. He comes out and helps me put the groceries in the back of the car. Inside the café, I buy ice cream for Emily and Willow, and a flat white – praise be! – then gaze wistfully at the chalk sign giving the Wi-Fi code for the devil's web. *Not today, Satan.*

'Are you having *caw-fee*?' Isiah calls over from where he's sitting with Marty.

I flash him a brief smile and adopt Faith's Teflon approach to negativity.

'Because we don't drink *caw-fee*.'

Marty smirks. By Monday, Faith will be recommending a caffeine detox to go with the digital detox. Next time, I'll buy a mini bottle of brandy and empty it into my flat white in front of them.

'Okay if I go to one more store?' I ask Marty, takeaway coffee held high.

'Sure,' he says.

I sip the coffee. 'Mmm, so good,' I say to the barista, even though it's too hot. Then I breeze off to the hardware store.

An older man stands behind a counter and studies me. 'Ma'am. What can I getcha?'

'Hi. I'm looking for a way to fit a padlock on this…' I pull out my phone and show him the photo I took of the wooden cabin door.

He squints at my phone screen. 'You new in town?'

I nod. 'Can you help with this?'

'Over at Lavender Ranch?'

'That's right.' I grimace.

'You'll need a heavy-duty hasp.' He nods to the phone screen. 'I have one that'll do the job.'

'What tools will I need?'

'Tools?' He looks at me like I'm an idiot.

If I'd had enough signal at the ranch, I'd have watched a YouTube video first. The old-fashioned bell dings over the door.

'Marty here will have whatever tools you need.'

I turn. He's behind me. 'Saw you come in. What you looking for?'

'She's after padlocking that there door.' He nods to my phone screen, making no attempt to get what's needed.

'S'okay, Pete, I have everything she needs.'

I walk out and stand on the street, defiantly chugging coffee. The culture clash is getting to me. This place is suffocating and why the bloody hell can't I lock my front door?

Chapter Twenty-Three

'Who's with the kids?' I ask Marty as he follows me out of the hardware shop.

'They're fine with their ice creams.'

'They're alone?' He's left an eleven-year-old in charge of four younger ones. Just because it's Utah, doesn't mean you can leave your kids to be snatched off the street.

I stride off and only let out a breath when I see that they're all accounted for. On the drive back, I ask Marty if he knows someone who can give me driving lessons.

'You don't need to drive.'

'It'll be easier if I learn.'

'Why? Someone goes to town every few days. You can either go along or give them a list.'

'I'm here to do a job. I don't want to be a burden.'

'We don't think like that. Everyone plays their part. We all make a contribution, and we help each other out. That's what a community like ours does.' He looks curiously at me. 'Guess you're more used to going it alone.'

Whatever. I can't live in a remote location with no means of transport.

Back home, Willow sees me putting a block of cheese in the fridge. 'Faith makes cheese from Myrtle's milk, Mommy. Faith's so nice and she makes nice food. Why don't we make cheese?'

Stick a knife in my heart, why don't you? Then a text comes through.

> What you playing at Mel? You busy kissing up to rich Mormons? Very sus

> Lay off.

> Do what you went there for or you'll be sorry

> If you don't give me space to do this, I'll leave and tell the police about your vendetta.

I sleep badly that night, Zac's messages preying on my mind. So much for lavender-scented calm.

He's been hassling me for a while. He worked briefly at the car dealership owned by Marty's brother, Asher Eversen, but he was fired for misuse of company computers and his sucky attitude. He told me he wanted to blow the place up. His hatred of the Eversen brothers goes deep. My own animosity towards them is behind my interest in Faith, since I'd been cyberstalking Marty via her socials.

Zac had pressured me to find a way in, so I contacted Faith with zero expectations. I'd intended to tell him I'd tried without success, hoping he'd give up. Then Faith offered me the job, which I accepted, partly in the hope of getting him off my back. If only. Coming here suits my purposes as well as Zac's. I'm looking for angles, ways to bring the Eversen brothers down. My threat of the police shut him up, but it's an empty threat, now that I'm complicit.

At early o'clock, Willow takes a flying jump onto the bed, giggling. 'Wake up!'

I groan and burrow deeper under the duvet. 'It's Sunday.'

'It's the Sabbath!' Her perky voice is only slightly muffled by the duvet. 'We have to go to church.'

Jesus.

Literally.

I open one eye and squint at her. 'We're not churchy.'

'Yes, we are,' she sing-songs. 'We go to church to feel the Saviour's love. I'm going to Sunday school.'

I rub my eyes. 'Who told you that?'

'Mrs Bone says we go to church so Jesus knows we care. I'm being baptised with Emily when we're eight.'

The hell you are. 'We're baking today. Don't you want to bake cookies and muffins with me? We can leave a cookie out for Jesus.' Hang on. I'm confusing him with the other make-believe beardy bloke.

'We can bake after church.' She bounces on the end of my bed. 'The Sabbath is important for us to be close to our heavenly Father.'

Who kidnapped my child and replaced her with a religious zealot? She's so adamant, I wonder if I've missed something, but no one mentioned it to me. I could take her for a hike instead and feign ignorance, but she won't comply with Jesus in the mix. What a drag, and why did I not see this coming? But Faith rarely mentioned religion on her socials, so I'd thought she was Mormon-lite. I'd even wondered if she only paid lip service to attract Christian followers, since there's loads of them with money for her products.

I'd been so wrapped up in getting Willow away from the bad influences and 'asshole boys' that I didn't consider the impact of an LDS education. It didn't rub off on to me, but in England I could balance it with critical thinking.

'What time's church?' I ask Willow.

'Morning time. No sluffing.'

'No *what*?'

'It means don't be lazy.'

If only. Sundays are supposed to be for exploring a mountain trail, a picnic lunch, then some unpressured baking. Maybe if we keep a low profile, they won't offer us a lift. That has to be a benefit of not having a car, but Willow hopscotches on the porch, determined not to miss the churchmobile.

I message Faith.

> Willow has it in her head that she's going to church. I told her we're not LDS and we're baking today.

> Everyone's welcome! The congregation will be thrilled to meet you both. See you outside at ten.

I groan. Why foist their religion on me? We can integrate to a point, but I'd only envisaged the occasional church barbecue with the kids running free, like she shows on her Insta. I haul myself up, hit the shower and make myself Jesus-ready.

Annoyance gnaws at me, but Willow's happy, and it's a change of scenery for a few hours. It's no bad thing for her to experience it, since I escaped unscathed. She'll make an educated decision when she's older.

We don't have Sunday best, so Willow wears her tartan dress and I put on the black dress and jacket I wore when we flew out for the podcast. Emily comes over in a soft-pink dress with a lacy collar.

'I'm riding in the car with you and Alice and Mrs Bone,' she tells us.

I wonder if there's room for us all in her small car, but it appears Alice's son, Jonny, has gone in Marty and Faith's minivan, filled with children. I'd like the opportunity to get to know Mrs Bone, since she's educating my child, sorry… *brainwashing* my child.

Zina Bone is in a well-cut lavender skirt suit and Alice wears a light blue dress. Both look expensive, so I guess they're Faith's cast-offs. I doubt she'll approve of my sombre outfit, more suited to a funeral, but my only other dress is the chambray one she gave me, which is too casual. Conversation from them is deadpan in the car, while Emily is thrilled to tell Willow about Sunday school.

'There it is,' Emily informs us. The church manages to be both picturesque and modern, standing pristine in the clear blue sky, with a white old-fashioned steeple. A big sign says *Church of Jesus Christ of Latter-day Saints*. Faith and Marty are there with the kids, chatting to an older couple and a subdued young woman in a lemony dress. Marty's smart in a tailored grey suit and matte silk tie, his hair neatly combed. He looks more at home in his workwear of brushed cotton shirts and blue jeans.

I'm hit by the lack of diversity, everyone white and nicely turned out. The women are dolled up in an array of pastels, with subtle make-up and neatly styled hair. It's a strange religion, the way it encourages modesty in women, yet they're expected to beautify themselves and their surroundings, since outward appearances matter. Faith embodies that. Gorgeousness is next to godliness. My brother would say that with a cheeky grin, back when Mum chivvied us into our Sunday best, smoothing out his neat haircut, telling him how handsome he looked.

Marty introduces us to members of the smiley, welcoming congregation. They're just like the super-friendly Mormons from my childhood. You can't fault their chirpiness. A middle-aged woman in a turquoise suit takes my hand in both of hers. 'Melissa, so lovely to meet you. We're all very happy to welcome you. Where was your church before moving here?'

'We don't go to church.'

She looks dumbfounded and pulls back, dropping my hand.

'We're not religious, but my daughter wanted to experience Sunday school.'

She looks at me like I'm an armed robber in a balaclava. I'm unsure if she'll speak at all.

'Bless your heart,' she says, recovering herself. 'I'm glad you found your way to Jesus Christ.' Then the others start filing into the main hall for the service.

'Why aren't you religious?' Marty asks.

'My dad was a missionary with the church,' I say.

He raises his eyebrows. I don't know if Faith's research on me stretched this far. It'll be on record with the church, but I never talk about it.

'He died.'

'Oh, I'm sorry. How'd he die?'

'Cancer.' There's a slight hesitation in my voice. What he had was *like* a cancer, really, eating away at him. 'He was sent to England, where he met my mum. They got married and I was raised LDS, but religion didn't stick for me.'

'That's too bad.' He studies my impassive face. I'm not revealing my story. Not yet. I don't tell him how my dad died, or how I then turned my back on church, fighting about it with my mum.

'Don't have girls,' she told me before I left for New York. 'They break your heart.'

Chapter Twenty-Four

'You're finding your way back to church as part of God's divine plan.' Marty guides me in to the service.

No chance. I didn't spend my teenage years escaping church to be press-ganged back in. We find seats for the service. An old man in a suit delivers a sermon about trusting in God's wisdom. They're following some divine blueprint they think will keep them safe. Spoiler alert: it won't. Wish I could scroll on my phone to break the numbing tedium. *Lord have mercy and let me mute the dull preacher.* At least Willow's low boredom threshold means I can talk her out of coming back.

The kids file out to Sunday school and Alice goes to help. I doubt she'll liven it up. The subdued young woman I saw outside is a few rows away. I wonder if it's Hel, who works at the ranch. Strange that we haven't spoken yet, given we're part of a small workforce.

'Do you have a break from teaching on Sundays?' I ask Zina Bone, who stays put when the kids leave.

'Satan works overtime on a Sunday, and we must too.'

'No rest for the wicked,' I say in my jauntiest voice.

'I taught Sunday school for twenty years while bringing up my eight kids.'

Twenty years? I shudder inwardly at them drafting me in for a lifetime of Sunday school. I'd teach them a thing or two. *Hey kids, did you know this is patriarchal bullshit to keep you all in line?*

'Have you always lived around here?' I ask.

'Born and raised. I taught in the local school until my oldest was born. The older ones have since moved out of the state.'

Anything to do with you?

'I didn't think Alice would come back either,' she continues.

'Come back from where?'

'Cornell. I expected her to work in New York or Silicon Valley.'

My mouth drops open. 'Cornell? Isn't that Ivy League?' How come the mousy, withdrawn Alice who shows no ambition has an elite education?

Zina nods. 'She had a scholarship, but it was a breeding ground for immorality.'

In other words, a hotbed of sex, drugs and alcohol, but it's not a nunnery. What's the point of uni if you can't get wasted and have a good time? I wonder if that's how she got pregnant.

'Should've stayed in Utah for college, like I'd said.' A hint of disapproval comes through. 'If it weren't for the scholarship, she would've.' The lack of teacherly pride in her daughter suggests she felt Alice had ideas above her station. The service starts so I can't probe more.

We're invited to a potluck lunch after the service. The trestle table groans under the weight of homebaking. Blessed be the carbs. The 'funeral potatoes' are a particular relic from my childhood, a Mormon delicacy of hash browns mushed with cheese and Campbell's condensed soup, topped off with cornflakes. Willow says they're lush.

Her face glows from making new friends. She's been given a kids' LDS book. 'It's the word of God,' she tells me, eyes bright. *Great*. Now the Sunday school brigade has its claws in her. They think we need saving, but I'm raising a free thinker. Round one to Jesus, but I'm going to win.

I'd hoped for Joel to distract me, but he's nowhere to be seen. Does that mean he's not religious? He doesn't present as a clean-cut Mormon. He's more of a playful lone wolf, the kind of guy a Mormon mum warns her daughter about. A whole new fantasy world opens out of boozy, unbridled dates, but the fun couldn't start until I learn to drive.

The young woman who I assume must be Hel stands in a corner, her body drooping as she eats a slice of pie. Her mouse-brown hair is in a limp bob, faded black dye at the ends, like she's a reformed Goth. I go over. 'Hi, I'm Melissa.'

She takes her time chewing, while her gaze drifts over me and away. She swallows. 'Uh huh.' The words come out slow. Is she stoned? Her cheery yellow dress has a big bow at the front and is from the same 'Mormon church lady' range as the other women wear on the ranch.

'Well, nice meeting you.' I back away. *And that dress looks ridiculous on you.* Baggy sweats are more her style. No wonder Faith didn't bother introducing us.

The time ebbs away. So much for preparing food for the week ahead. If I skip the baking, we won't have enough to eat, and I still have to milk the flipping cow. Church feels too much like work, putting on my best face to fit in with the prevailing culture.

'Melissa?' A smiling woman in her fifties approaches. I think we met earlier, but it's hard to pick out individuals in the sea of softly spoken, softly hued women. 'I'm so happy you've joined us.' She takes my hands lightly in hers and gazes into my eyes. 'All the way from England. That's quite something.'

I return her cheery smile.

'What sort of things are you interested in?' she asks with twinkling eyes.

'Well, my daughter and I like to explore and visit new places.'

'That's great! Come visit us.' She leans in conspiratorially. 'Us ladies have to look out for one another.' She gives a merry chuckle and looks delighted to make a new friend.

I can't help warming to her.

'Come to our Bible study group. We welcome newcomers.'

I take a breath. 'That's so kind, but I don't drive, and I have to look after my daughter.'

'We can find you a ride, and I'm sure someone will watch your daughter.' These women have weaponised kindness, so you're lulled into going along with them. 'Say you'll come. We'd love to get to know you better.' She nods in encouragement and I nearly mirror it back, lovebombed into agreeing.

As if by magic, Faith and Marty appear either side of me, Faith touching my arm in a protective gesture. The woman's gaze travels over them.

'And I'm not reli—'

'It's very kind of you, Dinah,' Marty speaks over me.

And I'm not religious. It's badass to say that around here, so I'll perfect it.

'But we have our ranch Bible group,' he says, 'which is more convenient, what with the kids.'

She concedes, her smile a little tight. 'It's lovely to meet you, Melissa.' Concern flickers across her face, then she turns to walk away.

The others close ranks around me. Maybe there's competition to suck in the new recruits. Multilevel marketing for Jesus: the more you recruit, the higher your tier in the afterlife.

'Our group is better,' Faith says softly. 'The kids watch a movie or do creative play.'

'But I'm not religious.'

'No Bible-bashing, I promise,' Marty says with a winning grin.

It's an ambush. They've cornered their prey, but the thought of spending an evening every week studying the Bible makes me want to scream and beg Hel for a spliff. I'll tackle Faith tomorrow, nip it in the bud. As we leave with the Bones for the ranch, I spot Hel getting in the back of Faith and Marty's people carrier with their kids.

Marty catches me staring after them. Our eyes lock before he gets into the driving seat. When I said my dad had cancer, he might have noticed me trying to keep my emotions in check. What looked like grief was suppressed rage burning in my chest. No way was I making small talk with him about the deaths in my family. Zac isn't the only one who hates the Eversen brothers and what they represent. I shudder at the ghost of a memory. Two people dead and two people I'm holding to account. That's why I'm here.

Chapter Twenty-Five

On Monday morning, we wake to a magical blanket of snow. This is nothing like NY snow, which turns to grey slush by the time we go out. The virgin snow is even more breathtaking on my walk to work, where Faith points out a package beside the door. It's my Wi-Fi box and says so on the packaging. She hasn't confiscated it, but another lecture might be brewing. I was ready to tell her I've no intention of becoming a Mormon, but I can only rock the boat so much in one day, and the Wi-Fi is enough.

'I made your drink.' She hands me a mug of witch's brew. 'Just how you like it.'

With a shot of vodka? How kind. I need to stay on the right side of her, so I go into the office and drink the tea while she takes a call. It's not so bad with added flavourings, but I prefer coffee.

She comes in and presents me with a large gift bag. 'For you.'

I delve in and lift out a carefully folded dress and jacket of the palest mint green. It's Sunday-best attire, so I'll fit right in with the Latter-day Saints in their matchy pastels. There's also a lightweight buttery-yellow jacket and a baby-blue dress. The jackets are feminine, the dresses modestly cut. So not me. She's included two dresses for Willow in soft vintage cotton, one in blue check and the other in a peachy shade with scalloped collar and cuffs.

'Those were Emily's. She's grown taller and wanted Willow to have them.'

'Thank you. We'll look smart for church.' Why did I say that? It's the opposite of what I meant to say, an auto-response to her charming ways. But I can't help being touched by the gesture when I'm so rarely given anything. I guess I'm easily bought, even with a bag of clothes I'd never choose for myself. Even with a gift that's really a manipulation. But it's that floaty feeling again. I quite like the airy bliss, even as it vaguely puzzles me. Why am I less inclined to argue? My instinct is to push back, while my mind and body say, *Chill, babe. Smell the lavender. Gaze at the mountains.*

Faith smiles as if I'm the one gifting her. I'm playing into her hands, but I'll fight my battles one at a time. I'll trade another week or two of church for the sake of Wi-Fi to help me feel connected. Besides, church visits might give me some intel for my secret mission.

Faith goes into town and Alice drops in with Jonny to watch the two youngest kids. She pours us some cold herbal tea.

'I hear you went to Cornell.'

She brushes a lock of hair from her face. 'Seems a long time ago now.'

'What did you study?'

'Economics and management.'

'Impressive. Do you miss it?'

She shakes her head. 'Cornell made me realise I don't like the world outside of Utah, and, you know…' Her voices trails off in regret.

I take a sip of the unflavoured cold tea and grimace at its foul taste. I'll tip it down the sink when she's gone. Alice doesn't elaborate. I guess she didn't belong, the naïve girl whose mother put the fear of God into her, as she's now doing to Willow.

'How did you end up here?'

'I know Marty's family from when I was at school. I wanted to build my own business at home, like Faith, so they said I could come here for some experience. Then they needed someone to educate the kids, so my mom moved in too.'

'Do you know his brother, Asher?'

She looks out at the mountains. 'His younger sister was my babysitter.'

I don't ask about Jonny's absent father. Maybe he's dead, since she's too devout to join me in the drunk-one-night-stand-mum club.

'What business will you set up?'

'I design data structures that use data efficiently. Indexing strategies are my thing.' Her eyes spark up for the first time, her face animated.

'Is that what you're working on?' She's wasted on minding babies and making school lunches instead of using the intellect that earned her a scholarship.

She turns away. 'You'd better get back to work.'

Back home that evening, Willow loves the dresses Faith passed on to her, even more because they were Emily's. This must be what it's like to have older sisters passing their stuff on, which is a new experience for us both.

'Faith's so pretty, isn't she, Mommy?'

'Yes, but we don't judge people on their looks. She's also smart and successful in business.'

'She wears pretty dresses. Now you can wear pretty dresses like Faith, because the other ladies here wear pretty dresses too.'

'And she focuses on her work.'

'And she has more kids than you, so she's closer to God.'

Brutal. You take my heart and rip it out. 'I'm not a Mormon, so I don't need to be closer to God.'

She looks stricken. 'You have to be, or at the end of days you'll burn to death and I'll be airlifted to heaven.'

I groan and pull her onto my lap. 'That's just a story church people tell so you'll stick with their religion. It's not true, like movies aren't true. They're just stories. No one gets airlifted to heaven. We just have to ace this life.'

I wait until she's in bed before setting up the Wi-Fi in my bedroom.

'Please work,' I plead. 'I call upon Jesus on his iCloud.' The flashing light shows it's trying to connect. 'I offer myself to the patron saint of the internet.' My laptop springs to life with a sudden influx of emails. I squeal, tempted to do a victory lap around the ranch. Our connection to the world is restored at the cost of Faith's disapproval and a church-going trade-off. I stay up late catching up on what I've missed. So yes, I am addicted.

The next morning, I stumble into the shower, then have two cups of coffee to clear the fuzziness of not enough sleep. At Willow's insistence I wear the 'it's so pretty' chambray dress that Faith gave me. It feels wrong, working in a floppy dress that billows around me, when a fitted shirt and trousers are more my style. 'Now you look like the other ladies,' Willow says, like it's a good thing. Like it's not weird for us to roam around the ranch in voluminous designer frocks.

Zina Bone gave her a journal to write, so after work and school we sit down to write. It's a Mormon quirk that kids document their lives with journals and scrapbooks. That's what gave Faith her grounding in influencing. This is the kind of homework I can get behind. I decide to journal with Willow to fill the podcasting gap. We'll write together through the long winter evenings and she'll grow into her own version of Jo March from *Little Women*.

We write at the kitchen table, then she reads hers aloud. 'We did cow math. Marty took us to a field and told us how much each cow cost and how much it costs to keep the cow and how much money he makes from the cow. He's like Nephi who followed God's commandments no matter what and guided his people by the scriptures. I wish I had a dad like Marty.'

I mean, what the fuck? I already feel traitorous for coming here, but I can't bear Willow seeing him as dad material. She has no idea, and all I can do is suck it up.

After dinner, I give her a pep talk about limited internet use. She's so tech starved that she readily agrees to any access whatsoever. We agree it's our experiment in a new way of living and pledge not to watch TV: '...since we're living a more natural and free life,' I say.

'We're living as God intended.' She beams at me. 'Mrs Bone said we're on earth to choose good over evil. Mommy, I'm praying for your soul.'

'And I'm praying for my sanity.' I feign a serene expression, the one that the women use around here. Seriously though. How has my child become brainwashed in a week? It's like she's been hijacked by fundamentalists. She's always been malleable. She imitated me from when she could first walk and talk. Now it seems Mrs Bone is the best thing since unsliced bread. She'd better not be a flat-earther. I'm in danger of losing myself to this strange way of life, and I'm already losing Willow. *I wish I had a dad like Marty* keeps hitting me like a gut punch.

As for my journal, I long to write the unvarnished truth, but it would open me to risk. Anyone could come into our *unlocked* home and root around. The hardware store incident left me mortified. It's probably going around town that the crazy Brit wanted to lock her front door when she went out. Marty never fitted the lock, *quelle surprise*. I've noticed my bedroom door has a keyhole and the windows are locked shut, but there are no keys in the cabin.

—

She's jumping the gun, taking liberties. Those city girls don't realise that you earn trust. Right now, we can't trust her with internet. But let her enjoy her little freedoms. She'll find out the hard way how it works.

Chapter Twenty-Six

There she is again. Hel. As Willow and I walk to the ranch house for Bible study, the young woman from church goes inside. I'd love to burst in waving a bottle of Absolut, shouting, 'Vodka, bitches!' I'd get the women wasted and bust us out of here to get matching tattoos of little red devils.

We arrive, *sans alcohol*, faces stinging from the cold night. Willow rushes to Emily and Eden who are making popcorn with Faith. Hel stands apart, like a bored teenager at a family gathering. I wave hello to Faith and go over to Hel. 'Hi. We met at church.'

Her gaze drifts away.

'Do you live around here?'

'In the duplex on the end of the big barn.' She looks dead behind the eyes.

It's strange I haven't seen her other than at church. I assume she's been press-ganged into this, same as me, but there's no ironic look to convey she doesn't buy into it either.

Faith brings an apple galette to the table. 'Apples are good this year.' She goes back for plates.

'There's too many apples,' Hel mutters as if the apples are oppressing her.

'Blessed be the fruit,' I say, wishing Beverley were here to share my nod to *The Handmaid's Tale*.

Zina and Alice arrive with Jonny, followed by Marty. The kids pile in the den with two big bowls of popcorn to watch Mormon propaganda for kids. So they do have TV. I'm sure she's said in interviews that they don't. It's rationed, so they'll gladly watch anything – even a cartoon of religious moralising. Zina sits at the kitchen table and takes a cross-stitch project from her roomy tapestry bag. I glance over, intending to say something nice.

> There will be no escape from the judgement
> of the Almighty.

I snort. She might as well stitch *fuck off and die*. She catches me looking and peers back at me through her glasses, her mouth set in a thin line.

'Is it… a gift?' I ask.

'It's to decorate the schoolhouse,' she says dourly.

I'm sure the kids love her cross-stitch scaremongering. 'Do the children do arts and crafts at school?'

'They're working on a craft project called Spirit Prison.'

'Which is…?'

'A place where the wicked are punished.'

That sounds fun. I imagine the cross-stitch homily hanging above Alice's bed at Cornell… *Harlots burn in hell*. Alice sits in silence. Her glassy blue eyes and porcelain skin combined with her stillness bring to mind a haunted china doll.

'How was your day, Hel?' We might as well bond since she looks like the second least godly person in the room. We could hang out and cross-stitch our sentiments, call ourselves *Sluts for Satan*.

'Her name's Helen,' Marty corrects. But Faith called her Hel.

'Um...' She scratches her head.

Zina barks out a cough, like she's clearing her throat.

'...Busy.' Hel flicks a look at her. 'Serving others.'

'Do you like your work?'

She gives me a withering glance to say *what do you think?* The others take their seats around us at the table, Marty at the head. I'd like to keep it chatty, but Marty kills that idea dead by placing one hand on the Bible in front of him. 'Let us pray.'

Dude, you said 'No Bible-bashing' when you pushed me into this. The mood turns sombre as we hold hands on the tabletop. Mine rest lightly in Marty's big paw and Alice's dainty one. I bow my head and close my eyes.

'Heavenly Father, we thank You for bringing Melissa and Willow to our ranch and we appreciate their unique presence in our community. Grant them the joy of embracing our lives as we welcome them with outstretched arms.'

I feel my face flush. My eyes flicker open to see Faith, sitting opposite, studying me with a head tilt. Our eyes meet, her gaze steady.

'Grant us the strength and wisdom to always take the right path together.'

I try to decode her look, inquisitive but not hostile, despite her husband holding both our hands and singling me out for his prayer. I close my eyes, pretty sure she'll keep watching me.

'And may it lead us away from outside forces.'

What outside forces? Is it a dig about my Wi-Fi?

'May we offer support and rejoice with them. In the name of Jesus Christ, amen.'

'Amen,' his minions say.

Alice slides her hand away, but Marty squeezes mine, rubbing his thumb over my skin. Faith keeps watching me.

Grant us the strength and wisdom to always take the right path together. Is that a veiled reference to becoming Mormons?

Zina Bone drops her creepy cross-stitch in her lap to give a Bible reading about every man loving his neighbour. It's odd to go along with this, and a shame that Willow has enough religious fervour for us both. Faith smiles and nods in blissed-out recognition of every biblical reference. The others are muted, possibly as bored as I am. If Marty weren't here, I'd steer the conversation away from religion. *So, who's on Prozac? Let's play Fuck, Marry, Kill. Show of hands: who wants to kill Marty? Be my guest, while I fuck Joel.*

'Helen,' he says, 'why don't you tell us about that book you're reading?'

Is it a cowboy romance? She looks in need of one.

'Yeah…' She hesitates for long enough that I think she won't continue. Then she clears her throat. 'It's about how a woman should admire her husband,' she says without conviction, her unfocused gaze drifting around the room. 'And let herself be protected by him.'

'Protected from what?' I ask. 'Bears?'

They're looking at me as if I'm supposed to go along with this bullshit, but if they want me here they get me *and* my opinions. With luck, I'll be banned.

The Patriarchy weighs in. 'It's about the woman embracing her feminine traits to bring out her husband's protective instincts. Anything else is damaging to a marriage.'

'Isn't that simplistic?' I ask. And creepy. He's her employer, so why are we even talking about how she should be a good wife? These people really know how to overstep. I glance around to check if anyone else agrees, but nope. This is fine. Just fine. Not weird at all.

Faith's smile is hazy. 'Simple is good. A man has to feel like a real man.' She gazes at him. 'I admire Marty's masculine ways without trying to change him.'

Is she for real? I still don't know.

Chapter Twenty-Seven

The Bible study readings continue while I think about renting an apartment in town. Willow can enrol in the local school, and I'll put a stop to church. Rentals are cheaper here, but I'll factor in the cost of driving lessons and car repayments. Then we can be ourselves again, with a lockable front door and walkable shops and cafés. It means returning to the old problem of school pickup times and what to do with her in the holidays, but I can deal with that. I don't know what Faith's reaction will be to us bailing out.

The Bible meeting ends after an hour, praise be. After milking the cow and cooking dinner, I'm ready to call it a night. Marty says he'll 'walk the ladies home'. Caleb has fallen asleep on the couch and Marty tenderly scoops him up and carries him to bed. He has an easy way with kids. I wonder if Jonny's lack of a dad makes Marty more paternal towards him.

He walks us towards the cabin, Zina holding the lantern torch.

'Great party,' Willow says.

'Where's the after-party?' I ask. *Let's get blackout drunk!* At the very least, it's wine o'clock. If Faith knows I'm sneaking booze back from the grocery store, it'll cause a full-blown panic attack, given her reaction to devil's bread from Walmart.

Willow gives us an account of the Mormon cartoon as if delivering a profound insight. 'It's about a boy who found out the hard way that church is better than having fun with friends who don't do church.'

Poor kid. I bet he's a bore. I go to say it's about having a balance, but Marty's telling her that she'll make friends for life at church. 'And you kids can have fun in "sharing time", when you sing songs, make music, plus you go on activity days and do creative play.'

Yeah, I've already heard about creative play from Zina, with her Spirit Prison.

'Cool,' Willow says.

Don't believe the hype, sweetheart. This is how they suck you in. They keep children occupied with activities same as they keep women occupied with housework. I adopt my serene expression, outnumbered by believers. Even my freethinking girl has crossed to the other side. She's too young for *His Dark Materials*, but I'd read it surreptitiously at twelve, knowing its sceptical view of religion wouldn't play well with the church that I was backing away from. I'm putting banned books at the top of our reading list.

'I'm teaching in school tomorrow,' Marty says before they peel off to the Bone residence. 'Entrepreneurial studies. We come up with business ideas and look at how to develop them.'

'Does Emily have a business?' Willow asks, eyes wide.

'Not yet, but I'm coaching her to be a success. I need all my kids to become millionaires so I can retire.'

Since you're already bankrolled by your millionaire wife.

He looks at me. 'They get to learn from a top business expert.'

'Faith?'

'Me.' His voice hardens with emphasis. 'I'm a really smart guy. I've worked real hard for what we have here. I'm the one who makes a success of the business.'

I'm the most successful person ever to run a ranch, by far. Tremendous success. Other guys' ranches? Disaster. I wonder how heavy his ego is to carry around.

'I didn't just fall off the turnip truck,' he says.

Could've fooled me.

'I can make a success of any business. I bring the real world into their studies. So, in math they learn to calculate interest payments.'

I'm the greatest entrepreneur God ever created. His bragging aside, this is the kind of learning I can get behind. Mormons are encouraged to make money. No vow of poverty for them. Another contradiction – the groupthink of religion yet it requires freethinking to create a successful business. Influencing is Faith's way of being a good Mormon with her own Holy Trinity of popping out kids while staying home and making money.

I try decoding the look she gave me when Marty said the prayer, as if she were weighing up my religiosity. But why? She knows I'm not into religion. There are trade-offs to living here, but I didn't expect to surrender myself to their beliefs. Nor did I expect to live a less authentic life. I'm treading a fine line, relying on them for work and a home.

We say good night to the others, and Marty carries Jonny to his barn conversion home with Alice and Zina. Willow takes my hand, and we walk the last little distance to the cabin with my phone torch. The darkness is absolute, unlike New York. I grit my teeth at the eerie calls of wildlife in the woodland. Back inside, I bolt the door. It's the first time we've returned to the unlocked cabin after dark. The night feels ominous and I'm a little spooked. I usher Willow into the bathroom to clean her teeth while I surreptitiously check under her bed and inside her cupboard, not wanting her paranoid about monsters hiding after dark.

How long until she's viewing Marty as a father figure? Back in Manhattan, she told her teacher that her dad was a florist. When the teacher asked me about him, I said he wasn't in our lives. He won't be arranging flowers where he is. That man will not be smelling of roses.

I sleep badly and wake at five a.m. remembering I didn't return the milking pail to Myrtle's barn. There's probably a spare, but I should take it back now in case it's needed for early morning milking. I pull on my boots and creep out in the chilled predawn darkness, a coat over my nightshirt. The temperature's dipped and there's a bite to the cold. I brace myself for a hard winter ahead.

After returning the pail, I walk back and hear a creak behind me. I crane my neck to see a shadowy figure walking away from Alice's barn. Marty. He goes to the ranch house, head bent. Maybe they needed his help with something first thing, but there are no lights on. Judging by his creepy tutoring of Hel, I wonder if he's taken it upon himself to educate the single women of the ranch on how to be good wife material. It's too ominous to consider when I have another looming menace to deal with. Zac was texting again last night.

> Why you ignoring me?

> I've nothing to say. If you keep hassling me, I'll change my number.

> Quit threatening me or you know what I'll do

Blocking him won't work as he'll message me from another number. I've had it with domineering men. It's bad enough handling Marty.

Chapter Twenty-Eight

'Mommy, you can't drink coffee.' Willow's little brow furrows earnestly as she eats her oatmeal with stewed apples.

'I can't?' I'm enjoying my Saturday morning pot of coffee.

'We follow the Word of Wisdom, so we eat healthy and don't drink coffee.'

'Well, good morning, Pastor Willow.' I've never felt more marginalised. It's me against the religious right, including my child.

'God is watching.'

'Hope He enjoys the show.' I take another sip, to her dismay.

'You need to repent,' she says with prim outrage.

'Can I repent after my second cup?'

'You'll live longer if you don't drink liquor or coffee.'

'I won't want to live longer.' And she'd never have been conceived without copious amounts of liquor. 'What's with the guilt trip?'

'Huh?'

She dishes it out but can't argue her point. Yet. 'I'm not a Mormon, so I make my own choices. It's called free will.' I could go on about the benefits to my well-being of moderate coffee intake.

'But this is a Mormon place.' Confusion clouds her face.

'Can you please dial down the religion? I'm not a believer.' I've put up with her other obsessions – bugs, dinosaurs, Hannah Montana – but I've a bad feeling my child is in the grip of religious fervour. Beverley was right about Jesus Camp. I just didn't realise we'd be living there. 'There are Mormons on the ranch, but we make our own decision about what we believe.' I could start a conversation about Mormon women lacking choices. We could talk about the expectation for them to marry young and give up career aspirations to be mothers and homemakers. It's the patriarchy on steroids, the man as undisputed head of the household. Faith gave birth to six children in eleven years. Despite managing a multimillion dollar brand, she stays home to raise the kids and keep house for her cowboy husband.

You would expect an army of helpers behind the scenes, but some Mormons have a suffering fetish. Suffering leads to growth, which sets things up for the afterlife. Faith can afford a housekeeper and nanny, but only has a twice-weekly cleaner so she's stuck with the relentless dross. The whole set-up is culty, including Marty's invasive prompting of Hel in Bible group. I still can't reorient my mind to living in this throwback parallel universe. I can't tell Willow in case she grasses me up to the Jesus brigade, but I'll find ways to help her work it out.

'Won't it be great to catch up with Coco and Tamsin?' I say as I set up her scheduled video call with her NY friends. 'You can tell them about milking Myrtle and you can show them your bedroom.' I log her in, and she jiggles with excitement. The other two come on-screen. I say hi to them and Coco's dad who's setting it up for her, then excuse myself to take a shower.

After the Zoom call, we step into the frosty bright outdoors for a trip into town with Marty and the kids. No Faith again. She makes her own trip during the week when the children are at school. On the way, I make innocent comments, but Marty doesn't indulge any chat and mostly drives in a stony silence. He's probably rattled by me calling his marriage views 'simplistic' at Bible study. I guess critical women don't exist in his domain.

In town, I avoid the hardware store, and sign Willow up for a library card. Emily plonks herself down with a picture book while we give our details at the counter.

'Are you new in town?' the cheery librarian asks Willow. Her name badge says 'Joan'.

'We're living on a ranch with Faith and Marty and all their kids.'

She looks perturbed for a moment, then regains her cheeriness. 'Over at Lavender Field?'

'That's right.' I try to read her look, which goes beyond small-town curiosity.

'Whatcha doing there?' she asks me in her upbeat voice.

'I'm working with Faith on her social media. What do you think of the ranch?'

'Oh… you know.' She purses her lips while tapping at the computer screen. 'Faith and Marty are very popular people.' She goes seamlessly into telling Willow how many books she can check out and asks what she likes to read.

We borrow *Little Women*. I've never liked the ending, but I'll read it with her to flag up Jo's ability to make her own choices. We can brainstorm better endings. As I side-eye the display of Mormon books, Emily veers towards it.

'Ice cream?' I suggest, ushering them away. Willow has a growing pile of churchy books that she brings home from school. I've told her she can read those herself.

'Take care,' Joan calls as we leave.

As we near the coffee shop, Joel pulls up in his truck. My heart lifts.

'Here.' I give Willow some money before she spots him, as I've something to ask him in private. 'Buy your ice creams and I'll see you in there.' I like the illusion of small-town safety. She can order and pay in the coffee shop, while I have sight of the front door. 'Joel, hi,' I say as he gets out of his truck. He's still gorgeous and I'm still wildly attracted to him.

'Hey, Melissa. Haven't seen you around. How's it going?'

'Good, thanks. I've been looking out for you.'

'Is that so?' He comes towards me.

In case I see you bare-chested in the field again, you lovely hunk of manhood.

'I wanted to ask if you'd give me driving lessons. I'll pay you, of course.'

He scratches his head. 'I guess. I'm not much of a teacher, but yeah…'

We're swapping numbers as Marty comes out of the coffee shop with the kids, Willow and Emily licking their ice creams. He looks quizzically at us.

Joel raises a sheepish hand in greeting. 'Catch you later,' he says and walks away.

On the drive home, I ask Marty about his entrepreneur classes, to stop him asking about Joel. Not that driving is on the list of banned activities, unlike podcasting.

'Do your siblings run businesses too?' I ask.

'My older brother Asher does, yes.'

'A ranch?'

'No, he sells cars.'

'Oh, used cars? I could buy one from him when I've learnt to drive.'

'You don't need a car,' he says. 'What about your family? Faith says you're not in contact with them.'

I glance back at Willow, but she's not listening. 'I fell out with my mum a while back over my brother when he went through a rough time. He got himself in trouble and wanted me to cover his back.'

'That's tough.' He flicks a glance at me.

'I'm not sure I handled it the best way. I guess we all do things we regret.' I bite my lip and look at him.

'You can ask God to forgive his sins and show you the way back to your family.'

'Is that what you do?' I say. 'Ask for forgiveness?'

He shoots me a questioning look. I return it with my best innocent face. Then the boys commandeer his attention, talking about horses for the rest of the way. I mentioned my brother as bait for Marty to say, 'That's nothing compared to my brother.' When he first mentioned Asher and how he looked up to him as a kid, there was no catch in his voice, or 'look how that turned out'. It strengthens my resolve.

When Willow and I are back home unpacking groceries, I remember her Zoom call from earlier. 'How'd the video call go?'

'Okay, I guess. I told them about school.'

I go into the group chat with Coco and Tamsin's mums.

> Hope the girls had fun catching up. Same time next Saturday? x

> Sorry, we've family visiting. x

Before I can respond to Marci, Amber's response flashes up.

> We can't make it either. Catch up soon. x

> Maybe the weekend after? x

It gets a love heart emoji from Amber and nothing from Marci.

The day goes in a whirl of housework and food prep for the week ahead. We start the bread on Saturday, using Faith's coveted sourdough starter. If I screw this up, it's on me. It won't be ready to bake until tomorrow, so we make a big batch of muffins, half of which we'll take to the lunch at church tomorrow. I've caved for now, but please God, let it be a novelty for Willow. Let her see the light and realise You don't exist.

On Sunday, she selects Faith's mint-green combo for me because 'it's so pretty'. The green fabric sucks the colour from my face and it's only when I have it on that I notice the hideous puffed sleeves. A jacket with puffed sleeves, for fuck's sake.

'I love it,' Willow says.

I loathe it.

Outside the church, Marty makes a beeline for us. 'Well, don't you two look like a summer's day?' He beams and Willow beams back. I blend in with the female congregation, who will know the outfit was Faith's. I sense their approval now I'm not in funereal black. Even the men mostly avoid wearing black suits to church.

After the service, the kindly Bible study woman approaches me again. Is her name Diana? 'Melissa, it's so good to have you as part of our church.'

I adopt my serene smile. I think Marty called her Dinah last week.

'Your outfit is lovely,' she says warmly. 'It's so becoming.'

We compare dresses and she radiates kindness. I'd like a friend, especially one who doesn't live on the ranch, if only I can avoid talking about religion.

'Have you been baptised?' she asks.

When I was eight, but I'm not telling her that. Faith's within earshot, so I bite the bullet. 'Thank you for asking, but I'm not religious.' I keep my voice sweet, like the surrendered women around here. 'We came because my daughter heard her classmates talking about church and she wanted to experience it.'

Dinah looks perturbed at me not following the script, so she nods and walks away. Sensing Faith's gaze on me, I turn. She's giving me that knowing look again. I smooth my hands over my waist.

'I'm sure I don't wear this as well as you.'

'Dress to impress!' She smiles and bounces the cooing baby. Wearing clothes she's chosen for me is another way to feel less like myself. Am I some kind of project? Did she create the job to recreate me, her own Eliza Doolittle trad wife?

Another message comes through from Zac.

> Fucking update me or else

Chapter Twenty-Nine

When Willow's in bed, I message Tamsin's mom.

> Thanks for the Zoom call yesterday. Can we make it a weekly thing? Maybe after school if you're busy on the weekend. We miss you. x

> I'm sorry Melissa, we don't want to hurt anyone's feelings, but the girls weren't interested in praying for forgiveness. They know to be respectful of religions and cultures, but they felt she was judging them.

My heart dives. I wish I'd kept an ear on their conversation instead of taking a shower. I fire a reply back.

> Oh, Marci, I'm the one who's sorry. She's immersed in the Mormon kids' lives. I'm pulling her back. What if we try again and they play one of their games? Promise I'll ban all mention of Jesus. x

Three wobbling dots appear, then disappear. I've given up on a reply when one pings through.

> She was mean to them and they don't want to talk to her. Kids are kids, but we always said we'd let them sort out their own disputes within the friendship group. I can't make Tamsin be friends with her. x

Tears prick the back of my eyes. My child has become someone only a Mormon would like. Enough of this 'I love Jesus' bullshit. I want to scoop Willow up and run for the hills. I pulse with guilt for bringing her here and now we're stuck until I learn to drive or they kick me out. How much damage will they do by then?

I go to my phone contacts.

> Hey Joel, are you still okay for that driving lesson tomorrow?

> You bet! See you at 4.30 p.m.

Praise be to the God of Driving Licences. Feeling better, I suggest to Faith on Monday that we add artful photos of the products they sell online, styled as an aspirational lifestyle feature.

'They can go alongside the studio shots.' I take a dainty sip of herbal tea to keep in with her. 'We'll add a photo of you making pancakes with a copper mixing bowl, and have a table laid out with a rustic lunch using the serving dishes and lavender in vases.'

I'm surprised she hasn't done this already. I could do far more to promote and extend her brand, which is why I thought she'd employed me. But she looks doubtful.

'Followers lap up your lifestyle content, so it's a natural extension. We can create the same feel for the products. It fits your aesthetic.'

'We can try it.'

Since it's a no-brainer. 'Let's start with a small range and compare the sales before and after.'

She doesn't need the extra revenue, but I have an ulterior motive. It gives me a reason to collect products to photograph from the big barn where Marty works, so I can dig around for inside info at the same time. And if I prove myself to her, she might see me as a confidante. It's unsettling that I still can't work her out. *Who are you*, I want to ask. *Who's the real you, because it can't be this.*

'I heard that Alice went to Cornell,' I say.

'Yeah.' Her face brightens. 'She's smart.'

'What does she do again?'

'She's overhauling the mail order operation.'

'That sounds short-term, but she's been with you, what… three years?' I wrinkle my face to show that I don't get it.

'She had a baby and she looks after him during work hours. She's finishing the overhaul and now she makes the school lunches and helps run the mail order. Marty needs a good team around him.'

Screw Marty. Alice is capable of more than dinner lady duties. 'Was she pregnant when you took her on?'

'Sure. It's fine. We're family-friendly, and Marty's known her since she was a kid.'

After work, Willow and I rush to milk Myrtle. I snort at the dream-life fantasy of milking a cow and baking bread from Faith's soft-focus content. Gritty reality doesn't get hits. The temperature's dropping. The days are still warmed by bright sunshine, but when winter sets in with heavier snowfall, my fingers will turn red raw and numb from freezing conditions in a draughty cow barn.

For now, I'm awash with the familiar zen-like calm as I milk Myrtle in the golden evening light. The place feels weird, but Willow's happy and I'm strangely okay, chilling the fuck out. Must be the slower pace of life. I'm always occupied, but without rushing from place to place through hordes of commuters.

Willow eats a muffin.

'How'd it go on Saturday with Coco and Tamsin?'

'They wanted to talk about their karaoke party. They didn't care about how I'm doing here.' She takes a contemplative bite of her muffin.

'That's a shame.'

'It's a shame they're not holy.'

'They're your friends. They don't have to be holy.'

'But they don't want to understand the word of God. I tried to get them to pray, and they said it was weird. I said they were dumb and they'd burn in hell.'

I turn my face away, hiding it behind Myrtle's bulk while I grimace and take a long breath. This isn't my child. She's never been preachy or a know-all.

'Sweetheart, that's not a nice thing to say to your friends. We don't call people "dumb" and say mean things. That's not even Christian.' Not that I'm coaching her in religious goodness. 'Your friends here wouldn't talk like that to a non-believer. You know Mormons can have friends who aren't in the church?'

She looks unimpressed. I leave it there. A little-and-often approach might chip away at her alarming new belief system.

'We're better off leaving New York behind,' she says with a world-weary shrug.

'How come?'

'God blesses Utah with children so we can save our country. Nobody else gets it.'

Christ on a bike. They've really done a number on me. Faith barely mentioned religion the first time we met, and now it's rammed down my throat via my daughter. 'You're a child. It's not your job to save our country. The world is made up of different people and we show understanding to others.'

'I love Jesus.'

Great. She always wanted a dad and now she has Sky Daddy.

'Jesus is way cool. He does miracles.'

'Like David Blaine?'

She shoots me a filthy look.

'You used to like him.'

We take the pail back to the cabin as Joel pulls up in his truck. I push down my attraction to him, since my priority is rescuing Willow from these fundie brainwashers and going far, far away. I settle her in the back and rush inside to tip the milk into a jug for the fridge. I'll have to throw out yesterday's milk, a daily occurrence. Maybe I can take half of it to the big barn where Marty employs a few locals like Joel. I can befriend Hel and deprogramme her by stealth along with Willow.

In the truck, I settle behind the steering wheel and Joel shows me how to bring the seat forward and adjust the rear-view mirror. I focus on the lesson, so I don't crash this thing. I'm all business to avoid turning into a hair-twirling, girlish flirt. Joel patiently explains the basics, we pull away and I whoop at making the huge lump of metal move. My brain's overloaded with co-ordinating my feet while steering and watching the road ahead. Joel directs me onto the main road.

'Can't we drive around the ranch where it's safer?'

'No, you're good. Turn left here.'

He encourages me to build up speed. I'm grinning widely. 'Hey, I'm driving.'

'Go you!' He grins. 'Your mom's driving,' he says to Willow.

I can pull this off. I can get my licence. 'Will you help me buy a car?' I ask. 'I've no idea what to look for.'

'Sure. Get something small for the two of you. So long as it can handle snow and ice, you'll be fine. Get it before you take your test, then it'll be easier than this big ole thing.'

I could spend my first month's salary on a down payment. 'Marty's brother sells used cars in Salt Lake. Would you take me there?'

'I guess.' He doesn't sound keen. 'There are other places.'

But I want to check out Asher. I could call ahead and arrange to see the man himself.

'Do you live on the ranch?'

'Nope. I have a place just the other side of town.'

We only pass a handful of vehicles. A few overtake us as I'm not ready to go fast on the open road, despite Joel egging me on.

'How you settling in?' he asks Willow.

'It's like *Second Chance at Philly Ranch*.'

'What's that?'

'A movie we watched.'

Willow had us watch it five times. Such is the allure of cowboy romance for city girls. I wouldn't mind playing around in the hayloft with Joel. I could stay up there indefinitely.

'What's it about?' he asks amiably.

'It's about a lady and her daughter who's like me, and they go to stay at a ranch and the lady falls in love with the cowboy and they live happily ever after.'

'Sounds good.' He gives me a look, his lips curling into a smile. I raise my eyebrows to say, 'Kids. What can you do?' I feel a blush creep up. I can't have him thinking I've a thing for cowboys, even if I'm in danger of losing my mind to his gorgeousness.

'Mom's a sucker for a cowboy.'

'Is that so?' He raises an amused eyebrow at me.

I laugh a little too loud. 'Please! You're the only cowboy I've ever met. That's if you really are one. I'm not sure they exist in real life.' My face burns. Stop digging this hole, you idiot.

'I guess... I mean, I'm a rancher, but go ahead if you want me to be a cowboy.' He winks at me and I melt a little. Are country boys less complicated and more reliable than city guys? Fortunately, we pull up at the cabin.

When I get out, my legs are shaking from being poised over the foot controls, and I'm buzzing with euphoria. I could hug Joel, but instead I hand him the money, which he refuses, so I tuck the notes in his shirt pocket. As I do, his hand brushes against mine and we exchange a meaningful look. He raises his eyebrow at me in what might be a suggestive way. I should ask for riding lessons next.

We arrange another lesson for two days' time, since I want my licence as soon as possible. As I help Willow out of the back seat, Faith's ushering Caleb in from playing outside. She's staring right at us. Joel waves goodbye and drives off, taking the track that snakes past the ranch house. She steps towards him, arms folded. He slows to a halt and lowers the window for her to lean in and speak to him. As we go into the cabin, I see him pull away. She looks back at me, arms still folded.

Chapter Thirty

> I can't give you any more driving lessons. Sorry.

I stare at Joel's message first thing on Tuesday morning.

> Is something wrong?

> I need to prioritise work.

Bullshit. Faith warned him off, but I won't drag him into it. Is she discouraging a potential romance, or doesn't she want me to drive? Marty had questioned my need to learn. But Faith and Alice drive, so why can't I?

> Okay, thanks for the lesson. I enjoyed it.

'What's up?' Willow notices my dismay.
'Joel says he can't teach me to drive after all.'
'Shall we pray?' she asks gravely, placing her little hand over mine.

I take her hand in both of mine and kiss it. 'What for?'

'We'll ask God to help you do the right thing and for it to all work out.'

I get up to make her breakfast. 'Thank you, but praying won't help. I'll work it out because that's what people do.' I could say that it's better to learn to help ourselves than rely on a false sense of a higher power, but I'm outnumbered on the religious front until I can drive us away from here.

After breakfast, Willow kisses me goodbye and scoots off to the indoctrination barn, pigtails bouncing. I've always loved the way she goes all in. Now, less so. When we came here, I marvelled at how much our commute had reduced, but our lives have too.

I stride off to the ranch house where Faith is preoccupied with wiping down the counters and avoiding eye contact.

'Good morning. How are you?' I say.

'Fine. And you?' She's still busy wiping.

'I'm good. Did you see me having a driving lesson yesterday?'

'Yes. I'm a little unhappy at you paying Joel to work extra hours.'

'It's just an hour here and there. He didn't mind.'

'He has a demanding job. Marty needs him focused. We don't encourage our team to work elsewhere. It's important to relax.'

'Do you relax outside of work?' It's a genuine question. I wait for her to stop cleaning. She glances at me, a trace of annoyance in her face.

'I'll find a driving instructor.'

'We have enough drivers here. Focus on spending time with Willow.'

I bristle. She's quite the dictator when it comes to my personal life. 'It's good for Willow if I'm independent, same as your kids see you working and driving a car, since this isn't Saudi Arabia.' I caved on church to keep the peace, but I'm digging in on this one.

She doesn't reply. The conversation's over. The old me might have pointed out that she's always in the kitchen and I bet she never does story time with her kids or crawls about on the floor playing with the little ones.

She pours us some herbal tea. I go to edit footage of her baking apple cake. Do they want to isolate me? I'm chaperoned into town, and they dissuaded me from joining a Bible group that wasn't theirs. But my annoyance eases. It keeps on doing that. I feel floaty, almost disengaged from the world. Does Faith feel this way too? She goes on about the calming effect of lavender, the aroma ever-present around the ranch house and in our cabin from lavender pouches, soap, laundry detergent. It's a subtle effect that takes the edge off me.

The final cut of the video looks good. Despite Faith's controlling tendencies, I still admire the way she showcases her cookery skills online. I don't need the limelight, but I miss the creative outlet of my podcast, from the planning and recording through to posting and promoting. I can do that for Faith, but it's her life, her voice, not mine.

In the absence of podcasting, Willow and I keep on journaling together. That evening, she says that Marty gave them another lesson in 'inter-pinner-ships'.

'Entrepreneurship,' I say. 'What did you learn?'

'Men go out and make money because they're the head of the household. And women stay home to look after the family, but they can still make money at home.'

So much for empowering her. 'Aren't women the lucky ones to do the housework *and* make money? But you can also go off and have a career. You can be a doctor, you can play in an orchestra or fly a plane. You can join NASA and go into space.'

She giggles. 'But who'll look after my kids?'

'It's a smart move to have a career before kids. If you decide to have a husband or a partner, that's something you'll work out between the two of you. Millions of women go out to work, so whatever Marty says the boys can do, you can do too.'

'But God put me on earth to be a wife and mother.'

'No.' I look deeply into her eyes. 'I brought you into the world so you can live your best life. When you're an adult, you're free to be a wife and mother, and you can be so much more besides.'

She hugs me sleepily and goes to get ready for bed.

'Dream big,' I call after her. *And outgrow that Mormon box they want to shut you in.* At least her journal entries are brimming with innocence and enthusiasm despite her telling her friends they'll burn in hell. I guess their lack of engagement frustrated her so she upped the stakes, unaware it would backfire.

It's just a phase. Her Jesus era. She'll move on to the next obsession once we leave, like that vile fixation she had on slime last year. Beverley thought it hilarious to buy her a slime lab so she could make her own. I miss Beverley and her cocktails. We've exchanged messages, but if I call her she'll know something's up and I'll feel even worse about coming here.

I need a stiff drink. I need cake made by someone other than me, and I need to cut loose. Marty's weirdness at the Bible night and Faith derailing my driving lessons has ramped up the urgency to get the hell out. The additional cost of a car and renting a flat will swallow my income, but I could pick up freelance work if I'm not wasting time on church, cow milking and baking. I'll pay whatever it costs for my independence and to reclaim my sweet girl. It's also a safer option, when Zac is hounding me. I bite the bullet and call him, since I don't want evidence of our actual conversation. He picks up at the first ring.

'Mel, the fuck are you playing at?'

I sigh audibly. 'It's not safe to message me. They hate me having tech as it is.'

'What've you found out?'

'He's not giving anything up yet. I've tried leading him into conversation about Asher, but he gives me strange looks. I'm working on it—'

'That won't cut it.'

'I'll find someone to drive me to Asher's car lot.' Zac knows all about Asher's car dealership since he was fired from there, so I say it to keep him off my back. 'Marty doesn't want me having a car, but—'

'He doesn't want you having a car?' he yells. 'The fuck's it got to do with him? Tell that cocksucker he doesn't get to dictate your life. Why you letting him push you around?'

'Like you push me around?' I talk in a low snarl. 'Back off or I'll leave because it's not safe, if you—'

'That's not a wise move, given the consequence.'

'Threaten me all you like, but if the truth comes out, you've lost your hold on me, and I'll tell the cops you're blackmailing me.'

'And they won't do shit.'

'They will when they know your plan for the car dealership. I'm sure Asher Eversen will help with their inquiries.'

'And you'll be finished. Marty Eversen will come after you hard for living on his ranch under false pretences. His lawyers will bankrupt you. Then you won't be able to rent a place to live, get a loan, nothing. And that's if he doesn't prefer rough justice, cos every redneck owns a gun.'

Chapter Thirty-One

While Faith's busy with the baby, I monitor online comments to last week's video. It's not just keyboard warriors who hate on Faith, podcasters have declared open season too. A feminist commentator has posted a link to her latest podcast, and I tune in.

'You never see trad wives over forty romanticising their lives,' she says. 'Not when they're exhausted, prematurely aged and resentful. When they stop having kids they lose their status. Next time you watch Faith Eversen's videos, consider what's going on that she doesn't share with us.'

I'm doing just that. I'm tempted to leave the offending link in Faith's comments, but I press 'delete'.

We shoot a video of her making apple jam. She has her detractors, but even when I'm engaged behind the camera, working out the best angle, I still find her tutorials weirdly inspiring. I could make a batch of apple jam with Willow on Saturday afternoon, along with apple sauce to go on her oatmeal. It's part of the back-to-basics experience and Willow enjoys helping me. We might as well immerse ourselves in the foodie aspect before we leave, and it's a distraction from the issue of Zac pressing in on me.

I'm still buying ready-made dairy products. I picture Faith sneaking into the cabin and opening the fridge, her face falling at the wrappers and plastic containers. Then she'll food shame me some more.

'Where are the jars for the jam?' I ask while the apples are stewing.

'Up in that high cupboard. I'll ask Marty to get them.'

I grab a chair to climb onto.

'Leave it,' she says with a smile, so I do.

She's natural on and off camera. But I can tell when she's annoyed and covering up with her Mormon lady face. She's serene but zoned out with a ghost of a smile. Is that how she avoids going on the rampage over everything that's wrong with her life? I wonder if they're taught it or learn from observing their mothers.

My own Mormon-lite mum followed the 'put up and shut up' school of housewifery, nurturing everyone but herself. Faith has perfected the art of acting like this is the only thing on earth she wishes to do, whereas my mum showed her irritation and she only had two kids.

'I was wondering about Bible study last week,' I say.

'Mmm?'

'Why did Marty ask Hel to read a book about being a good wife?'

'Well, she's only nineteen and Marty's so caring and paternal.'

We're between apple jam shots and she steps away to blow air upwards on to her face, wiping her brow with the back of her hand. The consummate performer feels tired like the rest of us, but she's reigning champ at the Trad Wife Olympics. It doesn't help that she's wearing yet another long-sleeved, long-skirted number while toiling over the Aga's heat.

'Where's her real dad?' I ask.

'Mmm...' She looks at me expectantly as if to say, 'You figure it out.'

She'd just said, 'Marty's so caring and paternal'. I narrow my eyes at her. 'Is Marty her dad?'

She looks out of the window. Speak of the devil, the cowboy comes stalking towards us. 'We can't talk about this. Please. Don't mention it again.' She looks flustered as he bursts in.

'Honey?' She gives him a pleading look. 'Melissa and I can't reach the jars. Can you please get them down for us?'

'Sure.' His chest puffs up. Her damsel-in-distress act is too much. Do they play sex games where he rescues her from being tied up on a train track? And if Hel's his daughter, why can't they just tell me? Either it's shameful that he had a child before marrying Faith, or they think it'll damage their brand.

Marty goes and I leave the camera out to capture the final shot later of her spreading apple jam on freshly baked bread for the kids. 'Where do you store the preserves?' I ask.

'I'll show you the storeroom.'

Faith looks for a key while I put on my coat and go outside. The children are singing, and I tune in to the odd melody. It sounds like a deathly hymn unsuited to their sweet little voices. Snatches of lyrics come to me about 'sinners slain' and someone deeply wailing who's nailed to a tree. My blood freezes.

'What are they singing?' I ask when Faith comes out.

She cocks her head to listen, then gives a hollow laugh. 'Zina's pretty hardcore.'

'What's wrong with "All Things Bright and Beautiful"?'

'She's good at keeping their attention. The kids like the drama of her hymns.'

Had I known they'd pay a religious nutjob to put the fear of God into my child, I'd never have come here. I'll double down on pop music and we'll dance to Taylor Swift.

Faith walks me to the storage barn, which is smaller than the big barn where the others work. It's used as a laundry and for storing sacks of wheat and potatoes. There's a washer and dryer in the ranch house, and I share the barn laundry with the Bone family and probably Hel too. One corner is a guy gym, set up with heavy weights and a punchbag hanging from the rafters.

'Is that your punchbag?' I ask.

'It's Marty's.'

'Who does he want to punch?'

She laughs daintily and unlocks a door inside the barn. I follow her down a wooden staircase to a cellar filled with foodstuffs in jars, bottles and sacks.

She's brought a string bag and selects what she needs from the shelves as if in a grocery store. 'We don't have to worry if we have a bad winter and get snowed in.'

Sensible, out here, I go to say, but she keeps talking.

'And Marty says when society breaks down, we'll be self-sufficient.'

What? 'Do you think society will break down?'

She reaches up for a jar of pickles. 'Marty says we only know what we can control.'

'But won't people try to loot what's here or take over the ranch?'

'Marty has guns,' she says in her mild, soft way.

My hairline prickles and unease tingles down my spine. 'Can you fire a gun?'

'Marty's a good shot. It's a divine mandate.'

'What does that mean?'

'We have the right to protect ourselves,' she says softly.

Guns go with the territory, but talking about it in their secret bunker makes me edgy. New Yorkers don't have guns, and I didn't grow up with them in the UK. After years of US school shootings and crazed gunmen on the loose, I don't trust anyone with firearms. And Zac's prediction of Marty the redneck coming after me with a gun might come true.

'Look at the sacks of grain,' Faith says. 'We're storing them for the apocalypse.'

'Zombie apocalypse?'

'Marty says society will break down before the Rapture, so we'll shelter here.'

We go back out into the open, thank God, and I breathe fresh air. So much to unpick, I barely know where to start. 'Jesus wouldn't be pro-gun.'

'Ask Marty,' Faith says. 'He knows about that. He's so wise.'

The wise man himself strides towards us, grinning widely at Faith's words. 'You ladies talking about me?'

Only because she's delulu.

She kisses him on the lips and lovingly brushes a smear of dirt from his chin. 'Melissa is asking if Jesus is pro-gun.'

'Heck, yeah.' He nods emphatically at me, fists planted on his hips. 'Jesus would be packing.'

I look from one to the other, both nodding in all seriousness.

'In Luke Twenty-Two,' he says, 'Jesus tells his disciples to buy swords. It would've been guns if they'd been invented back then.'

I picture Faith branching out from cookery videos to soft-focus instruction in shooting to kill. She takes aim and shoots. Killing for the Lord. Then I picture Willow at Jesus Camp, an army camp where children go for target practice. Perfecting her aim for the baby Jesus.

The kids spill out of school, so I walk away from the crazy. Willow and I take turns milking Myrtle. The air is crisp, and I take a photo of her on the low milking stool. My rosy-cheeked milkmaid looks born to it. Despite their crazy talk, I'm soothed by the repetition of milking, and talk about mindfulness.

She tilts her head in contemplation. 'That's good. You're making a space for God.'

'I'm making a space for me,' I say.

'So you can slow down and let God in. That's what we do before reading scripture.'

I try not to roll my eyes. 'How was school?'

'We sang a song. The others knew it by heart, but I had to read from a book.'

I recall the creepy lyrics about someone nailed to a tree. Poor Jesus, with no assault rifle. 'I heard you all singing.'

'It's about end days.'

I stop milking. 'The world isn't going to end. Religious people have said for a very long time that it's about to end, but it never does. Religions scare you into thinking you won't go to heaven if you don't believe.' We walk back with the pail of milk.

'But it's true. And you have to believe it or you're gonna catch fire and die.'

Enough of this end-of-days, burn-in-hell fuckwittery. I need another job, fast, then I'm grabbing her hand and running for the hills.

Chapter Thirty-Two

My first driving lesson is booked with an instructor on Bible study night. I tell Willow that we won't be going.

'Why do I have to come?' she whines.

'Because when you're not in school, you and I stick together. We milk Myrtle together, we bake cookies together—'

'Faith will let me come.'

'Faith wants you and me to spend more time together, and I want you with me.'

She goes to school in a huff. I tell Faith we can't make Bible study as I have other plans.

'Oh.' Her face drops. 'What do you have planned?'

'A driving lesson. Since Joel can't teach me, Thursday will be my regular lesson.' I half hope she relents and releases Joel for a little moonlighting.

'Why don't you book it on a Saturday so you can learn in daylight?'

'I'm having lessons on Saturdays too.'

'Marty will be sorry. Maybe he'll come over another evening for Bible study.'

'No thanks. I'm not religious. Do you remember me saying that when we first met?'

She looks passively at me.

'I made it clear that I came to church because Willow wanted to try it out, but it's not for me.'

She turns away as if offended.

'I'm sorry if you misunderstood.'

'I'm sorry too,' she says softly. 'I thought you wanted to be part of our community.'

'I wasn't aware I had to be Mormon. I've been honest about not sharing your belief, so I hope I can continue working here.' Until I have another job, that is.

'Of course.' She turns back, eyes wide. 'We wanted to welcome you. Our faith is central to our lives, so we worship together.'

'I don't believe in God.'

'You should talk to Marty about that. You know he's intuitive because he fell off his horse?'

'Did he get a brain injury?' I ask, deadpan.

'He got knocked clean out. That was the first time God visited him and told him he was a prophet and would speak through him.'

Fuck me, Marty thinks he's the Messiah. A God complex could work to my advantage, since I'm secretly looking for dirt on him, but it's even more reason to get Willow away from here.

'He always has a solution,' she adds.

'Is it always one that suits him?'

'And we love the way Willow's taken to it.'

'She wants to fit in,' I start saying.

Faith lights up. 'It's a perfect way to fit in. There are LDS communities all around the world so wherever you go, you can find a church. And Utah is the most welcoming community and that's so good for children.'

Yeah, but I'm hell-bent on clawing back my independence, and my two driving lessons a week will leave her in no doubt.

'I'll pray that someday you'll join us in feeling the spirit.'

After work, I rush to milk Myrtle, and Willow ambles over. 'Mrs Bone says I can come to Bible study without you. We're going to watch another show tonight.'

'I've already said you're coming with me.' She'll be happier with the others, but they indoctrinate her enough at school.

Their newest recruit folds her arms and stomps her cowboy-booted foot. 'I wanna go.'

I cut short the milking, carrying the pail in one hand, firmly leading her back to the cabin. She whines all the way. When the instructor pulls up, I chivvy her out to the car and buckle her up in the back. She pouts and refuses to look at me.

The lesson is more thorough than with Joel, so it's money well spent. I pay close attention, wanting to fast-track my way off Jesus Camp. After the session, my head spins and my leg muscles quiver again from my feet poised over the pedals.

Back in the cabin, Willow refuses to write her journal or read with me. 'Clean your teeth and go to bed then,' I say.

'It pains me that you're not seeing the good in our Lord,' she says in her indignant little voice.

I laugh. 'I'm not seeing the good in you right now. Clean your teeth.'

She bursts into tears. 'I wish Faith was my mom,' she wails. 'She's pretty and nice and close to God.'

I startle at a loud rap at the door.

'Do as you're told or there'll be consequences.' I give her a warning look and she huffs off to the bathroom. I want to sit with my head in my hands, but whoever's at the door raps on it again. I open it to find Marty.

Chapter Thirty-Three

Marty's on the porch and his trademark grin seems forced. He digs his hands into his pockets. 'We missed you earlier.'

'I had to switch evenings for my driving lessons.'

'Can I come in?'

I step back as Willow emerges from the bathroom, red-eyed.

'Hey, Willow. I was just telling your mom we missed you both at Bible study.'

'Mommy wouldn't let me come,' she says in a hurt voice.

I try to usher her up to bed but he jumps in. 'Let us pray now instead.'

I do not need to pray right now.

'May I?' He motions to the kitchen table, and Willow almost skips to it, triumphant that God Has Found A Way. There goes my parental authority. He pulls out a chair for her and one for me, then sits at the head of the table, of course. He serenely outstretches his hands, Jesus-like, palms upwards for us to join him in prayer.

Willow leans forward, stretching her free hand across the table to me. I hatch an idea to pull her back to me through my own sneaky brand of prayer. If they can manipulate her, I'll manipulate her back to me.

'Thank you, God, for this day and for Your blessings.' His voice is rich and confident. 'We thank You for the good times and the hard times that bring us important lessons to learn. Please protect us and those we love from fear and anxiety.'

And from guns and religious zealotry.

'Please guide Melissa and Willow. Help them to find the right path.'

The right path out of here.

'We pray for those who don't know You, God, and for those who need to know You.'

I squint one eye open and see my pious child nodding, eyes squeezed shut. All the time, Marty strokes my hand with his thumb, which should be creepy but is strangely comforting. An adult hasn't held my hand that way since before Willow was born. I forgot how good it feels, and then hate myself for it. But I've been feeling strange since coming here, less inclined to push back. Faith's serenity is rubbing off. At this rate, I'll catch God from these people, because something is going on inside me. A weird sensation is turning me more agreeable. Agreeable like a Mormon woman. What would happen if I lost my mind and turned into one of them?

'Amen,' Marty says.

Willow's 'amen' is emphatic. 'If God brings us lessons from hard times,' she says to him, 'what lesson do I learn from Mommy saying I can't come to Bible group?'

I chew the inside of my cheek and pull my hand from Marty's.

He furrows his brow. 'You're learning how much your faith means to you, and that's a beautiful thing.'

'Time for bed, Willow,' I say.

'Good night, sweet pea,' he says. She slides off the chair and gives him a hug, pushing herself into him, burying her face in his thick cotton shirt.

He looks fondly at her and wraps an arm around her shoulders. 'Sleep well.'

The tiny traitor heads for the stairs, not even looking at me. 'I'll be up in a minute,' I call after her.

'Could we speak on the porch?' he asks.

We go out the front where he pulls the door shut behind me.

'We've become awful fond of Willow,' he says, settling on the love seat and patting the space beside him.

I back off and lean against a wooden post holding up the porch.

'We all love you two being part of our community.'

'And we appreciate how welcoming you've been, but—'

'It's our way. I know it's different to the city and it's been a long time since you were involved in church. The two of you missing Bible group made us realise that we want you both around.'

I want to ask why, but he'll trot out some bullshit answer. My phone buzzes in my pocket and irritation flashes across his face.

'Faith and I were wondering if I can teach you to drive.'

'You? But you don't have time.' What about the sacred family time that Faith bangs on about?

'We take time for the people in our community who need us.' His voice is kindly, but lacking the sweetness deployed by females.

'Faith didn't want Joel teaching me in case he's less effective at work.'

He shrugs, leaning back on the wooden seat, legs splayed, thumbs hooked in his jeans. 'All I know is, you need lessons and I'm a good teacher.'

They're bringing me back into the fold. Do they have a thing for fallen women who need saving? Alice is a single mother who they brought on board, along with her mum. I shudder at the thought of my mum living with us. This place is smothering enough.

Whatever their motive, it's a temporary fix when Willow's threatening all-out war over the curtailment of her religious freedom. It's a battle I won't win for as long as we live here. 'Okay, if Faith doesn't mind.'

'That's settled then. You can drive us into town on Saturday.' He ambles away and lifts his hand in a goodbye. 'Sleep well.'

Like a true Mormon woman, I've been railroaded into the harmonious option, keeping the peace. I've lost the Bible study battle, which Willow will see as divine intervention, a gift from God who answered her prayers. But they're not the only ones on a mission. I turn off the porch light and stand in the cold semi-dark of the doorway. Marty would be less keen if he knew my rush to learn to drive is so we can get the hell away.

Then something catches in my peripheral vision. An outside light goes off at the big barn. I step off the porch and skirt round the cabin to see the barn's silhouette. A dim light is visible from an upstairs window. Maybe he went there to turn off a light, but there's no sign of him walking back down the gravel path.

Faith said he was paternal towards Hel. Is he her dad? Given the age gap, it's feasible, and she acts like their truculent teenager. Perhaps he's doing a prayer round at bedtime, bringing us black sheep back into the fold. I compare her to their batch of little blond cuties and wonder what went wrong. And where's her mum?

In the early hours, I startle awake, drenched in sweat after a vivid dream in which Marty drove me to the mountains and kissed me. I throw off the covers, since the bedroom window is locked and I can't get more air. The attraction felt dangerously bad. I lie drowsily in bed, trying to banish the sensations. I do not want to catch feelings for that man. I channel my thoughts towards Joel, to cancel out Marty. Will I ever get close to Joel with the Mormon vice squad on the prowl?

My drifting mind recalls my twelve-year-old self, the first time the church tried policing me as part of their unhealthy obsession with teen sex. My brother had tipped me off, saying to give them nothing. Twice a year from age twelve they forced 'worthiness' interviews on me, urging me to confess my sins. I acted innocent and pretended to only have pure thoughts.

Then I think of my aunt, my dad's sister, who I never met. She died at seventeen and my dad never got over it. I burn with the injustice and lack of karma. But I'm here to fix that. I'm here to expose the wrongdoings that tormented my family, driving more than one of them into early graves.

Chapter Thirty-Four

I'm determined to make the most of my driving lesson with Marty, but I'm creeped out by the remnants of my spicy dream, the freakishly wrong dream. I squash it down and focus on trying to drive their minivan. It's even harder than Joel's truck, with five noisy, distracting kids in the back.

'Why're we going so slow?' Isiah, the eldest, asks.

'Just keeping you all safe,' I call back, my eyes fixed on the road ahead.

'Go faster. It's boring.'

Marty gives him a warning stare that shuts him up. The driving is hard, especially coming into town where I sense everyone watching us. It's understandable that they're curious about Marty being with this new woman while his wife stays home.

I'm a bag of nerves with legs of jelly by the time I get out. It ruins the pleasure of getting away from the ranch, but I need to do this. An hour later, I drive us back and ask Marty for a second lesson every week. I suggest that I could ask to borrow Alice's car, since that's smaller.

'It's better to learn in a bigger vehicle,' he says. 'Alice doesn't drive her car when it snows, so there's no point learning in hers. You need to take it slow for the lessons to sink in. Once a week is fine.'

My little lady brain can only be taxed so much. I decide to go back to the instructor in town for another weekday lesson. I'll avoid Bible group night since Marty's lessons are in return for keeping that time sacred. But soon we'll be free of church commitments. Back at the cabin, I'm unpacking groceries when Willow asks if we're going to church tomorrow.

'We need to get one thing straight,' I say.

She looks up at me wide-eyed.

'I'm your mum and what I say goes. I'm allowing you to attend church and Bible study, but if I say you can't do something, you don't go crying to other people to get your own way. I don't care what Emily and her parents are doing. In our family, I decide and that's final, okay?'

She blinks at me. 'But God is our loving father in heaven.'

'And I am your loving mother on earth and what I say goes.'

'Does that mean we're going to church?'

'So long as you respect our rules. If you throw another tantrum or try to run off when I say no, there'll be consequences.'

'Obeying God's commandments brings peace.'

'So does obeying my commandments.'

She nods and pokes out her bottom lip. I resent being corralled into their religion. It sets a dangerous precedent with Willow when I've always tried to be one of those parents for whom no means no. I can only pull rank so much, or she'll call for divine backup. Beverley would be horrified. *I'm* horrified. The change in her shocks me to the core.

A thin layer of snow settles overnight. As we leave for church, Willow's wearing the second outfit that Faith gave her, and I appear at the last moment in my dark suit. Willow's face drops and she pleads with me to 'look nice'.

'It's too late to change.' I'm bringing my authentic self to church. She gives up and rushes out into the cold morning air, her Mormon fire burning bright. I squint through the blinding glare of sun on the snow. Zina's settling Jonny into the child seat.

'Alice isn't coming,' she says as Willow scootches into the back. 'She's not feeling well.'

'Will she be okay on her own?'

'She just needs to rest awhile.'

Emily joins us for the drive, and Willow chats happily with her in the back.

'How did you come to work here?' I ask Zina.

'Alice knew Marty's family. Then they offered her a job setting up the mail order operation. She can work flexibly, and we manage the childcare between us.'

Is Marty's brother the father of her child? It would figure, given his past, and explain why Marty and Faith took her in. Zina launches straight into teacherly mode, pointing out geographical features along the way as if the subject is closed.

At church, I adopt the serenely glazed expression that women around here have perfected. I smile and nod, say a few bland words when expected and let the tedious service wash over me. At one point, Faith catches my eye, signalling her disappointment in my non-churchy attire. Towards the end of lunch, Zina comes over to say she's leaving. My heart leaps. 'I'll find Willow.'

She's with a group of endearingly wholesome girls. I picture them holding hands and singing 'Kumbaya'. They have what my brother would call 'the Mormon glow' from their joyful spirits shining through.

'Willow,' I touch her shoulder, 'say goodbye. Mrs Bone is taking us home.'

She looks at me in dismay.

'You'll see everyone next Sunday.'

'I'll come home with the others.'

'We have to go,' I intone in the Mormon-esque firm yet soft way.

'Mommy—'

'Come with me.' I hold out my hand, my smile tight. She doesn't budge.

'Remember what we talked about?' I fire her a warning look.

She says goodbye and makes a show of huffing off. It would be easier to leave her, but the religious crackpots aren't getting their claws into her even more.

'I've hardly seen you today.' I rush to catch up.

Her face crumples and she's sobbing by the time we reach the door, turning heads. I've yet to see another child around here have a meltdown. Mormon kids don't play up in church. The judgemental stares burn into me as I guide her out with all the dignity I can muster. *Bad mother.* With luck, we'll be uninvited. By the time we reach the car, her shoulders heave in time with gulping sobs.

'Willow...'

'Stop crying,' Zina commands, her words cutting through mine. 'God hates whiners.' She shoots Willow a glacial stare. I go to tell her I've got this, but Willow stops crying instantly and slides into the back seat with Jonny.

We drive off and she wipes her eyes, then stares glassily out of the window. I reach back to hand her a tissue, but she ignores me, so I drop it in her lap. None of us speak. *God hates whiners.* Why so judgy, God? I stifle a guffaw and picture it as a cross-stitch, while smarting at Zina taking charge of my child, holding more sway than me.

She drops us at the door to the cabin and I give her a curt 'thank you'.

Once inside, Willow goes to stomp up to her room.

'Hey.' I reach out and lightly hold on to her arm, but she wriggles out of my grip.

She backs away with a mean look on her face. 'I frickin hate you!'

'Frickin?' I snort.

'Isiah says "frickin" and I do too.'

'We agreed to church and Bible group so long as you respect that I'm the parent. When I say we're leaving, that's what'll happen.'

'You're mean to me.'

'I want us to have time together on a Sunday. How about we go for a hike and work off those big emotions?'

'You took me from God's house for *a hike*?' She stands stiffly, her hands balled into fists. I always expected to fall out over her wanting a smartphone or pierced navel. But no, she wants Jesus. My daughter is a red-hot mess over religion.

'We've discussed this.' My voice takes on a warning tone. 'If you're going to—'

'It's not fair,' she screeches.

'Nor is religion. Children are killed all the time in the name of religion.'

Her little brow wrinkles.

'Children die in wars that are fought because of religion. Is that fair?'

Marty's car drives past. They must have left soon after us, so her outburst is all for nothing. She makes a beeline for the door. 'I'm going to see Emily.'

I rush after her to stop her tantrum spilling outside. She flings open the door. I slam it shut and lean against it, facing her down. 'Push me too far and I will take you away from here.'

'You can't.' She steps back and folds her arms.

'Yes, I can. I'm the boss of us.'

'Marty's the boss of us.'

'He's not the boss in our family.'

'He is too. He's the boss of everyone here.'

'I'm your parent, the only one you have, and I have the legal right to take you anywhere.' It's a mean thing to say when she needs stability. And she'll parrot it back to the others, making me a bad parent, bad Mormon and bad employee when they're expecting me to stay. But I have to get her back somehow.

'Asshole,' she snarls.

My eyes widen and my jaw drops open. I nearly laugh. 'What would God think of you using a word like that?' I try to keep the mocking tone from my voice.

'I hate you!' she yells at the top of her lungs. 'Let me out. I hate you.' She tries shoving me away so she can unbolt the door. I move behind her, both my hands over hers, trying to prise her from the bolt and restrain her until her anger subsides. She kicks back at me and screams.

Enough of this. I yank her away and go to haul her to my bedroom until she calms down. She screeches. A shadow passes the window followed by urgent rapping on the door. Willow keeps on. The door handle rattles.

'Melissa?' Marty shouts.

I haul my struggling child towards the bedroom.

'Open the door or I'll knock it down.'

Chapter Thirty-Five

Trust Marty to turn up during Willow's meltdown. I let go of her and unbolt the door. She throws herself on him and clings to his leg, wailing.

I take a frazzled breath, raking my fingers through my hair. He looks from me to her, then holds her by the shoulders, leaning down level with her face.

'I have it covered,' I say.

'Stop this right now,' he tells her in a low, commanding voice.

She immediately stops wailing. Fuck's sake. Why do the rest of them have more authority over her? She lets out a choked sob and wipes her nose on her sleeve. I grab her a tissue, which she sullenly takes.

'Why are you behaving this way?' he asks.

'She's mean to me,' she says in a petulant voice.

'Seems to me that you're the mean one. I come home and hear you hollering the place down, trying to leave your home while your mom's keeping you safe from yourself.'

She pokes out her lower lip and looks contrite.

'We must all respect our elders. It's your mom's job to look after you. You need to do as she says. You know what happens to kids who don't do as they're told?'

She looks at her feet and nods her head. What's he talking about? Will God strike her down for the sin of stroppiness?

'Say sorry to your mom for causing trouble.'

'Sorry,' she says in a choked voice, not looking at me.

'I want no more of this bad behaviour. You hear?' Marty says.

She nods and tears spill down her face.

'Now go to your room while I talk to your mom in private.' Marty releases his grip on her shoulders, and she goes quietly towards the stairs. He motions for us to go outside, where he sits on the love seat and I lean on the side of the porch.

'Thank you for that, but I could've handled it,' I say.

'Sure, but sometimes it helps to have backup.'

'We're stepping back from church activities. It's causing friction and I'm really not interested.'

He pushes himself slowly back and forth in the swing seat. 'Living on a ranch is hard. You rely more on your community, and church brings us together.'

Yeah, but we're not sticking around.

'We can take Willow to church and she can still come to Bible study nights.'

'No thanks. Faith says time outside of work is for family and I agree.'

'She'll miss out on having friends and doing fun stuff away from the ranch. The church organises a lot for kids.'

'I'll go check on her. Thanks for coming over.'

He stands up, confusion on his face. I guess women never say no to him. I go up to Willow, who's curled on the bed, turned away from me. I take *Little House on the Prairie* from the nightstand and scootch in close to read it aloud. After a while I feel her body relax. I finish the chapter and put the book down, thinking of something to say to rescue her back to me.

'Rats. I forgot to milk Myrtle.' So much for saying something meaningful. 'Wanna come?' I haul myself up.

She sits up too, hair a mess.

'Let's change into our jeans.' I kiss the top of her head. 'See you downstairs.'

I've got the hang of milking and the satisfying rhythm of squeezing the teats as the milk squirts into the pail. I look out on the shivery landscape, the scattering of snow. Willow takes a turn. She's listless, her eyes red from crying.

'Are we good now?'

She nods sadly.

Until our next religious run-in. 'Shall we make lasagna?'

She nods again. It's her favourite, and I'll make enough for two days of leftovers.

'Then we can write our journals.'

She shakes her head sadly. 'Not today.'

'Highs and lows make a good story. Real life isn't all apple pie and singing songs. Laura Ingalls had it tougher than us.'

She pokes out her lower lip. I'm tempted to offer her a movie, so we can snuggle up on the couch, but it goes against what I agreed. Walking back with the pail, I remember something.

'What did Marty mean when he said, "You know what happens when kids don't do as they're told"?'

'They get switched.'

'What?' I look at her, aghast. 'Has anyone hurt you?'

She shakes her head.

'Has he used it on anyone else?'

She shrugs. 'I don't know.'

The kids are well behaved because they're scared of him. He can silence Isiah with a single look. This is what they do, break a child's spirit until they comply. 'Have you seen it?'

'It's hanging up in the schoolroom.'

Along with the nasty cross-stitch. We're back at the cabin and I realise I'm shaking. I shut the door behind us and crouch down in front of her. 'Don't let anyone come near you with it, okay?'

She nods, eyes wide.

'No one is allowed to threaten you with violence. If anyone tries to hurt you when I'm not around, tell them they're not allowed, and you come and find me, okay?' I pull her into a hug, wishing we were back home.

What have I done bringing her to this throwback of a place? Mormon men have absolute authority in their homes, as decreed by God. I knew that, but I didn't plan on sharing my home with one. In the absence of a husband, Marty thinks he has authority over us, but he won't rule my child by fear. I'm so furious that I ditch the TV rules, and we watch *Just Add Magic*.

I did the right thing to leave their screwed-up religion in my teens. I did the wrong thing in bringing us here. I thought I could handle it, but we need to get out.

—

That fricking bitch. Who does she think she is? Coming here, judging us. Measuring us against her superior city ways. She needs re-educating. My way is the only way.

Chapter Thirty-Six

When Willow's asleep, I begin an online job search. My instinct is to leave right now, scoop her up and do a midnight flit. But we have no savings, no car, nowhere to go. I haven't even had my first month's wages.

The less nuclear option is to get my driving licence and move us to an apartment in town, then I can work while keeping Willow out of their clutches. I'm wary of driving through snow and ice now the cold weather's closing in. We've only had light snow, which doesn't settle for long while the days are still warm and sunny. But by December, the snowfall will be heavy and frequent. Shame we didn't come in spring.

My mind spins through the scenario of me as an inexperienced driver on a road turned to glass, spinning off an icy bend. If Willow's orphaned, what if Faith and Marty adopt her? She'd be defenceless, groomed to become a teen bride with a controlling husband. I'm spiralling. Deep breaths.

The local school will be more regulated than their home school, but we're better off leaving rural Utah. I need to get her away from the fundamentalists. New York's too expensive, so I scout out creative jobs in California, somewhere cheap and near a beach, where we won't be under snow for months of the year or threatened by wildfires or hurricanes. I scroll fervently through listings, then update my CV until midnight.

In the morning, Willow is her bouncy self, in her mostly Tiggerish approach to life. She wants us to say grace before breakfast, so I stay silent as she blesses the food and blesses our day and thank you, Jesus, amen. We come out of the cabin and she runs to Emily who's hopscotching outside.

On the way to the ranch house, the door to the storage barn is open and I spot Alice slumped over the dryer.

'Alice?' I come closer. 'You okay?'

She straightens a little and nods wearily. Jonny pushes a toy truck along on the ground, oblivious.

'What's wrong?'

She arches her back and tips her face up to the sky to take in some air.

'Mama sick,' Jonny says, barely glancing up.

'Your poor mama,' I say. 'You be kind to her when she's sick.'

'I'm fine.' She flaps an arm to say it's no big deal. 'Some kind of stomach upset. I'll go for a lie-down.'

'Shall I take Jonny to play with Caleb?'

'No, I'm okay if I'm sitting down. I was doing too much.' She walks listlessly back to her barn house. I follow a few steps behind, chatting to Jonny about his truck and whether he's been in a real truck.

'Daddy's truck.'

'Oh, your daddy has a truck?' I ask.

'Jonny, c'mon. We're fine from here.'

I watch them go. So, he has a daddy. I wonder where he is. It might be one of those things kids make up. Willow once told her first-grade teacher that her daddy flew a plane. That and flower arranging. Maybe he does,

I wanted to say, but I didn't get that impression the one time I met him.

At the homestead, Faith's on the phone, and I set to work on adding cute captions to her latest video on making your own natural lip balm with melted beeswax, shea butter and lavender.

She comes in a little later with a ghastly brew for us both. I need to ask about Marty, but can't launch straight in. 'I'm sorry about the situation with Willow yesterday,' I say.

She smiles and brushes it off as if to say, 'Kids, we've all been there.' But I've never heard hers indulge in more than minor squabbles. When their voices are raised, it's in youthful high spirits rather than calling their parents 'assholes'.

'Marty said something I didn't understand, and Willow said later that it was a threat of physical punishment.'

'Oh,' she says vaguely.

'Is it true?' I watch her reaction.

'He's never acted on it, and he never would against the girls. He was one of three boys in his family, and he says the threat kept them from getting in trouble.'

'But parenting is different now.' And the boys in his family did get in trouble, I know that much.

'When you have six kids, you can't do gentle parenting the whole time. Marty's fond of Willow. We know you're a gentle parent like me, so he just wanted to help you out. Oftentimes it just takes a stern voice to calm them down.'

'But does he understand that I'm the only one who makes decisions on discipline?'

'He sees it as his job to jump in and fix things. He was trying to help. Maybe he took it too far in talking to her the same way he does to our kids. He's a great guy.'

He's not. He's really not.

'He would never hurt Willow.'

'I don't want her physically punished.'

'She's safe here. Safer than in New York. I'm taking Emily to get new shoes after school tomorrow. Then we'll have afternoon tea. Would you and Willow like to come? It's nice to get away sometimes.'

'That'd be great, thank you. Willow will love that.' That went better than expected, given that Marty must have told her I've opted out of church. I take a sip of tea and it doesn't taste quite so bad now.

She stands, about to leave.

'Is Alice okay?' I ask.

Her face clouds. 'Why?'

'She didn't go to church yesterday and she looked sick just now.'

'She gets infections, but she'll be fine.'

'Jonny said something...'

She looks at me and blinks. She's holding her breath.

'He said his daddy had a truck. It made me wonder about his dad.'

She sits back down and sighs. 'Alice is a private person, so please don't repeat this to anyone, including her.'

I nod.

'Jonny is Marty's nephew. You might've noticed they look alike.'

They all look alike, the blond Aryan youth troop. 'So his dad is...?'

'Marty's older brother.'

'Asher?' My pulse races.

She pulls back. 'How do you know his name?'

My heart stutters. 'Marty mentioned him. Said he has a car lot.'

She goes to leave again. 'Like I said, don't mention it to anyone else.'

It all comes back to Asher, the man with so much to answer for, but Faith withheld some vital details. What's going on with Alice, the Cornell grad doing odd jobs around the ranch? I thought she was worn down by mothering a toddler, and maybe she has an ongoing health issue. But there's more to it.

Family is important to Mormons, including extended family. If Hel is Marty's daughter, they could just come out and say it for her sake. Non-religious followers won't care that he had a child before meeting Faith, but it tarnishes their wholesome brand.

If Asher fathered Jonny, it feeds into my secret mission. But I can't use it to bring the Eversen brothers down because it's not fair on Jonny, and Marty looks like the good guy for taking them in.

Poor Alice. She must be suffering eternal damnation, with recriminations raining down on her from Zina. But there's a story behind Alice's switched-off eyes about why she came here instead of fulfilling her potential. Why did a churchy girl get pregnant by an older married man? If Asher forced himself on her, why did she seek refuge with his brother?

Chapter Thirty-Seven

I take some products I'd been photographing back to the storage barn. My plan to pick up stock from the big barn as an excuse for a nose around hasn't panned out, since the right products magically appear in the smaller storage barn for me to collect and then deposit. Anyone would think they don't want me poking about in Marty's domain.

As I exit the barn, Joel walks towards me. My heart lifts. 'Hey, stranger,' I say with a smile. I feel instantly lighter around him.

'Hey yourself.' He grins back. Oh God, those dimples. 'I've been looking out for you to say sorry about the driving lessons.'

'It's okay. I'm covered. I don't want to get you in trouble.'

'I'm not worried about that, but when your boss tells you not to do something, you kinda have to comply.' He leans in and lowers his voice. 'There's other places to work, but I stick around because they won't run out of money to pay me. Will you walk with me to the maintenance shack?'

'Sure.' If anyone sees us, I'll spin a yarn about wanting to see it as part of my induction.

He squints up at the sky. 'Looks like snow. I'm gearing up for a powder day.'

'Powder day?'

'On the slopes. It's the greatest snow on earth, on account of the dry air. I snowboard.'

'Sounds good.' I'd like to talk more about his life off the ranch, but instead I ask what it's like working for Marty.

'He's weird.'

We exchange a look.

'Faith's a good person and Marty's okay, but he can be arrogant and domineering. I guess that's why he's a boss.' He says it matter-of-factly. 'The women don't do that well here.'

'How so?'

'It's like he's keeping them down or something. Faith deserves more recognition, but that's the way their marriage goes. Guess I'm saying that you can do better than stay here.' His brown eyes meet mine with a trace of concern.

I go to speak but we've reached a wooden hut that must be the maintenance shack, and he pulls open the door. I check no one's watching and go inside. It's cool and smells earthy, while he smells of a pine forest mingled with warm spice. A little daylight comes through the grimy windows. 'Nice place. Cosy.'

'I can think of better places to take you.' He shuts the door behind us. 'Several, actually, if only I had the chance.'

I lean one shoulder on the wooden panelling of the shack and suppress a smile. Never mind catching religion, I'm in danger of losing my mind to Joel.

'I've been wanting to get you alone.' He leans one arm on the door. 'Is that a bad thing?'

He's gazing into my eyes, our bodies close, but not touching.

'It's a good thing.'

'I liked you from the first day you came here, but I don't want to cross any lines.'

I indicate the space between us. 'There's no lines. Just us.' I know my decision-making is off, otherwise I wouldn't have moved here, but I like him. He's more than a distraction; it's a feeling that things are okay with him, while I don't trust the others. Joel's the only normal person here. I can relax around him.

'You're gorgeous.' His face is all mischief.

'Not so bad yourself.' I try playing it cool while fighting the desire to unbutton his shirt.

'So you into cowboy romance?' he asks, one eyebrow raised.

'So long as it's spicy.' I give him a suggestive smile.

'Spicy? Like sex scenes?' His eyes smoulder with interest.

I look at his lips and imagine kissing him. Then I am kissing him. His kiss tastes of hops. He wraps his arms around me and — sweet Jesus — it feels good. His hands and mouth so warm that I sink into him. I ease my hips towards his so we're pressed together.

He pulls back to see my face, his thumbs brushing over my cheeks. Feels good to be a sinner again. Endorphins win out over a commitment to God, not that it was ever in doubt. I get off on the illicit pleasure of screwing around with Joel, lovely Joel. He nuzzles his face in my hair. His leisurely approach rubs off. Feels like we have time to get to know each other, if not now, then next time.

'I'd like to carry this on someplace else.' I resist the urge to wrap my legs around him and give myself over to wild abandon. He's so fuckable, but I draw the line at sex in a shed.

'Fuck, yeah,' he murmurs. It's good to hear swearing again, except the swearing I do inside my head. I shouldn't be here with him in work time, but I'm like a Mormon girl again, regressing to teen rebel from the patriarchal control. Joel is the perfect antidote.

We eventually straighten ourselves up to exit the love shack. He brushes a cobweb from my hair and I reach for the door handle, but he pulls me back into his arms and holds me close. I bury my face in his soft shirt, feeling the heat of his body, then the heat of his kiss when I unbury my face. I have to tear myself away, or Faith will send out a search party.

Now I've had this taste of Joel, it'll be hard to keep my hands off him. His lips touch mine one last time in a kiss. I wish we could take off in his truck, bundle Willow in the back, feel the wind in my hair and go far, far away. We exit the shack and I scan around to check no one's watching, since it's obvious what we've been doing.

'Can I message you?' he asks.

'I'd like that.' I stop myself from pulling him back to me for another lingering kiss.

He winks, and walks backwards for a few steps, not taking his gaze from me. I smile and float back to work, tingling from the sensation of his fingers on my skin. It's exactly the illicit pleasure I needed. With him around, I might even make it through. My emotional support cowboy. He could be someone to confide in, but that wouldn't be fair on him when he works for Marty.

I long for a fun, boozy night out with Joel. My feel-good emotions keep flowing while I monitor Faith's socials in the little study. The illicit pleasure of hooking up with Joel glows warm inside me. I like having a secret, just between him and me, aside from that other darker secret of mine.

Chapter Thirty-Eight

My lips feel swollen from all the kissing with Joel, my face probably flushed from the blood pumping. Faith doesn't notice, unless she thinks my inner glow is from healthy living. When we finish work, she tells me her cleaner is staying late to feed the kids so we can head into town straight after they finish school. I'd forgotten due to my other excitement of the day. It's too much for Marty the Messiah to feed them, since he's off walking on water.

'I schedule one-on-one time with the older girls once a month,' she tells me. 'And Marty does the same with the boys.'

She drives us into town, and we talk about my driving lessons. She says it's good practice for Marty as he'll teach Isiah once his feet can reach the pedals.

'He'll drive around the ranch before he's old enough for a licence.'

This trip is a chance to bond with Faith outside of our work-home environment. I need to keep the fragile peace with both her and Willow until we can get away. In town, Willow and I head for the library while they go to buy shoes. We chat with Joan the librarian, mostly Willow enthusing about books.

'Do you go to our church?' Willow asks. 'I haven't seen you there.'

I'm hoping Joan's a Jedi, just for some variety.

'I've been to your church, if it's the one Marty and Faith go to. Our own church is in the city, where I was raised. All my family go there.' It figures as she has the trademark LDS friendliness.

When we meet up with Faith and Emily, I assume we're going to the coffee shop, but Faith ushers us back in the car.

'We're going to our favourite hotel.'

'Yay!' Emily says from the back seat.

'Yay!' Willow parrots. I'm stabbed with guilt to wrench her from another friendship group, but maybe we can repair the Coco and Tamsin bond once she's freed from religious control.

Faith takes us to a swanky hotel where we nibble on tiny sandwiches filled with delicacies. It's the first time I've eaten out since moving here, and the sandwiches taste ridiculously good. White bread, I notice. We're brought a pot of tepid herbal tea without anyone asking, when I'd have preferred a glass of fizz. The waitress then brings a cake stand filled with a tempting selection, along with a chocolate fondue.

Willow's face lights up and my heart swells. She's been to a birthday party that had a chocolate fountain, but those experiences have been lacking here. When Faith enquires after the waitress' family, I take a quick photo of the girls. She won't capture the moment as it doesn't fit with her homespun content.

I smile at Faith. 'What else do you and Emily do together?'

'Now she's older, we go on shopping trips to the city and she's a big fan of the theatre.' She smiles indulgently at the girls. 'I've promised her a weekend trip, just the two of us, before she's baptised.'

'Can Willow come too?' Emily asks.

'If Willow's being baptised, then we'll make it the four of us.'

'Mommy,' Willow says, licking chocolate sauce from her lips. 'I'm covered by God's grace now, but when I'm eight, I have to be baptised because I'll know the difference between right and wrong and I'm choosing to be right.'

Faith laughs melodically and turns to me.

'You can choose to be right without the baptism,' I say.

'But *you're* baptised,' she pleads.

I've never told her that. I only told Faith.

'We'd love to welcome Willow formally into the church,' she says.

It's a set-up. She's getting me back after I'd told Marty to count me out of their religion yesterday. I don't respond, since she knows my stance. Willow's eight in four months and the whole baptism rodeo will ramp up her religiosity. I'll give myself three months to land another job. It'll be her third home in quick succession and she'll hate me, but it's the only way.

Faith leans over, napkin in hand, to wipe a streak of chocolate sauce from Emily's chin. As she stetches, her sleeve slips down her arm, exposing a dark bruise. The kids go back to chattering to each other.

'How'd you get that?' I stare hard at the bruise.

She follows my gaze to her wrist and tugs the sleeve down. 'It's nothing. I bruise easily.'

It's a big bruise. The width of a man's hand. She casts her eyes down to her lap and I know she won't tell me more, even if the kids were elsewhere. I don't dig deeper as she'll shut me down, but it looks like she's been grabbed hard. Her detractors are right about her turning female oppression into an aesthetic. And how can I believe her assurance that Marty won't hurt Willow when he's possibly hurting his wife and kids?

I found my way to Faith via Marty. I cyberstalked him, not her. Back when she had a crappy WordPress blog, she made it easy for me to keep tabs on him, since Asher had zero online presence. Her blog was the gateway drug that led me here. Marty's a big reason why my teenage self turned away from the church. I'd never have guessed that he'd be the one luring me back.

—

Funny how Melissa pushes back, making her boundaries clear about church. Churchgoing is the least of her troubles and I can't frickin wait for her to find out. She'll be shocked when she learns the truth, but I don't know how hard she'll fight it. Soon as she pushes too far, she'll regret it. Bring on the fun and games. One thing's for sure: I'm coming out on top.

Chapter Thirty-Nine

Willow chatters away as I chop an onion on Saturday afternoon. I'd been indulging in happy thoughts of Joel, who I haven't seen since our tryst, although we've been messaging. I long to spend time with him, go for a coffee, but that's not possible without everyone knowing. I'd feel like a teenager trying to sneak out after curfew.

'I've had a personal revelation,' she says. Her speech is slowing into more of a drawl. She says 'moun'ain' instead of 'mountain', and her sentences end with the same singsong rise as Eden and Emily.

'A revelation?'

'God spoke to me.'

'What does God sound like?' I imagine a booming trailer voice for a Hollywood blockbuster. 'Is she a woman?'

'It wasn't a sound. It was in my head and I woke up knowing I'm on a journey of faith.'

I show my best poker face. 'A journey is great, because we're trailblazers. Remember our magic carpet trips to Arabia?' Seems so long ago. The pang of nostalgia hits hard.

'No, a *real* journey. My baptism journey. I make promises with the Father, and the Holy Ghost will bless my life. It's not like *Aladdin*. That's make-believe.'

'God is also make-believe. He's like *The Wizard of Oz*. That's the plot twist. You give your life to this sacred being.' I mime something vague in the sky with a waving arm. 'And guess what? He's not real.' She doesn't know what I know about their crooked faith, and she's not being baptised. I can't tell her as she'll throw another fit and the Mormon militia will weigh in. 'Who's telling you all this?'

'Emily's teaching me at lunch, because I'm way behind and I have to know it all before my baptism.'

I blame Faith for giving her the expectation during our afternoon tea. Why does it even matter to her? She knows I'm not a shoo-in for their faith and she's still alienating my child from me. She's a control freak under all those layers of serenity. I'll turn one of her kids atheist. That'll teach her.

A loud shot rings out. Willow and I jump and exchange surprised looks. I resist my instinct to grab her and shelter under the table in case a stray bullet comes through the window. That's what I'd do back home.

'Stay there.' I place a hand on her shoulder and look outside the front door. It's quiet. Then another shot rings out. I take a few steps beyond the porch in the direction of the gunshot. Marty stands in the distance, showing Isiah how to shoot a rifle. *What are you doing, shit for brains?* I want to yell. *He's a child.* What if Isiah takes potshots at the rest of us? Marty looks over and raises a hand in a hello. I turn and march back inside, making my stance clear about his kid pointing a loaded gun. In the kitchen, I take blueberry muffins from the oven and tell Willow it's just Marty doing some target practice. 'People on farms use guns to scare off wild animals. No big deal.'

Minutes later, there's a knock at the door. Willow flings it open to Marty.

'Hey, Willow. How's it going?'

'We're talking about my baptism.'

Here we go.

'Oh yeah? We need to get you an invite to a baptism so you can see what's expected.'

It might put her off to see it involves a man fully submerging her in water, but the culties will do an effective sales job. And there's a weekend trip with Emily as a bonus, not that she needs incentivising.

'Your baptism means promising to follow Jesus Christ.' He sits at the table with her.

'Mm-hmm.' She nods emphatically.

'It's the start of your new life with the Lord.'

Or the start of our new life elsewhere. He talks baptism while I size him up as a possible abuser. Did he give Faith that bruised wrist? I set a plate of muffins on the table. 'Careful, they're hot.'

'I hope we didn't scare you just now.' He takes a muffin.

'We were scared when we heard gunshots.'

'I guess you don't have target shooting in New York.'

I look at Willow. 'Sweetheart, why don't you read for a while? We're going to talk outside.'

Marty stuffs half a muffin in his mouth and waves bye to Willow. We go out onto the porch, and I pull the door shut.

'It worried me to see Isiah firing a gun.'

'He's a responsible shooter.'

I fold my arms and he folds his in our uneasy stand-off.

'It's unsafe with all the younger children around.'

He squints towards the mountain. 'As I said, this ain't New York, thank the Lord. We hunt. We protect our property with guns. I'm teaching Isiah because *I say* he's old enough. My daddy taught me to shoot when I was his age and nothing bad happened.' His tone takes on a harder edge. He's not used to someone like me challenging his supreme authority. I can see the hunter in him, eyes glinting as they fix on his prey.

'Fine.' I adopt a calm voice, but teaching a child to shoot is not fine. It's really not. 'You take responsibility for your children, and I'll take responsibility for mine.'

'Melissa,' he says in a sighing way. 'Don't you ever smile?'

Not around you, no. I'm not softening my words with a smile, falling into the Mormon lady trap of diluting my message by wrapping it in sweetness. He stands up and strides off, raking one agitated hand through his hair. I can handle a tricky boss and big egos at work, but not when it bleeds into our entire lives.

And the Earth's round, loser, I want to shout after him.

The gun-toting redneck is showing his true colours, and I can't ignore my growing sense that this is a bad situation. I think of Amy, the girl I never met. Age seventeen, my aunt Amy unwittingly set off a chain of events that led to her death and, I suspect, my dad's several years later. Marty and his brother Asher screwed her over. That's why I'm here. That's why I'm pissed off about Alice, and my anger is building.

Chapter Forty

When Willow's in the shower on Sunday morning, I message Joel, saying it'll be good to meet up again. His reply comes through minutes later.

> Been thinking the same. I need to get you away from the ranch... I don't think Faith likes me hanging out with you. x

> We'll have to wait until I have my licence then. x

Does she think it unseemly? I was going to ask him over for dinner as a friendly gesture, since Willow likes him. I'll invite Hel another evening, ply her with wine. But best to leave it if Joel's feeling the heat from Faith. No point in causing him grief when I won't be here much longer.

I tune in to a podcast that's just dropped from my favourite critic of Faith. I could listen to it at work under the guise of research, but I take solace from the podcaster. We harbour the same suspicions, and when listening in, I feel less alone.

'What's going on at Lavender Field Ranch? Beneath Faith Eversen's homespun persona there's a truth shades darker than her whiter-than-white life. Her fans say she chose that life, but Mormons either choose God or Satan. Choose God and you submit to a lifetime of putting your needs last. Is Faith living in a rural idyll or patriarchal prison?

'For a top influencer, she's unique in generating zero controversy other than her antifeminist values. But her husband, Marty, is a different matter. Which brings us to the Mormon boys' club. It's the woman's role to nurture her family, which Marty has turned to his advantage.

'Beneath the cowboy romance they portray on camera, he's known locally for his aggressive stance. He graduated from teenage fist fights to issuing threats against those who cross him. There's the small supplier who he threatened to put out of business for not agreeing to his punitive terms. And the disgruntled employee who tried reversing his NDA after his claims of unfair dismissal. Marty has his wife where he wants, in the kitchen with children tugging at her pretty apron. Maybe that's why he always looks smug. He plays up to his image of successful ranch owner and family man, but Faith is the provider. Why then is the ranch in his name only?'

I should alert Faith, since they can threaten the podcaster with a civil lawsuit if she doesn't take it down. Instead, I scroll through the comments.

> Does she really not own her ranch?
>
> What does it matter? She'll never get divorced. She'd be shunned by the church and lose her entire social circle as well as her trad wife income.
>
> No wonder they don't divorce if everything's in the husband's name.

> This can't be for real. Faith made that place what it is.

It is for real. I've seen the ranch deeds, having checked the land records. It's registered in Marty's name only, even though they bought it as a married couple. Faith runs the home and fronts the business empire while he owns it all.

—

It's the Sabbath and Willow is thrilled. We arrive at church in our Sunday best after she'd made a point of selecting a 'pretty' outfit to help me channel Faith. I only caved because I don't want her ashamed of me.

Marty pulls up with his carload just after us and nods stonily at me. Faith is all smiles, ever the peacekeeper. I should be happy for a change of scenery and a wider group of people after a week at the ranch, but I've never felt so out of step. I'll keep the fragile peace, even if I refuse to embrace it.

The boresville service drives me out of my mind. The rebel in me will go crazy if I don't switch things up. I want to sext Joel. *Hey, they're preaching about temptation and now I'm hot for you. xxx*

After the service, Willow is in the thick of an animated conversation with a group of girls, and I visit the restroom, passing a recessed area where a man's talking to his wife in a hushed voice. I catch her eye and see the look of a deeply unhappy person, blinking back tears.

'Are you okay?' I ask.

The man's head whips around. He glares at me. 'We're fine,' he snaps.

I give her a look of solidarity, waiting for an answer. She forces a sad smile and nods in reluctant agreement with him. He's still glaring. Jerk. I give him a measured stare, then return to the others who are socialising in clusters. I bet he tells Marty to keep his womenfolk in order.

Dinah catches my eye and waves. 'You okay?' she mouths, with friendly concern, not unlike my interaction with that other woman. I smile and nod, which she returns with a sunnier look. Then I spot that jerk coming back in with his wife.

'Who's that couple over there?' I say to the group.

Only Zina follows my gaze while the others are talking. 'That's Clara and Mattius Grenshore. They live in the next valley over.'

'He was giving her a hard time when I walked past.' He steers them to a little gathering and says something to the men of the group. She smiles stiffly at the woman next to her.

Zina turns back to the others. A man giving his wife a hard time merits no comment. I wonder how much Zina turns a blind eye to on the ranch, and I think again of what provoked Marty to give Faith that bruise.

The next day, I broach the subject with Faith when we take a break from work. 'Can I ask you something about church?'

'Sure.' She brightens, spotting a chance to convert me.

'What happens to women around here when marriages go wrong?'

Her face clouds. 'Why do you ask?'

'A man was being mean to his wife at church yesterday. She looked so unhappy but didn't say a word. What happens when a woman defers to her husband and it goes to his head so he dominates her?'

She looks confused.

'Say if it escalates to domestic abuse. What would a Mormon wife do in that situation?'

She turns thoughtful. 'She would pray.'

'And?'

'When we pray, we lift our mind to God and we receive revelation.' Her face turns serene again.

'So how will it help an abused wife?'

'A woman might feel encouraged to approach one of the bishops.'

'They're men, right?'

'Yes.' She nods.

'Doesn't a woman share her marriage concerns with the women close to her?'

She tilts her head and looks skyward. 'They could pray together, yes.' She smiles. 'I'll go wake Betsy from her nap.'

Faith glides swanlike on the surface, never tainted by the murky recesses. It started when she dodged tricky questions on my podcast. My unaired podcast. She and I could break out together, load all our kids in her car and find her a divorce lawyer. My getaway plan has escalated to taking them with me, since I might as well go out with a bang. I'd happily hire a bus and get all the women and children out.

I saw Marty going into Hel's duplex last night. Willow wanted to look for shooting stars, so we sat out on the porch sharing a blanket. As she stared up at the sky, I noticed him leave the ranch house and head towards the business barn. He followed the same pattern as I'd noticed before, walking there in the dark, letting himself in. He might be praying with her before bed, keeping an eye on his disengaged teenager.

I wonder about his relationship with Alice, given that he's Jonny's uncle. Perhaps he has white knight syndrome, covering his inadequacies by rehabilitating women in need. I bet he gets off on having more of us to control. Alice relies on their goodwill, since her child needs wrap-around care, and Zina's a widow in her late fifties who most likely needs to keep working.

When Willow and I open our journals, I want to write it down and blow the lid on these brainwashed women. But I write a neutral take on the day's events, place-marking for when I have freedom to tell the real story. I miss that. Words are the tools of my trade, but I've been silenced. There's power in words but danger in expressing them.

Willow reads her journal to me. '...Then in recess, Isiah said he was going to marry me when we're eighteen and I'll be his first wife.'

'His *first* wife?' I scoff. 'Is he planning on divorcing you? That can happen when people marry young.'

'No, Mommy. Mormons don't get divorced. Faith and Marty married young, and it'll last forever in heaven.'

Why would an eleven-year-old talk about his first wife? Mormons would rather someone die than divorce. I bet Isiah doesn't even know any divorced adults.

'We can have sister-wives, but when I marry Isiah, Emily won't be my sister-wife because she's his sister, not his other wife.'

I gawp at her. What in the name of sweet fucking Jesus...?

Chapter Forty-One

I'm still reeling the next morning from Willow's talk of sister-wives. Are they really polygamists? This is huge. It's my scoop that will blow up Faith and Marty's hashtag wholesome life.

But is it true? Isiah might be talking shit. Maybe multiple wives is their fantasy version of shagging around. Polygamy has been banned by the church for over a hundred years. But Marty's a law to himself. This is too weird. If we're in the midst of a polygamous sect, my exit plan has become more urgent. I wonder how long my first month's pay will last if we take off the morning after payday.

Act normal, I tell myself, at least for Willow's sake, even though it disturbs the hell out of me. That's what I do, staying watchful. On Thursday, I return some products I'd photographed to the storage barn. As I stride along the path with an armful of canisters and tea towels, Jonny runs out of his front door and scoots off in the same direction as me. No sign of Alice. The others would say Jonny's safe, but what if a delivery truck reversed into him? I speed up to keep him in my sights.

'Daddy!' he squeals.

Daddy?

I round the corner. He runs towards Marty, arms outstretched. Marty scoops him up and swings him around, then hoists a chortling Jonny onto his shoulders. Is he like an orphaned chick who sees his rescuer as a parent? Or maybe they've gone overboard with their ethos of 'it takes a village to raise a child'. Marty spots me at the exact moment it fits into place. Asher isn't Jonny's dad. I saw Alice throwing up and I clocked Marty's night-time visit to her. We lock eyes. Revulsion washes over me. I sway a little before steadying myself.

I want to turn back, but Faith's in the ranch house, so I can't go there. He's staring at me from twenty paces. If I keep walking, he'll walk with me and we'll have to keep it normal for Jonny. Screw that. I'm not pretending it's okay.

I take a breath, turn and walk to the cabin. Something was off all along, an unspoken tension from the women. Their code of silence. I sink into the seat outside, the products still in my arms, and stare straight ahead. I'm stunned, despite my creeping awareness that started as a whisper in my mind. Call it self-protection, but I couldn't acknowledge it, needing to keep the crazy at bay.

I've never seen him show Alice any attention, but she wears a wedding ring. She's his second 'wife'. Why does Faith tolerate it? The polygamist appears in front of me, minus Jonny. He sits beside me and we don't speak. Only a matter of time before he spews crap about God telling him to procreate with another woman.

'You wanna put those down?' he asks in a mild way.

I don't move.

'Here.' He tugs the products from my grasp. 'Allow me.'

My hands drop to my lap, and I look away.

'Guess the two of us need a talk, huh? We didn't want to explain about our family arrangement upfront as some people struggle to take it in. What with you being from the city and all.'

'What with you being a polygamist and all.'

'You're still getting reacquainted with our religion, so I don't expect you to feel the same as us. I'm just asking you to listen with an open heart.'

I stare ahead. 'I'm not a Mormon. Never will be.'

'Sure you are, honey. God has a plan for you.'

'No. *I* have a plan for me.'

He studies me in amused confusion. 'You're fighting God's plan. Just go with it. That's easiest.'

'Easiest for you.' I look towards the ranch house. 'Faith'll be wondering where I am.'

'This'll only take a minute, then you can go away and think about it.' He's angled towards me, his knee touching my leg. I want to shove him away.

I sense he's about to take my hand and lapse into prayer, so I shove both hands in my pockets.

'We believe that this life we've chosen brings us closer to God. It means our children grow up in a harmonious community.'

'And you get to have sex with another woman.'

'It's God's plan for us to have children.'

'Funny how God's plan benefits you.' Since he's not the one engaged in relentless childcare, and babies keep the women reliant. It's quite the scam.

'Faith struggles with going full term on her pregnancies, so this is God's way.'

'Alice doesn't seem happy. I guess she's pregnant and she's the broodmare. Not a great use of her elite education.' What does her mum, Zina, think? Maybe she's complicit. Otherwise, why wouldn't these two supposedly intelligent women leave? Who knows, certainly not me.

He sighs and plants his hands on his knees.

'It's not legal, is it? And it's banned by the church.'

'The Lord commanded me to raise up his seed unto him. There aren't enough children being born. Folks are working hard and can't afford it. Willow tells me she wants brothers and sisters, but I guess a single parent can't do everything – work, keep house, look after children. We support each other. We've enough money for all the kids to be raised according to God's will. That's a beautiful thing.' He looks imploringly at me. 'We want to absorb you in our blessings.'

'No thanks.'

'Willow needs a daddy.'

'Willow isn't up for grabs, not for you or Isiah.'

'Isiah?'

'He said he's taking her as his first wife.'

'He's a child. Faith wanted you and Willow to come here.'

I could ask what his plan is, but I can't bear to hear him say God told him to take me as a wife. My mistake for labelling Faith as the control freak. They've played a blinder in bringing me here. I think of the day we met, him on his horse, getting the measure of me. He must think I'm easy prey. But I also have an ulterior motive. They used the job as bait and I used it to infiltrate their inner circle. I came here for revenge, but this is more than I'd bargained for. Marty leaves, and I message Zac.

> I'm leaving.

> You're there to do a job

> It's done. I have dirt on Marty. It'll blow up their image.

> Tell me

> Not until I've left the ranch.

I delete the message trail. It's only safe to tell him once I'm gone. And Marty can't set his lawyers on me since the NDA is void if it covers illegal activity. A reason for coming here was to get Zac off my case. He's threatening to tell Willow the one thing I've been holding back from her.

Chapter Forty-Two

Marty left to go to the ranch house, most likely to tell Faith that I know their secret. I stay rooted to the spot. The implications crawl over me like ants. *We want to absorb you in our blessings... Willow needs a daddy.* But why drag me into it? Why not recruit a willing local to join their polygamous arrangement? I guess they don't want the locals finding out, but with Jonny calling him 'Daddy', it's only a matter of time. Faith said Asher was Jonny's dad, and maybe he is. It won't be the first time Marty's fixed one of Asher's fuck-ups. Does Marty want to claim all the stray children, including Willow? My job search hasn't led to any interviews, but I'll step it up, then I can abscond and start deradicalising my child.

I spot him leaving the ranch house to trudge back to the big barn, so I return to work. Faith's sitting at the kitchen table, fingertips resting on her forehead, but she lifts her head and looks towards me. I wait for her to speak. She stands and starts clearing things away.

'He told me about your marital set-up.'

She nods and checks on her rising sourdoughs.

'How does that affect you?'

'We make it work.' She gives me a sad smile.

'You make everything work, but what do you think about it?'

'It's God's will.'

'How do you know?'

'Marty goes to the mountains and prays. He started doing it when I had my first miscarriage.'

'I'm sorry.'

'Six kids on earth. Five in heaven.'

Eleven pregnancies? 'That must've been tough.'

'For both of us. Marty wanted a big family.'

'There's eight of you. That's big.'

'He wants more kids. It was taking its toll.'

'Count your blessings. Six healthy kids is good.'

'Marty went to pray after Martin Junior was born five years ago. God told him to bring another wife into our family.'

'That's convenient.'

I expect more Jesus bullshit, but she falls silent. I feel bad for her, knocked up eleven times and now the cowboy is impregnating another breeder. He sees women as cattle.

'I have two sister-wives. It's a community.'

'*Two* sister-wives?'

'Oh.' Her brow furrows. 'I thought you knew. Alice and Hel.'

'Hel? You said she was saving for college. You acted like he was her dad, but it's a big secret.'

'College was her original plan. It's what she told people until she decided to stay.'

I rub at my temples. 'What else have you lied about?'

Faith turns towards the window and covers her face with her hands. She's crying. It's dainty Mormon lady crying. No ugly sobbing around here. I bet she won't turn snotty and blotchy. I sigh and rub a consoling hand up and down her arm. She turns into me, so I hug her. We stay there for a while, until Faith pulls away and blows her nose. She takes a breath and returns to staring at the mountains in the distance.

'You don't have to live like this,' I say.

She looks at me, bewildered.

'You can live on your terms.'

'I have to take Caleb to the doctor.' She goes and scoops him up.

'You have a choice.'

She turns back to me. 'What about Marty? He's my husband.'

'What about you? You needn't put up with it.' It does my head in that she acts docile and compliant. Is there something in the water that'll infect me soon?

She takes her bag and goes to leave. 'You don't understand.'

Oh, but I do. And I want to expose it to the light.

Chapter Forty-Three

That evening, I tell Willow I need to ask Hel something. I say to bolt the door behind me and let me back in when I return. I'm tempted to call Joel, but I can't drag him into it, especially as it's convinced me to leave as soon as I can.

I hope Marty isn't at Hel's duplex. Alice spends time in the big barn with him, taking Jonny with her, so maybe that counts for family time in their weird world. Perhaps they have lunch, then he has dinner with Faith and breakfast with Hel. I bet he stayed over more often with Alice until she fell pregnant, and now he's shagging the younger model.

At Hel's, I take a breath and knock on the door. She opens it after a while, chewing an apple, half eaten in her hand.

'Hey.' I smile. 'Is this a good time?'

She steps back to let me in, and I follow her upstairs. Downstairs is just a bathroom, storage cupboard and hallway. Upstairs, I go to the kitchen counter where there's a window looking onto the back of our cabin, so I can check on Willow. Hel tosses the half-eaten apple in the bin.

'Nice place.' It's a little smaller than ours, with a modest open-plan kitchen-diner-living area that's more IKEA than the stand-alone ranch homes.

'I just found out about the arrangement with Marty.'

'Arrangement?' She stands listlessly at the furthest corner of the kitchen from me.

'What you and Alice have going on with him.' My jaw clenches.

'You seem hostile.' She narrows her eyes at me.

I exhale. 'I don't blame you or anything. I'm just trying to work it out. It's not my business, but it feels like a secret everyone's kept from me and I guess I'm here as wife number four.'

She sinks into a dining chair and chews on a fingernail.

'I know you don't like talking to me. It's like you avoid saying anything.'

'Well, yeah. We don't tell anyone what's going on.' She speaks in a slow monotone.

'I'm trying to get my head around it.' And the man's a creep. I want to know why she's going along with it, even grudgingly. 'Marty's acting like it's no big deal.'

She shrugs with one shoulder, like raising both is too much effort. 'Take it up with them.'

We stay silent for a few moments and I gaze out of the window. 'What about college?'

She leans back in her chair, arms dangling, looking at the ceiling.

'I guess I'm saying, don't give up on your dreams for a man.'

'You did,' she says plainly.

'Because I got pregnant? I already had a degree. I kept my job and my independence. College could make a difference.'

'What's the point? I'm LDS. They let us go to college as backup in case our future husband dies. Whatever career I choose, I'll give it up to start a family anyway, so why go into debt?'

'To get an education. To have choices. Even if you skip college, you don't have to marry until you find the right person, and you can carry on working.'

'I'm already married.'

'Where's your ring?'

She delves under her shirt and pulls out a thin gold ring on a flimsy chain.

'I'm pretty sure it's not legal. And what's the point of a marriage you have to hide?'

She shrugs, mouth downturned.

'How old are you?'

'Nineteen.'

'He's thirty-five. Don't you think that's gross? You're closer in age to Isiah.'

She stares glassily away.

'What did he do to you?'

'What?'

'To make you this way, because I bet you weren't always like this.'

She blows out a long breath and stares back at the ceiling, not fitting the cheery, surrendered wife category.

'Have you asked him to help you through college?'

'I don't think that's on the table.'

I agree that it's a wasted education if she returns here to the baby factory, but it's a way out.

'The world's falling apart. At least here, we're close to God. It's safe. He takes care of us. I wouldn't get that at college. The world's ending anyway.'

The world's ending anyway sounds like a cross-stitch project.

'You say you're LDS, but polygamy isn't legal. It's banned by the church. This isn't Mormonism. It's Martyism. If you stay, you're at his mercy.'

'The latter days are coming. Destruction and death. You only have to watch the news to know it's nearly here. We're protected and self-sufficient. We'll keep living this way until the Rapture.'

Is this what they're teaching Willow in school? Literally putting the fear of God into her. Frustration builds in me. No wonder Hel's depressed if she thinks the world's ending and her best option is a non-marriage to Marty. I want to shake her from her doomsday slump. It's their suffering fetish, tolerating a crappy situation, holding out for latter days and a so-called Rapture.

There's no getting through to Hel, who thinks it's God's will. No mention of love, and what about fun? *At least tell me he's a good shag*, I want to say, but abusers never are. They can't even go out together, since the townsfolk must suspect. When we drive there on a Saturday, do they assume I'm the next wife?

'Okay, so long as you're happy.' I nearly choke on my words. *May your womb be vigilant.* 'How do you get on with Faith?' I've never seen them alone together, only in a gathering at church or Bible group.

'She's a nice lady,' she says evenly, as if describing a casual acquaintance. Faith's the alpha wife, and nobody recruited to Marty's cause will match her brightness. How strange to live in her shadow.

I leave, giving her an open invitation to drop in at the cabin. *We have wine*, I nearly say. Back there on my laptop, I furiously register with employment agencies for creatives. Willow writes her journal and I widen my search to take in Washington state along with budget-friendly, family-friendly areas an hour or so from Manhattan. At least I'm justified in leaving so soon, since I'd never have come here had I known the truth. Thanks, Faith, but screwing your husband is beyond my remit.

—

She'll be ready to take flight, but that's not gonna happen. She knows too much. I'm bringing her round to my way of thinking, since my way is the only way. If she knows what's good for her, she'll take the path of least resistance.

Chapter Forty-Four

'Emily says we're watching a cool video tonight,' Willow chirps as we eat dinner.

Nooo. It's Bible night. My heart thuds downwards and my shoulders slump. That's all I need when I want distance from those freaks.

Willow sees the dismay on my face. 'Mommy, please!' she wails.

'What?' I arrange a more neutral Mormon mum look. 'It's fine.'

She relaxes and grins up at me. I'll send her without me, so I can search for a job far, far away. I've taken to drinking wine in the evenings, hidden in my lidded coffee cup, but I'm running low.

As I rush through washing the dishes, Willow answers the door to Marty. Bastard read my mind about bunking off. Maybe he does have God-like powers. 'Hey, you guys.' He's all smiles, since everything's fine and normal. 'Willow, Emily wants you to come over and make popcorn.'

'Yay!' Willow beams and jiggles around.

'Off you go then,' I say, knowing it's a ruse. She races off.

'Allow me to help.' He grabs a tea towel and begins drying the dishes, like we're a couple. Perhaps in his warped kingdom we already are. 'I hear you've been asking about me.'

That was quick. Hel's a compliant wife-lite.

'You visited Helen for a talk.'

'Sure,' I say. 'Since we're a community.'

'She says you were asking her about going to college.'

I give him the side-eye. He side-eyes me right back.

'Because Faith said she was going to college. I'm trying to get a handle on things, to understand how it works.'

'It all works fine if you trust in God. You think too much. Think less, trust more.' 'I'm working out the dynamics of polygamy.' I bet they never say that word aloud. What kind of mind control does he use on these women? It feeds into the real reason I'm here. I've a story to write, working around the NDA so he doesn't sue me into oblivion. I intend to unmask this vile man and tell the world how he exploits women.

He holds out his palm to me. 'Would you join me in a prayer?'

I step back and wipe my hands on a towel. 'No, thank you. I need some time.'

He holds up his hands in a surrender gesture. 'I'll walk you to Bible group. The others would like to see you.'

'I need to think things through.' *Think less, trust more.* Fuck that.

'Come to the house and we'll talk things through.'

I concede, only from curiosity at how they'll all act now it's in the open. He tells me a story on the way about an early member of the church who left in a dispute over milk and cream. He experienced hardship before 'setting his pride aside' to seek reconciliation. No use crying over spilt milk. No use leaving when he can control me with self-serving propaganda.

At the ranch house, Faith buzzes around the kitchen, cheery as ever, helping the girls heap popcorn into big wooden bowls. Alice and Zina sit in silence, and Hel looks away when I come in, the snitch.

Eleven-year-old Isiah strides out from the den, looking for all the world like his dad. 'Girls,' he barks to Willow and his sisters. He taps his watch. 'C'mon, we're on God's schedule.' He's deepened his voice to sound like Marty.

Isiah herds the compliant lambs through. How depressing that Mormon boys are raised to wield power in the home, while girls are conditioned to fall into line. I'm tempted to fuck with them and say God is a woman. But that would be ridiculous. She'd never let these men get away with so much.

Zina's at her cross-stitch again, busy with the Lord's work. It must be a new one as I catch a flash of red and orange thread. She sees me looking and peers beadily over her glasses.

'Another one,' I say. 'You could open an Etsy shop.' I read it and barely stifle my grimace.

> The day cometh that shall burn as an oven.

Maybe keep that one off Etsy.

When the older kids are settled in the den, we sit around the table. I position myself away from Marty. Hel still refuses to meet my eye, listless as ever. Does she feel bad for grassing me up?

The Patriarchy says, 'Let us pray,' so I hold hands with Zina and Faith. 'Dear Heavenly Father, we thank You for bringing us together. We ask You to bless Melissa with comfort and joy as she settles into our community. Please help us to support her.'

Faith squeezes my hand. I open my eyes and she's looking right at me as if trying to read me. She gives a small smile and nod. I give her nothing and close my eyes.

'We thank You for the joy that Melissa and Willow bring us as we pray to bring joy to them.'

Fat chance.

'Lord, please help Melissa find love and acceptance here, just as we open our hearts to her.'

'Amen,' I say firmly, to shut him down. The others murmur their amens. I can't be doing with these thinly veiled manipulations. 'Thank you, Marty, for asking me to come here this evening so we can talk things through.' I look around the table. The women all cast looks at him, since I'm not following the script. They expect him to control the narrative, but how do they feel about the set-up?

Zina does her throat-clearing bark.

'Zina,' Marty says. 'Would you read Mosiah Eighteen Twenty-One?'

She's already on it, thumbing through her Book of Mormon to expertly locate the passage. She peers at the page through her reading glasses. 'And he commanded them that there should be no contention one with another, but that they should look forward with one eye, having one faith and one baptism, having their hearts knit together in unity and in love one towards another.'

'Thy friends do stand by thee,' he says, 'with warm hearts and friendly hands.'

Keep your friendly hands off me. Faith makes contented 'mmm' sounds. I'd like to give them all a truth drug and let the accusations fly. This must be why alcohol is banned. I want to stand up and tell them it's mad, justifying this with religion when none of them are happy as his handmaidens.

What do they do with their anger? I imagine their silent prayers. *Sweet Jesus, help me offload this murderous rage before I kill the dickhead.*

'I think we can all find reassurance in those words,' he says, directing his conversation at me. 'When you feel isolated, there's comfort in knowing others stand by you.'

'What do you want from me?' I ask, emboldened by wine.

Faith stiffens and blinks at me, wide-eyed. The other three look down at the table.

'Jesus commands us to love one another. We are always accepted and loved by God.' He turns to Zina. 'Can you please read our favourite Bible passage?'

I push back my chair with a loud scrape on the wooden floor.

'Wait, please.' He reaches out and grabs my hand.

Zina's nimble fingers find the passage, ChatGPT in human form. 'For as the body is one, and hath many members, and all the members of that one body, being many, are one body: so also is Christ—'

'Here endeth the lesson,' I say. Enough Bible-bombing.

Zina looks daggers at me. I turn and march out, arms drawn around myself. I can't handle another scene with Willow right now, so I'll watch for when the others leave, then go back for her. Halfway to the cabin, Marty jogs up alongside me.

'Are those your only wives,' I motion back to the house, 'or are there more?'

'I have three wives,' he says amiably.

I stop dead. He stops too and I turn to face him.

'Do you want me as wife number four?' *Because it's not happening*, I want to say. *I'll never give myself or my child to you*. But I need him to tell me straight because I'm recording him.

Zac and I share a common goal of taking Marty and Asher down, but we clash in our approach. Zac favours direct action, an eye for an eye, while I came here to set the record straight by writing an exposé, a story of winners, losers and those who take what isn't theirs. It's more incendiary than I bargained for, feeding into my story of two upstanding Mormon brothers who ruin women's lives. The stakes are raised and Marty will want me silenced.

Chapter Forty-Five

Marty's unperturbed by my question about becoming his fourth wife. 'Faith wanted you here, and I agreed. Hel's only been part of our community for six months, so we're helping her to settle in before thinking about anyone else. Right now, we're just pleased you're here.'

I suspect he'll enjoy the challenge of turning me into another surrendered woman, same as Faith and Alice must have challenged him before he hijacked them, body and soul. Hel's still a work in progress.

Now I'm in on his grubby secret, he'll need to manage me. Meanwhile, this is all material I'm saving for my exposé, which is looking more dangerous by the day. I haven't spoken to Zina and Alice yet, but he'll tell them not to talk to me, other than quoting scriptures.

Willow comes running towards us. I smile.

'We played Celestial Pursuit.' She catches us up. 'It's like Trivial Pursuit. I was in Isiah's team. He knows the most and we won,' she gushes.

Stick with Isiah and you'll lose, sweet child of mine. You will be a loser in life. But it's a relief to focus on her. She takes both our hands and pulls us towards the cabin.

'Faith showed us how to make popcorn. She never gets mad, even when the boys are loud.'

That's because she's brainwashed, sweetie! She's a victim of the patriarchy. But that's the power of trad wife influencers.

They make you think it's harmless. I can't believe I was seduced by the romance of a simpler life. I thought we could escape here for a while, experience freedom while I held Zac at bay. I am the mother of all fuck-ups.

Before the polygamist can speak, I take charge. 'Thanks for walking us back.' I flash him the briefest glance. 'Sleep well.'

He says a reluctant good night as I usher Willow inside and bolt the door behind us.

I check on the job applications. One rejection and no interviews. I feverishly register with more recruitment sites for creatives. I'll consider temp contracts, no benefits, anything to get away from here. What if I pack up now and bundle Willow into a taxi? But she'll freak out and raise the alarm, even if I got the cab to wait on the road and we sneaked out after dark. In the meantime, I'm not Faith; I can't act like everything's fine. And what if he brainwashes me like he's done to the rest of them?

When I go to bed, sleep offers no relief. My dreams come laden with danger, fear and malice. I dream that Marty's coming for me. There's no escape. I slo-mo run through the woods, but I'm wading through mud, and Willow's still in bed, so escape is useless.

In the morning, I'm drained. I hustle Willow off to school and give the kitchen a quick clean. The door's ajar and it creaks open. I swing around, bracing myself for Marty. But it's Faith. She steps in, gives me a sad smile and sinks into a chair at the table. She looks like she hasn't slept. A red bump stands out above one eye.

'What happened?' I come close and peer at the bump.

'It's nothing. We got into an argument. It wasn't deliberate.'

'Faith—'

She waves it off with a wrist flick. 'I was tired and emotional.'

I sit opposite her. 'What happened?'

'He was a little hyper last night.'

'Hyper?'

'I don't know... crazed. He gets that way when his head's full of ideas. He wants you as his next wife.'

'This is insane. You know that, right? You're his wife. He can't keep doing this.'

She looks down at her hands. 'It's God's will.'

I groan and tip my head forward, resting it in my hands.

'I don't know what to do,' she says in a small voice. 'I feel bad for bringing you here.'

I raise my head. 'Why did you bring me here?'

'You reminded me of how I used to be. And I thought you'd know what to do.'

'I know exactly what to do. I refuse to be his wife, and I'll leave with Willow.'

'That's not wise. He'll get angry.'

'Leave with us. It's not safe for you or the kids.'

Her eyes widen. 'He won't let us leave.'

'What if we bundle the kids in the car? Drive away.'

'Where would we go?' She looks befuddled.

'Drive as far as we can, rent an Airbnb.'

'He'll come after us.'

'If we get a head start, he won't find us. And you can call the cops.'

'He's friends with the sheriff. The cops'll take his side.'

I should have known. 'They won't help him kidnap you.'

'The cops can help him take back the kids. And not just for this lifetime.'

'What?'

'When you marry, you're bound together for this lifetime and the afterlife.' She looks plaintively at me. 'If I leave him, the kids are bound to *him* in the afterlife, not me. I won't even get into their kingdom of glory unless he whispers my name.'

She can't really believe this shit? 'That's what the men made up to stop the women walking out.' It's insane that she's tolerating abuse in order to access Marty's VIP lounge in heaven. Anyway, that fucker is going straight to hell. 'Speak to a divorce lawyer who can help you in *this* lifetime.'

'Divorce?' She goes even paler. She hasn't thought this through at all.

'Then you'll know your rights. If you get some kind of court order, the cops can't touch the kids.'

'I don't think an order will work with Marty. The sheriff will still help him.'

'We'll go out of state.'

'I have to give him notice if I want to move the kids out of the state or I'll be in trouble with the court.'

I sigh and rub my forehead. 'We need a lawyer who can say if that rule still applies when you all need to escape him. Do you know someone a plane trip away? You can say you're taking the kids to visit. If we get a flight to say, California, you'll have some protection.'

'He'll suspect. We never go away without him. And what'll we do for money?'

I look quizzically at her. 'You have your social media income.'

'That's not mine.'

'What do you mean?'

'It's business money. I can access what I want for us as a family. Marty's generous with spending money, but he'll stop my bank card. Then we can't pay for a hotel.'

'But it's your income. All this is possible because of your socials.' I'm not surprised, when the ranch is in his name, but surely she'd have a bank account given all the money pouring in. No wonder she didn't care whether I increased revenue.

'He calls me the publicity whore.'

We exchange a long stare.

'Your accounts are in joint names, right?'

She gives a vague shake of her head. 'He can't stand me bringing in money, so it all goes into his account. Nothing's in my name.'

She's a millionaire influencer, an inspiration for living your best life and having it all. But she doesn't have it all. She has no money, no agency, no escape. She's trapped in the gilded cage he keeps her in. She has nothing.

Chapter Forty-Six

'Can you start siphoning money off?' I ask Faith. 'I'll help you set up a new account—'

'I can buy things. I have a debit card, but it's registered to the business.'

'Where does he keep the cash?'

'Locked in a safe. He has the key, but there isn't much.'

I try to come up with a plan. 'You're being controlled by an abusive husband who stops you having your own bank account. What if I leave with Willow and get advice from a domestic abuse charity?'

'No!' She clutches the sides of her face.

'I need you to drop us at the airport. Tell him I'm visiting a sick friend. If you transfer the pay I'm owed, I'll find a place to live, then I can help you when you're ready. We can fight this, prove the income is yours.'

'He'll blame me if you leave. He'll be angry I didn't involve him. He already blames me, but he thinks he can win you over.'

'What if we all leave in your minivan? I'll use my pay to rent us somewhere remote for a week. Bring your ID. You can see a lawyer who'll help you access your money. What comes in from social media is all down to you. Or at least, everything here is half yours.'

She slumps with her fingers over her face. 'You don't understand. It's not half mine. It's all his, and Mormon women don't go off and see divorce lawyers.'

The religious brainwashing is strong, same as when Willow spouts their doctrine as fact. It goes deep with Faith, after a lifetime of conditioning. If Faith leaves, the other two 'wives' might want a stab at alpha-wife status, keeping Marty occupied. Whoever steps up gets the house, which is quite the prize, not that I'd want what it entails. But he won't let her go without a fight. She's the cash cow and the empire will crumble without her fronting it. Whatever we do, we can't anger him. This is why guns should be banned, because I wish someone would shoot him.

'Let's go to the house and act normal,' I say. 'Can you do that? We'll shut ourselves in the editing room and pretend to work.'

She nods and pushes herself up from the table. I'm still in fightback mode when we reach the house, but she tells me she can't talk about it. 'I'm too stressed. I need to… y'know…' She waggles one hand in the air.

'Get back in character?' I venture.

She nods in our first ever acknowledgement that her persona isn't entirely genuine.

'This can't go on.'

She blinks at me, then turns away. Unlike most influencers, I guess she's not motivated by money, fame or success. It's an escape from reality, the only bit of creativity she's allowed. It's her validation, even if her posts are one big recruitment drive for trad wives. It's how she suckered me in, after all.

'Playing dress-up and baking cakes,' I say to her back while she wipes down the kitchen counters. 'Living in a fantasy to escape your real life.'

'I love him.'

'No you don't.'

'He's handsome and the kids look up to him.' Her voice is quiet and uncertain.

'So you'll keep doing the dom-sub role-play until he prefers one of the younger women and you'll have nothing?'

Her shoulders slump, but she doesn't turn back to me.

'You can fire me for that, so long as you call me a taxi to the airport.'

She doesn't respond, so I go to the editing room, where I'm supposed to work on the latest video. Instead, I look up divorce lawyers, then go through to the kitchen. 'Faith?'

She turns to me from the sink.

'I found you a family attorney in Salt Lake.' I point my phone screen in her direction, showing the home page. 'She promises a confidential service and says if you have a challenging financial situation, she'll defer fees until the divorce is final.'

Faith opens and closes her mouth. 'I can't,' she says shakily.

'I'll help you.'

'It's not safe. When he finds out...' The tremor in her voice worsens.

'It's confidential.'

'He'll find out. That's what happens around here. I'm telling you.'

'I'm calling her. I'll insist it stays confidential.' I click on the call button. 'Take the phone in the bedroom. If he shows up I'll say you stepped out somewhere.'

'Don't do that,' Faith says in a gasp as a woman answers the phone, giving the company name.

I back away, maintaining eye contact, hers panicked. I try to usher her towards her bedroom where she can talk in private, even though she's about to fall apart. 'Can I speak to your divorce lawyer, please? It's about setting up an appointment.'

'Hang up the phone.' Faith's voice goes up an octave as the woman on the call says she can help. 'I'm not talking to anyone,' Faith says. I'm struck by her rare show of emotion. It's the most real she's been.

'It's not a good idea—'

'*Hello?*' the woman says.

I'm so focused on Faith and the phone call, I don't notice Marty standing behind me. 'What's not a good idea?'

Chapter Forty-Seven

Fuck. Heart in mouth, I hang up the phone, hands shaking.

'Hi, sweetie,' Faith coos to Marty, her voice still high and a little wobbly. She goes to him for a kiss.

'What's not a good idea?' Even when she kisses him, he keeps staring at me.

I am so fucked. I shove the phone in my pocket, scrabbling for an answer. 'I wanted Faith to enter a Women in Business award.'

Anger radiates from him. 'That's not a good idea. No one cares about that crap and she's not a woman in business.'

'Okay.' I nod. 'I'll get back to work.' I go to the office.

As I close the door behind me, Faith's offering him a snack. I force myself to take slow breaths to stop my heart going crazy. Then I delete the entire call and search history from my phone. Thank God I thought to bullshit about a Women in Business award, knowing it would hack off the Patriarchy, but not as much as calling a divorce lawyer for his wife.

Moments later, I flinch as he flings open the door.

'Melissa. What are you doing?'

I gulp. He pulls up a chair, angling it towards me. Every cell in my body is repelled. I look at the computer screen. 'I'm editing this latest video on buttermilk cornbread.'

Faking it flies in the face of my principles, but it's knee-jerk when my entire self has switched to protection mode. That's why Faith does it. The doubters say her trad wife persona is a moneymaking scam, but it's for survival. She's too ingrained in the lie. Now I'm the one appeasing him. He inspects the knuckles of his clenched fist. Does he want to punch me? I offer to show him the video as Faith comes in, lugging a dining chair in one arm and Betsy in the other. We shuffle around and she sits between us, the small space thick with tension.

'Let us pray,' Marty says.

Gimme a break. Faith takes his hand and clutches mine, Betsy on her lap. Talk of a divorce lawyer totally freaked her out. She was convinced the call wouldn't be confidential. *He'll find out… that's what happens around here.* Has she tried to leave before and someone told Marty? It explains her sheer terror at my exit plan. The Patriarchy leans forward, his big hand clamping over mine. My skin crawls. It's all I can do to stop from shuddering.

'Heavenly Father…'

It's me, God, the dickhead with a Messiah complex.

I keep my eyes open. Faith's are closed. She squeezes my hand, either for support or a silent plea for me to rein it in.

'Thank You for all Your blessings and for Your love that binds us together…'

Is this how he brainwashes them, by holding their hands and talking about heavenly love? I have to leave, get a job, any job. We'll live in a trailer and I'll be a waitress until I'm back on my feet. We'll be gone by the weekend.

'…Thank You for our beautiful community, providing us with love and compassion…'

Willow will go ape. I'll pack what we can take on a flight when she's asleep, then I'll say it's a surprise trip, convince her Jesus gave us his blessing. She won't know we're never coming back.

'...Lord, grant us the ability to see each other as You see us, with understanding and forgiveness, so we may not look at one another in judgement and create divisions.'

Lord, shall I punch him in the face? I've known some control freaks, but coercive control in the name of God is next level. Prayer has a lot to answer for, and my grandparents are proof that you can't pray your way out of a bad situation.

Years ago, Marty's brother, Asher, attacked my aunt Amy. A naïve girl of seventeen didn't have a hope in hell against a rapist of twenty-one. Thanks to Marty's testimony, the gentle girl heading for a music scholarship was blamed for her own rape. She never made it to uni.

Amy was a talented pianist who liked ice-skating and going to the mall with friends. She fell pregnant, and my hapless grandparents turned to prayer. It should have been a straightforward case against Asher Eversen, since she was below the age of consent. Marty played his part in her downward spiral, lying to protect his rapey brother, making the classic dick move of calling her a slut who'd asked for it. I should be going after Asher, but I told Zac that's his job.

If Asher were known to millions, it would be easier to target him. But Marty was the smug git on my screen. He's the one with brand recognition. My exposé will hit Marty where it hurts by targeting his public image. Perhaps my anger is misplaced when Asher deserves my hate, but I can't help it. Every time I saw Marty living the dream on Faith's socials, I wanted to kill him. Asher raped my aunt.

He's the monster and I'm bringing them both down. It just so happens that Marty has further to fall.

He keeps praying and I keep seething. Prayers weren't answered for my aunt. Prayers didn't stop his rapist brother. They didn't stop Marty lying to discredit Amy, and they didn't stop her death. My grandparents doubled down on prayer. My dad couldn't handle the situation any better than the rest of them, a troubled boy who the church sent on a mission to England. They encouraged him to marry my mum and he only ever returned for short visits. Prayer didn't ease his guilt for not doing more for his sister before she killed herself.

We finally get to 'amen' and I hold his gaze with the steady, serene expression I've perfected from the Stepford Wives in church. I'll get my chance to call him out, but not with Faith squeezed between us on a knife-edge of emotions and in danger.

Chapter Forty-Eight

The kids come bursting in from school, and I let out a long breath. 'I'll get back to Willow.' I stand up.

'She's expecting me later. I said I'd pray with you,' Marty says.

Pray with us or prey on us? Unease snakes through me as I know this is a threat to keep me in line. Back at the cabin, I lean against the door to steady myself. Then Willow and I go to milk the cow.

As soon as she's in bed, I'll call Joel, so he hears it from me that we're leaving. He might give us a lift. Willow likes him, so it could be a way of getting her out by stealth, so long as I don't jeopardise his job. One thing's for sure: we're leaving ASAP with or without anyone's help.

When I'm rhythmically milking Myrtle, it creeps up on me that something was off about the cabin. Something wasn't right in my peripheral vision, but I didn't pick up on it. What was wrong in there?

Willow chatters away and we walk back. I'm shattered, but my real work's only just beginning. Soon as I've found us a temporary place to stay, we'll get a flight out of here. Then I can find a job and an apartment. So long as I'm paid what I'm owed, we'll scrape by until I find work.

Back in the cabin, I pour the milk into a jug and rinse out the pail. Willow runs back to the dairy shed with it. Then it hits me what's wrong. The mobile router is gone.

I spin around, my eyes searching for it. Has Willow taken it upstairs? But she only uses the laptop occasionally at the kitchen table.

I go in my room. The laptop's not on the chest of drawers where I left it. Where is it? I survey the place in a frenzied panic. Someone's been in here. I rush to my handbag in the cupboard, only used when I go to town and church. It's gone. I should never have caved on that lock for the door. Willow comes in chatting to someone. Marty. My heart's pounding into overdrive. I'm frantic and nearly in tears.

He stops dead and looks at me. 'What's wrong?'

'My laptop's gone. My purse. The Wi-Fi box—'

'I have it all.'

'What?' I screw up my face.

'I have them for safekeeping.'

I gawp at him. 'You took my stuff?'

'It's fine. Calm down.' He holds up his hands.

'What do you mean, calm down?' I snarl. 'Give me back my things.'

A smile plays on his lips. A fire lights inside me. I want to run at him, knock him to the ground with all my might and pummel the shit out of him.

'Sit down.' He pulls out a chair for me.

I stand with clenched fists. This man is a fucking lunatic, thinking he can walk into my home and steal from me. Willow looks from him to me, eyes wide.

'Willow, honey?' he says. 'Why don't you run over and play with Emily? Tell Faith I'm having a quiet word with your mom.'

She leaves, not needing to be asked twice. I stare him down in an absolute fury. 'I can't believe you're doing this. Give me back my property.'

'Would you please sit down and talk?' He goes to guide me by my elbow.

I yank it away. I could kill him with my bare hands, but instead I back up towards the door, where I stand with one fisted hand over my mouth. 'You can't steal from me.'

'I know.' He holds his hands up. 'We should've talked first, but I figured I'd come over and explain as soon as you were home.'

This is bad. Really fucking bad. He's a law to himself.

'None of this is your fault,' he says.

My heart's racing, my whole body on red alert. 'None of what?'

'Your lack of faith. You've come here from New York. You don't speak with your family. You don't know the bonds of community, of love. We love you, Melissa. You're with us now, but you're too influenced by outside voices. Let go and trust.'

'No one in New York ever walked into my home and stole my valuables,' I yell.

'It's for your own good, honey.' He gives me a baffled look as if expecting thanks. 'We're bringing you back into the church. Willow's already there. There's no stopping her. We'll bring you along with her.'

I splutter at his audacity. The most chilling part is the conviction that he's right. My heart thuds so hard against my ribcage that it hurts to breathe.

'Have you heard of free will?' I say. 'I make my own decisions. Willow's my child. *I* decide, not you.'

'That's the problem right there. You're making the wrong decisions because you've been poisoned by the outside world. You're not seeing the beauty of what we have here.' He holds his arms out, palms upwards. 'I'm showing you the way to purity.'

'Thou shalt not steal. You've no right.'

'I have divine right. God told me to marry you.'

'Did he mention I don't want to marry you?'

'Like that matters.' He smirks. 'You don't know what's good for you, so I'm bringing you into line.'

'Give me my things right now.' I enunciate each word, my voice low. 'Or I will call the cops.'

He swipes the phone from my hand. My last connection with the outside world. He tucks it in his back pocket. I lunge for it. He deftly spins me around and lifts me off the ground, arms pinned to my sides. I kick out with all my might. And I scream.

Chapter Forty-Nine

Marty manhandles me into the bedroom. I fight back in a frenzy of kicking at him while he grips my arms.

'Get off me!' I yell. 'Let me go.'

'Or what? Whatcha gonna do, crazy horse?'

His mocking tone makes me kick harder.

'Horses kick but they never win. Not on my ranch.'

If I can only break free, I'll knock Marty out, then call Joel and the cops. 'Put me down,' I snarl.

'Shhh. Shush now, honey,' he murmurs into my hair like a deluded horse whisperer. 'It's okay. It's all gonna be fine.'

'Jesus fucking Christ. Let go of me.' I want to kick out at him even more. 'I'm not a child.'

'Enough of your cussing. And no, you're not a child. You're a wild mare and I'll break you in. It's what I do best.'

He thinks he can bend me to his will. Fucking lunatic. You can't argue with crazy. Still in his grip, I stop fighting. He lowers me so my feet touch the ground. Still holding me firm.

'I'm gonna leave you for now and you'll stay here and read your Bible.'

Like hell I will. I spot my nail scissors on the chest of drawers and snatch them up, the sharp tips pointing outwards. I spin back, catching him off guard, taking aim at his heart.

He knocks my arm off target. His hand clamps hard on my wrist.

'Arrgghh!' I yell in pain and frustration.

'Let go.'

I drop the scissors and he grabs them up. I stand back rubbing my wrist.

'Careful, wild mare.' His voice is menacing. 'You don't want to sprain that dainty little wrist of yours.'

He hauls me to the far corner and makes me stand with my raised hands on the wall. I'm shaking uncontrollably, my skin burning hot.

'Stay there while I search the place. Move a muscle and you won't see Willow for a long time.' He turns the room upside down, emptying drawers and the wardrobe, looking for potential weapons. Then he goes to leave. 'Tidy your room, or you'll set a bad example to your child.'

He locks me in the bedroom. There wasn't a key for the lock. He'd kept it for this purpose, knowing from the outset he'd lock me in.

I shakily restore the ransacked room. My rage turns to fear as I hear him searching the rest of the place. Minutes later, he returns, locking us both in the bedroom, then he pockets the key. 'I should chain you up in the cellar for that little outburst, but I'm a reasonable man. I'm prepared to show you the error of your ways. If you disobey me, you're going in the cellar, and Willow will also be punished. Is that clear?'

It hits me like a gut punch that he can take Willow from me. I wish I'd grabbed a knife instead and gouged out his heart.

'I said, is that clear?'

'Yes,' I hiss through clenched teeth.

He rummages in my bedside cabinet. The Book of Mormon was in there when we arrived, which I'd shoved to the back. He pulls it out, and yanks me over to sit beside him on the bed while he thumbs through.

'Here.' He hands the open Bible to me. 'If you want Willow back this evening, you'll read this. When I come back, you'll tell me the story of Nephi and his family, and what lesson you learned. If you don't do it good enough, Willow's staying with us.'

Bastard. I want to lash out, scratch at his face with my fingernails. But I know he'll overpower me and keep Willow. I sit in mute fury, Bible in my lap, staring straight ahead, blinking away tears of frustration and the crushing shame of him reducing me to this.

He snakes an arm around my shoulders, pulls me into him and kisses my hair. 'You'll learn.' Then he strides out and locks me in.

I take gulpy breaths, trying to calm myself. I have to play his game until I can scoop Willow up and get away. He can't imprison me forever. When he takes us into town, I'll make a break for it. It might be a Mormon stronghold and he might have friends in high places, but surely no one will allow a man to take my child from me if I stand in the middle of town screaming.

A sudden noise startles me, a drilling sound right outside. The walls vibrate. I peer through the flimsy voile curtain. He's at the front door with an electric drill. I crane to see, but the view's limited. He must be fitting a lock. I lean back on the wall and slide to the floor, where I hug my knees to my chest.

What have I got us into? The enormity overwhelms me. I force myself to focus on Willow coming back. That bastard holds all the cards. This is how he sucked in the others, this man with absolute power. I've heard of trauma bonding, where victims fall in love with a captor who overpowers them 'with love'. He murmurs sweet nothings and kisses our hair. I think of Faith's bruised wrist as I rub my own.

Bitterness rises from my throat as I pick up the open book to read the bloody thing. Then I hurl it at the wall. It takes everything I have not to rip out the pages, tear them up and scatter biblical debris over this prison cell of a room. As soon as I get away from here there'll be hell to pay.

An hour later, a key rattles in the lock. When he opens the bedroom door, I'm on the edge of the bed, Bible beside me as I stare blankly ahead. He brings in a chill. The temperature drops.

'Melissa, honey, you gonna tell me a story about Nephi?'

'The Lord commanded Nephi to travel to the promised land.'

'Wait, wait, wait.'

In my peripheral vision, he holds up a hand. Irritation swarms through me.

'You can do better than that, sweet stuff. Tell it from your heart, otherwise I'll ask Willow to give you a lesson in learning your scriptures. She understands what you don't. These stories are our life lessons. They're a precious gift from the Lord.'

I stare ahead, listless. This is how it is for Hel, but she's not locked in, except in her mind.

'Go ahead, honey, make me proud.'

He holds a hand over his heart and I want to plunge a knife into it. Stab him and watch him bleed out. But I start again and explain how the good Lord commanded Nephi to build a ship that would carry him and his family across the ocean to the promised land. Nephi had no ship-building experience and could have been daunted by his task, but he took it on with faith and obedience. Because of that, God provided him with the strength and initiative to build the ship and sail away. Lucky bastard.

'Look at me, Melissa,' he says.

I'd also like to sail away, but I look at him, trying to make my face impassive when I want to run him down in his own truck and reverse over his broken body.

'And what lesson do we learn from Nephi?'

Had he brought his drill in, I'd have used it on him.

'We learn about God's power and Nephi's ability to trust.' My gaze drifts away. I fantasise about shooting him through his stone-cold heart with his own gun.

'Keep looking at me, honey. That's right.' He nods and smiles. 'You got the lesson. We all need to trust in the Lord, especially when times are tough and we question the road ahead. Let us pray.' He sits beside me and holds out a hand. I stiffen and take it. He closes his eyes. I keep staring at nothing. 'Dear Lord, we pray that our community is a place of love and harmony. We pray for Melissa, that her heart is open to Your teachings, that she will learn from her struggles and trust in my wisdom. Please guide me, Lord, to minister to her needs. Amen.'

'Amen.' My voice is choked.

He keeps holding my hand. 'Now, missy, I don't want any more of your gall, is that clear?'

I close my eyes and nod. Aside from everything else, I stifle the urge to gag at him infantilising me when he intends to take me as his wife. How do these women have sex with him? It's gross. I know he'll use access to Willow as a way of making me submit. Regardless, it'll be rape. I can't believe I've come here for my family history to repeat itself.

'Look at me, honey.'

I try to banish the loathing from my eyes as I look at him.

'If you put up a fight or disobey me in any way we'll keep Willow at the house and integrate her into our family. We'll take her on as our own, since we've remade her in God's name. I trust you'll be devout and show her by example how a good Mormon lady behaves at all times. If you can be a worthy mother, then I'll let you keep her.'

It's all I can do not to fly at him, scratch out his eyes. How dare he? I'll kill the bastard. If I had one of his guns, I'd shoot him right now.

—

Listen, honey, this can only end in one of two ways: total compliance or death. It's harsh, but we've revealed too much to let you go. Stop making that almighty fuss or it'll be the death of you.

Chapter Fifty

Marty stands up. 'I have work to do. While I'm gone, it's time for your first test. Because you learned your lesson today, I won't lock you in. If you stay in here, we'll bring Willow back and the two of you can live here so long as you always do as you're told. Is that clear?'

'Yes.' My jaw clenches. He'll pay for this. He might think I'll rot in hell for my ungodliness, but he'll rot in jail for false imprisonment and taking my child away.

'Good girl. I'll allow you three knives in the kitchen, but they have to be sticking out of the knife block at all times unless you're preparing food. Same as at the ranch house. No point in trying anything though. I'll always overpower you. And you need to be a proper mother and think of Willow.' He goes back to the drawer and pulls out another book, called *Daughters in my Kingdom*, also shoved to the back. I hadn't opened it despite knowing they'd left it there for me.

'It's about the divine nature of women and their spiritual strength. Start reading now while you're waiting for Willow. From tomorrow, you'll receive guidance from Zina on understanding your purpose and living in harmony with God. She'll report back to me on your progress.'

He leaves without locking the door. It's still a prison. Joel will have left for the weekend, but from Monday, I'll look out for him at every opportunity, try to flag him down. He'll help me. He's not sucked into the crazy like the rest of them. Even if he can't stand up to his bosses, he can lend me his phone.

I start speed-reading the book about women serving the church through history. The Bible-bashing is a means to an end. When Willow comes back, I'll spend my time with her, not on batshit brainwashing. I only take in the message on an intellectual level, since I refuse to lose my mind to Marty. It's a lot shorter than the Book of Mormon, so I'm nearly halfway through when little footsteps come towards the cabin. I reach the door as Willow bursts in. She flings herself in my arms for a quick hug. It's clear that she doesn't suspect anything. Faith follows her in carrying a covered bowl of leftovers.

'Willow had dinner with us, but I didn't know if you've eaten.'

I haven't even thought about food, but it smells good. She places it on the table and grabs cutlery. I'm torn between keeping hold of Willow, and urgently questioning Faith out of her earshot. They both sit at the table while I eat the casserole, Willow telling me about her day.

'Willow,' Faith says once I've finished dinner. 'Why don't you sit on your bed and write your journal while I talk to your mom?'

'Okay.'

'Were you going to try on that dress to show me?' she asks in her innocent voice, tilting her head towards the bedroom.

'Sure.' I go to bolt the front door but see that Marty's removed the bolt. I swear under my breath. When we're in the bedroom with the door shut, I turn to her. 'If he hurts Willow...' I say through gritted teeth.

'She's fine. He won't hurt her.'

'If anything happens to her, I'm holding you responsible. You need to get my phone back.'

She shakes her head sadly. 'That's how I got the bruise.' She brushes a finger over the mark on her forehead. 'He blamed me for letting you have Wi-Fi. He thinks you're influenced by "outside voices".'

God forbid that a world-famous influencer and her social media manager have the internet. He should relocate to North Korea.

'What he's doing is illegal. Even if you don't care about him abusing you, he's imprisoning me. I need your help. We can fix this.'

'I have to get back.'

'I've been praying,' I say, my voice softer as I lean into the crazy.

She looks at me, startled.

'I prayed and God told me we should all leave for the sake of our safety.'

'That's not true,' she says in a sighing voice.

'So why is it true when he says it?'

'Because he believes it. You don't.'

'And I believe we're all in danger, so let's leave.'

She looks exasperated, and I want to shake her.

'You know he's controlling you? Is this what he does with every woman until they comply?'

She touches the cover of the discarded Mormon misogyny book.

'We can stop this,' I whisper urgently. 'You have a car. You have a phone. I'll help you stop it for all our sakes.'

She looks sadly at me. 'It's no use.'

'Why didn't you believe that the call with the lawyer would be confidential?'

'He has influence. People know him. They know us. If word gets out that I talked about divorce…' She looks down, one hand covering her wrist, still hidden under a sleeve. I bet her dresses cover a multitude of Marty's sins. Long sleeves concealing a bruised wrist. Do her high necks ever cover the imprint of his grip on her throat? Do her long skirts hide a cut where he pushed her and she fell badly?

'Have you tried before now?' I ask.

She stiffens and clasps her hands together. 'It didn't work.' She goes to the bedroom door. 'Don't make him angry.'

She leaves the cabin, locking us in. What if there's a fire? I'd have to smash through a window. I call Willow down to finish her journal at the table, determined to act normal around her. When she reads out her journal entry for today, I listen intently for red flags.

At bedtime, I go up with her. 'Where's *Little Women*?' It's not on her nightstand.

'It's not holy.'

Normally I'd challenge this and raise the stakes with considerably more unholy reading material, but not now. I tell her I love her, no matter what, and she's the best thing that ever happened to me by a mile. Then I kiss her good night, otherwise I'll be sobbing all over her.

Downstairs, I survey my bleak landscape. I've no chance of getting away on my own. No more driving lessons and he won't allow me into town. If they keep Joel away from me, I'm relying on Faith to somehow free us. If she's too chicken to act, she only has to leave her laptop out and I'll alert the authorities. We just need someone official to come here to investigate, to insist on talking to me, then they can drive me and Willow away from here.

So long as it's not his sheriff friend, surely it's doable? And I'll get help for the others, because nobody's safe around that nutjob.

Now he has my phone, I'm terrified that Zac will keep texting. If the Patriarchy's monitoring it, he'll see a rogue message flash on the screen and everything will hit the fan. Zac and I have the same aim of taking down the Eversen brothers. But while I'd intended to expose the way they drove Amy to suicide, then let the court of public opinion decide, my co-conspirator wants full-out revenge. He took a job at the car dealership owned by Marty's brother, wanting to infiltrate the company. He told me he intended to blow the whole place up.

'You can't hurt innocent people,' I'd said.

'I'll do it when he's alone in there.' But he didn't last the week. They fired him and he never blew the place up, which was probably just bravado. He's known to everyone there so can't show his face. Part of me wished he had blown Asher up, then he'd be in prison and I wouldn't be here. But Zac failed to take revenge. The useless git blackmailed me to go in and finish the job. He wanted me as a honeytrap, to come on to Asher, the married man and upstanding pillar of his community. I called it a cheap shot. I said I'd take them down from a safe distance, writing the story of what happened and making it public.

I've been tracking Marty for years via Faith's social media. Their online fame is enough for the story to gain traction. Zac wanted more, exerting pressure on me, so I wrote to Faith, seeking an opening. It gave the story more credence for me to visit the ranch and meet them both. Then her job offer came out of the blue. It was a way to pacify Zac. Except it's made him impatient for results and I've landed in this clusterfuck.

Zac's been angry with the church for as long as I remember. He can't handle authority figures. He was always a rebel with a cause, any cause, so long as it fed the chip on his shoulder. He was never likeable, but as kids, I admired his anti-establishment stance.

He made Asher Eversen the focus of his anger and used blackmail to recruit me to the cause. If only I could shake him off, but you can't choose your family. There's no escaping my brother Zac.

Chapter Fifty-One

I sleep fitfully, nightmare scenarios playing out in my mind. Early on Saturday morning, I go to make coffee. My ground coffee is gone from the cupboard. I check around, even as I know the Patriarchy has swiped it, along with the cafetiere. Petty moron.

It's my fault for coming here, for caving to pressure from Zac. When I'd suspected something was off with Faith, my curiosity drove me to approach her for an interview. I'd picked up on her internal conflict, a dissonance that I doubt she was aware of projecting. It intrigued me when the interview raised more questions than it answered. I should've known someone like her wouldn't offer me a job without an ulterior motive, same as I wouldn't have accepted it without an ulterior motive. The job was my Trojan Horse, my way in to Marty.

I've always loved delving under the surface for the real story. She handed me the chance to do just that. In my wildest optimism, I saw myself teasing out the story like an undercover journalist. I had visions of serialising it, taking my podcast mainstream. It swayed my decision to come here, along with Zac's blackmail. What a dick move. The real story is worse than I ever imagined, leaving me more trapped than Faith. Now Willow's been sucked into the madness, I swear I'll use every trick I can to get us out.

She wakes up excited about the Saturday trip into town. My heart sinks at the thought of Marty keeping us both under house arrest for the weekend. I hold on to the sliver of hope that he'll let me come, albeit under supervision. The arrogant loon might think he can control me, even with others around. It's most likely that he'll take Willow without me, so I come up with a plan B.

'I might not go into town today,' I say to Willow, my voice casual.

My heart dives deeper at her quizzical look. 'Why not?'

I force a smile. 'Mrs Bone is helping me with something here. I need you to return your library book.' She goes upstairs for the book of short stories, and I write a note to the librarian.

> Dear Joan,
>
> I can't come into town and I'm afraid someone's taken our library card and the copy of 'Little Women' we borrowed. You know I read stories about heroines who escape from a difficult situation? What do you recommend?
>
> Melissa Fairbrock

She doesn't know I read those stories, but will she connect the dots? She's a librarian, so she'll understand subtext, and I have a good feeling about her. Even so, it's a risky move. I can handle the consequences of Marty finding the note, but I don't want any repercussions for Willow. She clomps downstairs.

'Put on your coat.' I fold up the letter so it's a small square that I fix in place with tape. 'Take your book back to the library.' I crouch in front of her so I have her full attention. 'Find Joan and give her this note.'

She eyes the square of paper I'm holding up between finger and thumb.

'Give her the book and the note. Can you do that?'

She nods. I slip the note into her pocket and hold both her hands.

'Don't give the note to Marty. Only give it to Joan or whoever else is working at the library, okay?'

Emily comes to the door before I can drill it in any more. The potential for disaster is high, but I have to find help wherever I can.

'My mom says you're to write a grocery list for us.'

I turn away to grab a pen and hide my upset. There was only the slimmest chance of him letting me out and it seems even Marty isn't that dumb.

'If you see Joel,' I say to Willow, 'tell him I lost my phone.' My voice catches but they don't notice. When I hand over the scribbled list, they tear off to the ranch house. I slump into a chair, hoping I haven't made another mistake. A minute later, their car starts up and drives off. I wonder who will buy my shopping, since Marty isn't the type for 'women's work'.

With them gone, I need to win over Zina Bone. She holds sway over my freedom too, but I won't go looking for her. If she wants to indoctrinate me, she can come and find me, but I'd prefer Faith so I can work on her some more.

A sharp rap at the door shakes me from my thoughts. Zina's there, radiating disapproval. I arrange my face into Mormon serenity. 'Zina, how nice to see you.'

She steps inside, arms folded across her chest, clutching her tapestry bag. Her lips press into an even thinner line than usual. She cough-barks and stares pointedly at the nearest chair.

'Have a seat.' None of these women act normally, from Faith's fawning to pass-agg Zina, and the blunted emotions of the other two.

She sits bolt upright with an austere look. Foreboding creeps over me, like my life depends on passing this test.

'Would you like a glass of water?'

'No.'

I grab one for myself, my mouth suddenly dry. 'How's Alice?' I ask.

'She went into town with the rest of them to fetch your groceries.'

'I don't want her to be put out. You know I'd rather get them myself.'

'She usually shops on a weekday, so in future she'll ask for your list when she goes.'

In future, like this will continue.

'And you... are you okay?' She creeps me out, but is it possible to get her on my side? I've no idea what's going on in her head. Having written her off as a religious zealot, I realise she's an enigma. An enigma who holds all the cards.

'We'll begin our lesson,' she snaps, taking a book from her bag. 'I have things to do.'

'I'm sure you do,' I coo in my soothing Mormon lady voice.

She's more formal than usual. Perhaps she's pissed off at having to teach on a Saturday. Has she considered the legal implications of colluding with a kidnapper? Doubtful, when she's already going along with a bully of a man wanting her daughter as his additional wife.

I grab my copy of the book to match hers and sit opposite her with an open expression. Am I pushing my religious conversion too far too soon? I need to convince these people without them thinking me fake, but the swift conversion worked for Willow, so they must believe in religious miracles.

She takes her creepy cross-stitch from her bag. Looks like a new project.

'You could teach me to sew.' It'll distract her from Bible-bashing. I'll call my first piece 'Stitched Up'.

'I'm not teaching you to sew.' She places a hand on the book. 'I'm here to discuss how these teachings shape our lives.'

I smile and nod. May God grant me serenity and an escape route.

'You can start by sharing an experience of your own. Tell me how faith in Christ has helped you or another woman you know to overcome an obstacle in life.'

'Well… the Lord is testing me.' It's important to bond, so I tap into her love language of retribution. 'My current obstacle in life is that Marty doesn't trust me. I've decided to place my faith in Christ and for Him to show us the way to overcome this.'

She peers at me over the top of her glasses, trying to ascertain the level of bullshit. It's DEFCON 1.

'How do you do that?'

'Prayer.' I nod decisively. 'I know that He listens and answers. Would you say a prayer for us now?' I tilt my head the way Faith does.

She straightens her spine even more and stretches her arm across the table for me to take her cold, bony hand. 'Dear Lord,' she says in her flat voice. 'Please help Melissa develop her faith in You. Please guide her to respond to the needs of those around her as they also respond to her needs. Help her, dear Lord, to feel Your love and to fill her home with the spirit. Amen.'

'Amen,' I say. 'Thank you.'

We keep talking in this way, with me asking innocent questions and deferring to her. Whenever I speak, she studies me through narrowed eyes, trying to work out whether I'm fucking with her. Of course I'm fucking with her.

Zina doubles down on Mormon mind control with a lot of scripture thrown in, but it's not as impassioned as I'd expected, given the profound effect she's had on Willow. She's going through the motions. Maybe she knows I'm a lost cause and isn't wasting her weekend headspace on me. Or maybe she knows imprisoning thy neighbour isn't godly.

I treat her as I would a client, a devout one, and it's my job to keep her onside by validating her choice and proving she's right to put her faith in me. It'll help me avoid brainwashing, as I'm leaving LDS behind when she walks out of the door.

Marty's car goes past, and she snatches up her book and shoves it in her bag with the cross-stitch.

'The schoolhouse must be full of your stitched art,' I say.

'This isn't for school. It's for you.'

I swallow. 'It is?'

'It's a wedding present.'

I catch my breath, then recover myself. 'How nice.'

I picture the end result hanging up here.

> Submit to your husband, bitch, as you do to the Lord.

Or Faith might inspire her to stay on-brand.

> On your wedding day and forever, may your
> shackles match your décor.

Zina stands abruptly, turns to go, then swivels back. 'The reassurance you need is out there.'

I assume she's talking about God, but her tone is confidential. Is it a coded message? Is Zina poised to lead a resistance movement? I'd like to think there's more to her than meets the eye. Perhaps she's working out whether I'm the one to save them.

'In what way is it out there?'

'Ask for reassurance and it will come to you.'

We lock eyes. 'Can I come to you for guidance?'

She nods curtly.

'Thank you for our time together,' I say.

Her face says *burn the witch*.

'Praise be!' I call as she walks out the door. 'Would you like to come again?'

'No.'

So much for me being the one to save them. Not even Christ Almighty can save this lot from themselves.

Chapter Fifty-Two

Zina leaves and I keep watch at the open door for Willow. *Please come back to me. Please.* What if the Patriarchy found the note? What if he decides to screw with me and keep her from me? It's gnawing at me that I have no say, but he turns up on the porch, carrying two bags of groceries. He's not angry, so maybe Willow managed to hand over the note without him knowing. I step back for him to come in and set the bags down on the table.

'Thank you.' I hate myself for every civil word when I'd rather slit his throat. I'll pretend to take his crap on board, the same as Faith pretends to be happy. But unlike her, I'm going to escape. 'How much do I owe you?'

'Nothing.' He grins. 'It's from the community fund. We pool our resources. You're one of us now.'

A shiver travels down my spine. I won't be paid now I'm his prisoner. Given that he controls Faith's finances, I've no chance. Of course I've no chance when the thieving bastard stole my purse. He's in no rush to leave, so I root through the bags, taking out what needs to go in the fridge. 'Is there butter? I put it on the list.'

'Our dairy comes from the cow. Alice got you the raw ingredients. There's a recipe book on the shelf with how to make butter and cheese.'

Living the trad wife dream. I rub at my temples. A headache forms from caffeine withdrawal. I'd like to waterboard him with Myrtle's milk. Or tie him to the ground and have Myrtle trample him to death. I go back to the groceries, rearranging my face into a serene expression. It's partly pride in not betraying how much he's getting to me.

'Faith can give you extra tips. Do you want her to bring you some rennet?'

'Yes please.' I say, sweet as apple pie. 'Willow and I can spend the day making butter, cheese and bread. She'll like that.' It'll make the situation less bad. And I want another chance to work on Faith.

'How'd your lesson go?'

When is my child coming back, you egotistical maniac? That's the only thing worth discussing, but I keep playing his game. 'I asked Zina to pray with me.'

He must know I don't share his beliefs, but Faith's faking it so I take that approach. He gets off on me telling him what he wants to hear.

'I'm satisfied with your progress for now, so you can have Willow back. You both need to pray at every meal and bedtime, as well as doing your scriptures together. She has a book that the two of you can work through with an exercise a day. I'll be asking Willow every day how it's going.'

Screw you for using my child against me. I picture taking an axe to lop his head clean off, spurting blood like in a horror movie. But first, I'd lock him up and teach him to respect women's reproductive rights and body autonomy. We'll have a read-along of *The Power* and discuss the impact of a world where women can generate electric shocks to keep the likes of him in line. I'm so caught up in my fantasy that I don't hear Willow approaching until she's tip-tapping over the wooden porch.

She rushes in, rosy-cheeked, book in hand. 'Mommy! You should've come. I've got a book that Marty says we can read together.'

'That's great. And Faith's going to bring us some rennet so we can make cheese.'

'Yay.'

The Patriarchy smiles indulgently at his rustic Mormon females. Bastard has me right where he wants, in the kitchen and learning scriptures. He stays for a while, and I buzz around to avoid looking at him. I put on the apron that Faith had left hanging on a hook when I arrived. I usually only wear it for baking, but I look more trad wifey in it. Willow will need lunch, so I set about making it. 'Are you joining us for lunch?' I ask in my most hospitable voice.

'Another time. I'll send Faith over after lunch.'

Good. Bugger off then. 'That would be lovely. Willow, won't it be nice for us to make our own cheese?'

'Mommy, when Lehi's family walked through the wilderness they had no food, just raw meat sometimes.'

'That's right.' Marty gets up.

Leave before I batter you to death with the rolling pin.

'God provided for them,' he said. 'He blessed them with the strength to go on.' He waves goodbye and leaves. I sigh and return to rubbing my temples as I slip out of trad wife mode. I can't take much more.

He didn't lock the door, so Willow can run free even if I can't. Has he put up an electric fence? The town is at least ten miles away. I can't walk her that far in the dark. If he found us gone, he'd hunt us down and manhandle me into his vehicle.

She shrugs off her coat. I take it to hang up and check the pocket. No note. 'Did you see Joan?'

'Isiah took the book back.'

I spin round from the coat hook. 'What about the note?'

Her mouth hangs open and I can see her mind whirring. 'Oh.' Her hand flies to her mouth. 'I forgot.'

'You didn't give the note to anyone?'

She shakes her head.

'So where is it? It's not in your pocket.'

'Maybe I lost it.'

Fuck. If it finds its way to Marty, I'm screwed. Maybe someone will see it's for Joan, even if they don't know her, it mentions a book and a loan—

A shot rings out. We both jump and exchange glances.

'It's just Marty. It's okay.' I want to wring his neck.

How else can we get away? I'm a good enough driver that I could take a car for us to escape in, but he'd get me banged up for stealing a car and driving unsupervised without a licence. Even if we made it to town during business hours, if I'm a fugitive from the law, he'll have me arrested. It's too risky. I'll put everything I have into working on Faith, even if she's too gaga to help.

There's a sharp rap on the door. Willow flings it open. No one's there, but her piercing scream goes right through me.

Chapter Fifty-Three

Heart in mouth, I spin around at Willow's anguished scream. She's frozen on the doorstep, hands clutching the sides of her face, staring down at a bloodied, furry corpse. It's a cottontail bunny, dripping with blood. I pull her away and sink down to her level. She smushes her face in my jumper, little hands clinging on.

'Surprise!' Marty jumps out at me brandishing a knife. He must have dumped the rabbit, rapped on the door and then stepped away to enjoy our reaction. I want to scream at him, call him a psycho, but I have to pacify Willow. She clutches me tighter and wails.

'It's okay,' I murmur, trying to soothe us both. I hold her firm to cover my own shaking. 'I know it's a shock.'

'Don't be a crybaby,' he barks. 'I'm gonna show you how to skin it, then you can make rabbit stew. I got my skinning knife.'

Willow turns more hysterical. Drunk on power, he pushes past us, brandishing the knife. He takes a glass dish from the kitchen. I'm kneeling, rocking her and murmuring in her hair, while my gaze stays fixed on him. I'd like to shoot him with his own rifle, then get to work with the skinning knife.

'C'mon out here. I'll show you how to skin a rabbit.'

She wails louder. I pick her up and settle her in the armchair, having to prise her fingers off me. 'Stay here, baby,' I whisper in her ear. 'Keep quiet for me, okay? I'll just be outside for a short while.' Her crying dials back to a whimper, and I tuck her in with a woollen throw.

Fists clenched, I go outside and try not to gag as I endure his warped masterclass. He doesn't force Willow to join in so long as I show willing. My stomach heaves as we skin it and locate the bullet. He hollows out the guts and I nearly puke mine up.

When the ordeal is over, he leaves me with bloodied hands and the skinned rabbit. The poor creature, running free until... Marty. I wash my hands then wrap it tightly in plastic bags saved from grocery shopping. We won't eat it, so I stash the wrapped carcass in the fridge until I can dispose of it. Then I scrub the bloodied patch on the porch and take a quick shower before going near Willow.

She's subdued, but I make her favourite comfort food of dippy egg for lunch, and she eats it all. Neither of us mention the rabbit.

'Mommy,' Willow says in a forlorn voice. 'What happened to the bolt?'

'Oh.' I look at the holes in the door where the Patriarchy removed the screws and bolt. 'Marty took it off so he can come in when he needs.' I smooth it over, tempted to urge caution but she might let it slip. She'll be drawing her own conclusions from the rabbit incident. Meanwhile, I want to tie him up and hold a knife to his throat, steadily exerting pressure as a trickle of blood turns into a torrent.

After lunch, Faith arrives with Emily, all smiles. She's carrying a bowl of vile brown liquid, which I assume is rennet, and some dresses draped over her arm. I take the bowl. She lays the dresses over the nearest armchair. Emily presents one to Willow, in pale lilac, and I'm relieved by the well-timed gesture of kindness. Willow yanks her plaid dress off over her head and tries on the lilac one. She smiles and twirls while we tell her she looks great in it.

'Why don't you two read together upstairs,' Faith says. 'Melissa will try on her dresses, then we'll make cheese.'

This is promising. The dresses are props so she can get me alone. They clatter upstairs, I crank up the volume on the radio and we go into the bedroom.

'What can I do?' I ask in an urgent, hushed voice.

'He wants to marry you as soon as you'll comply.' Faith closes the bedroom curtains and stands with her hands on her hips.

I sink onto the bed. 'I have to get away. Even if you don't want to leave, you can help me without him knowing. What if you leave your car keys in the ignition so we can escape?'

'That's not safe,' she says in her languid voice. 'You can't trust Willow not to make a noise. If it's at night, he'll hear and come after you. If it's in the day, either he'll see you go or someone else will.'

'Has he got any meetings elsewhere or is he going away?'

She shakes her head, no.

'Wait,' I say, a plan forming. 'Next Saturday when he goes into town, if you get the keys to the work truck, I'll take off in that.'

'He takes Willow into town.'

I sag. And it'll be a push to get Willow away without her kicking up.

'What if we get hold of a sleeping pill or something like that? I'll give it to her and pretend she's been ill all night and sleeping it off.' I'd hate to drug her, but it's safer than keeping her here with that monster. And what if Marty came after us and rammed the car, then forcibly took me back? It's better to hold off until I have a rock-solid plan.

'I don't know anyone who takes sleeping pills. And I can't get you the keys. He'll know it was me and he'll kill me.'

It's a figure of speech but maybe not. 'So, what do I do?'

'What if he has an accident?'

'An *accident*?' I stare at her.

'What if he dies in an accident? Like if someone shoots him.'

'That doesn't sound like an accident.'

'But it could look like one,' she says.

I search her face for answers, revising my view of her. Does she really want to kill him in a faked accident? The girls come tramping down the stairs and I reluctantly stand up and open the bedroom door.

'Hey, girls,' Faith says brightly. 'Ready to make cheese?'

This is insane. I can't believe she's switched from plotting to kill her husband to wholesome cheesemaking. Is she losing her mind? Fair enough, given her crazed double life. She's blown my escape plan out of the water with her own solution. The Mormon church would be seriously pissed off to know their poster girl is plotting to kill her husband. She's my only ally, but can I conspire to murder in order to stop this living nightmare?

She's already back in character and minutes later is stirring the pan. 'Let's get this straight,' I want to say, 'you can't loan me your car to escape, but we can kill your husband?' Like it's a viable option in the real world.

The girls talk about their baptism, which is unavoidable until we get away. Faith shows me how to make cheese from the cow she milked this morning, earth mother that she is. Anyone peering through the window would spy two aproned housewives from yesteryear, cooking with their daughters. Blessed are the cheesemakers.

'Girls,' Faith says. 'Can you go milk Myrtle while we finish off here?'

They go running off, leaving us alone. She acts untroubled as they pass by the window. I wipe down the kitchen table where we'd moulded the cheese into big lumps. 'Do you have a plan for this "accident"?'

She looks back at me from the fridge where she's placed the big bowl of cheese. 'I have one of his guns,' she says dreamily.

I open my mouth to speak, but heavy footsteps sound on the porch decking. The Patriarchy strides in carrying the baby, the toddler running behind. I seize up. Did he hear us?

Chapter Fifty-Four

Marty steps inside the cabin and I reflexively turn my stricken face away, my heart thudding since he might have overheard us.

'Hi, honey,' Faith trills, holding out her arms for Betsy. Caleb waddles over and grabs a handful of her flowing skirt in his fist. Marty's either checking up on us or dumping the kids back on her. He often carries the baby and holds Caleb's hand as he totters along, or talks with the older kids. But the real business of childcare is women's work. He spends most time with Isiah, teaching him the ways of the ranch, including shooting a rifle.

'Willow and I can make cheese, thanks to Faith.' I follow her lead and act like everything's peachy.

'Glad to hear it,' he says, perfectly content and why shouldn't he be? 'Did you drop something earlier?' Marty narrows his eyes at me.

I slowly shake my head.

He pulls a piece of paper from his pocket. I freeze. It's the folded note to Joan and it's been opened. 'I found your letter to the librarian. Interesting. *Veeery* interesting.'

Faith stands motionless and her eyes swivel to meet mine. My head swims. I feel sick. I could actually throw up from sheer terror.

'"Dear Joan,"' he reads aloud. '"I can't come into town and I'm afraid someone's taken our library card and the copy of *Little Women* we borrowed. You know I read stories about heroines who escape from a difficult situation? What do you recommend? Melissa Fairbrock.'"

It's all I can do to keep standing, since my legs have become jelly.

'Take the children outside,' he says to Faith. She ducks her head and ushers Caleb out. Marty cracks his knuckles.

Shit, shit, shit. What's he going to do?

He doesn't take his eyes from me. 'What in tarnation is this?'

I stare back, rigid and silent. Nothing I can say will fix this.

'I'm not putting up with any more of your crap,' he says.

Don't then. Let me go.

'Do you think our holy books are boring? Because we have females who achieve good things. Righteous ladies doing righteous things. You need to learn your scriptures and not waste time on trashy novels.'

What?

'You think I'm dumb or something?'

Yes. But I keep my mouth shut, trying to work out where he's going with this.

'Well, I'm not because I can see whatcha doing here. You think your nice lady librarian's gonna make home visits? That ain't gonna work because any visitors to my ranch have to get past me first. Understand?'

Yes, but you don't, peanut brain. Does he not realise the note was a coded cry for help?

'I'm disappointed in you.'

I'm disappointed in me too, mostly for coming here.

'What do you have to say for yourself?'

'I... um...' I force out the words through the tensed muscles in my throat. '...didn't want them to think we'd stolen the book. I just wanted to let the librarian know.'

'You don't contact anyone unless I say so. Is that clear?'

I nod gravely. Did he take the message literally? I know he's a chucklehead, but he can't be that stupid. He opens the door to leave. Faith's the other side, listening in. She steps back and smiles at him, bouncing the baby. 'Okay, sweetie?'

He turns back to me. 'You'll be doubling down on your scriptures from today.' He strides off, having both made his point and missed the point.

'I'll leave you to your baking.' Faith smiles sweetly. 'Now you have cheese, can you make savoury muffins for church tomorrow?'

'For church? Am I going to church?' Is he trusting me to leave the ranch, albeit heavily chaperoned and in the company of a brainwashed congregation?

Willow and Emily turn up with the pail of milk.

'Same time as usual.' I can tell she wants to say more, but she ushers Emily and Caleb away and makes a sad face as she holds up the padlock.

I sink into a chair, my hands flat on the tabletop to steady myself after the run-in with the Patriarchy. Even though I've dodged a bullet, my heart tightens as the padlock clicks into place. Willow doesn't notice, but she will.

The next morning, we're in our Sunday best and I'm praying for a miracle, like a non-fatal car crash on the way. Then I could fake a concussion and go to hospital where I'd tell the staff he's keeping me captive. I wouldn't have thought him dumb enough to let me go to church, but since he misread my letter to Joan, all bets are off.

Willow goes to open the door. I stiffen. But it's unlocked and I breathe out in relief. The Patriarchy must have come over after dawn and unlocked it, on his way back from whichever handmaiden he slept with.

Frosty air rushes in. 'It's cold,' Willow says.

It's okay, sweetie, we'll be warmed by fire and brimstone.

The kids are playing outside the schoolhouse, and she runs along the frosted path to join them. My heart speeds up at the prospect of escaping the ranch. I'll have to rely on someone in the congregation to save me, but I'll work it out.

No sign of any adults by the cars, which haven't been defrosted. The school door is wide open, and Hel appears from the side of the building with a huge dish of potatoes. A movement inside catches my eye.

Coming closer, I see that Marty and Faith are standing in their Sunday best, a semi-circle of chairs replacing the classroom layout. Zina and Alice are there too. The Patriarchy spots me. 'Welcome to our new church.'

Faith comes over, all smiles, and takes the plate of muffins from me. I'm crushed that we're not leaving the ranch. Bastard, getting my hopes up. He stands with the three sex dolls and Zina with her permanent scowl. Such a weird mix. Marty calls to the kids, who file in. The adults sit on chairs, the children cross-legged on a big rug in front of us. The Patriarchy stands before us on a wooden crate to deliver his sermon on the mount. He spreads his arms wide, Jesus before his devoted flock.

'Let us pray.'

Prayer is how he forces through his agenda, so I'm ready for his bullshit justifications. *Bring it on, Mr Holier-Than-Thou.* I'm working out his game so I can play him at it.

'Dear Lord, we ask You to bless our humble schoolroom where we worship You. Help our congregation to trust in my words, as I interpret Your will. Help me to channel Your guidance.'

Cowboy Marty, endorsed by God. Do the others buy into him as the middleman between God and us? Alice rubs her modest baby bump, Hel's pondering the meaninglessness of life, and Zina's lips pinch into a frown. I still can't work her out.

'Now we have separated from our wider congregation, we are bound together in love for You, dear Lord, and for each other. Help us strengthen our faith and commitment in harmony, despite our differences.'

I squint one eye open. There's a touch of theatre about his performance. He sways and holds his hands aloft, face tilted to the heavens. I turn my gaze on Faith, who's staring at me with that knowing look in her eyes. I raise my eyebrows in return. The wannabe televangelist keeps on. Maybe he plans to beam *The Marty Show* from his iCloud beside God, his lovely wife and kids on the front row. He's deluded enough, but the internet would die laughing. Meanwhile, the others are pretending this isn't the dumbest thing ever, allowing this clown to rule over them.

'Dear God, I am your prophet.'

God, is this man bothering you? I'm reminded of long-ago church sermons when Zac would cough and say 'Wanker' into his hand.

'If you don't follow the prophet, you give yourself to Satan. Grant us strength and courage in our challenges ahead in building this righteous new community. Amen.'

What righteous new society? When our saviour finishes his godly pep talk, the kids go off to one corner for Sunday school with Hel. Marty monologues about building a new society, in his position as God's right-hand man. We smile vaguely and nod while the demented sermon keeps on, managing to be both unhinged and boring, which sums up living in a cult.

Faith looks besotted with him. How does she do it? Is she imprinting Ryan Gosling's face onto his? Alice is trying to show polite interest, but it's entry-level acting. I glance over at Willow, her face rapt, hanging on Hel's every deadpan word.

Sounds like he's building his own kingdom, the cult of Marty, with his guns, a bunch of women and their growing band of kids. The underground storeroom that Faith showed me is part of it. Faith's social media fans think grinding your own wheat is wholesome, but the self-sufficiency kick is driven by his distrust of society. He's a doomsday prepper with a cache of weapons. Is he building his own apocalypse cult?

His self-glorified ego has free rein here. This is bigger than me. Tongues must be wagging in the town, what with Alice's pregnancy beginning to show, and the rising number of single women living at the ranch. If he's enacting a master plan for domination, it's a red flag to cut us off from the community. This is the tip of a dangerous iceberg and our combined existence is at stake.

Faith had said she saw something of herself in me. She brought me here to help her out of this shitshow. I'm still reeling from her suggestion of killing Marty. I need her to help me escape, while she wants to overthrow his crazy regime from the inside. If she thinks her plan to kill him is our only chance, it could escalate badly. He's freaked her out enough to believe the only way to stop him is murder.

Chapter Fifty-Five

After the makeshift church service, we stand awkwardly around a table in the corner laid out with lunch. Isiah stuffs one of my mini cheese muffins in his mouth and nearly spits it out. 'Ugh, gross!'

'Isiah,' Faith says mildly.

'What's wrong with this muffin?' He makes a grimacing show of swallowing like it's sawdust.

They all turn to me, as if they suspect a poisoning attempt. 'I usually set a timer, but I don't have my phone.' I look pointedly at Marty for confiscating it.

'Why do they taste so bad?' Isiah says. 'Mom's taste good.'

Yeah, rub it in. The kids look at me like a litter of bewildered golden retrievers, heads cocked this way and that. They can't compute bad baking. Willow's used to uneven results and is about to die of cringe, but the others have never tasted a muffin that wasn't baked to perfection.

'They're overcooked and might be a little dry,' I say.

We leave soon after. 'Sorry about the muffins,' I tell Willow.

She shrugs. 'God loves a trier.'

'Ha.'

She agrees to milk Myrtle on her own since I'm elbow deep in meal prepping for the week ahead. The milk is more important now I'm making cheese, yogurt and butter from scratch. Living the dream. I can't believe they've turned me into a trad wife.

While she's out, Faith turns up with what smells like a freshly baked pie, covered in a gingham cloth. She's come alone. I'm surprised Marty's allowing unsupervised access to me when I'm a bad influence, but she's world-class at faking. A mistress of deception, so the idiot trusts her. Epic fail.

She sets the pie on the table and lifts the cloth. 'Take a look.'

Something in her tone grabs my attention. The pie crust has a heart-shaped design on top. It's listing at an angle and I can't see any filling. I lift the crust with my forefinger and I'm struck dumb by disbelief. Then I check Willow's not going to burst back in, since I can't let her see what's nestling under the pie topping.

It's a handgun. I step back. I'd been wondering who was supposed to kill Marty, and now I know. It's me.

'Cover it up,' I say in a choked voice.

She watches me, head tilted, the way she watches me when we pray. This is the real Faith – appraising, knowing, murderous. In her shoes, I might have killed him long ago. I'm already murderous at him using my child to secure his chokehold on me. But…

'You can't leave it here,' I say. 'Willow's due back. You have to take it with you.'

'Trust in the good Lord.' She takes my hand and guides me to the bedroom, her other arm cradling the gun pie.

'Where'd it come from?'

'He keeps it in the house.'

I stare at the gun. 'Won't he miss it?'

'It's not one of his favourites.'

'What's his favourite?'

'Assault rifles, and he has another handgun he prefers in the bedroom.'

With six kids in the house? I don't trust myself to touch it, and I don't buy into her crazy scheme. Harbouring fantasies of killing him is one thing, but risking a murder charge is a whole new level of crazy. I'd love to blow his brains out in a no-consequence world, but it's not that simple, not in this backwater. He's a rich man, upstanding in his church, a boost to the local economy. He's friends with the sheriff and everyone else. Money talks around here and I'm skint. I can't afford legal representation, and I can't keep Willow safe if I'm in prison.

'It's not staying here,' I snarl. 'It's too risky with Willow. There's nowhere I can lock it away.'

'Hide it under the mattress. She won't go there. When he tries having sex with you, shoot him.'

It's unreal, Faith talking about her husband's plan to rape me. She's a lost cause, lost to this crazy life she's helped create. But where does that leave me?

'He might find it,' I say. 'He's already upended the room once because he doesn't trust me. What's to stop him checking under the mattress? He'll know you gave it to me.'

'Try it,' she says sweetly. 'This one doesn't have a safety. You just point and fire. Practise your aim. I'll show you.'

'No!' I want him dead, but this is nuts. 'I'm not going to prison for his murder.'

'You'll claim self-defence. I'll back you up and you'll be free.'

'Best case? I'll spend a year locked up waiting for a trial, separated from Willow.'

'If you kill him, I'll have access to the money, so I can pay for a good lawyer and look after Willow.'

'*You* kill him.'

'I thought you wanted help to end this situation.' She sounds hurt, as if I've rebuffed her cookies. How is it okay for me to shoot him dead, but she won't consider the safer option of helping us escape?

'Can't you poison him or something?'

She shakes her head sadly. 'It'd show up on an autopsy. Tox screening is standard in unexplained deaths.'

Wow. She's thought it through. 'Frozen leg of lamb?'

'Excuse me?'

'Hit him over the head with the leg of lamb. I know it's been done before, but it's an Instagrammable dish.' My voice drips with sarcasm. 'Do the deed, make a reel, eat the evidence.'

She blinks at me.

'Let's help each other,' I say. 'You help me get away. I'll raise the alarm. We'll say he's going mad, which he is.'

Willow comes in with the milk pail.

'Take that out of here,' I mouth, pointing at the gun, 'or I'll throw it out for him to find.'

I go to Willow and pour the milk into a big jug. Faith follows me out of the bedroom, holding the dish. I look pointedly at it, raising my eyebrows. She brushes a hand over the roomy pocket of her dress to show the gun's outline through the fabric.

'Would you take the pail back for me please?' I rinse it and hand it back.

Willow runs back out with it.

'Help me escape and I'll find you a good lawyer,' I say to her. 'They'll get you access to your money. You're rich. There's enough for you to start again with the kids somewhere else. If you want, you can sell your story and control the narrative. You'll have an instant income stream. The fans will lap it up.' I understand the logistical and emotional grief of uprooting six kids under twelve, but her social media income is in the millions. Even if it's controlled by him, it can be fixed and buy her freedom.

'If you get away, he'll blame me.'

'Then come with me, because I'm getting out, whether you help me or not. If you come, we've a better chance. Then he'll be locked up, since I'll give evidence and every normal, right-minded person will be on your side.'

'They'll say I was faking all this time.'

'They'll say you were in an impossible situation, keeping things stable for your children while he trapped you. It's what people do in relationships where they're abused and controlled. You can turn it around by showing you're making a stand on behalf of abused women.'

Willow comes tramping back.

'Do I come to work tomorrow,' I ask in a hushed tone, 'or am I under house arrest?'

'He says you can only come to the house and here. He wants me to lock you in now,' she says as Willow opens the door.

'Do it quietly,' I tell her, nodding towards Willow. 'Thanks for the pie,' I say brightly.

'You're welcome.' She beams and walks out.

I ask Willow to fetch my journal to distract her while Faith locks us in for the night. It's one thing to deal with Marty, but I'm also treading carefully with Faith. I'll search the bedroom later, making sure she didn't stash the gun out of the way and the one in her pocket was a spare. I'm putting Willow in terrible danger as it is. Faith and I are supposed to be on the same side, but a creeping sense of disquiet tells me to guard against her as well as him.

When I write my journal, it's factual as usual. The Patriarchy hasn't taken it, so I'm keeping it for a record. It's a sanitised version of the truth, but documenting the day-to-day serves as a reminder. I intend to write it as a memoir, weaving my family story with his, our downward slide with their upward trajectory. My story just turned explosive.

—

Nobody's perfect, not even me, queen of the trad wives, although I try my hardest. It took me a while to find the next sister-wife. I wanted to choose her even if my bonehead husband thought he was doing the choosing. I'd already tried it with Hel, expecting to unleash a homicidal firebrand, but he broke her. We keep her on Prozac now, or she wouldn't get out of bed.

This time, I needed a smart, resourceful woman on my side, one easily isolated – say, if she had no driver's licence. A single parent working in Manhattan without family backup had to be resourceful, especially as she wasn't earning big. Melissa was the one.

Smart people don't always do what you want, but she won't put up with Marty for long. One of them will kill the other, so Marty will either die or wind up in jail. There will be no blood on my *hands.*

Chapter Fifty-Six

As I leave for work in the morning, Marty's whooping on horseback in the distance, living the cowboy dream. Hashtag hero. I crane my neck, but there's no sign of Joel. My heart tugs. Has he messaged me? He'd help us escape, if only I could talk to him.

As before, someone unlocked our door first thing, probably our jailer. He pretends he's not a prison guard, same as he pretends to be a regular guy. He imposed this on me like I'm the one who's out of step, and he's just fixing the situation. Shame I didn't catch on earlier. Shame I didn't scoop up my child and run for the hills when my spidey senses kicked in. At least work allows more opportunity to raise the alarm.

'Good morning,' Faith chirps as I walk in, wheatgrass smoothie beside her, Betsy on her hip. Placid baby, placid mum.

'Shall I edit last week's video?'

'Sure.' She smiles widely, like it's a normal day.

She's unreadable. Will she turn away from confiding in me and start reporting to Marty on my dissent? Perhaps she's already a double agent, playing her own twisted game with me.

My heart pounds in the editing room as I call up emails on my work account. Nothing new loads for this week. I bite my lip and go online under the pretext of checking comments on Faith's socials, but the Wi-Fi router has gone from under the desk. I slump in the chair. They've cut off the internet. Of course they have.

I want to smash up the whole room and scream in frustration. And how can I edit the video when Faith's social media was the gateway to my abuse and disempowerment? I can't sucker in any more unwitting victims. My thwarted plan was to look up a domestic abuse charity and seek emergency help via email, since I can't trust the sheriff.

Why pick me when a devout country girl might swallow his bullshit and even like the lifestyle? It's still not acceptable, but Marty has a type. He targets bright, talented women like Faith, ones with a future involving college, like Hel, and in the case of Ivy League Alice, an assured career. And me, lured from my independent life. It's a sport to him, ensnaring women who fly free and turning us into caged birds.

Faith played his game to her advantage, and now she wants out. The others I'm less sure about. Hel could be the wild card. Alice's main concern is her child and pregnancy. As for Zina, time will tell, but I'm going crazy here. I'm not cut out for this. I won't hack it like the rest of them. I need to escape, fast.

I weigh up my two options: either risk a jailbreak or suck it up until he trusts me to go into town with Willow. But for him to trust me, I'll be forced into sex and faking affection when I'll never be a surrendered wife.

Mid-morning, I go to the kitchen for a drink of water. 'How are you feeling?' Faith tilts her head in empathy.

'Can we go outside for some air?' We stand on the doorstep, looking out at the mountains. 'You know this is against the law?' I say. 'I'm being kept prisoner.'

'Mmm,' she intones.

'How can we deal with this in a legal way? By "legal", I mean no guns.'

She stares into her herbal concoction. She hasn't offered me one, so that's something.

'If you were helping me get away,' I ask, 'how would you do it?'

'There's only one way to stop him,' she says mildly, and I want to brain her with a casserole dish.

'You could poison him with something natural, like deadly mushrooms, and pass it off as an accident.'

'He has a very strong constitution, and I can't risk the children being harmed.'

'You brought me here knowing this would happen. You know he's imprisoning me. Ignoring it isn't a defence.' I'm upping the stakes. If I get away despite her refusal to help, the fallout will ruin her, if Marty doesn't kill her first. It's all the more reason for her to take action against him.

She gives a small, sad sigh. 'We have to all stay safe and that means doing what Marty says.'

I stare hard at her. 'You don't believe that.'

She looks away.

'If he's a doomsday prepper, this'll escalate until we're living in a bunker. You can stop the craziness.'

She places a consoling hand on my arm.

'Listen,' I say. 'Let me online for ten minutes. Turn a blind eye. There's no risk to you. Marty won't even know.'

She gives me a pleading, sad puppy look. 'We have work to do. Let's get back to it.'

I'm so furious with her, with him, with this prison of a place, that I'm ready to take my riskiest move.

My husband loves a challenge and what better than bringing a lapsed Mormon back into the fold? That'll never happen. Melissa won't be finding her way to the light, but with God on my side, she'll be so mad at Marty, she'll snatch the gun from me and blow his head off.

Marty couldn't handle her refusing to go along with him. I suffered the accusations and the bruises for bringing her here, same as I suffer everything. But now he has her where he wants, she'll get the brunt of it, not me.

Melissa burns with rage, which only makes it worse. Want to know my secret? Turn sweetness into performance art. But she lacks patience. Anyway, I don't care what happens to her, so long as she eliminates my husband from my life.

Mormon women defer to their husbands, but online gentiles were picking up on it and making crass jokes. 'Gentile' is a slur, by the way, because we're better than you. Trolls made fun of me and questioned my life choices. As if I ever had a choice.

I learned manipulation from a young age. You get away with a lot when your sweet smile doesn't waver. Some might wonder how I kept it up, but having a plan to get rid of my husband calmed me. The more I plotted, the sweeter I became.

'Anything for you, honey,' I'd say. But it's time I had everything for me.

Chapter Fifty-Seven

I'm in the editing suite with the door open. I have to edit offline, then Faith will post the content from the big barn – the only place internet is still allowed. She comes and goes, milking the cow, collecting eggs and wafting around in a cloud of lavender. While she's in the land of make-believe, I'm busy adding a rogue message to the latest video.

> Help me.
>
> I work at Lavender Field Ranch. Faith's husband is holding me captive. Please enlist urgent help, but not the local sheriff who is friends with him. Seek advice from a Women's Centre. Don't post about this online until my child and I are safe.
>
> Thank you, Melissa Fairbrock

Even Marty can't misinterpret that one. Using the video editing software, I select the best places to add the written subliminal message between frames where it's more seamless. I lower the opacity to blend with the background. For each repeated subliminal, I set the duration to a tiny fraction of a second, so it's undetectable on a conscious level. Then I work on the audio, recording the same message in a low voice, hoping no one overhears. I lower the volume and layer it beneath Faith's voice and the background noise.

Content creators like me study successful reels and videos for signs of what makes them 'sticky', so viewers are glued to them. Just as I can use software to create subliminals, another pro can use it to detect them. I'll make it subtle enough that Faith and Marty won't notice as I silently will someone in the know to find it and raise the alarm.

After finishing my handiwork, I play back the video to check the message is suitably hidden. Faith appears in the doorway, Betsy on her hip. 'You finished it? Lemme see.'

My face flushes and I cringe inwardly. I play it from the start for her to watch over my shoulder. Halfway through, Marty comes tramping into the kitchen. *Shit.*

'We're in here,' she calls through. 'Rewind it for him.'

I close my eyes and heave in a breath. He comes in and I restart it. I can hardly bear to watch and resist the urge to gnaw on my nails and sink low in my chair. If I've been heavy-handed or screwed up the timings, they'll get a flash of something, enough to suspect I'm up to no good.

The twelve-minute video drags while I take shallow breaths and keep repeating *please please please* in my head. The Patriarchy hums and haws, a finger tapping his chin in contemplation. It's his trademark boss move, acting like he knows shit about content creation. Faith's the expert and he's an egotistical peanut brain. I was wrong to label her the control freak when she's going all out to avoid his backlash.

'We need it good so the faithful donate to our ministry,' he says, like he's running a mega-church.

'Do you take donations now?' I ask.

'He means the influencer payments.'

Dude, they aren't donations. Social media pays for the views and 'the faithful' follow her, not you.

Faith suggests some text overlay to highlight a key point.

'Yeah, I was thinking that too,' he says.

'Isn't he the smartest daddy in the world?' Faith coos to Betsy, who could be forgiven for throwing up a little.

Then they both go to leave, but he lingers. 'I'll be over this evening to check on your Bible studies,' he says with a glint in his eye.

My gut twists and I force a smile. 'Sure. We'll see you later.'

He leaves, and I slump in relief. They didn't pick up on the subliminal messaging, and nor will most people who watch the video. But surely someone in the know will look closely, suspect it's not quite right, then raise the alarm. My buzz of excitement is pierced with the very real danger of it backfiring.

Faith takes the laptop to post the video from the big barn, along with my hidden cry for help. A physical pain lodges in my chest at having an escape route so close. How does she square it in her mind? I couldn't stand by while someone else suffered this way. She only needs to let me send an email or send it herself. It's in her power to fix this, but if she was willing to help, she'd have done it already.

I'm realising why I've never pinned down Faith's real personality. It's because she doesn't have one. She was born to be a trad wife, raised to accept that persona. But beneath the surface lurks an arch manipulator. She lured me here as part of her grand plan, and she's not letting me go.

Alice is at the kitchen table with the youngest kids, where she's cutting up vintage flowery material for lavender sachets.

'Do you make them all by hand?' I ask.

She glances at me and nods, then huddles into herself like she wants to disappear.

'When's the baby due?' I ask.

'March, God willing.' She keeps cutting.

'If I asked to borrow your phone for a minute would you tell Faith and Marty?'

She stops and blinks at me, scissors in hand. Sharp scissors. Could I slit his throat with them?

'I don't have a phone,' she says.

'Do you have a tablet or computer?'

'Only the big barn computer, but I don't need the devil's web.'

Of course not, when she's squandering her education, cutting up bits of fabric. While we talk, I covertly scan the kitchen for the car key. Criminal charge or not, I'd take the car as a last resort. The key isn't anywhere obvious. Faith might keep it in her handbag, which is stashed away somewhere. I've already checked that it's not in the ignition. Funny that, when it's such a safe place that I needn't lock my door.

'Don't you mind being isolated?' I ask Alice.

She shakes her head and keeps fashioning her lavender pouches.

'Will you tell anyone I asked?'

'No.'

'Will you help me get away?'

'No.'

'You could send an email for me from the big barn.'

She looks at me with her clear blue eyes. 'I don't make Marty angry.'

'He wouldn't know it was you. Then if he goes to jail, you're free to make your own choices.'

She looks thrown by this. I bet she couldn't make a decision even if her life depended on it. I catch sight of Faith coming back along the path.

'You won't tell anyone I asked? Since it'll make Marty angry.'

She gives the smallest nod and hunches over her craft project. I return to the editing suite and, a minute later, Faith comes in to update me on the previous video we posted. 'Good engagement. The top comments are positive.'

I nod and purse my lips. *Bitch, where's the car key?*

As for the Patriarchy coming over later for Bible study, he'll be pushing me for sex soon enough. Cowboy Marty is a red-blooded lothario. In his weird world, I'm promised to him, and I nearly gag at the thought of his tongue in my mouth. I'm desperate to get out before he rapes me. My only hope right now is the video. I'm counting on an unknown expert – someone, anyone – alert to subliminals who's checking popular online content for telltale signs.

If Zac had been more reasonable, he could have been my safety net. He's the only person who knows why I'm here, so if I failed to keep in touch, he could have launched a rescue mission. He's vindictive enough to come steaming in, but he's not the rescuing type. Why look out for his sister when he can blackmail her instead?

He's threatening to tell Willow about her dad. And he's threatening to tell her dad, who has no idea Willow exists. I told her that he came to NY for a short visit, then left town before finding out about her. That much is true. But the deep, dark truth is that he's incarcerated in a federal prison.

Chapter Fifty-Eight

The Patriarchy turns up after dinner for Bible study. I'd quizzed Willow on her readings, so I can wing it if he questions me. She's delighted by my newfound belief, but her trust will be shattered one way or another. Marty's threat of taking her away clings to me. He discusses religious stories with Willow, while I want to gut him like that poor rabbit. I'm not expected to do anything except smile and nod. Faith is my warped role model, but I can't fathom how she sleeps with him while wanting him dead.

When Willow gets ready for bed, he makes small talk with me about his day, as if we're a couple. He's good at normalising the crazy. After Willow cleans her teeth, she climbs into bed and Marty says we should go up with her to say a prayer.

By now, I'm barely registering the religious bollocks. After his prayer, he kisses her lightly on the forehead. 'I want you to go to sleep now,' he says kindly. 'Your mama and I are gonna say our prayers in her room.'

I eye him with disgust. At least she doesn't suspect. My misguided child likes the idea of him saying a prayer with me. 'Night night, baby girl.' I kiss her and follow him stiffly downstairs and into my bedroom. He shuts the door. I'm at his mercy. He turns on the lamp, then tucks my hair behind my ears. A smile plays on his lips as he cups my face in his hands, then he leans forward for a kiss. Nausea roils inside me.

He takes my hand and pulls me towards the bed where he sits down. I step back and he pats the space beside him. Instead, I pull up the chair in the corner, sitting a few paces away. He chuckles like it's a game.

'Now then, Melissa, you know that you and Willow are part of our family now. It's God's will. He sent you to me and told me to take you as my wife. You and I can have family relations.'

I want to bolt but force myself to stay passive. 'Shouldn't we do things right for Willow?' I say. 'We can't teach her the sacred bond between man and wife without showing her that we're married. Let's not confuse her.'

He frowns, his forehead wrinkling.

'We need a wedding ceremony, so she understands.' Like hell we do, but anything to buy time.

His eyes narrow on mine. 'This Sunday then. We'll marry and I'll baptise Emily and Willow. Then you're both part of God's family here.'

At least Willow swallows the religious nonsense, so she'll accept it until I can untangle her mind from this culty headfuck. I bet he'll perform the ceremony, despite being the groom, which won't be the only bizarre aspect with his three other 'wives' looking on.

'C'mon over here and pray with me.' He lunges forward and grabs my hand, pulling us both down to a kneeling position facing the bed. Then he scoots behind me, forcing his knees either side of mine, his body pressed into me, big hands clamped prayer-like over mine. He angles my elbows onto the bed. I'm trapped and overwhelmed with panic.

'Dear Lord,' he murmurs into my hair, breathing heavily. 'Help our sister, Melissa, to lay down before You and accept Your divine wisdom.' More heavy breathing, the damp warmth close to my ear. 'Help her submit to Your will and be a conduit for Your blessings. Amen.'

My face is crumpled in a silent sob. He grasps my hands in one of his while his free hand roams over my body. He nudges my legs further apart with one knee. I try to control my shaking limbs and ragged breath, fighting off my emotions so Willow doesn't hear.

'This is allowed,' he says in a low voice. 'We're promised to one another so we can do heavy petting. You know it, honey.' His hand rubs back and forth between my thighs, then he starts dry-humping with his entitled dick. My eyes squeeze shut, my face contorted. Without warning, he hoists me up and deposits me on the bed.

I try to quell my revulsion to stop myself lashing out. I ball the sheets in my fists. My plan to channel Faith's cheerful acquiescence is way too optimistic. And wrong. I'm not giving him a happy face while he violates me. He climbs on top and grips my wrists, looming in for a sloppy kiss. *Stop it, stop it, make it stop, get off me you abuser, you vile fuck, you repulse me, fuck off and die, you fucking creep.*

No wonder Hel's so numbed out. My mind goes to a better place, far away from here. A tear trickles down my face, into my hair. I dig my nails into my palms, imagining tearing into his flesh. This man gets off on turning women submissive. Every fibre of my being rebels, but it's no use. My body's no longer my own. He's taken it and my mind takes flight. He wants my mind too, but I'm keeping it from him.

When he eventually leaves, I curl up, shaking. He didn't rape me, not yet, but he'll have me knocked up soon enough. No way do I want to bring another child into his grubby sex sect. Thank God I didn't hide the gun under the mattress. Faith knew how it would play out. She knew I could slide my hand under the mattress and reach for the gun. I'd have blown his brains out for sure.

Chapter Fifty-Nine

I wake up breathless in the night, convinced Marty's on top of me, suffocating me with his bulk. I'm a hot mess, but it's a nightmare. It's all one big nightmare. I lie awake for the rest of the night. If only I hadn't come here. If only I hadn't seen this as a way out from Zac blackmailing me.

My lowlife brother is threatening to shatter Willow's illusions about her dad. When I first moved to New York, Zac called out of the blue to say his friend was in town and would I meet him for a drink as he didn't know anyone else. My first mistake was saying yes. I met his friend in a bar, then he came back to my place where we drank shots and he laughed me into bed.

Turned out he was wanted by the Feds. He's now doing time for armed burglary and attacking the woman whose home he broke into when high on drugs. I can't even bring myself to call him by his name. He won't be bothering us for a while. But Zac is. The way it panned out, he might have stepped up and become a good uncle, but instead he used it against me. He's threatening to tell the convict and Willow about each other. I failed her before she was even born and I keep on failing her.

In the morning, Willow climbs into bed with me.

'Mommy?' she whispers.

'Mmm hmm.'

'Someone just unlocked the door. I think it was Marty.'

'I think you're right, sweetheart.' Might as well prepare her for the hellscape. I hate to normalise it the way Faith does, but I'll ease her in. 'He locks the door from the outside so no one can come in while we're sleeping. And you know what?'

'What?' She snuggles in.

I wrap my arms around her warm little body. 'You and I are a team. Always have been. I love you more than anything and I'm always looking out for you, no matter what.'

We stay like that until she asks for breakfast. I haul myself up. Five days until I'm 'married'. My deadline to get us the hell out. An impossible tension is building in me. At 8.30, I go to the ranch house with a revised plan to search harder for the car keys. Surely if the cops arrest me for car theft, I can convince them I had to escape.

We're due to shoot a video in the kitchen, but Faith's not there. I go straight to the dresser and pull open the nearest drawer. It's filled with string, batteries and household stuff. My heart races at the thought of finding an old mobile that I can get working. I pull open the second drawer.

'What are you doing?' Marty's staring at me.

I jump back from the drawer. He's come out of their bedroom. Shit. He's always gone from the house at this time in the morning.

'Scissors.' I paste on a grin. 'Where do you keep the scissors?'

His sandy eyebrows knit. I should've said tape, since I'd tried attacking him with scissors. 'I'm setting up the shoot for today. If we're using new products, I'll cut off the packaging.' My voice is breezy and light, but he's not buying it. 'How are you today?' I ask sweetly with a Faith-esque head tilt.

'I'm not trusting you with scissors after last time. Betsy has a fever. Faith's in bed with her. They can both rest this morning.'

'Oh, I'm sorry. Shall I take Faith some herbal tea?'

'She can manage.'

'Then I'll clear up the breakfast things.'

'You'll come to the barn with me.'

My heart races. I might see Joel. *Please God, let me see Joel.*

We take the path and draw level with the utility barn. 'What are you teaching the kids this week?' I make cheery small talk, God knows how.

He yanks me by the arm towards the open barn door. *No.* I'm not prepared. I can't have him assault me and then act like nothing's wrong. My brain's on fire. Rage pulses through my chest. I'm about to lose my shit. I could strangle him.

He pulls me inside as a little voice calls out to us.

He ignores Jonny and slams the door shut. He surveys me with a cold glint in his eye. His hands encircle my wrists, taking possession of me, holding me firm while he leans in to kiss me. I flinch. He smiles, like I'm a fun challenge.

I'm shaking. Even my lips tremble. He gives me what he thinks are teasing kisses. I want to scream in his face, to knee him, bite off his tongue, puncture his swelled ego. I'm furious with him, with Zac, and with myself for sabotaging my life with Willow to come here.

'Relax,' he croons. 'You're too tense.'

I try zoning out by tracing back to what point I should've grabbed her and bolted for the airport. But I toughed it out instead. My mistake for thinking like a normal person when dealing with nutjobs. Will someone figure out my subliminal message? The video must be racking up thousands of views. The more views, the more chance of the right person seeing it and putting a stop to this.

I keep telling myself to play the demure, surrendered female so he'll cut me some slack. But all my instincts scream at me to fight back. I ignored the impulse to run when I had the chance, and I can't ignore it now. He's acting like a randy teenager when I want to shoot him dead with the gun. The gun. The gun. I'm obsessed with Faith's gun.

Chapter Sixty

I'm desperately withstanding Marty's advances when the door handle squeaks and rattles. I try to move away, but he keeps me pinned to the door so it seems locked or stuck.

'Daddy?' Jonny's muffled voice comes through. He keeps pushing.

'He's only little,' I mouth, face to face with my abuser.

He traces his finger from my lips all the way down my body. It's meant to be seductive, but I swallow my nausea. He steps back and I open the door, relief flooding through me as I let the daylight in.

He scoops up a squealing Jonny and strides over to the big barn with him, while I trail a few steps behind. It would be safer for him to keep me locked up, but he's faking normality, acting like it's business as usual.

Joel's truck isn't parked with the others, but I spot a small figure in the distance, forking hay. 'Who's that?' I squint at the slight figure standing with a pitchfork on the back of a truck.

'It's Isaiah. I'll have him mending fences next. We have the most secure ranch and he has the best teaching.'

'Why isn't he in school?'

'Time he stepped up, seeing as Joel left.'

My heart sinks. 'Why'd he leave?'

'I inspired him to set up his own farm. I'm the best in the business. He learned so much from me that he wants to try it out for himself, since he's marrying his sweetheart soon. He's not one of us. It's better we keep it in the family.'

I can hardly bear it, losing my only ally. 'Sweetheart' or not, he could have helped free us.

Inside the big barn, two older workers fulfil warehouse orders. Marty points to the workstation in the corner. 'Go work with Helen.'

There's Eeyore in a flouncy polka-dot dress, at a computer with her back to us. I recognise the shell-pink dress with chocolate dots from one of Faith's reels. Faith can dress her as a trad wife, but it's not rubbing off.

I go over. 'Hey.'

She turns her head slowly, her eyes glazed. If she's on drugs, it figures.

'Marty says I'm to work with you.'

She shrugs one shoulder and turns back to the screen. I scoot a chair over. The desk is shoved against a wall, with no privacy. I sit sideways to her so I can see if anyone comes close. She listlessly inputs data. This isn't a two-person job or a training opportunity when Hel gives zero fucks, but it's a chance to work on her. She's the subversive black sheep of the flock. With Joel gone and Faith refusing to help, Hel's my next best bet.

'You okay?' I keep my voice low as Marty sings along to 'Born in the USA' on the radio. Jonny's stacking a pile of small boxes like they're building blocks.

She continues her low-energy tapping on the keyboard. It could go either way, but maybe we'll climb out of this hole together. Despite her sucky attitude, he lets her come and go. She has no kids and could break out of here with Willow and me riding shotgun.

'It's just that you seem...' I raise my eyebrows and blow out a long breath. '...either depressed or zoned out.'

She turns to me, dead-eyed. 'What do you care?'

'I care that you don't seem happy here. I also think you have more options than you realise.'

Another half-shrug. 'My meds make me spacey. I have to give them time.'

'How long have you been taking them?'

'Five months.'

That explains the unfocused eyes, her listless ways. 'You've given them enough time. What are they for?'

'Depression.'

'Try fixing it another way.'

'Like?'

'Taking control of your life.' My heart's nearly in my mouth. It's reckless, but if I can shake her from her drug-induced apathy, it'll be the breakthrough I need. She only has to help me send an email, then I can help her too.

She sneers. 'I've never had control of my life.'

'You will if you stop people controlling you.'

'Not around here. Sooner you get used to it the better.'

'And end up like you?' I say it kindly, but she looks over her shoulder as if seeking backup. I've overplayed my hand, pushed on by my desperate need to escape.

The Patriarchy strides towards us. I rearrange my face to a more agreeable version of me. He's still butchering Bruce Springsteen, then he performs a cringy air guitar. Hel ignores him. I force a half-arsed smile.

'How're you ladies getting on?'

'We're fine,' I say, while Hel hunches over the keyboard.

'What're you doing?' He peers at the screen.

'She's telling me not to put up with you controlling me.' She says it matter-of-fact, staring glassily at the screen.

I freeze. *Judas*. I've pushed it too far. I've endured his vile advances, submitted to him for the sake of getting through this, and it's all for nothing. I've blown it.

He looms over me. His nostrils flare as he takes an angry breath. I reel back. He grabs me by the arm, fury pouring off him. I'm in the eye of the storm.

'No!' I try pulling away, but he marches me towards the exit. He's stronger, hauling me out. Someone has to help me. 'Let me go,' I yell.

Heads turn. The couple stacking shelves gawp. He's dragging me out, I lock eyes with the woman, imploring her, but he yanks me harder.

'Help me!' I hold her stare, desperate. *Do something*. She can intervene. She looks towards the man and something passes between them, a warning look. She sags and turns away. I stumble, trip over my feet and fall awkwardly. Marty grabs me up, my feet not touching the ground. He bundles me out. 'He's keeping me locked up,' I shout as the door slams shut.

I want to lash out, but one muscled arm encircles me, trapping both my arms as he hauls me onto the path. He covers my mouth with his other hand. I bite down hard.

'Goddammit!' He drops me.

'He says he'll take my child,' I yell, on all fours on the frozen, stony ground. 'He's going to ra—'

'Ungrateful whore.' He pulls me up. I swing a punch at his face with all my might. It's the last thing I remember.

Chapter Sixty-One

Where am I? It's dark. Pain ricochets inside my skull. I go to rub my head and – ow, ow, ow – a red-hot poker jabs inside my skull. I'm on the floor, a storm raging in my ears. Then it comes back to me. Marty hauling me out, then I bit him. He must have thrown me to the ground, the impact knocking me out. Pain radiates from my head as I shift my lying position.

I blink through the darkness, eyes gritty and sore. At least I'm not tied up. *Yet*. It's his arrogance, thinking I'm no match for him. I'll prove him wrong. I pull myself up and lean against the wall until my head stops swimming. Pain engulfs me. Everything hurts. I think of waking up this morning and snuggling into Willow. My heart races, then thuds with dread. I choke back a sob.

Had I known how thoroughly the patriarchy trumps the sisterhood, I'd never have pulled that stunt with Hel. Her bad attitude spoke to my bad attitude, but hers said, 'Go fuck yourself.' My plan for one of these women to help me was flawed from the start. Cheers, girl gang.

Will the female employee report it? But the sheriff will believe Marty, and I caught the look that man gave her, signalling that it's not their problem. If he's her husband, I'm screwed. I'm screwed anyway. No one will help me when they're reliant on the Patriarchy one way or another. Men like Marty and his brother always come out on top.

I work out that he's locked me in an underground room adjoining the food store. Once his paranoia ramps up, will they all sleep in here, lined up on bunk beds, hunkered down for the end days? I bet there are more rooms down here. He's building his own cult, with Willow in his clutches. I can't bear to think of his vision for her if I don't get out alive.

To escape, I'd have to get through two locked doors and out of the barn, which won't happen unless I overpower Marty or someone helps me. I slump against the wall. The bump on my head throbs over a pounding bassline.

A sound from above startles me. I freeze. Light spills through the keyhole and around the edge of the door. Fast tapping footsteps come closer and a key turns in the lock. I haul myself up, one hand pressed against the wall, braced for what comes next. I'm ready. I've got this. I'll come out fighting.

The door creaks open. Dazzled by the light, I blink and cup both hands over my sore eyes. I squint at whoever's silhouetted in the doorway, surrounded by yellow light like a heavenly vision of Jesus. Maybe this really is a celestial kingdom. The figure swims before me, my double vision seesawing. The person comes into focus. It's Faith and she's pointing a gun at me.

Heart in mouth, I shield my eyes from the overhead glare. But nothing will shield me from a gunshot wound. I blink in the dazzling light. My heart's punching out of my chest. I've blown up my whole life and now a crazed influencer might shoot me. Faith, the golden girl of influencers, is aiming a gun at me.

So, Faith, shall we shoot a gun-toting video? Ever the pro, I picture a meme of her, the deadly assassin in a cute outfit. *#LifeGoals!* Her trolls would go crazy for this unseen cut. Her Insta followers would be blindsided by their trad queen. Despite everything, I'm still goggle-eyed at her transformation from sweet earth mother. She keeps presenting herself as a puzzle to solve, which is partly why I'm locked in her cellar.

'How are you?' she says in her sweet voice.

'I don't think much of the accommodation.' My voice is clotted. 'One star on Tripadvisor.'

She tilts her head to one side.

'How's Willow?'

She lowers the gun. 'She's fine. She's at the house. Don't worry.'

'Don't worry? Your husband locks me up, you've taken my child and you're aiming a gun at me.' But hey, don't worry.

She watches me, her face impassive.

'Did he send you?' My voice slurs like a drunk. Am I concussed?

She shakes her head, holding the gun in her gloved hand. Her other hand clutches her egg basket. This would make a great TikTok post.

'How'd you get the key?' I'm surprised she has access to it, given that he's dumped me here like radioactive waste. I arch my aching back from lying on the cold floor and rub my stiff neck.

'I have a spare he doesn't know about.' She hands me a metal drinking bottle. 'I've added glucose so you can stay strong. Don't drink anything Marty gives you.'

'Why not?'

'He has an ancient herbal remedy for Hel. It's quite strong.'

Is he turning me into Hel? 'I thought she was on antidepressants.'

'She is. The herbal concoction makes her more agreeable.'

'It's not working.'

She smooths out the gingham cloth.

Something hits me. 'Have you been drugging *me* all this time? Making me "more agreeable"?'

She looks like a startled fawn. 'It's just my grandma's herbal tea,' she says breathily.

Bullshit.

'It has special properties.'

'Let me go.' I blink at her. '*Please.*'

'He'll know I helped you and it'll put us all in danger.'

'You're my only—'

'God told him to keep us all safe. He's on a mission. I've never seen him like this. He's putting up an electric fence and keeping the gates shut. He's taken all our car keys to protect us from outside forces.' She's talking like she believes his lunatic conspiracy theories. 'He's making Davy in the warehouse go out for our provisions and told him to say we have a virus. We're all trapped.'

This is bad. A virus excuse will only work for a couple of weeks. Then what... will he take us all down in his death cult?

'If you're in here with a key that he kept from you,' I say, 'you can get your car key back.'

'I had this one before it turned bad. You have to trust me.'

Trust her? She's done a number on me by bringing me here and pretending her nutjob husband is a good guy.

'Will you protect Willow?'

She nods quickly. My soul crushes with every thought of her. Can I overpower Faith and grab the gun? I won't shoot her, just lock her in. My fingers itch at the prospect, but she's stronger than she looks, while I can hardly stand. And what's the point if Marty has the place on lockdown? I won't get far on foot before he comes after me. Even if I make it to town, I'll risk someone calling him.

'We don't have much time. He's having a ceremony on Sunday.'

'What day is it?'

'Tuesday.'

Still Tuesday. I can't hold out until Sunday. I'll go crazy.

'He'll let me see her on Sunday?'

'He thinks he'll break you by then.' She places the egg basket beside the door and takes out a chunk of cornbread smeared with butter and apple jam. I let out a mirthless laugh. Even in this dire situation, she's serving up wholesome fare. She leans forward and hands it to me. 'Sharing is caring,' she says.

She's definitely screwing with me now.

'Don't leave crumbs.'

It's a lifeline of sorts, even if she's not letting me out.

'I'm giving you the gun to hide in your coat pocket. If he finds it, he'll go crazy.' She makes strong eye contact. 'Promise me you won't try to escape if I come back... on Willow's life.'

I wince but place a fist on my heart. 'I swear on Willow's life. I won't try to escape if you come back.' *And I swear that if she's harmed, I'll fucking kill you.*

She crouches and places the gun on the ground, then sends it skittering across the floor away from me. 'Hide it from him.'

'I shoot reels, not guns,' I say.

She steps deftly out and locks the door. The light flicks off and I sit motionless. It's not so hopeless if she has a key.

I doubt she'll let me die in here, but who knows? She'll feed me for as long as it takes me to shoot her husband.

My stomach growls from the cornbread I'm holding. My appetite's gone and the Patriarchy wants me weak. But I have to fight back. I bite into it and realise how hungry I am. When I've finished, I crawl along the floor in the direction of the gun. She didn't give me it for self-defence. She wants him dead and knows I'm desperate enough to kill him.

Chapter Sixty-Two

I must have fallen asleep as I startle awake at a noise above me. A sudden line of light appears around the door. My heart seizes up, then stutters to life as the door's flung open. In the blinding light, I know it's Marty before seeing him.

I try to focus while my vision swims. He comes closer and I flinch. My heart's punching out of my chest. He's nursing his bitten hand in a performative way. A plaster covers the bite mark, the skin around it a livid red. He's ready to come at me if I make a move. No chance of that when I'll fall over if I stand up to him.

'Melissa, Melissa. When will you learn?' He looms over me, tone mocking, legs splayed. 'This really won't do, little lady. Have you thought about the bad example you're setting to your child?'

My body's turned to cotton wool, otherwise I'd wring his neck.

'On your knees.' He inspects his hand where I bit him.

I don't move, overcome with a bone-deep chill.

'You heard me. On your knees, ungodly slut, or I'll force you.'

I fight the roiling waves of nausea and fear. If I had the strength, I'd run at him screaming, then scratch his eyes out. Instead, I laboriously shift onto my knees, trying to minimise the wincing pain from every move.

'Don't go thinking anyone'll rescue you after witnessing your tantrum. I explained to them how New York made you mentally unstable. You came here for respite but it's not working, so we'll get you help. We all prayed for you.'

That's right, blame a crazy woman. Crazy woman from the crazy city. The woman who turned away from me can ease her guilt through prayer.

He grips the top of my bumped head. I let out a strangled yelp.

'Lord, help me redeem this Jezebel for refusing to follow her divine path.'

You're the one who needs redeeming, mate. But I'm too fixated on the cutting pain to take in the exorcism.

After a minute that seems like an hour, he releases his grip. 'These are for you.' He motions to a plastic bucket and a metal water bottle that he must have dumped on the floor while I was shielding my eyes from the blinding light. I guess the bucket is my toilet. He's watching me hawk-like, ready to pounce. 'You need to learn some manners before we trust you around decent folk again.'

I want to tell him there are laws against what he's doing. Whether his patriarchal stance will hold up in a law court is another matter. That's if I don't end up dead and buried somewhere I'll never be found.

His voice turns mean. 'I'll break you in like a broodmare. You're gonna buck up your ideas and watch your attitude. When I come back, you'd better be begging me for forgiveness. I'm not allowing you food. Fasting will bring you closer to God. Then we'll talk some more.'

The weaker I am the more I'll yield. If I die in here, someone might still discover my subliminal message implanted in Faith's video. Even if it's too late for me, they can take Willow and charge Marty. I don't want her in foster care, but if she stays here, they'll crush her spirit and turn her into Isiah's teen bride.

'We're praying for your soul,' he says before locking me in.

The knock to my head has fuzzied my brain. It's only when I'm alone again in the dark that I remember the gun. If he pushes me too far, I'll use it, but the cops won't see my side of the story if he's convinced everyone I'm mentally unstable. And if I murder him, I'll lose Willow.

Being kept away from her is ripping out my heart. All my fault for coming here on a futile mission. I wanted the inside track on his family's misogyny, and now I'm locked up because of a half-arsed plan to dig for dirt, then take sloppy revenge.

The case against Asher and Marty is thin on facts, only what's on public record. The rest I know from my dad. Marty lied about Amy to absolve his brother. After her suicide, the authorities brushed it under the carpet, since why ruin the life of an upstanding young Mormon male?

Has her suicide stayed with him? We all do regrettable things when we're young, but unless you're a sociopath, if your actions led a girl to suicide, then your older self would feel remorse. I didn't expect a tearful confession, but if he'd alluded to it when I'd prompted him on the drive into town, if he'd shown a trace of guilt at the terrible thing his brother had involved him in, it would have been something, for Amy's sake. He didn't care. Of course he didn't care. Colluding against a dead girl was ancient history, but not for me.

I open the water bottle and sniff inside, then I take a tiny sip. It's bitter. Definitely spiked, but my dry throat and raging headache need water. I remember the soothing effect of Faith's tea, so I drink it and let the anger, fear and pain melt into exhaustion.

I doze on and off, sometimes slumped against the wall, other times lying on the cold, hard floor, my sore head resting on my folded scarf. I slip into a fever dream of a forced wedding, but it's not me getting married, it's Willow, a child bride. I wake up sobbing and shaking, then I startle at the metallic clunk of a key turning in the lock.

—

Marty was against taking on someone else's child, but once he saw how pliable Willow was, it only took a mild suggestion of her becoming a wife for Isiah, and what do you know? God told him to take them both on. The Lord moves in mysterious ways. Marty liked the idea of expanding the gene pool, and it makes sense for him to control her upbringing along with the other kids.

Obviously Melissa would never comply, that's why I've been giving her my grandma's herbal concoction. It's a gift from God, helping us wives stay agreeable. It stops newcomers pushing against the regime until they're entrenched. I had to keep Melissa on board while we indoctrinated Willow.

I microdose myself, just enough to keep me sweet while staying present. I even slip a daily dose to Marty, heavily concealed in his oatmeal and honey, to take the edge off him. But it sends him on these ridiculous flights of fancy. And no more herbal remedy for Melissa now she's imprisoned with the gun. I need her angry.

Chapter Sixty-Three

Marty returns. I must be feeling stronger as my instinct is to come out punching, but I switch to trad wife mode, weak from fasting and meek from the religious experience, even though Faith has smuggled food in. He crouches beside me and plants his hand on top of my head.

'Dear Lord, provide atonement to Melissa for she has sinned and falls short before Your glory.' His eyes are closed.

My fingers stroke the gun through the fabric of my parka.

'Though her sins be as scarlet, they shall be white as snow.'

Ooh, poetic. I'll save that one for my headstone.

'Help her to repent her sins.'

How easy would it be to take him out? In my mind's eye, I aim and fire. *Bang. Splat.*

'...and help me, as Your earthly lord and saviour...'

That's right, holy man. Use your God to oppress me. Brag about breaking me like a skittish mare. Let me know when you're done.

'...steer her through repentance in order to heal and become our devout sister. Amen.'

Would I rather be knocked out or endure his endless sermonising? Are his prayers worse than concussion from his violence? Tough call.

The gun is an ominous presence in my deep pocket. If he gets handsy, he might find it and I'd have no choice but to shoot him. If I shoot him, he'll have to die, otherwise the cops will believe him over me. I want to kill him. I really do, but even in self-defence, I'll risk jail time.

Marty brings another bottle of drinking water, which I leave this time. I'd like to send it to a lab and find out what's in it. I stay in the far corner, not wanting him near me while I'm hiding the gun. If he touches me up, I'll slip off the parka before he notices its bulk and weight. Meanwhile, I pretend to be weaker today than yesterday, which pleases him.

Sometime later, Faith returns. I'm seething that she can sneak in here but didn't sneak me out before it came to this. She gives me a thermos of warm milk with blended oats and honey, which I drink.

'How's Willow?' I say, my heart contracting. 'Has she asked about me?'

'Of course. We're saying you have a virus and you're in quarantine.'

'The only thing she'll catch is rational thinking.'

She doesn't reply. Is she armed too? If not, it's a big risk when I have a gun and a desperate need to escape this hellhole.

'Tell her I love her.' My voice is thick with emotion.

'I'll tell her.'

'I'm scared of where this is going... what he'll do.'

She toys with a loose thread on her pinafore dress. Monster. I could never keep another parent from their child.

'He's crazy. Someone has to raise the alarm, for all our sakes,' I say.

She tips Marty's spiked water into her empty smoothie cup. 'You'll be out soon, God willing.'

'When?'

'He's bringing the ceremony forward to Friday, after the workers finish for the weekend.' She replaces the spiked drink with glucose water from her own metal bottle. 'That's two days. You can hang on, right?'

Two days shaved off my jail term. She calls it the ceremony, not a wedding. I wonder if she even recognises Alice and Hel as her sister-wives. Before leaving, she gives me a paper bag of pecans. It's like she's fattening me for market or giving me strength to fight.

I've made it this far without shooting him. I ache for Willow too much to risk it. I don't care about the fake wedding and baptism. I just want her. I hope my appearance won't scare her, since I'll look a fright after a battering from Marty and three long days and nights in here. But she's been told I'm sick, so that'll explain it.

I have no window or any way to tell the time, but on what I assume is the next day, it feels like I really do have a virus. Perhaps it's keto flu from restricted eating, combined with lying on a hard floor and existing in a state of fear, despair and blind panic. Two days feel like two months.

In my reduced state, Marty comes and kneels before me. I stiffen, painfully aware of the gun in my pocket. Before I can shrug off my parka, he takes both my hands to guide me into a kneeling position which he mirrors before me. He sandwiches my hands in a prayer position. I'm praying he doesn't find the gun.

'Dear Lord, please exorcise the demons within Melissa. Give her faith and wisdom to know the right path.'

The right path to escape.

The God botherer speaks fast, fervour in his voice. I squint one eye open to spy him, deep in the prayer zone, eyes closed, face scrunched in the effort of channelling God. I imagine shooting him point-blank when he lets go of my hands, but I'd be covered in his blood and brain matter. Then I couldn't see Willow while dripping in blood, even if I could find her.

'Allow her to know she has found eternal love and companionship. Help her love to grow as we are sealed together in these end days and for all eternity.'

My jailer's voice is tremulous and loud before his congregation of one. He's shuddering in what I assume is a fake religious experience, spewing fire and brimstone. It's raining down on me, an apocalyptic storm. I picture him spontaneously combusting, leaving a pile of smouldering ash. He lets go of me to hold one hand up to the ceiling like an evangelical preacher, then slaps it on top of my head. I flinch. His fingers dig into my aching skull.

'Demons begone!' He's full-on televangelist now, his voice taking on the twang of a Deep South preacher. 'Dear Lord, guide Melissa towards the light. Melissa, have you found the light?'

'Um… yes?' I mumble, not remotely on board with his batshittery.

'Thank You, Lord, for bringing Melissa back to us. Thank You for bestowing me with divine skills to guide her, for she will be joined to me in Your heavenly name. Amen.'

The man is possessed.

Chapter Sixty-Four

After Marty exorcised my demons yesterday, he left without feeling me up. That's one advantage of his pious mode, although I'm a sure thing for after the ceremony. And today's the day.

He turns up in his usual ranch wear, bringing me a covered bowl of porridge with honey and yogurt swirled in. 'Your wedding breakfast. But first, we pray.' He sets down the bowl, a spoon balanced on top.

'Dear Lord, we thank You on this day for the bond of marriage and Your eternal blessing. Thank You for granting patience and understanding to Melissa. Give me the strength and wisdom to guide her along her new path.'

He paces around the small space while I eat. He might have spiked the food, so I'll only have half, despite wanting to wolf the lot. I pick up on his manic intensity.

'I see the signs,' he mutters.

'What signs?'

'The storm of fire is nearly upon us.' He walks out, distracted, locking me in. His poor, sweet children. What'll happen to them?

I wonder if he'll come back, now he's off fighting satanic forces, but ages later he returns with Faith. He stands by the door while she crouches before me. 'Oh, honey,' she soothes. 'Let's get you over to the house. You can take a shower and I'll dress you.' She helps me stand, then runs a hand down the side of my parka to locate the gun. She's smart enough to know I'm right-handed and would keep it on that side. She clings to my right arm, having me lean on her for strength.

We come out into thin daylight. I rapid-blink and squint in the natural light, flooded with relief at my release, even if my prison is just a change of scenery. I survey the lonely landscape, looking for raging fires after Marty prophesising the end of the world, but there's been light snowfall. Faith guides me to the house, Marty on my other side, still wired with his strange intensity.

'Where are the children?' I ask.

'In school,' he says. 'We're having the ceremony after we close up the business at four.'

When Faith and I go inside the ranch house, he stays outside and locks us in. We exchange a dark look. I bet she'll have a key to get out. It's just a case of keeping me contained, since they can't have the wild mare bolting.

She nods to the table where a glass of milk waits for me. I sit down and drink it, infantilised as if I'm one of her kids. Before this week, I hadn't drunk a glass of milk since my childhood. She goes to the Aga and brings me a cheese toastie she's been keeping warm.

'What's the plan?' I ask between mouthfuls.

'School finishes soon and Alice will have the kids. I'll get you ready for the ceremony. It starts around five. I have a dress you can wear.'

Sitting in Faith's warm kitchen eating hot food after three days in the bunker would have me in raptures if it weren't for the sickly dread that's seeped into me. I've no idea how today will pan out, only that my actions will affect Willow's life for better or worse. Either I'll finish the day in bed with that monster, or I'll finish it off once and for all.

Chapter Sixty-Five

Faith ushers me to the bathroom to take a shower. 'Use whatever you want,' she says, hanging a velvety-soft bathrobe in dove grey on the back of the door. I catch sight of myself in the mirror. A woman with a gaunt face stares back. She's wild-haired with feral eyes haunted by dark shadows.

I stand under the jet of hot water for the longest time. It soothes the constant throb in my head and the ache in my neck that travels down my spine. I try reviving myself so I look normal for Willow. Not long until school finishes. I wrap myself in the soft bathrobe, my skin tingling and fragrant from the expensively natural lavender products.

Faith sits me at the dressing table in her bedroom and blasts my hair with her hairdryer, styling it with her fingers. I close my scratchy eyes, wishing I could curl up with Willow and escape into sleep.

Faith applies make-up for a surprisingly dewy effect. But you can see the darkness in my eyes, the shadows beneath them.

'Just need a little concealer.'

'You're good at that...'

'Thank you.'

'...Concealing the dark reality.'

She smooths it across my under-eye shadows. 'What do you think?' she asks breezily, smiling at me in the mirror.

I look like the world's most murderous bride.

'No time for a manicure.' She peers at my fingernails that are as ragged as my nerves.

She's laid out a matching set of underwear from my chest of drawers, the one I used to wear on dates. I wriggle into it, and she reaches for a long white gown on a padded hanger. This whole situation is surreal. She's acting like a close friend or sister, helping the giddy bride get ready. She's changed into a billowy white cheesecloth number, last seen online when she drifted through her lavender field.

The wedding dress is ridiculously stunning, with a silk bodice and full long skirt. It's fit for a Disney princess waltzing up the aisle to her Prince Charming, not a doom-laden bride in a forced marriage. I look at the framed photo on the dressing table of her and the abuser on their wedding day. It's the same dress.

'Um.' I scratch my neck. 'Do you have something simpler?' I'd expected a prairie dress, not her own wedding gown from the supposedly happier occasion at Salt Lake Temple.

'Marty wants you in this,' she says without emotion.

I doubt she's sentimental, given that she'd like him blasted to death. With an air of resignation, I step into the ornate skirt and slide my arms into the silken sleeves. She does up the mother-of-pearl buttons that run from my lower back to my neck.

'Pretty,' she murmurs, leading me to the full-length mirror. I've lost weight, highlighted by the snug fit of the dress. It's more fitted than anything I've worn since coming here, and it drags on the floor because she's a little taller than me. She takes a pair of heeled ankle boots in beige from her walk-in wardrobe.

I peer at the size marked inside. 'They're two sizes too big.'

She stuffs some kind of cushion wadding in the toe. I sigh and wordlessly try them on, demonstrating how hard it is to walk in them. 'My church shoes are better. No one will see them under the dress.'

'They'll do,' she says.

'Why? Because you don't want me to run?'

She looks at me, head cocked. 'Where will you run to?'

It's what I call 'Faith logic', designed to shut me down with a Bambi-eyed look and an innocent remark. She knows I'm on to her, but I'm playing her game as well as his until I can break free. Soon. Please let it be soon. Meanwhile, I'm their puppet, dressed up and made to perform.

'Your church shoes are flat. You need heels or you'll trip over the dress.'

I'd rather walk on tiptoes in my own shoes, but this serves her twisted agenda. The foofy dress is another barrier to my escape.

'Will Willow come back to the cabin tonight?' I need to prepare her for this madness.

'It's your wedding night. She'll stay here another night.'

At that moment, I hear the familiar shouts and whooping of the boys. They're out of school. 'Is Willow coming back?' I'm itching to see her. If only we could skip the ceremony. I'm tired of it all, bone-tired and worn down.

'The girls are going to Alice's barn to get ready for their baptism, and the boys will get ready in your cabin with Marty.'

At least Willow can be happy about the fake baptism, although the wedding is a lot to deal with when I haven't prepared her. My eyes scan through the window, but the kids are elsewhere. 'Can I see her before the ceremony?'

'We have to stay here until Marty collects us. He's locked us in.'

'But you have a key.'

She shakes her head sadly. 'He changed the locks. Only he keeps the keys now.'

'Doesn't he trust you?' I know I'm a loose cannon, but the escalation with security is more than that.

'He's turning unhinged. Paranoid. Word got around that Alice is pregnant and there's no daddy. People are talking. It's awkward at church, so I guess we're not going back.'

I doubt the church buys into his vision as the new Messiah. I think of Dinah trying to befriend me. Did she have an inkling when she said us ladies should stick together?

'He says we're self-sufficient now.'

I sigh and rub at my temples. The odds of getting away are diminishing if we're all confined here. 'You're telling me he doesn't trust you to drive your own car or have the keys to your home? That's controlling. It's abuse.'

'That's why I gave you the gun. You're the only one who stands up to him. You're not safe.'

Which reminds me... I check the dress for pockets, but it would spoil the line of the delicate fabric. I needn't worry about her foisting the gun on me, which I'd never fire near the kids.

'Aren't you worried for the children?'

'Of course, but they're his children too.'

'Willow's not.'

'She is. The ceremony is to seal your family with ours. We're all one family for all eternity.'

Zac would love that. I'm on hyper-alert scanning outside. 'Why can't I see her?'

'It's what he wants.'

'What's wrong?' Panic sounds in my voice. 'Is she okay?'

She tells me Willow's fine as Marty comes striding towards us in a white onesie with short sleeves. What the fuck? If the situation weren't dire, I'd laugh.

'What's he wearing?'

'It's a baptismal outfit. Come.' She tugs at my wrist and positions us a few paces inside the door, as if presenting ourselves to him. I remind myself to pick my battles. I've nearly got Willow back and can't jeopardise it.

He unlocks the door and steps inside. 'Well, looky here.'

Faith presents me to him in a ta-da gesture. She gives zero fucks that he's marrying me. One more woman to service his needs.

The thick fabric of his outfit is dripping wet. He must have done the baptism without us. He locks us in and kicks off his cowboy boots. 'I'll take a quick shower.'

Faith follows him, while I stand at the window looking for Willow. Everyone's indoors somewhere. Maybe the girls are having showers before the wedding. Faith returns with a dusky pink coat. It's better than my grubby parka which smells musty after nights of sleeping on the bunker floor. She helps me into it and I'm aware of a weightiness in the right hand pocket.

'Not the gun.' I'm too desperate to be armed. It's dangerous.

I was a good girl who became a good wife. But I've had it. There's gossip in town. I need to take charge before the rumours move online. Divorce will damage my brand, but what if I'm a trad widow? So tragic! Marty has to die.

Chapter Sixty-Six

'You wanna practise aiming it?' Faith asks in a sweet whisper.

'You want a shoot-out in front of everyone? Is that what you want?' I whisper back, staring hard at her.

She turns away and I go to take the gun and press it on her, but Marty appears in his Sunday best, hair still wet, tucking in his shirt beneath the jacket.

'How do I look?' he asks, without commenting on the bride in her exquisite gown. He raises his palms heavenward, Jesus with open arms.

'Like our beloved prophet,' Faith says in awed reverence.

'Thank you.'

Lay it on thick, traddie. He's dumb enough to accept the shameless ego plumping.

'I think we have a wedding to go to,' he says.

Showtime. He holds out his arm, like the father of the bride. He'll walk me up the aisle, perform the ceremony and become my fake husband in a multitasking feat.

I take his arm with no resistance. Faith takes my other arm, on the gun side. Will we recreate *The Handmaid's Tale*, the wife holding on to the handmaid while the husband rapes her? I grimace. Outside, the wind whips my hair in my face. I breathe a lungful of cold air, needing it to revive me while my insides burn with silent rage.

Marty walks with righteous confidence. Why didn't they drown him in the baptism plunge pool? With teamwork, they could've held him under. I catch sight of Isiah and Martin, having a cowboy shoot-out in the distance. My gown trails in the dirt of the stony path, the skirt already coated in ranch dust. A faint buzzing hovers on the edge of my consciousness, like someone strimming grass in the distance, but barely perceptible. Must be inside my ears, a lingering side effect of the head injury.

We go in the schoolhouse to the hard silence of Zina and Alice. Are they angry with me or him? They're wearing similar white cheesecloth dresses to Faith, reluctant bridesmaids. Zina doesn't meet my eye. Does she disapprove, since he's 'married' to her daughter? Alice's head is bowed as if already praying, or letting it slide along with everything else. They knew he had me locked up for days until I was crazed with desperation, taking the path of no resistance. Any one of them could have called the police. But they're world-class at tuning out.

The baptism pool takes up one corner, puddles of water around it.

'Where are the children?' I ask.

'With Helen,' he says, walking me to the wooden lectern that's been added since the church service last Sunday, a makeshift pulpit for our Messiah's sermons. A huge wooden crucifix hangs on the wall behind it.

'I want to see Willow.' She doesn't belong with that weirdo.

'She needed a hot shower and a change of clothes after the baptism.'

I tell myself it's for the best, so she doesn't witness this screwed-up ceremony. But frustration bites. How do I even know she's okay when I don't trust a single person here?

'Take her coat,' he says to Faith.

She slides it from my shoulders and stands with the other two women.

Marty holds his palms aloft, our blond Jesus. 'Sisters, the world outside our home is lost to darkness.' His voice is tremulous. 'Yet fear not, as I have been chosen to guide us towards the divine light. You too have been chosen to serve me in these end days. My word is the word of God.'

A throat-clearing cough comes from Zina. I try to catch her eye, but she's focused on the wooden floor. The four of us can overpower him, but I'm on my own in resisting his bullshit. Surely Zina knows this is a bastardised version of church. I guess she approves of the top-tier scaremongering.

'Today we strengthen our bonds by welcoming our sister Melissa and our daughter Willow.'

My daughter. Mine, not yours.

He takes my hand and guides me so I'm facing him. The others watch while he preaches, mostly at me. I look passively at him, but my mind is elsewhere. I imagine escaping to a Californian beach with Willow, or taking her to England. So easy to take flight in my mind, but I have to keep acting. It's possible to fool him, since Faith does it all the time. He only wants complicit women, and hammy acting doesn't matter.

'Melissa,' he commands.

I snap back to attention.

'Do you proclaim that your love for me is pure and unconditional?'

I cast a sideways glance at Faith, who gives a tiny nod.

'I do.' Like fuck I do.

'Do you swear that your faith in me, the chosen one, is without limits?'

'I do.'

'Do you promise to obey me, your master, in all things?'

'I do.' I guess this is a one-way street.

'Do you embrace your role as my divine vessel?'

Get real, you abuser. It takes every fibre of my being not to shove him away. I picture him falling backwards onto the lectern, smashing his head open, blood staining through his pure white shirt. If only. He narrows his eyes on me, tightening his grip on my hands.

'I do.' *I want to kill you. I do. I do. I do.*

After fervent prayers and hymns, he slides a plain gold wedding band on my finger and leans forward to kiss my forehead. The others stand in silence, because what would they say?

'Ladies, will you return to our children?'

Zina looks me in the eye. 'Wickedness was never happiness. Ye must repent and be born again.' Not the warmest of wedding congratulations. She and Alice file out.

Does she mean I'm wicked for having a child out of wedlock? *Bitch, you're wrong.* Willow's my biggest source of joy, and my 'wickedness' brought happiness. Zina's the wicked one, along with Marty the false Messiah. She won't save me from this horror show. She thinks it's what I need.

'Don't forget your coat.' Faith points to the pink coat on a chair by the door. I stare blankly at her. She follows the others. I guess there's no celebration.

Tension crackles. I shrink inside my wedding gown, a sacrificial lamb. Marty runs his fingers through my hair and kisses me on the lips. My heart rattles under my ribs. The kiss turns urgent. Will he demand sex in the schoolhouse church? He's twisted enough to consummate it at the altar.

I hope my dad's not watching from the afterlife while history repeats itself. Amy's death plunged him into a depression that never left. Alcohol became his medication of choice until the night he drank two bottles of whiskey and threw himself off a bridge. Two members of my family died as a result of Asher and Marty's actions. Ever since Dad died, Zac blamed Asher and was eaten away with a need for revenge.

Chapter Sixty-Seven

Marty pulls me to the lectern, before the open Bible. He stands behind me, breathing heavily on the back of my neck, and then he starts kissing it.

'Don't be too proud to submit. Pride is a sin.'

So is rape. Waves of revulsion sweep through me. I cling to the lectern, stomach lurching, a tight knot of agony filling my chest as he murmurs scripture in a fevered voice. Any of the kids could walk in. I'm itching to batter him to death, Bible-bash him with the heavy one on the lectern.

'You gurna have another baby, honey.' Spoken like a true redneck.

Monster.

'Not here,' I say demurely. 'This is a place of God.'

He walks towards the door. 'Let's go.'

I wipe away a stray tear. 'Will we celebrate with the others?' I ask in a small voice.

He doesn't answer. I pull on the coat, the gun a weighty presence in the pocket. I follow him out and scan around, but it's just us in the eerie stillness. He takes my hand in his firm grip and strides away from the cluster of homes. 'Come with me.'

'I want to see Willow.' I'm pulled along with him striding ahead.

'Do as I say.'

He's not going to let me see her. What's he done with her? I dig in my heels and stiffen against his forward motion. His head whips around, face thunderous, like he's about to slap me. I resist the impulse to recoil and instead adopt Faith's fawning ways.

'Are you okay?' I say in a sweet, soft voice, fighting every instinct to lash out. 'I want us to be okay.'

He lets out a sigh, ready to reason with me, the difficult one.

'I'd love to see Willow.' I hide the alarm in my voice. 'We can tell her we're married.'

There's a moment of silence where he's working out how best to control me. I hear that buzzing in my ears again.

'When you earn my trust.' He turns and pulls me along. 'I need to be satisfied you've learned your lesson.'

Then I realise. He's throwing me back in the bunker. No way am I going back. No fucking way. I try digging in, pulling back against his iron grip but I stumble and fall.

'What've you done to her?' I yell, kicking my legs, trying to lash out. He drags me along the ground by my arm, the stony path ripping the dress fabric, scraping against my legs. Pain tears into me. One boot catches on a stone that drags it from my foot. 'Let me go!' I scream.

He hauls me upright and carries me like a sack of wheat with my arms clamped to my sides.

Adrenaline surges. 'Your murdering rapist of a brother is bad enough. But it runs in the family, and you're worse.'

He stops dead, drops me to the ground and looks down on me, eyes glinting. He lunges at me, grabbing my wrist hard. 'What did you say?'

'Your fucking lowlife brother raped my aunt.' I blurt it out to buy time, the longer I'm out in the open the better. Anything to stay out of the bunker. If I shout loud enough, one of his brainwashed flock might have second thoughts about their collusion.

'You crazy bitch,' he snarls. 'What're you talking about?'

'Your brother dated Amy Fairbrock. He raped her and the two of you lied about it. You said she was the liar and she'd come on to him, but you weren't even there.'

He scratches the side of his head, still clutching my wrist with his other hand. 'Oh, yeah. I remember now. That harlot. You'd better watch your mouth. Unbecoming female behaviour runs in *your family*.'

I launch myself at him in a burst of rage. I swing a punch at his face, putting all my might into it. He stumbles back, letting go of me. I scramble to my feet and run. I take a few strides, but he rugby tackles me to the ground. I fall flat, stones and gravel grazing my chin, cutting into my palms.

'Watch your mouth, harlot.' He's on top of me, spitting out the words. 'My brother's no murderer. I'll make you sorry for that.' He yanks me up again and pain sears down my back.

I scream. He slaps me across the face. I stumble and fall, but he still drags me by my arm. My feet scramble for purchase, one bare foot, the other boot threatening to come loose. I struggle to find my footing to stop him taking the skin off my shins. I make it upright, stumbling to keep up.

The gun is in my right pocket and he's dragging me by my right arm. I can't shoot him left-handed. He'll see and knock it from my hand. I gasp for air. My eyes turn heavenward. And there it is, a drone hovering around the treeline. Hasn't he noticed it?

I squint at it, eagle-eyed and predatory. Is it monitoring us? It must be, since I heard it buzzing when we went into the schoolhouse. From my knowledge of drones, it probably isn't recording audio, but I scream anyway. I wish it were military grade with the power to take Marty out. I dig in my heels again, leaning away from him, flailing to escape his clutches. I try yanking my arm from his grip, pulling it this way and that to show the drone operator my desperation to escape. *Call the cops, drone guy*.

'You little bitch.' He grabs me in an armlock. I shriek. He pins my arms to my sides to manhandle me back to the bunker. Fear and fury combine. Propelled by rage, I twist my body and slam the pointed heel of Faith's remaining boot into his junk, kicking out with more force than I knew I possessed.

'Arrrgh!' He drops me like a lead weight and doubles over.

In a heap on the ground, I go to scrabble upright, but he lurches forward and grabs a fistful of the wedding gown, holding me in place. Then he looks up, spotting the drone. While he's distracted, I make a grab for the gun in the deep pocket of the coat that's twisted around me.

His attention snaps back to me. He yanks off my remaining boot and starts dragging me by one ankle, his face a determined snarl. Ignoring the gravel tearing at my skin, my hand closes over the gun handle. I've one chance to shoot him before he snatches the gun. I pull it out, my finger finding the trigger. The shot rings out. He falls backwards. I drag myself up to kneeling. His body splays out. Blood everywhere from a shot to his chest. Screaming. It's me who's screaming.

Chapter Sixty-Eight

He's splayed out and I spiral into an abyss, my mind disconnecting. It's too much. It's all too much.

Faith's voice cuts through. Urgent footsteps come closer. 'Keep the kids away,' she shouts to someone. I'm pulled back to reality as she stops and leans over Marty. 'Looks dead,' she says, matter-of-fact. She deftly plucks a bunch of keys from his trouser pocket, then helps me up.

I clutch at the sides of my face. 'Does he have a phone?'

'He left it behind. Come.' She heads back to the house.

'Wait.' He makes a throaty sound. He's still alive.

Blood spurts from his mouth and streams down the side of his face. She leans forward, hands on hips, peering at him like he's a dead bug. He takes a last gurgling breath as she looks stonily down. His glassy eyes stare heavenward. *Forget it, dipshit. You're not going up there.*

'Let's go,' she says, all business. 'He locked my phone in a drawer. We have to call nine one one.'

I stumble after her. 'You make the call. I'll go to Willow.'

'She can't see you like that.' She glances back at me.

My filthy, torn wedding dress will take some explaining. Then I look down and see I'm covered in his blood.

'You can't shower until the cops and medics have checked you over, but you can change into something of mine. They'll take the dress. It'll help prove self-defence.'

'How?'

'It shows you struggled and he was unhinged to force a wedding on you when he's married to me.'

Inside the ranch house, Faith goes in search of her phone and I sit dazedly in a dining chair. My head swims. I'm shaking all over and lean forward, hands planted on my knees as I try to breathe through it. Faith comes out, phone clamped to her ear, answering questions. Then the distant wail of a police siren gets louder. We exchange a glance.

Her eyes are wide. 'Someone called it in already.'

Blue lights flash in the distance, and she goes out there. A minute later, a cop bursts in.

'Hands in the air.'

I freeze.

'I said put your hands in the air *now*.'

My shaky hands rise above my head. The cop approaches and handcuffs me. I must look like some madwoman, hair all over the place, in a blood-spattered wedding dress.

'Where's Faith?' I ask. She'll help clear it up.

'She's gone with my partner to the victim.'

It's okay, I tell myself. I just have to explain. A man died, and they need to investigate. The cop leads me out to the car and puts me in the back. Alice watches anxiously from the doorway, but no sign of any kids. It sinks in that I won't see Willow until I can prove my innocence. But surely that's a formality. I might spend the night in a police cell, but it can be cleared up.

Another police car pulls up behind us with a lone officer behind the wheel. The two of them confer, talk on a handheld radio, and the one who cuffed me opens the door and reads me my rights, including the right to an attorney. I definitely need an attorney. He gets back in the front seat. 'I'm driving you to county jail.'

This is bad. Really bad. At the jail, they take my fingerprints and mugshot. My thoughts veer wildly. They'll release the photo, then how long will it take the internet sleuths to notice I'm wearing Faith's wedding dress? Mugshots are usually head and shoulders, but given my striking attire, I bet they'll show me against the height chart in my bloodied bridal gown.

It's several hours later when I stop telling myself the arrest is a formality. That's when I'm told a witness said I was deranged and stole Faith's wedding gown. I also stole the gun from Marty's locked bedroom cabinet. The only prints found on the gun were Marty's and mine. And that's not the only confusing aspect. I don't recall pulling the trigger.

Chapter Sixty-Nine

I tell them over and over that I didn't shoot Marty.

'Then who did?' a different officer asks on Friday night.

'I don't know. But he had a lot of guns.'

'You were in a fight with him. You had a gun in your hand.'

'I wasn't in a fight. I was defending myself from him. He wanted to lock me up again and rape me.' I'm certain the gun didn't fire. There wasn't a kickback from the bullet discharging. I didn't even aim the bloody thing, so no way did I shoot him in the chest. I keep telling them this. I know I should shut up for my own sake, but I won't get an attorney until I appear before a judge on Monday. If I can somehow set the record straight, I might get out before then.

'What about the drone?' I suddenly remember. 'Has anyone come forward with the footage?'

'What drone?'

'I heard it flying overhead when Marty and Faith took me from their ranch house to the marriage ceremony in the schoolhouse. It was up there again when he tried forcing me back to the underground bunker to lock me up.'

He looks blank.

'If someone operated the drone,' I keep on, 'it might've been Hel, another sister-wife. She did computer stuff. She's the only adult living there who I didn't see yesterday, so she was somewhere behind the scenes. If it was her, the drone could've been dumped in the forest, but can someone look for the footage?'

'We'll look into it.' His voice is flat. I store it up for my attorney, my non-existent attorney, my 'I can't afford an attorney, so they'll be shit' attorney.

'Because it'll show what happened, which'll save time proving who shot him.'

'We have your cell phone. What's the code to unlock it?'

I try not to look stricken. If they go through my deleted messages, they'll find the threatening ones from Zac. And I bet he's messaged me since Marty took the phone.

'I need an attorney first.'

'We can compel you to give us access. Failure to comply can result in a fine or imprisonment.'

I need to hold them off, since the case against me is bad enough. 'I'm being set up. They confiscated my phone when Marty locked me up, so they might have planted false evidence. I'll wait for an attorney. Will you release me tonight?'

'You'll spend the night here.'

'What about Willow?' My voice trembles. I'm losing it. 'It's not safe for her if the family blame me for his death.'

'She's here and she won't be going back to the ranch.'

'Will you let me out on bail so I can look after her?'

'She'll go into an emergency foster home.'

I crumple, slumping onto the table, head in my hands. It's killing me that I can't keep her safe all the time I'm locked up. 'Please.' I lift my head. 'She'll be scared without me. I've no money and no transport so I'm not a flight risk. I promise I'll stay put.'

He looks away. It's what I'd dreaded, but I cling to the hope of straightening it out.

Back in my concrete cell, I pull my knees to my chest and sob into them. Then I pace around and try to see the positives. He's dead. I didn't shoot him. Whoever the drone operator is, they have footage.

A different cop interviews me on Saturday morning. 'Tell me about Amy Fairbrock.'

My heart sinks.

'She was your aunt. Is that correct?'

I swallow. 'She died before I was born. What's she got to do with this?'

'We've been informed that you came to the ranch to get revenge on Marty Eversen. Is that true?'

'I'm not answering any more questions until I have an attorney.' I've been co-operating in the hope of them releasing me, but there's no chance now.

'A witness heard you accuse Marty Eversen of colluding in your aunt's murder. Can you tell me about that?'

'Who said that? Was it Faith?' So much for her promise of paying for a lawyer to defend me.

'She says you targeted them and befriended her. You made her feel sorry for you, so they offered you a job.'

It's true that I targeted them, but not for murder. Now the police know about Amy, it gives me a motive and puts a different slant on my self-defence plea. I'm being set up as a madwoman on a murderous mission. But I didn't go there to kill anyone.

'Melissa, you need to tell me what happened.'

'Faith's set me up. I need a lawyer.' I am so fucked.

Back in my cell, terror consumes me. I could get life and Willow will be damaged for life, abandoned to the care system.

On Sunday, I don't expect to be interviewed, but the officer who first questioned me turns up and walks me to the interview room. Is he going to brief me before court tomorrow? I wish someone would bring me my own clothes to wear to court, so I don't appear before a judge wearing standard-issue jail sweats. But nobody at the ranch will help me. Faith's the ranch mafia queen and the others have closed ranks behind her.

'How's my daughter?' I ask when we're seated at the table.

'We'll get to her in a moment,' he says grimly. 'There's been a development. We have preliminary evidence to support your account of what happened.'

Oh thank God. If I weren't sitting down, my legs would buckle beneath me.

'We're waiting for ballistics analysis, but given aspects such as the angle and distance of the shot, the entry and exit wound, it's likely the victim was shot from further away. We know from blood spatter on your clothing that you were in close range. And it appears he was shot with a different firearm to the pistol you were carrying.'

That's why I don't remember firing it. Someone else shot him. Relief washes over me.

'Will I get out today?'

He nods and my heart surges.

'Where's Willow? I need to get her back.'

'You won't get her back just yet.'

'Why?' I search his face in desperation.

'It appears your daughter was the shooter.'

Milking Myrtle used to be quiet time for planning my videos. Something about the rhythmical action made the ideas flow along with the milk. But lately I've been planning my husband's death, covering every eventuality.

Willow was always central to the plan. I instructed Zina to bring her to God, and for the older kids to show her the way to Jesus, knowing it would drive Melissa crazy. I knew all along that Willow would help my cause, I just didn't know how much until it all came together at the end.

Chapter Seventy

The blood drains from me. 'She's seven.' I tell the cop. 'She's tiny. She's never seen a real gun. No way could she shoot a moving target from a distance and kill them with one shot.'

'It's not impossible. Little kids have killed plenty of times. Another witness says Willow saw him dragging you and she was trying to stop him. The firearm's recoil sent it flying out of her hands and she fell backwards. Then she ran and hid. Her prints are on the gun.'

What? Had I known, I'd have confessed. 'What'll happen to her?'

'She's in protective custody, which means people are taking care of her welfare. We're mindful of her age. She's under the age of criminal responsibility and can't be charged.'

That's something, but she'll be scarred from the trauma. 'Surely you don't believe this? Faith tried setting me up. I had ample opportunities and I made it clear that I wouldn't kill him. Then the evidence shows I didn't do it, so she blames my child instead?'

'We'll be looking at the child protection issue, and we're talking to the adults in the situation regarding how your daughter came to have access to a gun. Did you take any additional guns from the ranch?'

'I didn't take any guns at all. Faith kept forcing the handgun on me. I had a disagreement with Marty a few weeks ago when he was teaching his eleven-year-old to shoot. I made it clear I thought it dangerous and irresponsible.'

'Did anyone show your daughter how to shoot?'

'No.'

He stands up. 'That's all for now.'

'What about the drone?'

'There's no evidence of a drone or any footage at the crime scene.'

I sigh. Did I imagine the drone? Maybe I have brain damage from the head injury. 'When can I see Willow?'

'There's a process to go through with Child and Family Services. They'll be in contact, and we still need to finish our investigation. If it's found you didn't shoot the gun, then the prosecutor can dismiss the charges against you. There may be charges of negligence regarding your child having access to a firearm.'

'Did she actually say she'd shot him?'

'I can't give you details just yet. We have a lot to establish.'

My head's spinning. How could I not know my child was within sight, brandishing a gun? But I didn't see her in the manic blur of chaos, fighting off that brute.

They release me. I've no idea where to go, since I have no money on me and no phone or laptop, so I can't contact anyone. But they hand over my bag, not seen since Marty stole it. Someone stuffed it with some of my clothes and toiletries. My bank cards are in my purse, so I head to the nearest cheap motel where I check in for one night.

The next morning, after my worst night yet, I drink complimentary bad coffee from the motel's percolator and ready myself to find legal representation. Then a cop walks in and says he's driving me to the police department, without saying why. He deposits me in an interview room, where I expect the worst.

The officer from yesterday bursts in, looking triumphant. Is that good or bad? He sits down and angles his laptop towards me on the table. 'Take a look at this.'

I stare at the screen, unsure of what I'm looking at. The officer sits back, arms folded, watching my reaction. Then I realise it's aerial footage of me being led to the schoolhouse by Marty and Faith. I'm in the white wedding gown, long train dragging over the dirt track. They're each guiding me by the arm, Faith looks like she's holding me up.

The footage cuts. *Please let there be more.* The screen comes to life again. Marty's dragging me away, just the two of us. I'm putting up a determined fight, digging in while he manhandles me in a fury. I fight back and start running away, but he tackles me to the ground, then drags me by my leg. Marty looks up at the drone and I frantically wrench the gun from my pocket. I'm flailing, not even pointing it when he's blasted with a shot and thrown backwards.

I hold my breath the whole way through. The real perp is out of shot. But the camera swoops and pans wider to catch two small figures pelting away. Willow and Isiah. Isiah's carrying a rifle. The drone backs off, but the footage continues. Faith appears and stonily leans over his body. Even from that angle and distance, you can tell she's dispassionate about her husband taking his dying breath. Then I follow her back to the house, me a wreck, her in total control. The footage cuts. The cop reaches over and closes the laptop lid.

'That's Isiah with the gun,' I say, one hand covering my mouth.

He nods firmly. 'He said Willow shot Marty then dropped the gun. He picked it up, then they both ran away in fear. Faith backed him up.'

'Faith wanted her husband dead. That's why she kept insisting I have the gun, first in our home, then when he locked me in the bunker and when she dressed me for the wedding.' I'd already told him this. 'Isiah did target practice with Marty. Surely she didn't...' I say it to myself, but he's pursing his lips and nodding gravely. 'Who shot the footage?' I ask.

'Some tech bro from California and a man who used to work on the ranch.'

'*Joel?*'

'That's right. Marty paid him off, said his services were no longer required, and reminded him of his NDA. The two of them were going to come forward sooner but they were conflicted about getting the kids in trouble and tainting them for life.'

Willow must already be tainted for life.

'Then they saw news reports that said you'd shot him, and it wasn't looking good for you, so they did the right thing.'

'Wait... a tech bro from California?'

'That's right. He showed us the subliminal message you put up on YouTube.'

Epilogue

Marty died three months ago and we're still picking up the threads of our lives. With the help of Dan, our tech bro saviour, we've rented a beautiful little place in Sacramento. Dan's a digital persuasion geek with a PhD in cultural studies. He specialises in unconscious cues that help social media posts go viral. He analysed Faith's videos for clues to how she influenced followers. I wasn't the only professional who viewed her posts with suspicion.

Dan picked up my covert cry for help on the video. He didn't want the sheriff to tip Marty off, so for the cost of a $50 flight, he flew out to discover more. Luckily for me, he's big on further exploration. He didn't know if the message was legit, but given that Faith had ten million followers, he grasped the potentially explosive story.

Someone in town hooked him up with Joel, who knew things were going rapidly downhill at the ranch. They procured a drone, intending to check if I was still living in the cabin, in which case, Joel planned to sneak in and get the two of us out.

He hesitated over the footage because it showed Isiah and Willow with the gun, but when the charge against me was made public, they went to the police. The cops took a dim view of Dan's amateur sleuthing, but he was heeding my warning to avoid the sheriff. As for Joel, he'd tried to contact me when I was under arrest, wanting to help me get an attorney.

The NDA I signed was deemed unenforceable since it was used to cover up criminal activity. Faith's unlikely to challenge that, since she has far bigger problems, and I have the might of a top New York publisher and their lawyers behind me. Did I mention my book deal? They want the story of how Faith tried setting me up to kill her husband. I have to keep saying that so it sinks in.

Faith and Marty stifled my voice on the ranch, and now I won't stop until I've finished my side of the story. I hesitated over the impact on Faith's kids, but they're shielded, and that horse has already bolted. It's been open season online, all over the mainstream news and true crime podcasts. And don't get me started on the Reddit threads. So I'm writing a rational account, making sense of the crazy.

I'm not blameless, since I went looking for trouble and found it. Now I'm weaving a narrative of Marty's birth family and mine. I don't need the full picture from every angle. I'm honouring my dad and his sister, showing the darkness that lurked behind the upstanding Eversen brothers.

It won't be published until after Faith's trial. I only talk about the children collectively in the book, and gloss over the killing. Everyone with a shred of interest already saw the shooting play out, dubbed the wedding day massacre. The drone footage was all over national TV news and racked up millions of online views. The tech bro did good. He and Joel made a mint for their troubles.

The children are the victims, not Marty. Faith's parents and sister in Salt Lake are caring for the kids. It's a Mormon stronghold, but they're going to a regular school, and I hope the city gives them a better life than that isolated ranch.

Isiah came clean and said he tried shooting his dad in the arm, in a desperate bid to stop him hurting me. I bet he saw his childhood years stretching ahead, filled with feeding hay to the cattle in lieu of a real education. He's been placed under juvenile court supervision and ordered to attend school and therapy.

The court refused bail to Faith. She's fighting accusations of murder and conspiracy to commit murder, along with coercion, child endangerment, illegal firearm possession and distribution to a minor, plus false imprisonment. The cops even traced her original background search of me, in which she found out my connection to Marty and Asher. She was two steps ahead of me the whole time. So smart, yet forever 2-D, a living, breathing trad doll.

The Mormon church turned its back on their poster girl. Her defence will come in strongly on Marty's coercion of her, which won't absolve her of every crime. The drone footage and lies she fed the police are damning, not least because she set up an innocent seven-year-old.

The other women pleaded ignorance. They might have been free to leave the ranch, but they were up to their necks in mental quicksand. There must be a programme to deradicalise them, like they do with ISIS brides. Hel has a lawsuit pending against the ranch, so she might taste freedom after all, and I hope Alice does the same.

Willow and I have booked a summer holiday in England, and we're reclaiming our lives. She's made new friends and God has loosened His grip. I told her about her dad, but she has good men in her life. We video-call Beverley and our old friends in Manhattan, who we'll visit for Halloween. Beverley has a new neighbour in our old apartment, a recently retired woman with a taste for cocktails.

As for Joel, it turns out he's a surf dude. He's visited, showing us how to catch a wave. Oh, and Marty lied about him marrying a sweetheart. In the aftermath, he took us in and gave us a sanctuary. He knew we couldn't stay in the area after what happened, but it's only a short flight to meet up. I'm often distracted by a mental image of him in swimming shorts, cutting through the waves, but that's another story. A cowboy romance. Meanwhile, I'm feverishly rewriting our future, telling the story of the podcaster and the murderous trad queen.

A Letter from Carrie

Dear reader,

Have you ever been enchanted by a trad wife online? It's easy to be seduced by their lovely dresses and baking superpowers, but who knows what goes on when the camera stops rolling? Whether you've heard of trad wives or not, you're very welcome here.

I first came across the trad wife movement when someone online made fun of a trad wife's Instagram photo. The cinematic image showed a beautiful woman and her young daughters in vintage prairie dresses looking dreamily photogenic in a homespun scene. I didn't get it. Why make fun of models in a heritage-chic photoshoot? But no, it was their real life. I still didn't get it. Did they always waft around in a charming time warp? So began my deep dive into why women live that way, since I love going down weird rabbit holes of research. The result is Faith as The Trad Wife, and Melissa who doesn't fathom her out until it's too late.

Thank you so much for reading *The Trad Wife*. The late, great Alan Rickman said, 'the more we're governed by idiots and have no control over our destinies, the more we need to tell stories to each other about who we are, why we are, where we come from and what might be possible'. Stories help me make sense of the world, and this is my story of a picturesque ranch whose inhabitants are governed by an idiot. Thanks for jumping down the rabbit hole with me!

I had so much fun writing *The Trad Wife*. If you enjoyed reading it, please do leave an online review.

Carrie x

Acknowledgements

Thank you to my powerhouse of a literary agent, Jade Kavanagh. I've gained so much from your enthusiastic support. Thanks also to the rest of Darley Anderson, including Camilla Bolton, Georgia Fuller, Ilaria Albani and Francesca Edwards.

Thank you to my unfailingly wonderful editor and partner in crime, Jennie Ayres. Thanks also to proofreader Vicki Vrint, and Ross Dickinson for copyediting prowess. Sorry for my 90% failure rate on hyphens.

Thank you to Head Design for a gorgeous cover. And thanks to the team at Hera and Canelo including Keshini Naidoo, Iain Millar, Kate Shepherd, Hannah Cowie, Dan O'Brien, Rebecca McInerney and Kim Yudelowitz.

Lastly, thanks to my family and friends, including the wonderfully book-centric Becky Edwards and Chris Moore.

Meet Our Writers

Carolyn Heller
@CarolynBHeller

Carolyn fell in love with long-distance walking – and with PEI – after spending five days on the Island Walk (p128). Based in Vancouver, she writes about culture, food, and all sorts of offbeat adventures from her travels across Canada.

Jennifer Bain
@thesaucylady

As a puffin lover, thinking about the Elliston Puffin Viewing Site makes Jennifer giddy. It's one of the only spots in Canada where you can get a great (and free) view of these nesting seabirds from land instead of from a moving tour boat. You don't even need binoculars or a zoom lens to watch them interact, though of course those things help.

Joel Balsam
@joelbalsam

While growing up in Ottawa and living in Montréal, Joel loved taking off to the Laurentians for a day trip or to spend the weekend snowboarding at Mont-Tremblant. Seeing the snow blanket the evergreens while cruising down from above the clouds is among his most cherished winter memories. And the best part of any ski day? Warming up in the lodge with an ooey-gooey poutine.

Isabella Noble
@isabellamnoble

Isabella is a bilingual Spain-raised, British-Australian travel journalist who often spends time in Ontario. She loves wandering around Toronto's colorful neighborhoods for hours, escaping into on-the-doorstep urban greenery for walks and yoga, and seeking out fabulous places to eat (p43) all over Canada's largest city.

Debbie Olsen
@wanderwoman_Deb

Debbie loves driving the Icefields Parkway (p184) that connects Banff National Park with Jasper National Park. The scenery is awe-inspiring and you pass more than a hundred glaciers. There's no place like it in the world. There are also a number of incredible viewpoints and hikes along the way.

Lonely Planet

CANADA

Carolyn Heller, Jennifer Bain, Joel Balsam, Isabella Noble, Debbie Olsen, Kelsey Olsen, Darcy Rhyno, Brendan Sainsbury, Barbara Woolsey

▰▰▰ Trek beneath snow-topped mountains, along sandy beaches and through dense green forests. Check out the art, food and eclectic neighborhoods in some of the world's most diverse cities. Adventure in the snow and marvel at the colors of the northern lights. Learn about the traditions and cultures of the Indigenous Peoples who've lived on this land for millennia. Sample regional specialties from poutine to perogies, and cycle through verdant vineyards. Explore islands offering everything from surfing lessons to one-of-a-kind cultural experiences.

This is Canada.

TURN THE PAGE AND START PLANNING YOUR NEXT BEST TRIP →

'On a recent trip to Algonquin Provincial Park, I paddled out across the glassy lake first thing with only a few flapping loons for company.'

ISABELLA NOBLE

'You can't beat screaming along the Ingraham Trail in the Northwest Territories on a e-bike at 45km/h.'

BRENDAN SAINSBURY

'That time I cycled the Bow Valley Parkway and met Split Lip, one of the biggest grizzlies in Banff National Park and the biggest grizzly I have ever seen.'

DEBBIE OLSEN

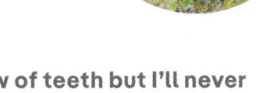

'While wandering Granville Island, I sampled so many treats that I skipped lunch entirely.'

KELSEY OLSEN

'My first iceberg was puny and looked like a row of teeth but I'll never forget it.'

JENNIFER BAIN

'I took my mom to Îles-de-la-Madeleine with me and she found it as magical as I do.'

JOEL BALSAM

FROM TOP LEFT: ISABELLA NOBLE/LONELY PLANET, RICHARD WAYNE COLLENS/SHUTTERSTOCK

Although the authors and Lonely Planet have taken all reasonable care in preparing this book, we make no warranty about the accuracy or completeness of its content and, to the maximum extent permitted, disclaim all liability arising from its use.

All rights reserved. No part of this publication may be copied, stored in a retrieval system, or transmitted in any form by any means, electronic, mechanical, recording or otherwise, except brief extracts for the purpose of review, and no part of this publication may be sold or hired, without the written permission of the publisher. Lonely Planet and the Lonely Planet logo are trademarks of Lonely Planet and are registered in the US Patent and Trademark Office and in other countries. Lonely Planet does not allow its name or logo to be appropriated by commercial establishments, such as retailers, restaurants or hotels. Please let us know of any misuses: lonelyplanet.com/legal/intellectual-property.

THIS BOOK

The 1st edition of Lonely Planet's *Experience Canada* guidebook was researched and written by Carolyn Heller, Jennifer Bain, Joel Balsam, Isabella Noble, Debbie Olsen, Kelsey Olsen, Darcy Rhyno.

Brendan Sainsbury and Barbara Woolsey.

This guidebook was produced by the following:

Destination editor
Caroline Trefler

Production editor
Katie Connolly

Cartographer Corey Hutchison

Image researcher
Virginia Moreno

Assisting editor Sally Davies

Cover researcher Daisy Korpics

Thanks Sofie Andersen, Melanie Dankel, Kate James, Darren O'Connell

Sea to Sky Gondola 215
seafood 124-5
Sentier des Cimes 75
sheep 213
shopping, see markets, *individual locations*
skating 245
ski resorts 75, 193, 204-5, 215
skiing & snowboarding, see snowsports
sleeper trains 246
smoking 248
snowshoeing, see snowsports
snowsports 10, 193
   Callaghan Valley 205
   Les Laurentides 74-5
   Mont Tremblant Resort 75
   Whistler-Blackcomb 10, 204-5, 215
social media 37
spas 83, 114, 133, 167, 171
sports, see *individual sports*
Squamish Adventure Centre 215
Squamish Canyon 214
SS *Keno* 224
SS *Klondike* 223
Ste-Flavie 77
Sulphur Mountain 183
sunscreens 245
surfing 13, 200-1

T

Taproom Trail 9
taxes 238, 243, 248
taxis 239
television 37
territorial parks, see national & provincial parks
Territories, the 216-35, **218-19**
   accommodations 221
   activities 222-3, 228-9, 234-5
   boat trips 222-3
   costs 220
   drinking 221

food 221, 231, 235
history 224-5, 226-7, 230-1, 233, 235
Indigenous cultures 232-3
itineraries 32-3, 228-9, **32-3, 229**
money 221
navigation 221
planning 218-19
road trips 228-9, **229**
shopping 234
travel seasons 220
travel to & within the Territories 220
Thanksgiving 16
theater 46, 68-9, 120, 180-1, 225
theft 242
Thousand Islands, the 13
Tilting 145
time zones 248
Tintamarre 110-11
tipping 243
Tofino 13, 26, 200-1
toilets 248
toonie 243
Toronto 8-9, 22, 44-5, 46-7
Toronto Islands 47
totem poles 207
tours 125, 133, 141, 187, 205, see also road trips, walking tours
train travel 239, 240, 246
travel seasons 14-21
travel to/from Canada 238-9
travel within Canada 240-1
trekking, see hiking
Trout River 143
Tsiigehtchic 229

V

Valley of 1000 Devils 163
Vancouver 8-9, 27
viewpoints 184, 227
visas 239, 248
volunteering 244

W

walking, see hiking
walking tours
   Newfoundland & Labrador 148, 151
   Prince Edward Island 120-1, 132, **121**
water, drinking 242
waterfalls 83, 95, 184-5, 214
weather 14-21, see also *individual locations*
websites 37, 245, 247
whale blubber, see *muktuk*
whale-watching 73, 212
   New Brunswick 115
   Newfoundland & Labrador 150
   Nova Scotia 100
Whistler 27, 204-5, 215
Whitehorse 32, 222-3
wi-fi 238
wildlife 7, 100, 182, 210-11, 212-13, 242
wine 48-9, 83, 171, 208-9
wineries 11
   British Columbia 209
   Manitoba & Saskatchewan 171
   New Brunswick 115
   Ontario 49
Winnipeg 29
wolves 213
world's largest monuments 107, 190-1

Y

Yellowknife 33, 226-7
Yukon River 222-3

Nova Scotia *continued*
 navigation 89
 planning 86-7
 road trips 90-1, **91**
 shopping 101
 tours 100
 travel seasons 88
 travel to & within Nova Scotia 88
Nunavut Territory 230-1

O
observatories 83
Okanagan Valley 11, 208-9
Olympic Games 9, 193
Ontario 38-61, **40-1**
 accommodations 43, 51
 activities 50-1, 52-3, 56-7, 60
 boat travel 50-1
 costs 42
 drinking 43, 48-9, 60-1
 food 43, 44-5, 60, 61
 history 54-5, 58-9
 itineraries 22-3, 52-3, **22-3**, **53**
 LGBTIQ+ travelers 46-7
 money 43
 navigation 43
 planning 40-1
 road trips 52-3, **53**
 shopping 61
 travel seasons 42
 travel to & within Ontario 42
orcas 212
Osoyoos 27
Ottawa 23, 54-5
oysters 83, 125

P
paddleboarding 133
paddle-steamers 223, 224

000 Map pages

parks & gardens
 Butchart Gardens 214
 Irving Nature Park 109
 Jardins de Métis 77
 Parc Jean-Drapeau 73
 Riverfront Park 109
 Rotary Peace Park 222
 Shipyards Park 222
Peace Meeting Site 161
Percé 77
petroglyphs 97, 189
picaroons 113
Place Royale 71
podcasts 36
potatoes 130-1
poutine 11, 72
prairie dogs 163
prairies, the 162-3
Pride festivals 15, 47
Prince Edward Island 24, 117-33, **118**
 accommodations 119, 133
 activities 122-3, 126-7, 128-9
 drinking 119
 food 119, 124-5, 131, 132
 history 120-1, 130-1
 Indigenous cultures 122-3
 itineraries 24-5, 120-1, **24-5**, **121**
 money 119
 navigation 119
 planning 118, 129
 tours 133
 travel seasons 119
 travel to & within from Prince Edward Island 119
 walking tours 120-1, **121**
provincial parks, *see* national & provincial parks
puffins 25, 100, 140-1

Q
Québec 63-83, **64-5**
 accommodations 67
 activities 74-5, 76-7, 78-9, 83

 costs 66
 drinking 67, 82-3
 entertainment 80-1
 festivals & events 83
 food 67, 72, 82
 history 70-1, 76-7
 itineraries 22-3, **22-3**
 LGBTIQ+ travelers 68-9
 money 67
 navigation 67
 planning 64-5
 road trips 76-7, **77**
 travel seasons 66
 travel to & within Québec 66
Québec City 23, 70-1, 82

R
reservations 247
responsible travel 210-11, 244-5
Rideau Canal 54
ridesharing services 239
road distance chart 241
road trips
 New Brunswick 109
 Alberta 30, 182-3, 184-5, **183**
 British Columbia 208-9, **209**
 Manitoba & Saskatchewan 163, 164-5, **165**
 Newfoundland & Labrador 144-5, **145**
 Nova Scotia 90-1, 93, **91**
 Ontario 52-3, **53**
 Québec 76-7, 83, **77**
 Territories, the 33, 228-9, **229**
Rocher Percé 77
rodeos 179

S
safe travel 242
salmon 212
Saskatchewan River Crossing 184
sea otters 213
sea stacks 95

N

national & provincial parks, see also ecological reserves
Algonquin Provincial Park 56-7
Auyuittuq National Park 234
Banff National Park 7, 31, 182-3, 193
Blomidon Provincial Park 101
Bruce Peninsula National Park 53
Canmore Nordic Centre Provincial Park 193
Cape Breton Highlands National Park 93, 97
Cape Chignecto Provincial Park 95
Cliffs of Fundy UNESCO Global Geopark 94-5
Elk Island National Park 193
Fathom Five National Marine Park 53
Five Islands Provincial Park 95
Forillon National Park 77
Fort Smith Mission Territorial Park 235
Fundy National Park 109
Georgian Bay Islands National Park 53
Grasslands National Park 28, 162-3
Gros Morne National Park 25, 142-3
Hopewell Rocks Provincial Park 109
Jasper National Park 30, 193
Joffre Lakes Park 214
Kananaskis Country 193
Kejimkujik National Park 97
Killarney Provincial Park 7, 53
Kluane National Park Reserve 234
Kouchibouguac National Park 111
Mactaquac Provincial Park 106
Nahanni National Park Reserve 234
New River Beach Provincial Park 109
Parc Marin du Saguenay-St-Laurent 83
Parc National de la Gaspésie 76
Parc National de la Mauricie 75
Parc National des Hautes-Gorges-de-la-Rivière-Malbaie 83
Parc National du Mont-Tremblant 75
Pinery Provincial Park 60
Pituamkek National Park Reserve 123
Prince Edward Island National Park 126-7
Qaummaarviit Territorial Park 235
Roosevelt Campobello International Park 109
Sandbanks Provincial Park 60
Shuswap Lake Provincial Park 214
Sylvia Grinnell Territorial Park 231
Taylor Head Provincial Park 101
Thousand Islands National Park 60
Tombstone Territorial Park 229
Waterton Lakes National Park 193
Wood Buffalo National Park 234
Writing-on-Stone Provincial Park/Áísínai'pi 189
New Brunswick 103-15, **104**
 accommodations 105, 106-7
 activities 106-7, 108-9, 115
 boat trips 106-7, **107**
 drinking 105, 112-13, 115
 festivals 110-11, 114
 food 105, 115
 history 107, 111, 114-15
 itineraries 24-5, 106-7, **24-5**, **107**
 money 105
 planning 104
 travel seasons 105
 travel to & within New Brunswick 105
Newfoundland & Labrador 135-51, **136-7**
 accommodations 139
 activities 140-1, 142-3, 146-7, 150-1
 bird-watching 140-1
 costs 138
 drinking 139
 food 139, 148
 history 148, 150
 Indigenous cultures 150-1
 itineraries 144-5, **145**
 language 148-9
 money 139
 navigation 139
 planning 136-7
 road trips 144-5, **145**
 shopping 151
 tours 141, 147
 travel seasons 138
 travel to & within Newfoundland & Labrador 138
 walking tours 151
nightlife, see drinking & nightlife, individual locations
northern lights 18, 221
Nova Scotia 84-101, **86-7**
 accommodations 89
 activities 94-5, 100-1
 art 96-7
 costs 88
 drinking 89, 100
 festivals & events 92-3
 food 89, 98-9, 101
 geology 94, 94-5
 history 90-1, 94-5, 98-9, **91**
 Indigenous cultures 96-7
 itineraries 24-5, 90-1, **24-5**, **91**
 money 89

M

Magdalen Islands 78-9
Manitoba & Saskatchewan 28-9, 153-71, **154-5**
  accommodations 157
  activities 160-1, 162-3, 166-7, 171
  costs 156
  drinking 157, 158-9, 170-1
  festivals & events 164-5, **165**
  food 157
  history 168-9
  itineraries 28-9, 164-5, **28-9, 165**
  money 157
  navigation 157
  planning 154-5
  population 168-9
  road trips 164-5, **165**
  shopping 171
  travel seasons 156
  travel to & within Manitoba & Saskatchewan 156
Manitoulin Island 53
maple syrup 20, 72
maple taffy 72
markets 51, 245
  Gimli Fish Market 165
  Granville Island Public Market 11, 202-3
  Kingston Public Market 55
  Prince Edward Island 132
  St Lawrence Market Complex 61
  Treasure Valley Markets 171
Métis Crossing 12, 189
mining 226-7
mobile phones 238
money 243
Montgomery, Lucy Maud 120-1
Montréal 8-9, 23, 68-9, 82
Mont-Tremblant 74

000 Map pages

moose 76
mosquitoes 21
muktuk 11, 221
multiculturalism 35
museums & galleries, *see also* cultural centers
  #2 Mine Tour & Museum 150
  Acadian Museum 133
  Âjagemô 55
  Anne of Green Gables Museum 121
  Art Gallery of Ontario 60
  Blackfoot Crossing Historical Park 189
  Canadian Canoe Museum 59
  Canadian Glove Museum 150
  Canadian Museum for Human Rights 9, 160-1
  Canadian Museum of History 54-5
  Canadian Potato Museum 130
  Centre d'Art Marcel Gagnon 77
  Dawson City Museum 225
  Deep South Pioneer Museum 171
  Durrell Museum 151
  Espace Pour La Vie 83
  Fort Edmonton Indigenous Peoples Experience 189
  Fundy Geological Museum 95
  Green Gables Heritage Place 121
  Herring Cove Art Gallery & Studio 145
  Highland Village Museum 92-3
  Île-aux-Marins 151
  International Fox Museum 133
  Jack London Museum 235
  Jardins de Métis 77
  Johnson Geo Centre 146
  Kings Landing 107
  Le Musée Heritage 151
  Little Manitou Art Gallery 167

Lucy Maud Montgomery Birthplace 121
Lucy Maud Montgomery's Cavendish Homestead 121
Maison de la Nature et de l'Environnement 151
McMichael Canadian Art Collection 60
Musée de la Gaspésie 77
Musée des Plaines d'Abraham 71
Myrick Wireless Interpretation Centre 146
National Gallery of Canada 60
New Iceland Heritage Museum 165
North Atlantic Aviation Museum 150
Nunatta Sunakkutaangit Museum 231
Prince of Wales Northern Heritage Centre 227
Royal Tyrrell Museum of Palaeontology 187
Sheffield Park Black History & Cultural Museum 53
Site d'Interprétation Micmac de Gespeg 77
Stompin' Tom Centre 131, 133
T-Rex Discovery Centre 171
Tunnels of Moose Jaw 171
Unikkaarvik Visitor Centre 231
Yellowknife Historical Museum 227
music 36, 73, 132
music festivals
  Festival d'Été de Québec 83
  Festival International de Jazz de Montréal 83
  Harvest Music Festival 114
  Manitou Music Fest 167
  Montreal International Jazz Festival 15
  Vancouver Folk Music Festival 15

KidsFringe 181
Montréal Complètement Cirque 81
National Day for Truth & Reconciliation 16
National Indigenous Peoples Day 14 Pride 9, 15, 249
Tintamarre 110-11
films 37
First Nations peoples, see Indigenous culture, Indigenous Peoples
fishing 98-9, 165
fjords 143
Fogo Island 13, 144-5
food 11, 35, 60, 125, see also individual locations
forts 91, 92-3, 229, 235
fossils 186-7
foxes 133
French language 250
Fundy Trail Parkway 109

G

galleries, see museums & galleries
Gander International Airport 149, 150
gardens, see parks & gardens
Gaspésie 76-7, **77**
gay travelers 8, 46-7, 68-9, 161, 249
Georgian Bay 52-3, **53**
Gimli Ice Festival 164-5
gîtes 246
glaciers 185
GMC Stadium 179
goats 133, 213
gold rushes 224-5, 226-7, 235
gondolas 183, 215
Grand Colombier 141
Granville Island 11, 202-3
Grasslands National Park 28
Gros Morne Mountain 7, 143

H

Haida Gwaii 12, 26, 206-7, 211
Halifax 25
Hay River 235
health 242
Hecla Heritage Village 165
hiking 6-7
 Alberta 185
 British Columbia 201
 Newfoundland & Labrador 143, 145, 150
 Nova Scotia 100-1
 Ontario 52, 57
 Prince Edward Island 7, 121, 127, 128-9
 Québec 83
 Territories, the 222, 234
historic sites, see also forts
 Alberta 189
 Manitoba & Saskatchewan 161
 New Brunswick 107, 110, 114
 Newfoundland & Labrador 141, 150
 Nova Scotia 91, 95
 Québec 71, 77
history 130-1, 148, 233
hot springs 10, 183, 214
houseboats 106-7
human rights 160-1

I

icebergs 146-7
Icefields Parkway 30, 184-5
Icelandic heritage 164-5
icewine 49
igloos 231
immigration 35
Indigenous culture 12, 34, 55, 122-3, 214-15
 Alberta 188-9
 Haida Gwaii 206-7
 Mi'kmaq 96-7
Indigenous Peoples 12, 34
 Cree Peoples 167

Inuit peoples 232-3
Lennox Island Mi'kmaq First Nation 122-3
Mi'kmaq 96-7
Saulteaux Peoples 167
Indigenous tours 97, 114, 123, 150-1
insurance 242
Iqaluit 12, 33, 230-1
Island Walk 7, 128-9
itineraries 22-33, **22-3**, **24-5**, **26-7**, **28-9**, **30-1**, **32-3**, see also individual regions

J

Jewetts Cove 107
Joggins Fossil Cliffs 95
Johnston Canyon 183

K

kayaking, see canoeing & kayaking
Kelowna 27
Kingston 23, 54-5
kitesurfing 79

L

lakes 183, 184, 214
languages 35, 148-9, 250
Laurentians, the 74-5
Le Jeune, Olivier 71
Les Îles-de-la-Madeleine 13, 78-9
 food 82
Les Laurentides 74-5
LGBTIQ+ travelers 8, 46-7, 68-9, 161, 249
light shows 75
lighthouses 76, 79, 133, 146
literature 36
Little Fogo Islands 141
Little Manitou Lake 29, 166-7
lobster 101
loonie 243
loons 57

camping 57, 244, 247
Canadian Museum for Human Rights 160-1
cannabis 242
canoeing & kayaking 12, 58-9, 244
  British Columbia 12, 207, 211
  Nova Scotia 97
  Ontario 57
  Prince Edward Island 125
  Québec 75
  Territories, the 223
car travel 240
Caraquet 110-11
carbon footprint 241
Carcross 235
caribou 76, 144
Carnaval de Québec 10, 73, 83
castle hotels 246
Cathedral Grove 214
Cavendish 120-1
caves 163
cell phones 238
Celtic Colours International Festival 17, 92-3
children, travel with 181, 249
churches 71, 231
cinemas 167
circuses 9, 80-1
Cirrus Mountain 184
Cliffs of Fundy UNESCO Global Geopark 94-5
climate 14-21
climate change 245
cocktails 61, 192
coffee 60-1
Collingwood 53
conservation efforts 210-11
costs 239, 240, 243, 246
cougars 212
courses 93, 123
credit cards 243

000 Map pages

cultural centers
  Black Loyalist Heritage Centre 91
  Change Islands Interpretation & Craft Centre 149, 151
  French Shore Interpretation Centre 150
  Greenwich Interpretation Centre 127
  Haida Heritage Centre 215
  Lennox Island Cultural Centre 123
  Metepenagiag Heritage Park 114
  Millbrook Cultural & Heritage Centre 91, 97
  Nk'Mip Desert Cultural Centre 215
  Squamish Lil'wat Cultural Centre 215
  Tilting Heritage Centre 145
  Unikkaarvik Visitor Centre 231
currency 243
currency exchange 238
custom regulations 238
cycling
  Beausoleil Island 13
  La Route des Vins 83
  Le P'tit Train du Nord 75
  Prince Edward Island 128-9
Cypress Lookout 214

D
Dalvay by the Sea 127
dangers 240
Dark-Sky Preserve 17, 163
Dawson 32, 224-5
Dempster Hwy 33, 228-9
diamonds 227
Dinosaur Provincial Park 31, 186-7
disabilities, travelers with 248
distilleries, see breweries & distilleries

dogsledding 10
drag shows 47, 68-9
Dredge No 4 225
drinking & nightlife 9, 48-9, 248, 249, see also individual locations
drinks 11, see also beer, wine
driving, see car travel, road trips
drugs 242

E
eagles 213
ecological reserves, see also national & provincial parks
  Cape St Mary's Ecological Reserve 141
  Mistaken Point Ecological Reserve 150
  Witless Bay Ecological Reserve 141
Edmonton International Fringe Theatre Festival 9, 31, 180-1
electric vehicles 240
electricity 248
Elliston Puffin Viewing Site 141
etiquette 34, 245
events, see festivals & events, music festivals
exchange rates 238

F
family travel 181, 249
ferry travel 239
festivals & events 14-21, 83, 114, see also music festivals
  Calgary Stampede 15, 178-9
  Carnaval de Québec 10, 73, 83
  Celtic Colours International Festival 17, 92-3
  Edmonton International Fringe Theatre Festival 9, 180-1
  Festival Acadien de Caraquet 14, 110-11
  Fierté Montréal 68
  Gimli Ice Festival 164-5

Index

A
Acadian Historic Village 110
accessible travel 248
accommodations 246-7
activities 14-21, *see also individual activities, locations*
agriculture 168-9
air quality 242
air travel 241
Alberta 172-93, **174-5**
 accommodations 177
 activities 182-3, 186-7, 193
 costs 176
 drinking 177, 192, 192-3
 festivals & events 178-81
 food 177, 192
 history 186-7
 Indigenous cultures 188-9
 itineraries 30-1, 182-3, **30-1, 183**
 money 177
 navigation 177
 planning 174-5, 179
 road trips 182-3, 184-5, **183**
 shopping 179
 travel seasons 176, 177
 travel to & within Alberta 176
amusement parks 111, 107
animals 7, 182-3, 210-11, 212-13, 242, *see also individual animals*
Anne of Green Gables 13, 120-1
Arctic, the 228-9
area codes 248
art galleries, *see* museums & galleries
arts 97, 171, 214-15, 232, 234, *see also* music, theatre
AstroLab 83
Athabasca Glacier 185

ATMs 238, 243
aurora borealis 18, 221

B
B&Bs 246
Baffin Island 13, 230-1
bagels 72
Banff National Park 7, 31, 182-3
bank notes 243
bathrooms 248
battlefields 71
Bay of Fundy 24
beaches
 Georgian Bay 53
 Les Îles-de-la-Madeleine 79
 Little Manitou Lake 167
 Prince Edward Island National Park 127
 St Vincent's 150
 Tofino 201
 Toronto Islands 47
Beaconsfield Historic House 132
bears 34, 210-11, 212
Beausoleil Island 13, 53
beer 112-13, 158-9, 170-1
bicycle travel, *see* cycling
bird-watching
 Algonquin Provincial Park 57
 New Brunswick 108-9
 Newfoundland & Labrador 140-1
 Nova Scotia 100
bison 163
Blackcomb 215
boat travel 50-1, 241
boat trips 106-7
 Les Îles-de-la-Madeleine 83
 New Brunswick 106-7, **107**
 Territories, the 222-3

books 36
border crossings 239
Bow Valley Parkway 183
breweries & distilleries
 British Columbia 215
 Manitoba & Saskatchewan 158-9, 170-1
 New Brunswick 107, 112-13, 115
 Nova Scotia 100
 Territories, the 231
bridges 112, 114-15, 222
Brimstone Head 145
British Columbia 194-215, **196-7**
 accommodations 199
 activities 200-1, 204-5, 206-7, 214-15
 costs 198
 drinking 199, 208-9, 215
 food 199, 201, 215
 Indigenous cultures 206-7, 214-15
 itineraries 26-7, 208-9, **26-7, 209**
 money 199
 navigation 199
 planning 196-7
 responsible travel 210-11
 road trips 208-9, **209**
 shopping 202-3
 travel seasons 198
 travel to & within British Columbia 198
bus travel 239, 241
bushwalking, *see* hiking

C
Calgary Stampede 15, 31, 178-9
Cambridge Bay 235

000 Map pages

LANGUAGE

Canada is a bilingual country with French and English as its official languages at the federal level, which means you'll see both English and French on highway signs, maps, tourist brochures, packaging etc. French is the official language in Québec though many people in Montréal and Québec City also speak English. Students in Québec are taught the French of France in school but the local tongue is known as 'Québecois', which has a few differences from the French of France. New Brunswick is the only officially bilingual province and there are pockets of French-speaking populations in most of the other provinces. You'll have no problems if you use standard French phrases.

BASICS

Hello.	Bonjour.	*bon·zhoor*
Goodbye.	Au revoir.	*o·rer·vwa*
Yes.	Oui.	*wee*
No.	Non.	*non*
Please.	S'il vous plaît.	*seel voo play*
Thank you.	Merci.	*mair·see*
Excuse me.	Excusez-moi.	*ek·skew·zay·mwa*
Sorry.	Pardon.	*par·don*

What's your name?
Comment vous appelez-vous? *ko·mon voo· za·play voo*

My name is...
Je m'appelle... *zher ma·pel...*

Do you speak English?
Parlez-vous anglais? *par·lay·voo ong·glay*

I don't understand.
Je ne comprends pas. *zher ner kom·pron pa*

TIME & NUMBERS

What time is it?	Quelle heure est-il?	*kel er ay til*
It's (8) o'clock.	Il est (huit) heures.	*il ay (weet) er*
Half past (10).	Il est (dix) heures et demie.	*il ay (deez) er ay day·mee*
morning	matin	*ma·tun*
afternoon	après-midi	*a·pray·mee·dee*
evening	soir	*swar*
yesterday	hier	*yair*
today	aujourd'hui	*o·zhoor·dwee*
tomorrow	demain	*der·mun*

1	un	*un*	6	six	*sees*
2	deux	*der*	7	sept	*set*
3	trois	*trwa*	8	huit	*weet*
4	quatre	*ka·trer*	9	neuf	*nerf*
5	cinq	*sungk*	10	dix	*dees*

EMERGENCIES

Help!	Au secours!	*o skoor*
Call...	Appelez	*a·play*
the police!	la police!	*la po·lees*
a doctor!	un médecin!	*un mayd·sun*
I'm ill.	Je suis malade.	*zher swee ma·lad*

SMALL TALK
'Shooting the breeze' is a beloved Canadian art form. Engage as much or as little as you like.

PUBLIC DRINKING
Generally prohibited except in Québec parks (food must be present). At bring-your-own-bottle restaurants, a corkage fee usually applies.

LAST CALL
Servers come around for final drink or food orders around 30 minutes before closing bars and kitchens.

FAMILY TRAVEL
Attraction admission is usually free for children five and under.
Youth tickets are usually half the adult price. Age ranges vary but it's usually 17 and under.
Family tickets usually cover two adults and two children.
Public transport is generally discounted for those aged 17 and under and free for those aged five and under (12 and under in cities such as Toronto, Vancouver and Calgary).
Restaurants' bars and lounges prohibit children even when accompanied.

FAMILY DINING is well-catered to at mid-range restaurants and popular Canadian chains. Often, kids' menus are standard and sometimes little ones will get crayons and coloring sheets. High-end restaurants are often not junior-friendly except for a couple of chain exceptions, such as The Keg steakhouses and Earl's.

TRAVELING ESSENTIALS Families should call ahead before traveling for essentials like child car seats (hire them ahead of time from your vehicle rental provider) and cots or rollaways in hotels. Sometimes, cots have an additional charge. Many budget properties, including Hostelling International Canada hostels, offer good family rooms.

LGBTIQ+ TRAVELERS
Canada's 'Big Three' of Pride parades are in Vancouver, Toronto and Montréal (August).
Winnipeg's Canadian Museum for Human Rights covers LGBTIQ+ history in the exhibits 'Love in a Dangerous Time: Canada's LGBT Purge' and 'Examining the Holocaust.'
The largest 'Gayborhoods' are Vancouver's Davie Village; Montréal's Le Village (also, around Rue Ste-Catherine) and Toronto's Church-Wellesley Village.
Dating apps Grindr and Scruff are popular; apps like HER (for queer women) and Lex (queer community networking) are catching on.

ESSENTIAL NUTS-AND-BOLTS

SMOKING
Smoking in enclosed public spaces as well as on transit and in bars and restaurants (also patios and terraces) is not allowed. The ban includes vaping.

NATIONAL PARKS
Canada's 37 national parks and 11 national park reserves are found in every province and territory.

PUBLIC TOILETS
Not always easy to find but always available in shopping malls. The GoHere: Washroom Locator app *(crohnsandcolitis.ca)*, initiated by Crohn's and Colitis Canada, maps washrooms nationwide.

FAST FACTS

Time Zone GMT -3½–8

Country Code +1

Electricity 120V/60Hz

GOOD TO KNOW

EU, British and Australian citizens must apply for an eTA (Electronic Travel Authorization) before entering Canada. United States citizens are exempt.

Many retailers in Canada offer tax refunds on certain goods. Amounts and eligibility vary by province.

Legal drinking age varies by province: 18 in Alberta, Manitoba, and Québec; 19 elsewhere.

Try out the heartwarming tradition of 'Paying it Forward' in a drive-thru – buy a coffee for the driver behind you.

ACCESSIBLE TRAVEL

Canada's main airports have strong and well-resourced disability-access strategies, including dedicated support services and facilities. For assistance, contact your airline at least 48 hours before flying.

Hand-controlled vehicles and vans with wheelchair lifts are available from rental agencies at no extra cost; reserve well in advance. Highway service stations usually have accessible toilets and designated parking.

Public transit buses with unfolding electronic ramps are standard in many Canadian cities, with bus stops often featuring Braille signs and rumble-strip areas.

Newer hotels offer adapted rooms with full wheelchair access. Older properties are less likely to be accessible, but Parks Canada has cabins for travelers with autism and wheelchair accessibility needs.

Canadian museums are mostly accessible. Some also provide free wheelchairs and electric scooters.

Canada's national parks have some excellent accessible trails. These typically include smoothly paved or wooden boardwalk routes and range from forest pathways to beachside tracks. Favorites include the 1km Marsh Boardwalk Trail in Point Pelee National Park, home to turtles and amazing birdlife.

GREAT CANADIAN CAMPING

Canada is filled with campgrounds – some federal or provincial, others privately owned. Alongside its traditional campgrounds, Parks Canada offers some distinctive alternative accommodations at many of its sites. As well as log cabins, there are tipis, yurts, teardrop-shaped micro-cabins, A-frame wood-and-canvas glamping oTENTiks and kitted-out RVs. There are some in special locations; for example, tucked into stargazing preserves or in one-of-a-kind rooms in preserved historic buildings.

Facilities vary widely. Backcountry sites offer little more than pit toilets and fire rings.

Unserviced (tent) campgrounds offer drinking water, toilets and usually showers. The best-equipped sites feature wi-fi, flush toilets and hot showers, and water, electrical and sewer hookups for recreational vehicles (RVs).

Locals snap up spots at popular Canadian campsites as soon as booking opens in May. Most government-run sites are first-come, first-served and fill up quickly (especially the more unusual sleepovers). The official season runs from May to September, but exact dates vary by location. Some campgrounds offer off-season (late October to April) camping at reduced rates. Winter camping is only for the hardy.

If Parks Canada lodgings are snapped up, check out private campgrounds (although these sometimes cater only to caravans and RVs). Or, consider staking your tent on parkland off the beaten path. Waking alongside a deserted beach or in a tranquil forest clearing makes for freedom-filled adventures.

BOOKING

Most hotels are part of international chains – take advantage of loyalty and membership programs. It's best to book ahead during summer (June through August), as well as during ski season at winter resorts, and during holidays and major events.

Destination Canada (en.destinationcanada.com) Official tourism site – resources on accommodations and packages.

Destination Indigenous (destinationindigenous.ca/accommodations) Indigenous-owned and -operated lodgings.

Parks Canada Reservations (reservation.pc.gc.ca) Campsite reservations take place from May to September; book well ahead.

Hostelling International Canada (hihostels.ca) Nonprofit, national hostel network.

BBCanada (bbcanada.com) Listings website for B&Bs, inns and vacation homes.

Super, Natural British Columbia (supernaturalbc.com) Skiing and snowboarding lodging info in BC.

Travel Alberta (travelalberta.com) Skiing and snowboarding lodging info in Alberta.

Ontario Parks (reservations.ontarioparks.ca) Book a campsite in one of Ontario's more than 340 provincial parks.

Cottages in Canada (cottagesincanada.com) Lakefront property rentals.

Chalets au Québec (chaletsauquebec.com) Vacation cottages and cabins in recreational areas.

UNIVERSITY ROOMS

Visit University Rooms' website (universityrooms.com) for under-the-radar budget stays on campus during the lecture-free season. In Montréal, McGill and Université de Montréal's dorms (private rooms with shared bathrooms) offer prime locations with easy access to public transport.

UNIQUE AND LOCAL WAYS TO STAY

In popular destinations, such as Ottawa, Banff and Jasper, it pays to book ahead during summer, especially during major festivals, and for ski season. In many rural destinations (for example, in small towns in the prairies), your options of where to stay will generally be limited to one or two midrange inns or motels. Hotel chains are common nationwide.

HOW MUCH FOR A...

Castle hotel $400

Cabin $100

Backcountry campsite $30

CASTLE HOTELS

To lure wealthy passengers onto their fledgling railroad lines, early train operators built turreted, castle-like grand hotels throughout Canada. Many are around today, offering stays in splendid heritage properties with spectacular views – iconic landscapes or expansive city center panoramas, for example. Look for top options in Québec City (pictured above left), Banff, Victoria and beyond.

B&BS

B&Bs (*gîtes* in French) are essentially converted or purpose-built private homes whose owners live on-site. From purpose-built villas to heritage homes or someone's spare room, B&Bs are often the most atmospheric lodgings. At the most simple, budget ones, bathrooms might be shared; more commonly, B&Bs are midrange accommodations with a private bathroom, and, as the name suggests, free breakfast (usually continental). People who like privacy may find B&Bs too intimate, as walls are rarely soundproof. Overall though, they offer the best value for your travel money.

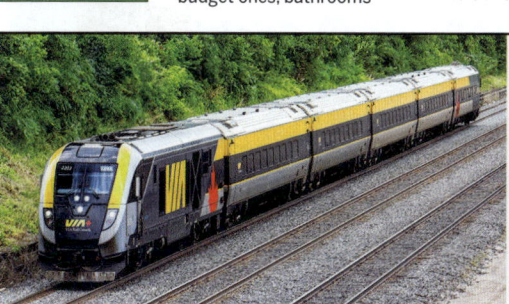

SLEEPER TRAINS

VIA Rail offers several overnight services where you can roll over in the early morning and watch the sun rising over some spellbinding Canadian vistas. Consider the cross-country Canadian service, which takes four days to trundle from Toronto to Vancouver, and choose from curtained bunks to plush cabins with private washrooms and gourmet meal plans.

DOS & DON'TS

Do be mindful of Indigenous customs and traditions.

Don't bring food or drink into ceremonial spaces.

Do bring an offering to a sweat lodge ceremony. Tobacco is traditional.

Do seek out Indigenous perspectives. Visit Indigenous-run museums and galleries, join Indigenous-led tours. Check **Indigenous Tourism Association of Canada** (indigenoustourism.ca).

LEAVE A SMALL FOOTPRINT

Canada's Dead Sea, Little Manitou Lake, is sensitive to human intervention. Wear eco-friendly sunscreens to avoid contaminating these mineral-rich waters.

Shop at farmers markets for locally grown berries and go for wild game instead of imported products.

Sample 'grain-to-glass' distilling in Manitoba. Stumbletown Distilling and Farmery produce spirits with native grains and fruit.

Skate on naturally formed ice as opposed to refrigerated rinks or artificial, resource- and energy-intensive surfaces. Every year, Ottawa's Rideau Canal freezes on its own into the world's longest ice-skating rink.

SUPPORT LOCAL

Seek out Indigenous-led tours empowering communities financially and magnifying lesser-known perspectives.

Choose family-run, independent rural accommodations such as homestays, or B&Bs in heritage buildings, instead of chains.

Shop unique, Inuit-designed souvenirs from First Nations–owned galleries and boutiques in the Yukon and Northwest Territories, such as Gallery of the Midnight Sun.

CLIMATE CHANGE & TRAVEL

Lonely Planet urges all travellers to engage with their travel carbon footprint, which will mainly come from air travel. While there often isn't an alternative, travellers can look to minimise the number of flights they take, opt for newer aircrafts and use cleaner ground transport, such as trains.

One proposed solution – purchasing carbon offsets – unfortunately does not cancel out the impact of individual flights. While most destinations will depend on air travel for the foreseeable future, for now, pursuing ground-based travel where possible is the best course of action.

The UN Carbon Offset Calculator shows how flying impacts a household's emissions:

The ICAO's carbon emissions calculator allows visitors to analyse the CO2 generated by point-to-point journeys:

RESOURCES

davidsuzuki.org
goodwork.ca/volunteer
naturecanada.ca
parks.canada.ca
indigenoustourism.ca

RESPONSIBLE TRAVEL

Tips to leave a lighter footprint, support local, and have a positive impact on local communities.

ON THE ROAD
Canoeing has a long history in Canada through its Indigenous Peoples. Today, it's a fantastic, ecologically sound means of exploring waterscapes. Recreational operators abound across rivers and lakes.

Consider wild camping on Parks Canada sites (where this is allowed). Along with carrying a low carbon footprint, these can be some of the more memorable adventures Canada's wilderness has to offer.

Winter travel offers some of Canada's most unique, zero-emissions experiences. Discover snowy terrains with non-motorised activities such as snowshoeing or cross-country skiing.

Scenic nature tours, for example, lake cruises and around nature parks, are increasingly incorporating e-vehicles into sightseeing fleets. Inquire ahead.

Green transport in Vancouver makes fully sustainable sightseeing easy. Hop on an e-bike, e-scooter or into an electric rideshare – 90% of Van City's electricity is hydro-powered.

GIVE BACK
Contribute to the community-driven retreat Auberge Yoga Salamandre Lac-Brome in Lac-Brome, Québec. Enjoy volunteer-led yoga classes and return the favor by helping with daily activities or organizing a creative session.

Get your hands dirty and get to know locals volunteering on a rural organic farm via Worldwide Opportunities on Organic Farms (wwoof.ca). Stays are available across Canada and offer fascinating, firsthand experiences into harvesting and horticulture.

Share your story at the Canadian Museum for Human Rights in Winnipeg by writing down or recording your thoughts, reflections, or experiences at designated stations. If a language you speak is not represented on the 'Welcome' wall, museum staff will ensure it gets added.

QUICK TIPS TO HELP YOU MANAGE YOUR MONEY

The Canadian dollar (CAD/$) is the only accepted currency throughout Canada. Most banks will exchange American dollars.

TAXES

Taxes include Goods and Services Tax (GST) and Provincial Sales Tax (PST), sometimes combined into a Harmonized Sales Tax (HST). These can add up to 15% to store purchases, hotel rates or restaurant bills. They're never included in the sticker or menu price. Tax rates and their calculations will be presented in your final bill; always be prepared for a higher total price.

LOONIES & TOONIES

Canada's $1 coin are called a 'loonie' (after the loon bird) while the $2 dollar coin is called a 'toonie' (a playful reference to the 'loonie' – they depict a polar bear).

BANKNOTE ARTWORKS

Canada's banknotes depict important citizens and themes. The newest banknotes, made from shiny polymer and with a vertical orientation, include a purple $10 bill portraying Canadian Black civil rights icon Viola Desmond. The newest $20 bills feature His Majesty King Charles III; older circulations still depict Queen Elizabeth II.

CURRENCY

Canadian Dollar

HOW MUCH FOR A...

Parks Canada Family Discovery Pass $150

Public transit day pass $8-15

Overnight hotel parking $30-50

Single adult entry to many of museums can range up to $30, most also offer free-entry days. Check the 'Hours & Admission' tab of institutions' websites.

CREDIT CARDS

Visa, MasterCard and, to a lesser extent, American Express are almost universally accepted in Canada. Remote communities prefer cash. A card is essential for hotel reservations and car rentals.

ATMS

Canadian ATMs typically charge a service fee of up to $5, an exchange fee and possibly a fee from your own bank. Using bank ATMs helps avoid hidden fees found at standalone machines. Some banks have 24/7 drive-thru ATMs.

CASH & TIPPING

Standard tipping is 15% to 20% in restaurants, bars, salons and cafés and 15% for taxis. Paying cash, $1 or $2 per drink is standard in bars.
Cash tips are always preferred.
Tip creep Many restaurants pre-suggest tip levels on their card terminals, often starting at 18%. You can accept or, alternatively, key in your own amount.
Loose change Pennies were discontinued in 2013, so when paying in cash round up or down by the nickel (5 cents).

SAFE TRAVEL

In Canadian cities, crime rates vary widely by neighborhood. Factors include socio-economic disparities and population density, highlighting the need for targeted community support and policing. Rural areas experience lower reported crime rates, though, due to increasing urbanization, are affected by limited, delayed emergency response.

CAR THEFTS
Canada is a safe country but major city centers such as Vancouver, Montréal and Toronto struggle with petty crime. Rental-car break-ins (usually at night) are the most common for travelers. Don't leave valuables in gloveboxes or visible items in backseats; parking garages with video surveillance offer peace of mind.

CANNABIS
Canada legalized the personal use of cannabis in 2018, and you will likely see licensed 'pot shops' alongside regular stores on many streets here. Taking cannabis across Canada's international borders is illegal and taken very seriously, as is smoking in public areas.

HEALTH INSURANCE
Canada is world-renowned for its universal health-care system, but as a non-resident, medical care is expensive to access. Long wait times in ERs are a serious problem. Booking travel insurance that includes health care/medical coverage is essential. Call your credit card provider beforehand, as travel insurance might already be included.

AIR QUALITY
A surge in the number and severity of Canadian wildfires stokes increasing air-quality warnings. Watery eyes, trouble sleeping and respiratory challenges can occur. Check Environment Canada's online weather forecasts (weather.gc.ca) for regional alerts.

Nature's remedy Canada's national PaRx program enables doctors to prescribe nature as medicine. Prescriptions typically treat mental health issues with visits to parks, gardens or green spaces. More than 15,000 prescribers participate in the program.

Wildlife Look out for yellow diamond-shaped signs on country roads. They indicate nearby wildlife presence. A leaping deer, moose (broad, flat antlers, not leaping), caribou (large, higher-reaching, branch-like antlers) and bear images warn of these animals respectively.

TAP WATER
Don't waste money on bottled water. Canada's tap water is generally excellent and a refillable bottle is all you need. Water fountains are everywhere. Don't be shy to ask for iced tap water in restaurants..

PLANES Canadians often complain about exorbitantly priced Air Canada and WestJet domestic flights and overall unavailability of budget providers/routes. Budget carriers include Flair Airlines (flyflair.com) and Porter Airlines (fly porter.com); Rouge (flyrouge.com) is Air Canada's budget brand. Several northern destinations are only reachable by air.

BUS In recent years, Greyhound Canada has cut services dramatically, offering only a handful of connections, primarily in the east and to Vancouver. Regional carriers pick up the slack but not everywhere. Some routes are cleaner, more comfortable and reliable than others.

FREIGHTERS An adventurous (though not necessarily inexpensive nor widely available), travel option within Canada (or heading abroad) is a cargo ship. Though considerably less cushy than the experience on cruise ships, they offer a salty, unique perspective on regional seafaring. Maris Freighter Cruises (freightercruises.com) has good info on routes (they're ever-changing).

KNOW YOUR CARBON FOOTPRINT
A domestic flight from Toronto to Montreal emits roughly 137kg of CO_2 per passenger, while taking a bus produces about 50kg, and traveling by train generates only 18kg. There are a number of carbon calculators online. We use Resurgence at resurgence.org/resources/carbon-calculator.

ROAD DISTANCE CHART (KMS)

	Ottawa	Toronto	Montréal	Québec City	Fredericton	Victoria	Vancouver	Calgary	Edmonton
Toronto	405								
Montréal	200	541							
Québec City	464	802	251						
Fredericton	1026	1364	812	589					
Victoria	4370	4370	4567	4835	5392				
Vancouver	4360	4360	4557	4825	5382	118			
Calgary	3330	3414	3527	3849	4421	1050	971		
Edmonton	3388	3377	3588	3819	4390	1238	1159	299	
Winnipeg	2140	2062	2273	2509	3075	2379	2300	1332	1353

TRANSPORTATION TIPS TO HELP YOU GET AROUND

Canada's vastness makes flying the most efficient (though expensive) transport. Beware, extreme weather can affect flight schedules significantly. If you have time to spare, driving – or even better, train-tripping – can be a more rewarding and reliable way to explore within provinces. Limited public transport in rural areas will also require your own set of wheels.

CAR RENTAL
All the major rental companies operate in Canada, most conveniently at airport kiosks. Book before arriving for best prices and vehicle selection. A valid driver's license or International Driving Permit (IDP) is required. Expect to pay more if aged under 25.

ELECTRIC VEHICLES
Canada's car rental companies are generally behind the US and Europe in offering EVs. Standard rentals typically cost $50 per day, EVs are usually $125 or above. The vast majority (88%) of charging stations are in three provinces (Québec, Ontario, British Columbia). Check plugshare.com for locations.

TRANSPORT COSTS

Car rental $50 per day

Petrol approx $1.35/litre

Plane ticket cost from Toronto to Vancouver $500

TRAINS Canada is a slow-travel dream. From the iconic cross-country Canadian service (four days from Toronto to Vancouver) to scenery-hugging regional routes in the Rockies, Québec or out to the Maritimes, these photogenic weaves are entirely memorable. VIA Rail's website often offers deals. Visit viarail.ca/en/offers/deals-discounts.

DRIVING ESSENTIALS

Drive on the right side of the road.

Speed limit on Canadian highways varies from 100km/h to 120km/h.

Unless indicated otherwise, it is legal to make a right-hand turn at a red light after coming to a complete stop.

.08 Blood alcohol limit varies by province from 0.00% to 0.08%.

It is illegal to make a U-turn at an intersection with traffic lights.

EXTREME CONDITIONS Canada's well-maintained highways make long-distance driving an epic experience. But winter storms and summer wildfires can dangerously affect road conditions and visibility. Having the appropriate (winter) tires on your vehicle is essential. If you have limited experience with winter driving, refrain from driving on highways and gravel roads due to drifting snow and black ice.

GETTING TO THE CITY CENTER

TRAIN
Toronto Pearson and Vancouver airports offer rapid rail transit (pictured left) to downtown. In Vancouver and Montréal, shuttle buses connect to public train stations heading into the city center (at an additional fare cost).

BUS
Shuttle buses, as well as regular bus (public transit) routes, connect most Canadian airports to their respective city centers. Duration can be anywhere from 30 minutes to an hour, depending on traffic. Service frequency varies, and nighttime (typically between midnight and 6am) is mostly unavailable.

REGIONAL AIRPORTS
Regional airports might not have taxis waiting for arrivals after midnight. In case of flight delays (common in winter), have a local taxi number ready.

HOW MUCH FOR A...

Train
$12.35
25 minutes

Bus
$3.30
1 hour

Taxi
$60
1 hour

TAXI AND RIDESHARING
Taxi and ridesharing services (Uber and Lyft) are available at major Canadian airports. Both operate in designated areas – typically, taxi stands and ridesharing pickup zones (both are clearly marked). Final fares are dependent on distance and traffic.

HOPP
Since 2025, an additional ridesharing company services Toronto Pearson. Run by the Estonian ridesharing company Bolt (best known in Europe and Asia), Hopp operates in Toronto and the Greater Toronto Area. At the time of writing, there were no public plans for further Canada expansion.

AIRPORT SURCHARGE
Taxis leaving from Canadian airports typically charge an extra $5 to $10 in addition to the regular meter fare.

OTHER POINTS OF ENTRY
Land crossings The almost 9000km US–Canada land border has dozens of official road crossings, the busiest of which are open 24 hours a day. Visit cbsa-asfc.gc.ca/bwt-taf for locations and wait times. When arriving by vehicle, you'll still be required to fill out a declaration form. Based on your answers, border staff will ask you questions regarding the nature and length of your visit. Account for extra time at road crossings during higher-traffic times such as summer (June to August), holiday weekends (especially on Mondays) and, generally, afternoons and evenings.

Ferry crossings Ferry crossings on the coasts connect the USA and Canada, including several ferries running between Washington and British Columbia, from Maine to Maritimes destinations, and Alaska to Prince Rupert, British Columbia.

Advanced declaration forms On the border agency's ArriveCAN app, filling out your declaration up to 72 hours pre-arrival is recommended. You can list up to four people living at the same address on one card, but each traveler is responsible for their own declaration. The service is available at 10 Canadian airports (including Toronto Pearson, Vancouver and Montréal-Trudeau).

EASY STEPS FROM THE AIRPORT TO THE CITY CENTER

Toronto, Vancouver and Montréal are Canada's busiest international airports, with smaller options and connecting airports located throughout the country. You can also arrive via multiple road, rail and even ocean crossings from the US. Major airports are typically connected to downtown centers by rail, taxi or public transit services, with major car rental providers also operating counters for incoming passengers.

AT THE AIRPORT

SIM CARDS
Sim cards for unlocked phones can be purchased at airports, convenience stores and in malls at mobile providers' kiosks. Rogers offers the best nationwide coverage, while Telus, Bell and regional providers offer good rural (or region-specific) coverage. Most carriers provide pre-paid eSIMs.

INTERNATIONAL CURRENCY EXCHANGE (ICE)
The exchange rates at airport outlets are not as good as those at local banks. Exchanging cash here will be more convenient than finding a bank as the outlets have longer opening times and less chance of a queue. However, it's probably easiest to get some cash from your home bank pre-departure.

Wi-fi Free wi-fi is available in Canada's major hub airports (Toronto, Vancouver, Montréal, Edmonton, Halifax) and most other airports.

ATMs ATMs from Canadian banks (TD, CIBC, Scotiabank, RBC) in airports are best for avoiding hidden fees (compared to standalone machines).

Charging devices Free charging stations are common, you'll also find standard (non-USB port) outlets around gates (these require a travel adapter).

CUSTOM REGULATIONS

Duty-free Use your Declaration Form (provided as paper on international flights or to be completed at electronic kiosks upon landing). Allowance limits include 1.5L of wine and 200 cigarettes; bringing cannabis into Canada is illegal.

Paying tax and duty If you exceed limits, you are required to pay tax on items or forfeit them. Customs officers perform random baggage checks.

Practicalities

ARRIVING
238

GETTING AROUND
240

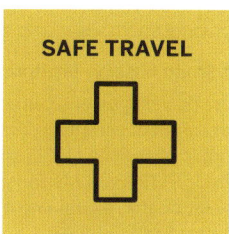
SAFE TRAVEL
242

MONEY
243

RESPONSIBLE TRAVEL
244

ACCOMMODATIONS
246

ESSENTIALS
248

LANGUAGE
250

Right Lakeside camping, Yukon Territory (p216)

📖 Historic Sites & Heirlooms

Qaummaarviit Territorial Park
On an island 12km west of Iqaluit, this site preserves a 750-year-old Inuit (Thule) winter camp where you can see 11 well-preserved traditional sod houses and a grave site.

Fort Smith Mission Territorial Park
Contains vestiges of a Catholic mission first established at the site in 1876, including a bishop's residence (1911), the town's original cathedral (1923), a Marian grotto, and numerous signboards explaining its erstwhile role and function.

Bonanza Creek Discovery Claim
The place that sparked the Klondike gold rush is now a national historic site 14km south of Dawson City. An interpretive trail with info boards leads visitors around the eerily quiet creek surrounded by brush and trees.

Jack London Museum
This literary labour of love in Dawson City contains a reconstructed portion of the writer's original cabin found at Henderson Creek by the museum's former curator, Dick North, in the 1960s.

🍴 A Taste of the Territories

Wildcat Café $$
Encased in one of Yellowknife's oldest buildings dating from 1937 with a menu that serves everything from British scotch eggs to Indigenous bannock.

Antoinette's $$$
Tackling a full gamut of global cuisine with a strong bias towards Caribbean flavors, this colorfully attired Whitehorse restaurant takes you on a tasty around-the-world journey.

Anna's Home Cooking $$
Superb smalltown home away from home in tiny Fort Smith with warmly welcoming

Akshayuk Pass Route

owners, delectable daily soups and a giant pizza oven.

Grandma's Kitchen $$
The only reliable place to eat in Arctic Tuktoyaktuk, this family-run restaurant serves musk-ox burgers and the dare-to-try dish, *muktuk* (whale blubber).

Small Northern Communities

Hay River, NWT
The southern gateway to the Northwest Territories, Hay River is an old fur-trading post on Great Slave Lake.

Carcross, Yukon
Home to a history-defining railroad, gold rush memorabilia, the finest American beach north of 60°, and a lavish manifestation of Tagish First Nation culture.

Fort Smith, NWT
Fort Smith has amassed a wealth of heirlooms at its Northern Life Museum, which has one of the largest collections of Indigenous and settler artifacts in Northern Canada.

Cambridge Bay, Nunavut
Cold, blustery regional center acts as a brief stopover for small cruise ships navigating the Northwest Passage. Its best attraction is the Canadian High Arctic Research Station.

Listings

BEST OF THE REST

Accessible National Parks

Kluane National Park Reserve
Vast, wild and mostly roadless, Kluane guards 17 of Canada's 20 highest mountains, over 2000 glaciers and endless tracts of unadulterated backcountry.

Auyuittuq National Park
Highlights of Nunavut's most accessible park include views of the sheer face of Mt Thor and the flat-topped countenance of Mt Asgard, where James Bond famously base-jumped off a cliff in his skis in the film *The Spy Who Loved Me*.

Nahanni National Park Reserve
The most spectacular of the NWT's six national parks, Nahanni is a roadless wilderness famed for its untamed rivers, deep canyons, huge waterfalls and karst topography riddled with intricate cave systems.

Wood Buffalo National Park
Canada's largest national park covers an area the size of Switzerland and is home to around 3500 hybridized wood-plains bison, the world's largest free-roaming herd.

Indigenous Art & Culture

Carvings Nunavut
Displays a diverse selection of Inuit serpentine and whalebone sculptures in Iqaluit.

Gallery of the Midnight Sun
A Yellowknife shop well-stocked with Inuit and First Nations art, including ornately decorated Dene moccasins and small stone sculptures by Inuvialuit artists.

Carcross Commons
An artistic celebration of Indigenous culture replete with totem poles, a wood-carving house and various cabins turned into souvenir shops and decorated with striking Tagish motifs.

Northern Collectables
An old curiosity shop in Iqaluit stuffed with prints from Kinngait luminaries.

Hiking above 60° North

Apex Trail
Contouring a rocky bluff overlooking Frobisher Bay in Iqaluit, this path meanders between a diminutive cemetery and a sandy beach that lies below the outlying hamlet of Apex, juxtaposing boggy muskeg with minor rock scrambles.

Akshayuk Pass Route
Nunavut's most defined and doable long-distance hike follows a broad open valley, climbing to a height of 500m and crossing the Arctic Circle en route.

Canol Heritage Trail
A wild, challenging hiking/biking trek that stretches for 355km between Norman Wells and the Yukon border along the route of the erstwhile Canol pipeline.

Grizzly Lake Trail
A gutsy 22km round-trip backpacking adventure in Tombstone Territorial Park, much of it along a stony but spectacular ridgetop with inspiring views of Mt Monolith.

Boot Lake Trail
This 5km loop around a tree-lined lake in Inuvik marks one of the most northerly portions of the Trans-Canada Trail.

lands span the boreal regions immediately south of the Arctic. Dene Nations include the Yellowknives and the Slavey whose homelands abut Great Slave Lake. The caribou was the cornerstone of the Dene economy, although moose, musk oxen and fish were also harvested.

The Yukon counts 14 First Nations including the Vuntut Gwitchin, the most northerly non-Inuit people in North America, who co-own Air North, the Yukon's main airline. The Gwitchin were one of the first Indigenous groups in Canada to sign a successful claims agreement in 1995. After investing in Air North in 2002, the Vuntut Development Corporation bought several Boeing jets and expanded the airline's services to BC, Alberta and Ontario, making air travel for Yukoners much more affordable.

Further south, the Tagish are a self-governing First Nation based mainly around Carcross in the Southern Lakes region of the Yukon. They maintain a learning center in the Carcross Commons where you can admire a selection of their totem poles representing the Nation's six clans, along with other art pieces emblazoned on the local buildings. With deep ancestral roots in the region, the Tagish are central to the Yukon story on many levels. Three of the four prospectors responsible for the original gold discovery at Bonanza Creek in the Klondike in 1896 were Tagish: Keish (usually known as Skookum Jim), his nephew Káa Goox (Dawson Charlie), and his oft-forgotten sister, Shaaw Tláa (Kate Carmack).

The largest of the Yukon's First Nations is the Kwanlin Dün. Based in a longhouse-style cultural center in Whitehorse, the Kwanlin is a diverse nation whose members include people of Tagish, Inland Tlingit and South Tutchone heritage with whom they share strong linguistic ties and overlapping territory.

Shared Knowledge

A crucial component of Inuit culture is *qauijimajatuqangit*, or shared knowledge. When, in September 2014, Parks Canada, after 169 years of mostly fruitless searching, found HMS *Erebus*, the 'lost' ship captained by Sir John Franklin on his fateful 1845 voyage to chart the Northwest Passage, it wasn't purely because of modern side-scan sonar technology. Equally important were remarkably accurate Inuit oral testimonies passed down through generations that referenced erstwhile encounters with stricken sailors and their ice-bound ships.

Today, the Kitikmeot Inuit Association collaborates closely with Parks Canada to co-manage both HMS *Erebus* and its sister ship, HMS *Terror* (found in 2016) as a National Historic Site.

Indigenous Culture in the Territories

THE DESCENDANTS OF CANADA'S ORIGINAL INHABITANTS

If you want to appreciate the complex nuances of Canada's Indigenous culture, the territories is a good place to start. Almost half of the people living north of 60 degrees are Indigenous – either First Nations, Métis or Inuit – ranging from 22.3% in the Yukon to 86% in Nunavut.

The Inuit

The Inuit are descendants of the Thule people, a civilization that has inhabited the Arctic regions of Northern Canada since around 1000 CE. They number about 70,000, most of them in Nunavut, and make up around 0.2% of Canada's total population.

The Inuit are famed for their world-renowned art, no more so than in Kinngait, a small community of around 1400 people off Baffin Island's Foxe Peninsula that has more artists per total population than Florence or Paris. Kinngait's artistic renaissance dates from the late 1950s, when residents pioneered modern printmaking techniques and began to successfully market their work worldwide. Their skills have since been passed down through family lineage, with artists like the late Kenojuak Ashevak having garnered international acclaim. Kinngait upped the ante in 2018 with the opening of the Kenojuak Cultural Centre & Print Shop, a facility divided between an exhibition space and a state-of-the-art print workshop where visitors can watch the masters at work employing dexterous stone-cut, lithograph and stenciling techniques.

First Nations

While Nunavut is dominated by Inuit people, the Northwest Territories and the Yukon are mostly the preserve of the First Nations and, to a lesser extent the Métis (people of mixed Indigenous and European ancestry).

Large numbers of Indigenous people living in the NWT are classified as Dene; a loosely defined group of Athabaskan-speaking First Nations whose traditional

Left Inuit woman wearing a traditional seal-skin smock **Center** Eagle totem pole, Carcross **Right** Dene drummers

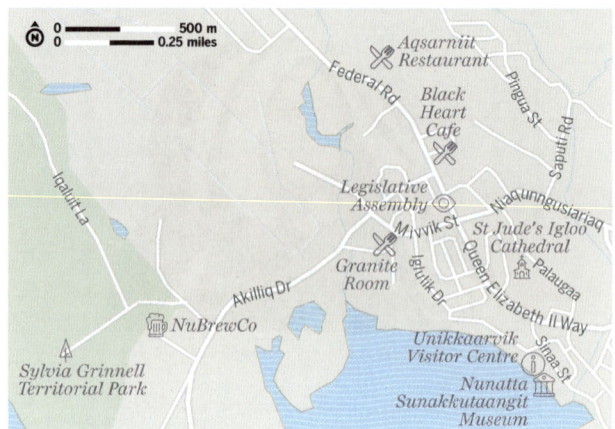

Top left Sylvia Grinnell Territorial Park
Bottom left St Jude's Igloo Cathedral

Northern Exposure

Iqaluit has an unusual non-linear layout, interrupted by various hills and crags, and crossed by a mix of asphalt and dirt streets. The best place to get orientated is the **Unikkaarvik Visitor Centre** (destinationnunavut.ca) by the waterfront – this is also the town's most encyclopedic museum, with exhibits of Inuit culture and a fearsome stuffed polar bear. Next door is the **Nunatta Sunakkutaangit Museum** (nunattasunakkutaangit.ca), with a small permanent collection presenting Indigenous clothing, kayaks and tools.

The city's most emblematic edifice is **St Jude's Igloo Cathedral** (iqaluitcathedral.ca), the second incarnation of a similar church that burnt down in 2005. The circular interior is illuminated by a rooftop skylight. Nearby, a small sculpture garden next to the post office is anchored by a mermaid-like Sedna (sea goddess) statue fashioned out of scrap metal.

The **Legislative Assembly** (assembly.nu.ca) offers entertaining free tours (by appointment) of Nunavut's handsome parliament building with its Indigenous touches. You can admire its igloo-like interior, sealskin benches and seats for community elders.

Cusp of the Wilderness

For a taste of the Baffin wilderness, walk over to **Sylvia Grinnell Territorial Park**, 2km from downtown, the city's window into the vast emptiness of the tundra. You can contemplate its dizzying scale at a bleakly beautiful viewpoint overlooking two mini waterfalls that adorn the mouth of the Sylvia Grinnell River. On the way back, warm up at **NuBrewCo** (nubrewbeer.ca), Canada's most northerly brewery.

Eating Places

Iqaluit's best eating places are in its hotels. Expect big portions at inflated prices. Arctic specials like char and musk ox are widely available. **The Granite Room** in the Discovery Hotel gives gourmet a go with caribou medallions, escargot and rack of lamb. The **Aqsarniit Restaurant** in the namesake hotel has a succinct international menu that includes esoteric dishes like Haitian chicken.

For more casual fare, there are several fast-food joints, the cozy caffeine-replenishing **Black Heart Cafe**, and one of Canada's most northerly Tim Hortons. There's also one large, expensive supermarket.

49 A Taste of NUNAVUT

INNUIT CULTURE | ARCTIC LANDSCAPES | BEER

■ Despite its location in Nunavut Territory near Baffin Island's southern tip, **Iqaluit** exudes a definitive Arctic feel with its tundra landscapes, moon-base architecture and a perennial chilliness, even in summer. Come here to taste the slightly retro essence of a very different Canada where children still play in the streets, dogs roam untethered and harsh winters are softened by a charitable help-thy-neighbor ethos.

How to

Getting here/around Iqaluit is tricky to get to. Your only options are to fly from Yellowknife or Ottawa with Canadian North. Fights aren't cheap.

When to go July and August when the temperature might creep above 10°C.

Apex Trail Enjoy this 2.5km trail around a rocky bluff overlooking Frobisher Bay southeast of downtown.

Astro Hill Complex Contains Nunavut's tallest buildings, including the Frobisher Inn, a modern supermarket, a cinema and several restaurants.

48 Journey into the ARCTIC

WILDLIFE | BARREN TUNDRA | REMOTE COMMUNITIES

▬▬ The only public road in North America to cross the Arctic Circle, the daunting Dempster Highway stretches for 740km from just east of Dawson City to Inuvik. En route, you'll drive from tussocky tundra to the lake-dotted Mackenzie River delta.

Trip Notes

Getting there/around To get to the start of the Dempster, fly into Whitehorse, rent a car and drive 493km north on the Klondike Hwy to Dempster Corner.

When to go June to September.

Supplies Bring plenty of food and water; the only decent restaurant on the Dempster is at Eagle Plains.

The road is gravel Travel with extra gas and tires, and expect to use them.

Dempster Rest Stops

It takes around 10 to 12 hours to drive to Inuvik without stopping. However, it's much nicer to split the journey over two days, followed by a night in Inuvik and two extra days on the way back.

The Yukon government maintains three roadside campgrounds and there are another three across the border in the Northwest Territories.

Top left Giant Mine
Bottom left Prince of Wales Northern Heritage Centre

Giant Mine's Mixed Legacy

Modern Yellowknife's pièce de résistance is the **Prince of Wales Northern Heritage Centre** (pwnhc.ca) a free-to-enter homage to the Northwest Territories that provides an excellent precis of the region's mining history, including its erstwhile Giant Mine.

Located 5km north of town, the Giant Mine went a long way in making the town rich in the late 20th century but not without a litany of toxic side-effects. The site's clean-up or 'remediation' is ongoing and expected to last until at least 2038 and ultimately cost $4.4 billion. Not surprisingly, access to the hazardous site is prohibited. The closest you can get is the **Yellowknife Historical Museum** (yellowknifehistory.com), whose exhibits place a strong emphasis on the mine's bittersweet history. They're laid out in the mineworker's old recreation hall 2km beyond the airport turn-off. Also on show is a revolving film about Yellowknife's evolution and a small restaurant offering lunch. Outside, you can sift through a jumble of rusty industrial machinery and absorb some info pertaining to the ecological recovery of adjacent Baker Creek.

For a safe, if distant, glimpse of the mine site and its stark industrial buildings, rent an e-bike from **Overlander Sports** (overlandersports.com) and pull over at the **Giant Mine Scenic Viewpoint** at Km 5 on the Ingraham Trail. Further along the road, you'll pass the abandoned shaft of the Ptarmigan Mine poking above the trees.

◇ Diamonds

The main diamond mines are located around 300km northeast of Yellowknife in isolated terrain with hostile winter temperatures. They include the Diavik, Gahcho Kué and Ekati mines, the oldest dating from 1998. In 2018, Diavik unearthed the largest diamond ever found in North America, a 552-carat beauty roughly the size of a chicken's egg.

In town, the **NWT Diamond Centre** (nwtdiamondcentre.com) presents Yellowknife's premier mineral in all its crystalline glory with an A to Z of diamond intel and a short, fascinating film about the territory's mines. Assorted jewelry in glass cases tempts those with money to burn.

47 Built on Gold & DIAPERSMONDS

MINING HISTORY | CYCLING | MUSEUMS

The territory's main settlement and capital, **Yellowknife**, is a city born of gold that's since shifted its focus to the equally lucrative business of diamonds. In the disparate lands above 60º north, Yellowknife is the main hub and orientation point, a place that, despite its generic conference hotels and legislative assembly, retains a palpable frontier spirit and plenty of engrossing mining paraphernalia.

How to

Getting there/around
Yellowknife is pretty isolated and most people arrive by plane. The international airport has good connections to other Canadian cities. The city is small and walking is the easiest way to get around.

When to go June to August is the best time. Stick around until September to see the Northern Lights.

Ingraham Trail Rent an e-bike and explore this 70km-long road with its abundant campgrounds, boat launches, lakes and trails.

Dredge No 4

The Klondike's initial prospectors came armed with only the most rudimentary of tools (a gold pan and shovel were standard), but as big business and smarter technology took over in the early 1900s, dredges became the primary modus operandi. Beginning in 1905, the dredge era lasted over 50 years and introduced the concept of gold mining on an industrial scale to Dawson. The era's legacy can be investigated at **Dredge No 4**, a floating sluice plant turned historical site near Bonanza Creek, 14km south of Dawson. The dredge served for 46 years, repaying its investment by digging up nine tonnes of gold.

were constructed in the decade after the gold boom. Some, such as the **Palace Grand Theatre** *(parks.canada.ca/lhn-nhs/yt/klondike)*, are faithful replicas of the originals. Helping you piece together the story, the whole town is chock-a-block with pictorial signboards documenting the historical significance of the various tenements and the charismatic characters who once frequented them.

Museum Overview

Historically speaking, the 'rug' that ties the historical site together is the **Dawson City Museum** *(dawsonmuseum.ca)* housed in the landmark 1901 Old Territorial Administration building. Inside, fascinating gold-rush paraphernalia (including old gold pans) is complemented by numerous Indigenous artifacts.

Above Dredge No 4

46 DAWSON'S
Gold Rush History

ARCHITECTURE | HISTORY | GUIDED TOURS

Dawson is western Canada's historical highlight, a richly evocative gold-mining town whose rags-to-riches, boom-bust story glows with an unsullied authenticity. This is where the legendary Klondike gold rush reached its heady apex between 1897 and 1900, as more than 35,000 hungry prospectors rafted into the region. Today, the town is a quirky crossroads of mavericks, tourists and miners still working the goldfields.

How To

Getting there/around Drive in on the Klondike Hwy (an epic road trip) or fly in with Air North from Whitehorse. The town itself is tiny and easy to negotiate on foot.

When to go June to September, with bearable temperatures and long hours of daylight.

Klondike Experience (klondikeexperience.com) This fabulous Dawson-based company offers day trips around the town center before heading out to the historic goldfields. Transport's included.

The Historical Hub

For those feverish for juicy gold-rush stories, the best place to get acquainted with Dawson and its historical heirlooms is the wooden **Visitor Information Centre** on Front St, where you'll find costumed guides dispensing precious nuggets of advice, along with a mini-museum of exhibits and a small theater showing a revolving reel of four Klondike-related films.

Guided tours led by Parks Canada docents dressed in period garb allow you to enter some of the buildings (of which there are 26), and examine the century-old paddle-steamer **SS Keno** (pc.gc.ca; guided tour $11). A good half-dozen tours leave daily in the summer. Alternatively, it's perfectly feasible to roam the town's tight downtown grid on your own and get a superficial view of the manic happenings of 1897–98. Most of the surviving buildings

SS Klondike

Whitehorse's historical pièce de résistance is the **SS Klondike** (pc.gc.ca) a paddle-steamer built in 1937 to carry freight along the Yukon River. Decommissioned in 1955 after the Klondike Highway was opened, the steamer has been rehabilitated and made into a national historic site. The boat, with its giant stern wheel, has its own visitor center and sits handsomely in dry dock next to the Robert Campbell Bridge. It is undergoing renovations through 2027 but you can still peruse the visitor center and admire the sternwheeler from outside, where interpretive panels tell its story.

Above SS Klondike

Getting Out on the River

North of the Whitehorse dam, the Yukon River is navigable as far as the Bering Sea, and Whitehorse is a popular embarkation point for canoeists heading solo or in groups to Carmacks, Dawson City and beyond. For trip logistics, rentals and intriguing day paddles, head to the riverside office of **Kanoe People** (kanoepeople.com).

Because of the fast flow of the Yukon River, it's practically impossible to paddle upstream. For this reason, Kanoe People arranges bus transfers back to Whitehorse from the confluence of the Takhini and Yukon Rivers, a four-hour paddle from downtown Whitehorse.

45 WHITEHORSE & the Yukon River

CANOEING | HIKING | HISTORIC SITES

In the days before a coherent settlement existed, 'White Horse' was the name given to a set of ferocious rapids on the Yukon River that gold rush prospectors had to portage around or attempt to 'shoot' in hastily built rafts. Dams pacified the river in the 1920s and the mighty waterway is now a hub for recreational activities.

How to

Getting here/around You can drive to Whitehorse on the Alaska Hwy or fly into Erik Nielsen International Airport which has regular connections to Vancouver. The city is small and highly walkable.

When to go June to September when the river is ice-free.

Yukon Transportation Museum Got a layover, or a long wait for a plane? Check out this superb museum within walking distance of the airport.

The River from the Shore

These days a sense of calm pervades over Whitehorse's riverside and you can stroll its wooded banks on the paved **Millennium Trail**, a short 5km loop that traces a rough circle between downtown's Robert Campbell Bridge and the Rotary Centennial Bridge. For a longer 15km loop, carry on south to the **Miles Canyon Suspension Bridge** where the Yukon River is pushed through a narrow gorge. The canyon hike involves some road walking on the river's west bank complemented by prettier forest trails on the east side.

Further north, the Yukon flows directly through downtown with most of the metro action centered on the west bank, where a paved trail hugs the waterside. Here, you'll find many of Whitehorse's premier sights sandwiched between **Rotary Peace Park** at the southern end and **Shipyards Park** in the north.

EATING & DRINKING

There's no real signature dish in the territories. One of the most ubiquitous menu items is Arctic char (pictured top right) best served pan-seared in a citrus-based sauce. Other popular fish include lake trout, whitefish and the longstanding Indigenous staple, salmon. *Muktuk* is a must try (pictured bottom right; narwhal being prepared) as long as it's legally harvested.

As well as beef, pork and chicken, restaurants often serve more unusual local meat items such as caribou, musk ox and bison in their burgers, stews or pasta. In some of the more remote communities, the best eating options are in the hotels.

Best restaurant
Bullocks Bistro, Yellowknife (p226)

Must try *muktuk* (whale blubber) bites Grandma's Kitchen (p235), Tuktoyaktuk

FIND YOUR WAY

The remote territories have a pretty scant public transportation network. Cars and planes are the main means of getting around. Outside of Yellowknife and Whitehorse, there are no year-round public buses or scheduled trains. To visit national parks and other adventurous locations, it's worth considering an organized tour with companies like Black Feather *(blackfeather.com)*.

WHERE TO STAY

Hotel accommodations are expensive and options are often limited. Outside of the Yukon there are no real hostels or cheap backpacker facilities. Camping is possible only in the summer.

Town/City	Pros/Cons
Iqaluit	Most hotels have their own restaurants and gyms; no cheap options.
Yellowknife	Several large chain hotels plus a couple of good campgrounds; places lack character and personal touches.
Whitehorse	The territory's largest and most varied sleeping choices; limited deluxe hotels.
Dawson City	Quirky hotels in heritage buildings; books up fast in the summer.

NORTHERN LIGHTS

The territories are a world hot spot for viewing the aurora borealis. Come in September when the nights are longer but it's not yet too cold.

MONEY

Everything is more expensive in the territories from supermarket food to flights. Budget accordingly. The main cities accept credit and debit cards but in more isolated communities it pays to carry a little cash.

Practicalities

ARRIVING

Erik Nielsen Whitehorse International Airport Good links to Edmonton, Vancouver and Calgary with Air Canada and Air North. Bus route 3 connects to downtown.

Yellowknife Airport (pictured) Daily flights to Edmonton, Vancouver and Toronto with Air Canada and Air North. Most hotels have free airport shuttles.

Iqaluit Airport Regular connections to Ottawa and Yellowknife with Canadian North.

HOW MUCH FOR A

Beer
$7-10

Main course meal $25-35

Bike rental per day $80

GETTING AROUND

Plane Many towns and villages in the territories are only reachable by air. The region's main carriers are Air North, Canadian Northern and Air Tindi.

Car The Yukon is accessible via the Alaska and Klondike Highways, which link Whitehorse, Dawson City and Haines Junction. Yellowknife can be reached from Edmonton in the south via the MacKenzie (Hwy 35) and Yellowknife (Hwy 3) Highways.

Bicycle In the summer, you can rent bikes to navigate the uncongested cities of Whitehorse and Yellowknife or forge further afield and explore the sights around Dawson City and the Ingraham Trail. Some diehards plan cycling excursions along the Klondike and Dempster Highways.

WHEN TO GO

SPRING
Watch the spectacular ice break-up on the Yukon River in Dawson City.

SUMMER
Warm temperatures, midnight sun and limitless hiking and canoeing.

FALL
Longer nights make for better stargazing. Rivers and lakes start to freeze over.

WINTER
Dog-sledding, snowmobiling and watching the Northern Lights.

Attend a church service in Iqaluit's unique **Igloo Cathedral** (p231)
✈ *5hr from Yellowknife*

Enjoy the silence amid the stunted forests of **Tombstone Territorial Park** (p229)
🚗 *1½hr from Dawson City*

Uncover the less glittery history of gold at the **Yellowknife Historical Museum** (p227)
🚗 *6min from Yellowknife*

Sally forth across the arctic tundra in **Sylvia Grinnell Territorial Park** (p231) near Iqaluit
🚶 *30min from Iqaluit*

THE TERRITORIES
Trip Builder

Only a small percentage of Canadians ever venture north of 60°N, yet the nation's three sparsely populated territories comprise 40% of the country's total land mass and contain some of its most untamed and starkly beautiful scenery.

Test your driving skills on the gravelly Dempster Highway all the way to the **Arctic Circle** (p228)
🚗 7hr from Dawson City

See where the Klondike gold rush reached its heady climax in **Dawson City** (p224)
🚗 6½hr from Whitehorse

Rent a canoe and plan an adventurous paddle along the Yukon River from **Whitehorse** (p222)
🚗 6½hr from Dawson City

Admire the steam-powered mechanics of the **SS Klondike** (p223) in Whitehorse
🚗 6½hr from Dawson City

CLOCKWISE FROM BOTTOM LEFT: MARK-WU/SHUTTERSTOCK, CRISTINA RAMOS HERNANDO/SHUTTERSTOCK, CAROLYN HELLER/LONELY PLANET, DAVID STANLEY FROM NANAIMO, CANADA, CC BY 2.0/WIKIMEDIA COMMONS

- **Trip Builder** (p218)
- **Practicalities** (p220)
- **Whitehorse & the Yukon River** (p222)
- **Dawson's Gold Rush History** (p224)
- **Built on Gold & Diamonds** (p226)
- **Journey into the Arctic** (p228)
- **A Taste of Nunavut** (p230)
- **Indigenous Culture in the Territories** (p232)
- **Listings** (p234)

THE TERRITORIES

GOLD RUSHES | WILDERNESS | INDIGENOUS CULTURE

RESEARCHED BY BRENDAN SAINSBURY

Haida Heritage Centre

To learn about the Haida People of Haida Gwaii, visit this heritage centre at Kay 'Llnagaay. The award-winning exhibits share traditional stories, elaborate totem poles and more.

Nk'Mip Desert Cultural Centre

In Osoyoos, learn the traditions of the Osoyoos Indian Band through a variety of exhibits, displays and several trails through the only desert in Canada.

Squamish Lil'wat Cultural Centre

Visit this cultural center in Whistler to learn about both the Squamish and Lil'wat Nations through free guided tours, interactive experiences and performances.

Eating & Drinking Highlights

Granville Island Brewing Taproom $$

One of Vancouver's best breweries. Stop by for a craft beer or some light bites.

Old Vines Restaurant $$$

Located at Quails' Gate Winery in the Okanagan, Old Vines serves farm-to-table fare in a beautiful setting with views of the vineyard and Okanagan Lake below.

Red Fish Blue Fish $

For sustainable, fresh seafood in Victoria, this waterfront eatery serves favorites like fish tacos and chowder from a converted shipping container.

Tacofino $

The iconic taco truck that started in Tofino now also has locations in Vancouver, where you can try its variety of creative tacos made from local ingredients.

Pointe Restaurant $$$

The location is just as phenomenal as the food. Dine on freshly caught seafood and other seasonal dishes while admiring the 360-degree views of rocky shorelines and beaches.

Teahouse in Stanley Park $$$

This upscale restaurant, located right in Vancouver's iconic Stanley Park, serves Pacific Northwest fare with beautiful forest and ocean views.

Sea to Sky Gondola

Epic Adventures

Capilano Suspension Bridge Park

The main 137m-long suspension bridge spans over Capilano River Canyon and there are seven other smaller bridges as part of the Treetops Adventure.

Sea to Sky Gondola

Located in Squamish, the Sea to Sky Gondola soars dramatically over Howe Sound, giving endless views of mountain peaks, sparkling fjords and forested valleys.

Squamish Adventure Centre

The gateway to outdoor adventures in Squamish, this large timber-framed building is a visitor hub that offers information on the countless outdoor adventures nearby.

Whistler Blackcomb Peak

In winter, you can ski and snowboard at North America's largest ski resort and in summer you can hike alpine trails and mountain bike at Whistler Mountain Bike Park.

Listings

BEST OF THE REST

Scenic Stops

Brandywine Falls
If you're headed to Whistler, take the easy trail to the dramatic 70m waterfall located just south of town. It's a great photo op and ideal for families.

Butchart Gardens
The 55-acre gardens are one of Victoria's most popular attractions. The vibrant flower displays, gorgeous pathways and beautiful fountains are fun for the whole family.

Cathedral Grove
This old-growth forest on Vancouver Island is worth stopping at to admire the massive Douglas fir trees, some more than 800 years old, that tower overhead like a giant canopy.

Cypress Lookout
Just 30 minutes from downtown Vancouver, Cypress Lookout offers one of the best views of Vancouver's dramatic city skyline. From this viewpoint you can see the ocean, mountains and city, all at once.

Emerald Lake
In Yoho National Park, Emerald Lake's pure turquoise waters, framed by rugged mountain peaks, make it one of the most picturesque spots in British Columbia.

Harrison Hot Springs
The mineral-rich hot pools are a great place to stop for a relaxing dip. The views of Harrison Lake and the surrounding mountains add to the tranquility.

Joffre Lakes Park
These vibrant turquoise lakes near Whistler are a popular spot for hiking and camping. Trails take you past glaciers, waterfalls and through striking alpine scenery.

Shuswap Lake Provincial Park
In the heart of BC's interior, this mountain lake is a popular spot for water sports and houseboating. If you're driving through, it's also a beautiful picnic stop.

Squamish Canyon
Elevated wooden walkways take you high above the dramatic canyon, carved over thousands of years by glaciers and rushing water.

Takakkaw Falls
In Yoho National Park and one of the highest waterfalls in Canada, the short trail leads you to a viewpoint of the 253m misty, dramatic falls.

Indigenous Culture & Heritage

Bill Reid Gallery
The extensive art collection at the Bill Reid Gallery in Vancouver is the only public gallery in Canada dedicated to Indigenous Northwest Coast artwork. It showcases Bill Reid's artwork alongside other contemporary Indigenous artists.

Cathedral Grove

07 Sea Otter
Once extinct in BC, the sea otter has been reintroduced into the waters near Tofino, Barkley Sound and Haida Gwaii.

08 Bald Eagle
Found all across the province, these birds of prey are most easily spotted along rivers or near bodies of water.

09 Sea Lion
This playful marine mammal can be spotted on rocky shores along BC's coast from Vancouver Island to the Sunshine Coast.

10 Mountain Goat
Usually found in higher altitudes navigating rocky ledges, the white alpine mammal is found in the Rockies and Coast Mountains.

11 Bighorn Sheep
Known for their incredible climbing skills and massive, round horns, bighorn sheep can be spotted in rocky areas and near grasslands.

12 Wolf
Another rare wildlife encounter, the wolf can be found in BC's mountains and forested areas.

01 ARIEL CELESTE PHOTOGRAPHY/SHUTTERSTOCK, 02 ANAN KAEWKHAMMUL/SHUTTERSTOCK, 03 AMINE CHAKOUR/SHUTTERSTOCK, 04 CHRISTIAN MUSAT/SHUTTERSTOCK, 05 RAIMUNDA-LOSANTOS/SHUTTERSTOCK, 06 NATURESMOMENTSUK/SHUTTERSTOCK, 07 KENEVA PHOTOGRAPHY/SHUTTERSTOCK, 08 SERGEI MIRONENKO/SHUTTERSTOCK, 09 ERIC ISSELEE/SHUTTERSTOCK, 10 JENNY CC CARTER/SHUTTERSTOCK, 11 GEORGIA EVANS/SHUTTERSTOCK, 12 PHOTOMASTER/SHUTTERSTOCK

Wildlife ROUNDUP

01 Grizzly Bear
With the largest population of grizzly bears in Canada, these animals are a sight to see. Just make sure you follow local guidelines and keep a safe distance.

02 Cougar
Though you likely won't see a cougar while in BC, as they tend to avoid people, it's good to remember they're out there and stay alert while on trails.

03 Humpback Whale
The largest whales in the area can be found in the summer months before they migrate south for fall and winter.

04 Orca
These iconic British Columbia whales can sometimes be sighted in coastal areas. Book a whale-watching tour for your best chances.

05 Pacific Salmon
The reddish-hued fish migrate upstream during spawning season and are an important part of Indigenous culture and history.

06 Spirit Bear
Indigenous Peoples have held beliefs about these light-coloured black bears for generations. If you're lucky, you might be able to catch a glimpse of one in the Great Bear Rainforest.

ecosystems. Partnerships like this are proof that tourism and conservation can coexist.

Pacific Rim National Park Reserve encompasses 511 sq km on Vancouver Island's west coast. BC Parks focuses on maintaining the pristine areas within the park as well as restoring damaged areas. Recent restorations include repairing salmon streams that had been damaged due to industrial logging practices and restoring sand dunes by removing invasive plant species that threaten and invade other important species. In terms of tourism initiatives, visitors can enjoy guided hikes, surfing lessons and other activities that are carefully guided to ensure protection of the surrounding environment.

> Small efforts like staying on trails, respecting wildlife and carrying out trash, all add up to make a big difference.

The Indigenous communities on Haida Gwaii provide numerous tourism opportunities that emphasize cultural education and environmental stewardship. Visitors can take part in guided kayaking tours, wildlife tours, and workshops that highlight traditional fishing and foraging techniques. Through these experiences, not only are visitors investing in Indigenous communities to help conservation efforts moving forward, but also participating in authentic tourism experiences. This is another great example of how tourism and sustainability can exist together. By making mindful decisions and supporting ecotourism initiatives like the above examples, visitors can ensure the beautiful, undisturbed areas of British Columbia will stay intact for years to come.

Responsible Travel Tips

Traveling sustainably is more of a mindset than a checklist of things. Being conscientious in your daily decisions can go a long way. For example, bringing reusable cups, bottles and containers is one step you can take to reduce the disposal of plastic containers that contribute to the buildup of harmful microplastics in the environment. When you can, consider walking, biking or taking public transport to reduce harmful emissions. If you do end up flying, opt for flights that have lower CO_2 emissions. When choosing accommodations, opt for one that prioritizes sustainability. Small decisions like these can all work to reduce your travel footprint.

Exploring BC Responsibly

SEE THE BEAUTY BUT KEEP IT WILD.

British Columbia's vast landscapes, untouched rainforests and rugged coastlines attract millions of visitors each year. People flock here to enjoy its pristine wilderness, and with so many travelers comes a responsibility to protect these delicate ecosystems. Conservation efforts and ecotourism are important, now more than ever, in order to protect these special places and wildlife for years to come.

Left Spirit bear, Great Bear Rainforest **Center** Surfers, Pacific Rim National Park Reserve **Right** Sea lions, Gwaii Haanas National Park Reserve

British Columbia is Canada's most visited province and while the province relies greatly on the tourism industry for economic growth, the environmental impacts of tourism are a serious concern. The fragile ecosystems are being affected by increased foot traffic and pollution from littering, as well as disturbances to wildlife habitat. Ecotourism and education play a key role in addressing these concerns. By staying at sustainable accommodations, enjoying guided tours, and learning about Indigenous stewardship, visitors can enjoy BC's beauty without causing lasting harm. Small efforts like staying on trails, respecting wildlife and carrying out trash, all add up to make a big difference.

Conservation Efforts in British Columbia

Through a variety of initiatives, the province is working to protect its landscapes and wildlife, all while promoting sustainable tourism. BC Parks protects 15.4% of the province's land base and 3.4% of its marine areas. Partnerships with Indigenous communities also play a key role in conservation, as Indigenous people have been stewards of the land for generations, caring for and practicing traditional ways of knowledge that help preserve the land and its wildlife.

The Great Bear Rainforest is a perfect example of how tourism and conservation can go hand in hand. An agreement between the province of BC, the Coastal First Nations, and the Nanwakolas Council, protects over six million hectares of rainforest. Indigenous-led tours and ecolodges allow guests to explore the area, and even responsibly see wildlife like grizzly bears and the elusive spirit bears, while preventing harm to the delicate

44 Sip Through the OKANAGAN

VINEYARDS | SCENIC VIEWS | WINE TASTINGS

The Okanagan Valley is home to over 200 wineries. Sprawling vineyards ascend hillsides that overlook the expansive Okanagan Lake, giving spectacular views while you sip some of Canada's best wines. You can casually sip at a local family-owned winery or visit a luxurious award-winning estate – either way, tastings are as much about the scenery as they are the wine.

Trip Notes

Getting around Wineries are spaced across the valley so having a vehicle is ideal. You can book a guided wine tour to explore multiple wineries without having to worry about driving or you can opt to tour on your own. Just make sure someone in your group is the designated driver.

When to go Prime wine touring runs from late spring through early fall when vineyards are the most vibrant.

Tasting fees Some wineries charge a small tasting fee that's often waived with purchase.

Sommelier Tip

One great hidden gem is actually the region just next to the Okanagan Valley, the Similkameen Valley. Here there are no large corporate wineries, just small, quality-focused operations. And because they don't get anywhere near the number of visitors as Okanagan wineries, you often get a more immersive tasting experience.

■ **Rhys Pender,** *Master of Wine*
@rhyspendermw

Totem Poles

The Haida are renowned carvers. Even today, many of the Haida are skilled artisans continuing the craft traditions of their ancestors. When you visit village sites on Haida Gwaii, you'll see remarkable craftsmanship with deep spiritual and cultural meaning. Totems tell stories, honor ancestors or represent a family or place. Guided tours can offer more insight into the symbolism and meaning of these cultural artifacts, including those in SGang Gwaay, a UNESCO World Heritage Site.

through the water, you'll notice seabirds soaring high above you and the occasional seal weaving through kelp. Inlets reveal tidal pools with agile crabs and other shore creatures.

Choose your Adventure
Beginner paddlers can start with a short tour or half-day kayak rental to get the feel for the water. More experienced paddlers or those wanting a longer trip can plan for a multi-day trek. Multi-day tours explore deeper into the islands, reaching more remote areas, secluded driftwood-strewn beaches, and quiet coves away from people. These trips are the best way to explore the local ecosystems, as they aim to take participants far away from civilization.

Left Kayaking, Haida Gwaii **Above** Totem poles, Haida Gwaii

43 Indigenous Shores of **HAIDA GWAII**

CULTURE | PADDLING | NATURE

This archipelago off the west coast of British Columbia is a cultural and natural treasure. Exploring the islands by kayak is one of the best ways to view its rugged coastlines, see wildlife up close, and experience the rich Indigenous culture that has shaped Haida Gwaii for centuries. Paddle through open ocean waters and secluded inlets where both outdoor and culture lovers can enjoy this special place.

How to

Getting here Haida Gwaii can only be reached by air or ferry. There are direct flights from Vancouver to the islands and BC Ferries operates a seasonal route from Prince Rupert.

When to go For the best kayaking conditions and weather, travel from May to September.

Costs Kayak rentals range from $85 to $120 per day with discounts for multi-day rentals. Guided tours start at $190 for a day tour, with multi-day trips costing significantly more depending on duration.

Stories on the Water The Haida are the Indigenous people who have lived on these islands for at least 6000 to 8000 years. In the Haida language, Haida Gwaii means 'islands of the people.' When you paddle along the shores, you are paddling the same routes used for generations. Indigenous guides share stories, legends and oral traditions that have been passed down and bring Haida culture to life as you navigate the storied waters.

Living Landscapes Exploring Haida Gwaii is a multi-sensory experience. Each paddle connects you to the land. The cedars rise majestically from the shore, reflecting off the calm ocean surface. As you slowly move

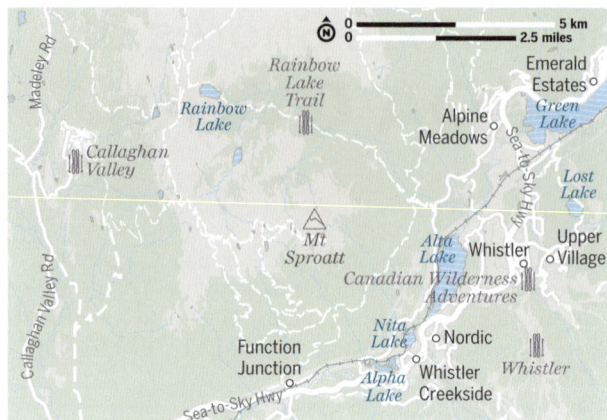

Ease into the Trails

Start your snowshoeing on gentler routes before tackling your steepest climbs, especially if you're a beginner. You can check out **Callaghan Valley's** wide network of snowshoe trails, where there are many easy trails to choose from, or you can challenge yourself by picking an intermediate or advanced trail. If you opt for a guided tour, local guides can help you decide which trails are a good fit for you and share stories about the trails along the way.

It's About the Journey

Slow down and take in the sights, sounds and smells. Watch for signs of wildlife – on guided tours, local guides will often stop and point out animal tracks hidden in the forest. Take breaks not only to catch your breath, but to stop and take in the stillness of winter. It's a magical part of Canada that many people don't get a chance to witness.

Guided Tours for Local Insight

The best way to learn about the Whistler area is by booking a guided snowshoeing experience. **Canadian Wilderness Adventures** has been offering tours for over 30 years and guides know the terrain inside and out. Whether you enjoy an evening stargazing by snowshoe or combine your trek with a wood-fired sauna experience, being guided can add local knowledge to your experience.

Top left Snowshoeing Whistler's backcountry **Bottom left** Snowshoes

⚠ Be Prepared

Canadian winters are beautiful but they can be unpredictable and frigid. Wear warm, moisture-wicking layers, waterproof boots, and bring enough water and snacks for your day. Remember that daylight hours are much shorter, so plan your route accordingly, or bring headlamps to avoid being caught out after dark. Despite it being winter, sun protection is important as UV rays reflect off the snow and can be surprisingly strong. Lastly, bringing a small first aid kit is also recommended, just in case.

42 Wintery WHISTLER

SNOWSHOEING | SCENIC | ADVENTURE

This mountain town is one of the top ski towns in North America, and while the skiing is phenomenal, there are slower ways to explore Whistler's backcountry. Snowshoeing takes you away from the long chairlift lines and into a quiet winter wonderland of frozen lakes and phenomenal mountain viewpoints. Whether you take off on your own or with a tour guide, snowshoeing is a great way to take in Whistler at your own pace.

How to

Getting here From Vancouver, it's a two-hour drive to Whistler on the scenic Sea-to-Sky Highway. There are also buses that run from Vancouver to Whistler daily.

When to go For the best snow coverage, visit from December through March.

Pro tip Start early to avoid crowds or enjoy quieter trails like **Rainbow Lake Trail** for a peaceful escape.

or creamy gelato from **GI Gelato & Coffee House**.

Admire Artwork

Granville Island is known for its artsy vibe, and visitors can often watch artists working in their studios. It's one of the endearing things about the island, allowing you to not only admire and purchase artwork, but also chat with the artists themselves. One of the most fascinating aspects of art is the story behind the piece – learning what inspired someone adds a whole new layer to the experience. Notable galleries, such as **Blue Seas Gallery** and **Karen Cooper Gallery**, offer a deeper look into Granville Island's creative community.

From Industry to Arts

In the 1970s, Granville Island was a mostly deserted industrial area of Vancouver full of sawmills, warehouses and factories that were mostly abandoned. The city decided to revitalize this area and transform it into the vibrant cultural hub it is today. When you visit, you can still see the industrial remnants of the past that give Granville Island part of its unique charm.

Above Waterfront, Granville Island

41 Granville Island
LIKE A LOCAL

SHOPPING | FOOD | WALKS

A former industrial site, Granville Island has been transformed into one of Vancouver's best neighborhoods, a cultural wonderland with art galleries, quirky shops, restaurants and breweries, and an indoor market that attracts the city's best chefs. **Granville Island Public Market** is a multi-sensory experience with more than 50 permanent vendors and a variety of daily rotating vendors selling everything from seafood to produce and baked goods.

How to

Getting here Walk, take the bus or board the False Creek Ferry in downtown Vancouver to avoid the hassle of parking. Driving is an option, though parking may be limited during peak times.

When to go Granville Island's regular hours are from 10am to 6pm every day. Summer hours are from 9am to 7pm.

Early bird Getting to the public market early helps to beat the crowds. Plus, many of the bakeries sell out of their most popular items by late morning.

Meander the shops

The best way to explore Granville Island is to just let the wind take you. It's the perfect place to wander without any timeline or expectations. Follow the scents of freshly baked bread or the sounds of buskers playing along the waterfront and you'll come across an assortment of galleries, artisanal shops, the public market and eateries to explore.

Sip & Savour

From waterfront cafes to craft breweries, there is no shortage of watering holes on Granville Island. You can grab a drink to go or sip one at a cafe by the water – either way make sure to sample some of Granville Island's specialties, like fresh oysters from a market stall, handmade chocolates from **Kasama Chocolates**

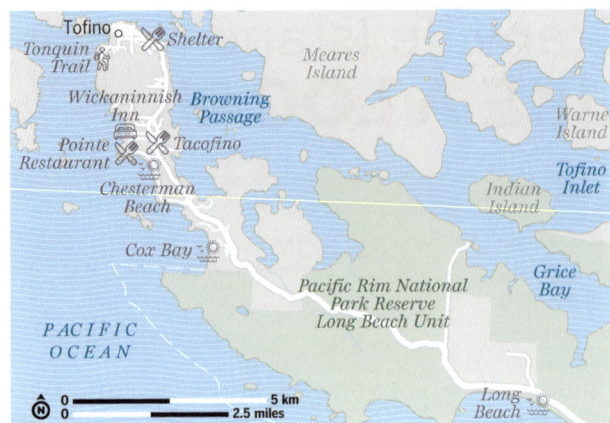

Surf the Pacific & More

Surf Lessons There are several surf schools to choose from that offer lessons for first-time surfers to advanced surfers. Instructors will provide you with your equipment and help set you up for success by helping you find the right location and providing practical tips. If you're not into booking a lesson, opt to just rent your gear and surf on your own at one of the many stunning beaches. Just keep in mind the water is cold year-round, so wetsuits are a must. Summer is the ideal time to visit if you're a beginner, while fall and winter bring bigger waves for more experienced surfers. Top spots include **Chesterman Beach**, **Long Beach** or **Cox Bay**.

Refuel Nearby When you inevitably get tired and need a break, take in the scenery from the beach. If you're up for a light adventure, try the easy **Tonquin Trail** that winds through the forest and takes you to a gorgeous, secluded beach. Keep your eyes peeled for wildlife as you adventure, especially in the sea, whales, otters and even sea lions can sometimes be spotted from shore. If you get hungry, there are several world-class restaurants to check out, most offering fresh local seafood and coastal views. The **Pointe Restaurant** at the Wickaninnish Inn pairs West Coast cuisine with views of Chesterman Beach, while **Shelter** serves local dishes in a more relaxed setting. When you're refuelled and ready to hit the waves again, consider timing it so you can catch one of Tofino's famous honey-hued sunsets.

Top left Surfers, Chesterman Beach
Bottom left Tonquin Trail

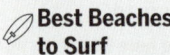

Best Beaches to Surf

For the most consistent and clean waves, Cox Bay and Long Beach are top spots among beginners and advanced surfers. Even if you're not surfing, it's worth visiting them for their beauty. If the swell is too big, try going to **Chesterman Beach** where the waves are almost always smaller. For the best conditions, aim for high tide or moving from low to high tide.

 ■ **Kat Morgan**, *Office Manager at Tofino Surf School*
@tofinosurfschool

40 Catch Tofino WAVES

ADVENTURE | SURFING | BEACHES

The little town of Tofino on Vancouver Island is often called the 'surf capital of Canada'. Visitors and locals alike don wetsuits and grab their surfboards to ride the Pacific waves. Braver souls surf all year-round, even when the winter storms invoke massive swells, but summertime attracts warmer waters and gentler waves perfect for beginners and casual surfers. The town itself is known for its endearing surfer vibe and its rugged coastlines and beaches framed by dense rainforests.

How to

Getting here Getting to Tofino takes a little planning. You can fly into Vancouver, then either rent a car and take the ferry to Nanaimo for the three-hour drive, or hop on a direct flight from Vancouver to Tofino on a Pacific Coastal Airlines flight. Another option is flying into Nanaimo and driving from there.

When to go June to September brings milder weather ideal for surfing. While fall and winter showcase bigger swells that attract more experienced surfers.

Quick lunch stop Tofino's legendary **Tacofino** truck is a must.

EATING & DRINKING

British Columbia's diverse landscapes also bring a range of flavours that reflect the province's coastal, mountain and urban areas. In Vancouver, stop for craft coffee, fresh seafood and innovative fusion food. The Okanagan is famous for producing award-winning wines. Vancouver Island's locally caught salmon and Dungeness crab are must-tries especially when eaten at a gorgeous waterfront restaurant in Tofino or Victoria.

Best wines Mission Hill Family Estate (pictured top right; p209), Okanagan

Must-try Dungeness crab Pointe Restaurant (p201), Tofino

CONNECT & FIND YOUR WAY

Wi-fi Most restaurants, hotels and cafes offer free public wi-fi.

Navigation Driving is the best way to get around British Columbia and navigation is straightforward using apps like Google Maps. Trails and bicycle routes are usually well marked and local visitor centers can help with maps for scenic routes or backcountry experiences.

PARKS CANADA DISCOVERY PASS

Explore British Columbia's national parks and historic sites with the Parks Canada Discovery Pass. It's valid for unlimited visits for a full year.

WHERE TO STAY

Pricing varies throughout British Columbia. Popular tourist destinations like Whistler, Vancouver and Tofino can be pricey. If you're looking to save some money, look at staying in a nearby town for lower prices.

City/Town	Pros/Cons
Vancouver	Offers many accommodation options. Downtown locations can be pricey so book early or look at boutique hotels for less-expensive options.
Kelowna	A common basecamp for exploring the Okanagan, Kelowna has many accommodations to choose from.
Victoria	British Columbia's capital city offers a range of accommodations from luxurious waterfront hotels to more affordable options.
Tofino	This popular surf town can be pricey, but it offers luxurious hotels and boutique lodges. You can stay in nearby Ucluelet for lower prices.
Whistler Village	There is a wide range of hotels in this popular mountain destination. Many hotels are ski-in/ski-out in the winter and steps away from the mountains for summer activities.
Kamloops	For adventures in the interior, Kamloops has numerous hotels at a lower price point than other cities.

MONEY

Most establishments in British Columbia accept credit cards and Apple Pay. Some smaller shops in artisanal and farmers markets may only accept cash.

Practicalities

ARRIVING

Vancouver International Airport (YVR) Most international flights arrive at British Columbia's largest airport. There are connecting flights from this airport to other small airports in the province. From YVR, you can catch the **Sky Train** *(translink.ca)* to the downtown waterfront on the Canada Line in about 25 minutes. Tickets can be purchased at kiosks near the boarding area.

HOW MUCH FOR A

Latte $5.50

Craft beer $8.00

Ferry ride $15.50

WHEN TO GO

DEC-MAR
Ski season in alpine regions, rainy season along the coast.

APR-MAY
Cherry blossom and spring flower season.

JUN-AUG
Warm, dry season.

SEP-NOV
Fall foliage in interior and alpine regions, rainy season returns to coastal areas.

GETTING AROUND

Driving The best way to get around British Columbia is by car. There are many scenic highways, like the Sea-to-Sky and Trans-Canada, that are worth driving to take in the breathtaking views. Having your own vehicle gives you the flexibility to stop at roadside attractions like waterfalls, lakes and viewpoints along the way. Car rentals are available at most major cities including Vancouver, Victoria and Kelowna.

Public transit Vancouver and Victoria offer public buses, ferries and light rail to get around the cities.

Ferries BC Ferries provides connections to Vancouver Island and the gulf islands.

BRITISH COLUMBIA
Trip Builder

Ride the Pacific Coast waves near **Tofino** (p200), Canada's coolest hippie surf town
🚗 3hr from Nanaimo

Experience the culture and history of the Haida People in **Haida Gwaii** (p206), a UNESCO World Heritage Site
✈ 2hr from Vancouver

Hike through lush coastal rainforest to get to a secluded beach on **Tonquin Trail** (p201)
🚗 3hr from Nanaimo

■ Canada's westernmost province has miles of Pacific coastline, ancient forests, glacier-fed rivers and breathtaking mountains. It offers some of Canada's best skiing in winter and incredible hiking, cycling, paddling and mountaineering in seven national parks in summer. It's also home to sophisticated cities, quaint small towns and Indigenous communities with fascinating history and cultures.

CLOCKWISE FROM BOTTOM LEFT: BOB HILSCHER/GETTY IMAGES, FOKKE BAARSSEN/SHUTTERSTOCK, JOSEF HANUS/SHUTTERSTOCK, SUN_SHINE/SHUTTERSTOCK

- ▶ **Trip Builder** (p196)
- ▶ **Practicalities** (p198)
- ▶ **Catch Tofino Waves** (p200)
- ▶ **Granville Island Like a Local** (p202)
- ▶ **Wintery Whistler** (p204)
- ▶ **Indigenous Shores of Haida Gwaii** (p206)
- ▶ **Sip Through the Okanagan** (p208)
- ▶ **Exploring BC Responsibly** (p210)
- ▶ **Wildlife Roundup** (p212)
- ▶ **Listings** (p214)

BRITISH COLUMBIA

TRAILS | TASTES | TIDES

RESEARCHED BY KELSEY OLSEN

produces spontaneous and mixed fermentation beers inspired by Belgian lambics.

Best Parks in Alberta

Banff National Park
Canada's first national park is in the heart of the Canadian Rockies, with remarkable scenery – craggy mountain peaks, turquoise blue lakes, hot springs, glaciers and accommodations, shops and restaurants.

Jasper National Park
The largest national park in the Canadian Rockies protects miles of wilderness, rugged mountains, lakes, rivers and an abundant amount of wildlife. There's also a ski resort and hot springs inside the park.

Waterton Lakes National Park
In the southwest corner of the province, Waterton Lakes National Park is one of the smallest Rocky Mountain Parks and one of the most beautiful, sheltering plants and animals of the Crown of the Continent region.

Elk Island National Park
This 194-sq-km park 48km east of Edmonton has the highest concentration of hoofed mammals of any national park in Canada with thriving populations of bison, elk, moose and deer.

Canmore Nordic Centre Provincial Park
Developed to host the Nordic events for the 1988 Winter Olympics, this provincial park is a great destination for novice and expert cross-country skiers with trails, equipment rentals and lessons.

Kananaskis Country
K Country is a network of provincial parks and protected areas in the foothills and the front ranges of the Canadian Rockies that are a great place for hiking, cross-country skiing, horseback riding and paddling.

Lake Louise Ski Resort

Alberta's Best Ski Resorts

Lake Louise Ski Resort
Located near the village of Lake Louise in Banff National Park, this ski resort has 4200 acres of terrain spread across four mountains. The gondola operates in summer for hiking and bear viewing.

Banff Norquay
The closest ski resort to the Town of Banff, this resort has night skiing and a tube park in winter and a sightseeing chairlift and climbing via ferrata in summer.

Sunshine Village
Just 15 minutes from the Town of Banff, this resort has more than 3300 acres of terrain on three mountains. In summer, there's an extensive trail network and hiking trails.

Marmot Basin
Located in Jasper National Park, this ski resort has 91 named runs on four mountain faces and a lift capacity of close to 12,000 skiers per hour on seven lifts.

Nakiska Ski Area
This ski area was designed and built to host the alpine events of the 1988 Winter Olympics. There's great terrain for beginner, intermediate and expert skiers.

Listings

BEST OF THE REST

Best Places to Eat Alberta Beef

Caesar's Steakhouse & Lounge $$$

For more than 50 years, Caesar's has been the place to go for a steak dinner in Calgary. Steaks are grilled to perfection and Caesar salad is made tableside.

Major Tom $$$

This stylish award-winning restaurant has sweeping city views, a global menu and great craft cocktails. Alberta beef is on the menu along with other items. Book well in advance.

Rge Rd $$$

Farm-to-fork dining is at the heart of Chef Blair Lebsack's menu, which features locally sourced beef, wild game, seasonal vegetables and grains served with local craft beer or BC wines.

Barbacoa $$$

At this restaurant just outside Edmonton, Alberta beef is cooked over wood and charcoal to give a delicious blend of smoke and char. Fish and seafood, chicken, pork and roasted veggies are also on the menu.

Chuck's Steakhouse $$$

Angus and Wagyu beef steaks are sourced from Alberta ranches at this Banff restaurant. Then they are dry-aged, started on a mesquite-wood grill, and finished in a copper pan with butter and herbs.

Where to Try Canada's Cocktail

The Beltliner $

This Calgary diner has an iceberg vodka Caesar bar with three different versions of the drink and seven different toppings ranging from pepperoni and bacon to a cupcake.

Walter's Pop Up Bar $

If you want to have a Caesar cocktail in the place where it was invented, this bar at the Westin hotel in Calgary is the place to go. The beloved drink was invented in 1969 by Walter Chell.

Craft Beer Please

Big Rock Brewery $

Canada's largest independent craft brewery has been producing premium, all-natural craft beers since 1985. Located in Calgary, it is named after the Okotoks Erratic boulder in nearby Okotoks.

Village Brewery $

The taproom at this Calgary microbrewery offers 16 beers on tap and a full BBQ-inspired menu. Reasonably priced flights let you sample four different beers.

Alley Kat Brewing Company $

Founded in 1995, there are 14 house beers on tap at this Edmonton brewery, which is known for double IPAs and smooth brews.

Blind Enthusiasm Brewery $

This Edmonton taproom runs one of largest barrel-fermented beer programs in Canada. It

Rge Rd

12.8m Ukrainian sausage was named in honour of Stawnichy's Ukrainian Sausage.

07 World's Largest Mallard Duck
This giant duck, found in Andrew, weighs one tonne and has a wingspan of 7m.

08 Saamis Teepee
Find the world's largest teepee in Medicine Hat; it's 65.5m tall and has a diameter of 49m.

09 Giant replica of the *USS Enterprise*
Head to Vulcan, where this attraction celebrates the coincidental similarity between the town's name and the fictional planet of Vulcan in the Star Trek franchise.

10 World's Largest Mushrooms
Vilna's giant mushrooms stand 6m tall; a tribute to the area's heritage of harvesting wild mushrooms.

11 World's Largest Lamp
In Donalda, this 13m-tall lamp sits across the street from a museum that houses the world's largest collection of oil lamps.

01 SCHNEPFDESIGN/SHUTTERSTOCK, 02 TETYANAT/SHUTTERSTOCK, 03 RICK RUDNICKI/ALAMY, 04 ALBERTA BEAUTY/SHUTTERSTOCK, 05 VINCENT JIANG/SHUTTERSTOCK, 06 BUSKER909/SHUTTERSTOCK, 07 WHEATLEY/ALAMY, 08 EWY MEDIA/SHUTTERSTOCK, 09 JORDAN FEEG/SHUTTERSTOCK, 10 AL HUNT/FLICKR, 11 GUNTER MARX/TA/ALAMY

ALBERTA
Giants of the Prairies

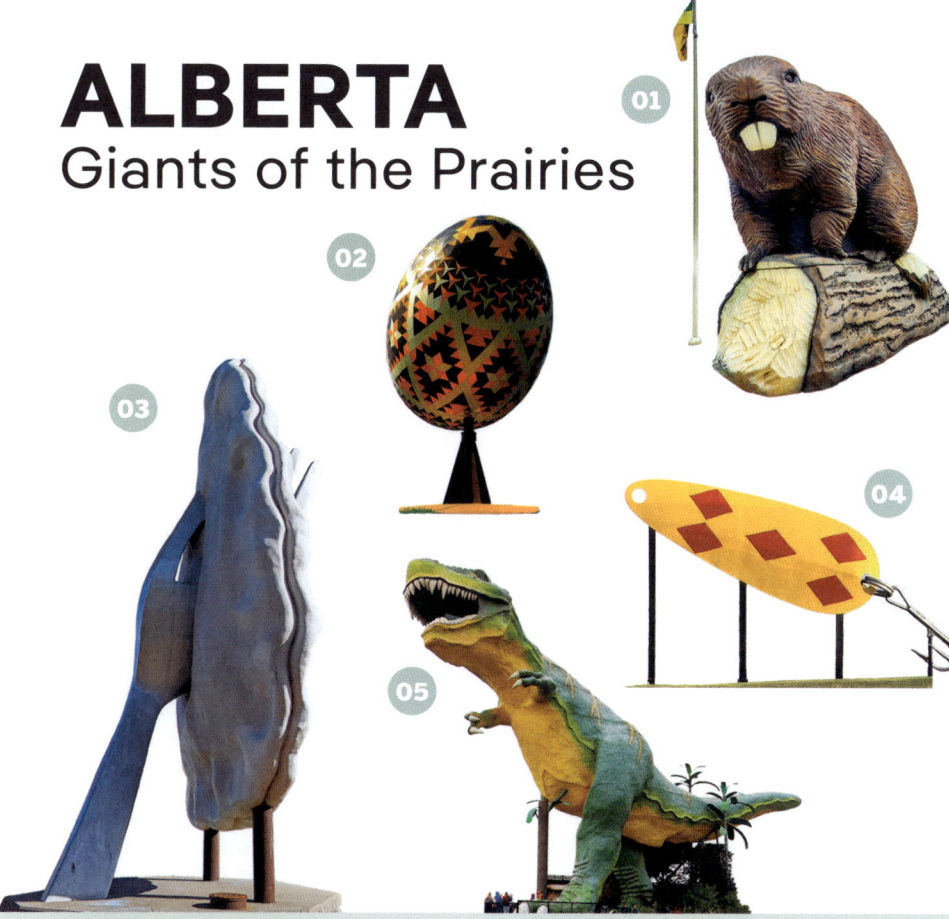

01 World's Largest Beaver
Found in Beaverlodge, the world's largest beaver is 4.6m high and 5.5m long.

02 Vegreville Pysanka
Vegreville has the world's largest Ukrainian Easter egg, with 524 star patterns, rotating on a giant pedestal.

03 World's Largest Pierogi
This giant pierogi, in Glendon, is perched on a fork and stands 8.2m tall and weighs 2700kg.

04 World's Largest Fishing Lure
In Lacombe, this Yellow and Red Five of Diamonds fishing lure was built by Len Thompson Lures, which has been in business since 1929.

05 World's Largest Dinosaur
Visit Drumheller to climb inside the mouth of 'Tyra', a female T-Rex that is 26m tall and 46m long.

06 World's Largest Kielbasa
Affectionately dubbed 'the turd' by locals, this

Canadians and Albertans today are engaged in reconciliation, working to acknowledge the wrongs of the past and restore Indigenous rights and cultures. Every time someone participates in an Indigenous tourism experience or some other activity that shares culture and builds understanding, they contribute to reconciliation. The healing process takes time, but it is the best way to ensure a future of equity and mutual respect.

> Canadians and Albertans today are engaged in reconciliation, working to acknowledge the wrongs of the past and restore Indigenous rights and cultures.

Best Indigenous Tourism Sites in Alberta

Writing-on-Stone Provincial Park/Áísínai'pi This site has the largest collection of Indigenous pictographs and petroglyphs on the Great Plains of North America.

Head-Smashed-In Buffalo Jump This buffalo jump was used for nearly 6000 years for hunting bison.

Blackfoot Crossing Historical Park Located where Treaty 7 was signed, this site has an interactive museum that helps explain the culture and history of the Blackfoot (Siksika) People.

Fort Edmonton Indigenous Peoples Experience Learn about the customs and traditions of First Nations and Métis Peoples at this walkthrough exhibit at Fort Edmonton Park.

Métis Crossing Learn about Métis culture at this site that was designed, built and is operated by Métis Peoples.

Rocky Mountain House National Historic Site This archaeological site and park tell the story of the fur trade and the role of Indigenous Peoples.

Find Authentic Indigenous Tourism Experiences

There are many excellent companies that offer guided Indigenous experiences and tours in Alberta including **Mahikan Trails** (mahikan.ca), **Painted Warriors** (paintedwarriors.ca), **Talking Rock Tours** (talkingrocktours.com) and **Warrior Women** (warriorwomen.ca) – to name a few. Find more authentic Indigenous tourism experiences on the **Indigenous Tourism Alberta website** (indigenoustourismalberta.ca) and on the **Indigenous Tourism Association of Canada website** (destinationindigenous.ca).

Indigenous Culture in Alberta

THE INDIGENOUS PEOPLES OF ALBERTA ARE DEEPLY CONNECTED TO THE LAND.

Indigenous Peoples are the original inhabitants of what we now call Canada and about 6% of Alberta's population is Indigenous. Treaties 6, 7 and 8 cover the Alberta region. There are many different nations, cultures and languages spoken by Indigenous Peoples who reside in Alberta. Experiencing these unique cultures is fascinating and rewarding.

Left Chiefs' eagle-feathered headdresses
Center Head-Smashed-In Buffalo Jump
Right Petroglyphs, Writing-on-Stone Provincial Park/Áísínai'pi

There are almost 285,000 Indigenous People in Alberta. Three distinct groups of Indigenous Peoples are recognized by the Canadian Constitution: First Nations, Inuit and Métis. Within these three broad groups are many different nations, each with their own unique culture and traditions. The majority of the Indigenous People in the province are First Nations (52.8%) and Métis (44.2%). About 1% of the Indigenous population is Inuit.

There are 48 First Nations and 138 First Nations reserves in Alberta. There was a time when First Nations People were confined to reservations and could be arrested if they left without a pass. From 1884 to 1951, a federal law also prohibited them from dressing in traditional clothing and performing traditional dances and ceremonies. The *Indian Act* was amended in 1951 to lift the ban on Indigenous cultural and religious ceremonies and amended again in 1985 to remove restrictions that prevented First Nations People from living off reservations. Today some First Nations live on reserves and some choose to live off the reservation. The most commonly spoken First Nations languages in the province are Blackfoot, Cree, Chipewyan, Dene, Sarcee and Stoney (Nakoda Sioux).

The Métis are people of mixed European and Indigenous ancestry. In 1938, Alberta enacted the *Métis Betterment Act,* which led to the creation of 12 Métis settlements – the first and only secure land base for Métis People in all of Canada. The Métis were officially recognized as Indigenous Peoples in the 1982 Canadian Constitution. In 1990, Alberta passed legislation that protected Métis land under Alberta law and officially recognized Métis governance. There are eight Métis settlements in Alberta today.

Top far left Dinosaur Provincial Park
Bottom far left Dinosaur fossil
Left Badlands, Dinosaur Provincial Park

Guided Excavation

A one or two-day guided excavation isn't easy, but it's an experience of a lifetime. There are few places in the world where you can work alongside scientists meticulously uncovering and collecting 75-million-year-old fossils from an active excavation site. The work done on excavations contributes to ongoing research conducted by the **Royal Tyrrell Museum of Palaeontology** *(tyrrellmuseum.com)*. It's an opportunity to experience the wonder and challenges of working in the field of palaeontology and to gain valuable hands-on experience with palaeontological field techniques.

The day starts with a hike to the excavation site. Participants must be able to hike up to 5km. Fossils start to disintegrate once they are exposed to open air, so scientists only uncover what they can collect in a reasonable amount of time. The work involves chiselling away at stone and dirt and working with brushes to clear debris around the fossils. Palaeontology technicians impart knowledge about dinosaur species and collection techniques used to uncover fossils.

The work isn't easy physically and often involves sitting on the ground, hunching over the work area or getting onto your hands and knees. You must be physically fit to participate in an excavation and you must wear closed-toed and closed-heeled shoes and dress for the weather.

A guided excavation is a chance to be part of the thrill of discovery. It's a glimpse into the everyday life of those working in the field of palaeontology.

Best Tours in Dinosaur Provincial Park

Since active fossil excavations are ongoing, some areas of the park can only be accessed on guided tours that leave from the Dinosaur Provincial Park Visitor Centre.

Explorer's Bus Tour (2 hours, easy) Take a bus tour through the heart of the park.

Golden Hour Photography Tour (2 hours, easy) Photograph stunning badlands vistas in optimal light on this bus tour.

Fossil Safari (1¾ hours, easy) Develop your fossil spotting and identification skills on this hike.

Bonebed Express Hike (2¼ hours, moderate) Trek to a renowned horned dinosaur excavation site.

Great Badlands Hike (4 hours, difficult) Conquer challenging terrain and be rewarded with panoramic badlands views.

39 DINOSAUR Provincial Park

FOSSILS | BADLANDS SCENERY | PALAEONTOLOGY

This UNESCO World Heritage Site contains the highest concentration of late Cretaceous period fossils in the world in a starkly beautiful landscape of semi-arid steppes, gorges, buttes and hoodoos. In the restricted area that can only be accessed on tours, you can see dinosaur fossils still partially buried in the ground and on a special tour, work beside scientists to uncover them.

How to

When to go Guided tours are available from April through October. Some areas of the park cannot be seen unless you are on a guided tour.

Getting there Dinosaur Provincial Park is 217km east of Calgary on Trans-Canada Hwy/AB-1 E.

Book tours in advance Programs frequently sell out, but extra tours are often added to meet demand. The cost for a one-day guided excavation is $200 per person. It is only available for ages 14 years and up. Youths aged 14 to 17 must be accompanied by a paying adult. Limit of two youths per adult.

mountain that weeps. The **Weeping Wall** is a series of waterfalls that cascade more than 100m down the mountain.

Athabasca Glacier The Athabasca Glacier is the most visited glacier in North America. It sits across from the Columbia Icefield Glacier Discovery Centre, which houses educational displays, a restaurant, a gift shop, a cafe and a restaurant. There's also a tour desk where you can book tours onto the glacier and onto a glass walkway overlooking the area (banffjaspercollection.com/attractions/columbia-icefield-adventure).

Athabasca Falls This beautiful 23m waterfall is one of the most powerful in the Canadian Rockies.

Best Hikes on the Icefields Parkway

Mistaya Canyon Hike A 1.9km easy loop trail brings you past a stunning, steep-walled canyon and multiple waterfalls.

Parker Ridge Trail A steep 5.4km trail leads to one of the best hikes in the Canadian Rockies with dramatic views of the Saskatchewan Glacier and the peaks that surround it.

Sunwapta Falls Lower Falls Hike View beautiful waterfalls on this short 2.6km return hike.

Above Deer, Athabasca Falls

38 The World's Most SCENIC ROAD

MOUNTAINS | GLACIERS | WATERFALLS

You'll be immersed in the Canadian Rockies and pass more than 100 glaciers as you drive the 232km **Icefields Parkway** (Hwy 93 North) that connects the community of Lake Louise in Banff National Park with the town of Jasper in Jasper National Park. There are craggy peaks, powerful waterfalls, turquoise blue lakes, flowing rivers, incredible wildlife and epic hikes all along the way.

How to

When to go Road conditions are best from June through September. The road is cleared in winter, but there are few patrols to assist if your vehicle breaks down.

Getting there A vehicle rental is the best and most convenient way to explore. **SunDog Tours** (sundogtours.com) and **Brewster Express** (banffjaspercollection.com/brewster-express) offer tours and transportation along the route.

Stay Our picks on the Icefields Parkway include **Glacier View Lodge** (banffjaspercollection.com) and the **Lodge At Bow Lake** (lodgeatbowlake.com).

Highlights of the Journey

Plan to take at least one full day for this drive, so you can stop often. Here are just a few of the best stops.

Bow Lake The Crowfoot Glacier rests on a peak above this beautiful lake about 30 minutes north of Lake Louise. It's one of the largest lakes in Banff National Park.

Bow Summit and Peyto Lake Lookout Peyto Lake is one of the bluest lakes you will ever see. And at 2070m, Bow Summit is the highest point along the Icefields Parkway.

Saskatchewan River Crossing This spot has the only gas station on the route. Fill up before you set out.

Waterfall Heaven Cirrus Mountain is known as the

01 Take the Parks Canada shuttle or Roam public transit to one of the most beautiful turquoise blue lakes in the Canadian Rockies and meander the **Lake Louise** lakeshore, a great spot for canoeing and hiking.

02 Explore a winding canyon on a trail that hugs the canyon walls high above a bubbling stream and towering waterfalls at **Johnston Canyon**.

03 Drive around **Lake Minnewanka** and the **Bow Valley Parkway** near dusk watching for deer, bighorn sheep, moose, elk, eagles and bears.

04 Summit a mountain without breaking a sweat – when you ride the **Banff Gondola** to the top of **Sulphur Mountain**, there are countless peaks as far as the eye can see.

05 Banff Upper Hot Springs is Canada's highest-elevation operational hot spring, and the reason Banff became a national park. Soak in soothing waters surrounded by mountains.

FROM LEFT: ELMUNDODEG/SHUTTERSTOCK, JORDAN FEEG/SHUTTERSTOCK

37 Canada's Oldest NATIONAL PARK

MOUNTAINS | LAKES | WILDLIFE

Established in 1885, **Banff National Park** was Canada's first national park and the world's third. It is a place of rugged Rocky Mountain peaks, impossibly blue lakes, glaciers, forests, hot springs, diverse wildlife and one of the prettiest mountain towns on the planet.

Trip Notes

Getting around: A car rental is the most convenient way to explore, but there are several companies that offer transfers from Calgary Airport (YYC) to the town of Banff including **Banff Airporter** *(banffairporter.com)*, **Brewster Express** *(banffjaspercollection.com/brewster-express)* and **Discover Banff Tours** *(banfftours.com)*.

When to go: June through August for hiking, September through October for fall colors, November through April for skiing and snow activities.

Top tip: Shoulder season travel – late spring or early fall – will have fewer crowds and slightly lower prices.

Wildlife Watching

For the best wildlife watching in Banff, head out at dawn or dusk when animals are most active. Keep binoculars handy and observe from a safe distance. Travel with a local guide for insider knowledge, and always respect park rules to protect both wildlife and yourself.

■ **Bastiaan De Bruijne**, *senior driver/guide at Discover Banff Tours*
@banfftours

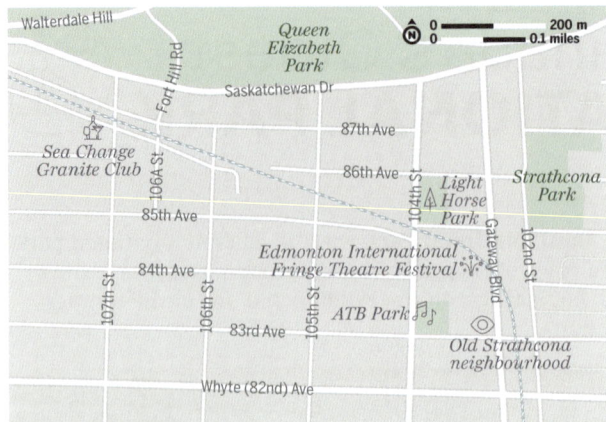

Top left Fringe festival sign
Bottom left Street performer

Get Your Fringe On

There's more than one way to fringe. Check out the shows online *(fringetheatre.ca)* and purchase tickets to the top shows in advance. Next, put on some comfy shoes and head to the **Old Strathcona neighborhood**, a funky historic area of the city that is at the heart of the Edmonton International Fringe Theatre Festival. Stop at the ATB Community Patio and pick up a festival guide with a map of the area and a list of events and performance times. Be sure to ask a volunteer for info and recommendations. There are more than a thousand volunteers at the festival. Stop at the **ATB Stage** to watch free one-minute previews by fringe artists. Purchase tickets at the **Central Box Office** – if you haven't already got some. There are hundreds of shows for theatregoers of all ages and there's something for every budget. Watch jugglers, acrobats and other artists perform stunts at the outdoor street performance pitches. Fuel up at a food truck and relax with a glass of wine at the wine tent. Enjoy free music at **ATB Park** throughout the day and in the evening. If you're still down for a party, fringe after dark at Rapid Fire Theatre's infamous Late Night Cabaret at the **Sea Change Granite Club**. Cool fact: fringe artists decide the ticket prices and make all the profits.

A Festival Within a Festival

KidsFringe is the Edmonton International Fringe Theatre Festival's 'Festival-within-a-Festival' designed especially for children 12 and under. Be sure to collect your KidsFringe Passport when you arrive at **Light Horse Park** – it'll guide you through all the magic. There are workshops, interactive performances and storytelling adventures that spark imaginations. Everything is free to help nurture the next generation of artists and arts lovers. KidsFringe opens before the rest of the festival site. Get there early to beat the rush and take in a morning of free play, then stay for the day and explore all the festival has to offer. You'll find Fringe family itineraries on the festival website.

■ **Megan Dart,** *Executive Director of the Edmonton Fringe Theatre*

36 Fringe Theatre FESTIVAL

THEATER | MUSIC | STREET ARTISTS

At its heart, fringe theater is unconventional and experimental. It's a platform for innovative, boundary-pushing theatrical performances and for 11 days every August, Alberta's capital city becomes the fringe capital of North America. There are ticketed and free performances including more than 180 indoor theatrical performances in 37 different venues, outdoor entertainment, live music, street entertainers, food and fun for all ages.

How to

When to go The **Edmonton International Fringe Theatre Festival** has been held for 11 days in mid-August annually since 1982.

Getting there Edmonton International Airport (YEG) receives flights from all over the world. The city has a great public transit system and it's best to use it to get to the festival to avoid the challenge of finding parking.

Buy tickets in advance on the fringe website (*fringetheatre.ca*) or on the SeatGeek website (*seatgeek.com*).

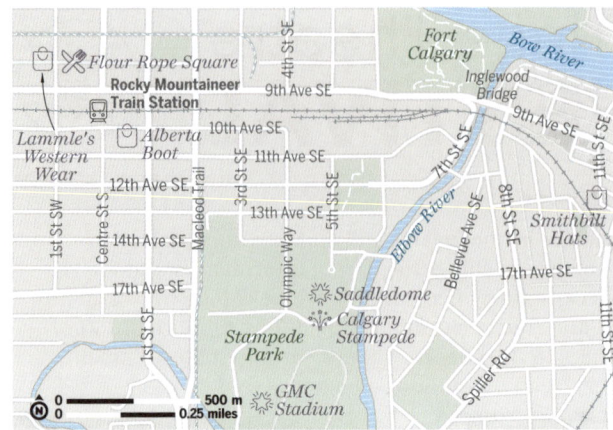

Top left Powwow ceremony at the Saddledome **Bottom left** Pancake breakfast

How to Embrace Stampede Spirit

Stampede spirit is a feeling of western energy and hospitality that is almost tangible during the Calgary Stampede. Here's how to embrace it.

Dress the Part Wear authentic western attire – jeans, a cowboy hat and boots. Top shops: **Alberta Boot**, **Smithbilt Hats** and **Lammle's Western Wear** in Calgary.

Rock Out Calgary turns into a city-wide music festival during the Calgary Stampede – in a wide variety of music genres. Over 150 artists play in multiple venues over 10 days. Some concerts are included with Stampede gate admission. Check the music schedule on the Coca-Cola Stage and the Nashville North tent for concerts that are included with no extra charge.

Attend a Powwow The three-day Powwow at the **Saddledome** is open to everyone who attends Stampede and it features some of the top dancers and drummers in North America.

More Amazing Adventures The Calgary Stampede is a multi-day event with many experiences to enjoy. Attend the world's largest outdoor rodeo at **GMC Stadium**. Visit an Indigenous village and explore the cultures of the Kainai, Piikani, Siksika, Tsuut'ina, and Stoney Nakoda First Nations of Treaty 7. Enjoy the midway and unusual midway foods. Enjoy agricultural displays and competitions, and attend The Grandstand Show at GMC Stadium, the 90-minute nightly culmination of the Stampede celebrations with music, dancing, gravity-defying stunts, a drone show and nightly fireworks.

Attending the Stampede

Hotels go up in price during Stampede and they sell out. Book well in advance.

Parking is limited near the Stampede Grounds. Consider taking public transit.

The Stampede offers special days where you can get free or discounted admission if you arrive early.

Top-tier concerts sell out during Stampede. It's best to book well in advance.

Bring a refillable water bottle. There are water bottle filling stations throughout the park.

There are events all over the city during the Stampede like cowboy trivia nights, cabarets, line dance events, chef cook-offs and western art exhibits.

35 CELEBRATE
Calgary Stampede

COWBOY CULTURE | MUSIC | RODEO

The **Calgary Stampede** is an epic celebration of western culture that transforms the city of Calgary for 10 days every July. There's a rodeo, an agricultural exhibition, a parade, a midway, a powwow, an Indigenous village, concerts, free pancake breakfasts and all kinds of entertainment that attracts over a million people every year. Locals and visitors alike don cowboy hats, jeans and boots.

How to

When to go The Calgary Stampede is held for 10 days annually in early July.

Getting there Fly into Calgary International Airport. Once in Calgary, it's best to use public transportation to get to the Stampede Grounds. Calgary Transit operates C-Train and bus routes throughout the city – including bus service from the Calgary Airport. Taxis and ride-sharing services like Uber and Lyft are also available.

Free pancake breakfast Free pancake breakfasts are a Stampede tradition and there are hundreds of them all over the city – including one every morning at **Flour Rope Square** on Stephen Avenue. Check the local newspapers or visit stampedebreakfast.ca for a comprehensive list of pancake breakfasts.

EATING & DRINKING

Restaurants in popular tourist destinations in the Alberta Rockies like Banff and Jasper tend to focus on Rocky Mountain cuisine which emphasizes ingredients like bison, elk, Alberta beef (pictured top right), native berries, prairie grains and local fish. In major cities, you'll find many types of cuisine thanks to the multicultural nature of the province. Alberta is famed for its beef and for being the place the Caesar cocktail (pictured bottom right) was invented. There's also a fantastic craft brewery scene.

Best steak house
Chuck's Steakhouse (p192), Banff

Must try Caesar cocktail
The Beltliner (p192), Calgary

CONNECT & FIND YOUR WAY

Wi-fi is available in many hotels, shops, restaurants and visitor centers in Alberta. You'll also find free wi-fi and computer access at public libraries.

Navigation Finding your way around Alberta is fairly straightforward – especially with the help of navigation apps. Most destinations are well marked. Vehicles drive on the right side of the road.

WHERE TO STAY

Prices for accommodations in Alberta vary depending on where you stay. They are highest in Banff and Jasper, followed by Calgary and Edmonton. Smaller communities like Drumheller or Brooks have lower prices.

Place	Pros/Cons
Calgary	Alberta's largest city has great public transportation and a wide range of accommodations at different price points.
Edmonton	The capital city has good public transit and accommodations at a range of prices.
Banff	The most popular tourist destination in Alberta has some of the most luxurious accommodations and higher prices for all accommodation levels.
Jasper	Accommodations in the Rockies tend to have a higher price point than other places. Jasper has a wide range of accommodations.
Drumheller	There are a lot of family-style accommodations in Drumheller at reasonable prices.
Brooks	Less-traveled towns and cities like Brooks, which is close to Dinosaur Provincial Park, tend to have lower prices and family-style accommodations.

SHOULDER SEASON

Traveling during the shoulder season (May/June or September/October) tends to yield lower accommodations prices and fewer people.

MONEY

Most shops and restaurants in Alberta accept credit cards including Apple Pay and Tap. Some vendors in craft markets might require cash.

Practicalities

ARRIVING

Calgary International Airport (YYC) This is the busiest airport in Alberta and the fourth busiest airport in Canada – both in terms of passenger traffic and aircraft movements. It is also the hub airport for WestJet and the closest airport to Banff National Park and Kananaskis.

Edmonton International Airport (YEG) This airport is just outside Alberta's capital city and it's the closest airport to Jasper National Park.

HOW MUCH FOR A

Coffee $3-5

Craft beer $6-12

Casual meal $15-20

WHEN TO GO

NOV-APR
Ski season in alpine regions.

MAY-AUG
Warm, dry season.

SEP-OCT
Harvest season and autumn colours.

GETTING AROUND

Car Having your own vehicle is by far the best option for exploring Alberta. This allows you the freedom to stop at roadside pullouts, trailheads, attractions, parks, towns and cities.

Bus Most major cities have public bus services. Red Arrow connects Calgary and Edmonton with several other communities in Alberta and British Columbia. Banff Airporter and Brewster Inc offer bus services from Calgary Airport to the mountain parks. SunDog Tours connects Edmonton with Jasper and Banff.

Train Via Rail has scheduled train services from Edmonton to Jasper twice per week. **Rocky Mountaineer** offers luxury train service that connects Vancouver with Banff and Jasper and motorcoach service to Calgary or Edmonton.

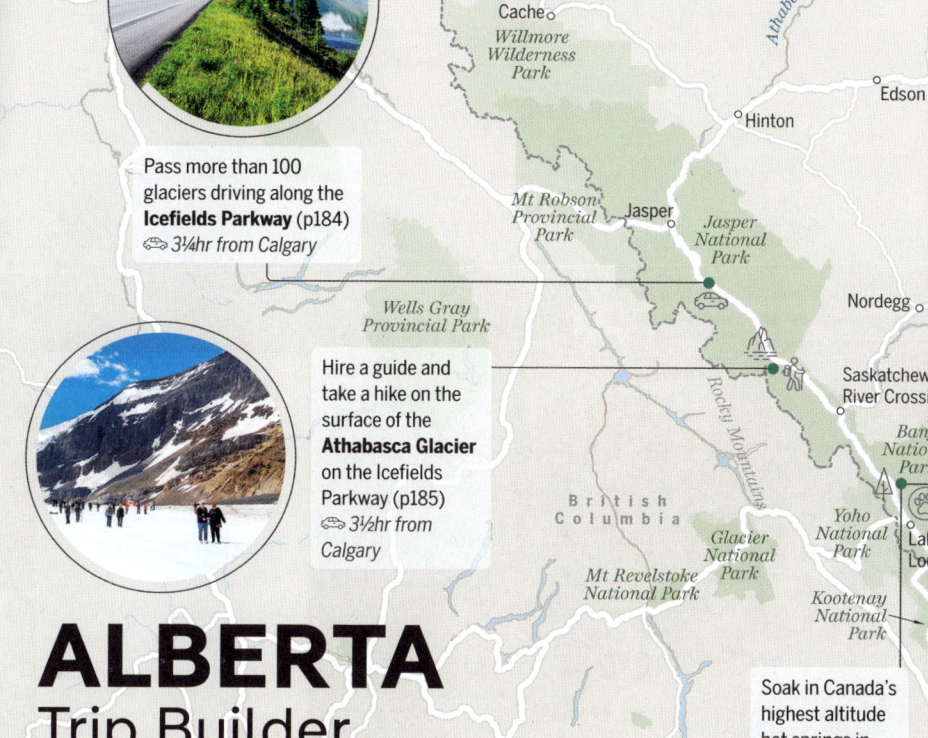

Pass more than 100 glaciers driving along the **Icefields Parkway** (p184)
🚗 3¼hr from Calgary

Hire a guide and take a hike on the surface of the **Athabasca Glacier** on the Icefields Parkway (p185)
🚗 3½hr from Calgary

Soak in Canada's highest altitude hot springs in **Banff National Park** (p183)
🚗 1½hr from Calgary

ALBERTA
Trip Builder

Alberta is all about adventure. It is home to some of the most dramatic scenery in Canada – rugged mountains, hundreds of glaciers, impossibly blue lakes, rivers and streams, vast prairies and otherworldly badlands and hoodoos. Within these dramatic landscapes, countless experiences and adventures await.

- ▶ **Trip Builder** (p174)
- ▶ **Practicalities** (p176)
- ▶ **Celebrate Calgary Stampede** (p178)
- ▶ **Fringe Theatre Festival** (p180)
- ▶ **Canada's Oldest National Park** (p182)
- ▶ **The World's Most Scenic Road** (p184)
- ▶ **Dinosaur Provincial Park** (p186)
- ▶ **Indigenous Culture in Alberta** (p188)
- ▶ **Alberta Giants of the Prairies** (p190)
- ▶ **Listings** (p192)

ALBERTA

MOUNTAINS | BADLANDS | CITIES

RESEARCHED BY DEBBIE OLSEN

Saskatchewan purple wheat. Tour a distillery and microbrewery (City Limits Brewing) here in one stop.

Patent 5 Distillery $$

A former stable is now the home of a craft distillery and one of Winnipeg's most atmospheric cocktail bars. Gin-based mixology is a specialty here.

 Wineries

Over the Hills Orchards and Winery $$

'Supper in the Orchard' sees local chefs drop in for pop-up menus with fruit wine pairings. Delicious gastronomy against scenic valley views (near Lumsden).

Shrugging Doctor Beverage Company $$

Winnipeg-based winery with a tasting room for wines and ciders. Everything's made from 100% province-grown crops. Sometimes offers tours out to its vineyards in Pembina Valley.

Prairie History Museums

Tunnels of Moose Jaw

Guided historical tours disguised in theatrical, role-playing adventures take you into Moose Jaw's underground tunnels. Discover bootlegging and Capone's connection to Saskatchewan during Prohibition (near Regina).

T-Rex Discovery Centre

Southern Saskatchewan's palaeontology history is worth a two-hour drive from Grasslands National Park to Eastend. Visit the biggest, most complete Tyrannosaurus rex skeleton ever found.

Deep South Pioneer Museum

An hour outside of Regina in Ogema, this small-town museum offers a fascinating peek into the province's earliest days through preserved buildings, farming equipment and more historical artifacts.

Artisanal Wares

Indigenous 1st Designs

Prince Albert–based art hub for Indigenous artists to showcase and sell. Clothing, homeware and traditional handmade jewellery.

Manitobah

Métis-owned footwear brand selling cozy moccasins, slippers and high-quality *mukluks* (some do use rabbit fur). Locations in Winnipeg (flagship in Forks Market), Regina and Saskatoon.

Treasure Valley Markets

In Cadillac (one hour from Val Marie/Grasslands), orchard picking and a shop with a huge selection of take-home preserves promise family-friendly fun. Stay all day and delight in paddleboat rides and a petting zoo.

CreeAtions & Artist Showcase

Métis-owned gallery-workshop for made-to-measure *mukluks* and moccasins, one-of-a-kind artwork, jewellery, star blankets and more by Cree and First Nations artists from around Manitoba.

Thermal Spas

Temple Gardens Mineral Spa

An hour's drive from Regina, Moose Jaw indoor-outdoor pool complex offers steamy dips into geothermal mineral waters. It's the perfect winter reprieve for a day visit or overnight resort stay (book well ahead).

Therměa Spa Village

Scandinavian-inspired, modern wellness center in Winnipeg. Savor outdoor thermal baths, eucalyptus-infused saunas, cold plunge pools, a full spa menu of massages and facials, and much more. A 'simulated' thermal experience (water sourced from Shoal Lake).

Listings

BEST OF THE REST

Urban Microbreweries

Bonzzini's $$

Serious hidden gem in Regina. Don't let the strip-mall fool you; beyond 'Bonzo's' heavy door is a rustic, charming surprise. Fantastic brews and pub fare.

Bushwakker $$

Chase down a Wild Boar Burger with endless IPAs and blackberry mead in a circa-1913 converted warehouse-turned-Irish Regina pub. Live music and open-mic nights.

Rebellion Brewing $$

Saskatchewan's best microbrewery has a stylish taproom in Regina's Warehouse District. The beer list is long and changing – plus, there's tacos.

Pile O' Bones Brewing $$

This spacious brewpub located near the stadium boasts vintage pinball machines and a pop-up kitchen. Try the 'Prairie Pilsner'.

Nonsuch Brewing Co $$

This Winnipeg brewery's German *Kölsch* is a national, gold-medal winner. Fruity beers and sharing plates round out a decadent foodie experience.

Little Brown Jug $$

Winnipeg's favourite beer brewed with a little history: a Belgian-style pale ale named after the city's famous 1919 strike.

Trans-Canada Brewing Co $$

Raucous beer hall popular with groups. A bewilderingly big beer selection (some very experimental), plus gourmet pizza to sober up.

Torque Brewing $$

Sampling a pint of Witty Belgian at this award-winning brewery. Live music on Friday evenings; catch sporting games on big flat-screens too.

Brazen Hall Kitchen & Brewery $$

Crowd-pleasing microbrewery and bistro with experimental small-batch brews every Thursday, brewery tours and great food.

Rural Microbreweries

Crossmount Cider Company $$

A sucker for cider? South of Saskatoon, sip inventive ciders – from rosé to jalapeño pear – among orchards. Skating pond in winter.

Farmery Estate Brewery $$

Manitoba's first estate brewery in Neepawa does 'farm-to-glass' craft brewing grounded in sustainability. Craft beers and excellent non-alcoholic sips, too – try a virgin or beer caesar.

Craft Distilleries

Last Mountain Distillery $$

Outside Regina, must-try vodka flavors include pickle (made with dill, cucumber and garlic grown in Qu'Appelle Valley) and Saskatoon berry.

Black Fox Farm and Distillery $$

On a distillery tour, peek into copper stills and relax on a barn patio sampling favorites like Rhubarb Gin and Boreal Mint Gin made from grown and forest-foraged ingredients.

Stumbletown Distilling $$

In Saskatoon, sip on 'grain-to-glass' gin and vodka distilled from antioxidant-packed

ulation. European newcomers came early, Asians and Africans dominated later waves. Consequently, the prairies have become sweepingly diverse in urban centers (Winnipeg and Regina count over 100 different ethnic communities); new immigrants sustain rural workforces, too.

These provinces are changing economically. The agriculture industry faces challenges such as chronic labor shortages and climate change. Increasing wildfires are a serious threat.

> In the earliest decades, agriculture became these provinces' lifeblood. For rural communities, that's still true today.

While the majority of urban Saskatchewan and Manitoba still have their rural roots back one or two generations, other immigrants might feel disconnected from farming heritage overall. Demographics remain ever-shifting, including recent Ukrainian refugees. A 2023 census found Tagalog (Filipino) is now Saskatchewan's 'second language'.

Seeds of Change

Such a climate can breed misunderstanding, especially in Indigenous rights. Intergenerational traumas from residential schools to the reserve system have resulted in a disproportionately lower life quality for Indigenous Peoples. They endure higher rates of homicide, incarceration and victimization. Reconciliation, the ongoing repairing of relationships between Indigenous and non-Indigenous peoples, is a defining challenge for the nation, and especially, the prairies' treaty lands. Favorably, a hard-working mentality is deeply ingrained in Saskatchewan and Manitoba's DNA. The future will surely depend on planting new seeds.

Reaping Violence

Sowing provincial sovereignty was bloody and violent. The fur trade between the Hudson's Bay Company and Indigenous Peoples marked earlier days, but peaceful negotiations were short-lived. It took only a decade for homesteaders and hunters to slash Saskatchewan's wild bison population from 60 million to 500 by the 1890s, decimating Indigenous Peoples' most integral resource. Most Cree, Dene and Assiniboine moved to reserves. In neighboring Manitoba, conflict over land rights launched a Métis (people of mixed Aboriginal and European backgrounds) rebellion. Negotiations between their leader, Louis Riel, and the federal government saw Manitoba join Canada in 1870, though Riel was later executed for treason.

Seeds of Community

IN CANADA'S BREADBASKET, THE CROP ECONOMY SEEDS AN UNDERSTANDING OF THE SOCIAL LANDSCAPE THAT'S STILL MATURING.

In Saskatchewan and Manitoba, the agricultural industry is the root of everything – politics, culture and history. Still, harvesting an understanding of Canada's prairies provinces is sweaty work. Wide-open plains are well-culled with misconceptions about living here. Plowing deeper reveals a fascinating landscape where yields, economic and otherwise, are dynamically changing.

Left Canola fields in bloom, Saskatchewan **Center** Storytelling with a Métis cultural speaker **Right** Bison, Grasslands National Park

Canada's Breadbasket

Canada's grain belt finds its identity still in a ripening phase. Saskatchewan and Manitoba are among Canada's youngest provinces (by a few decades only), though that matters in today's culture and society. Nationally, the prairies has historically felt, at times, forgotten and like a footnote. Meanwhile, writing a new chapter provincially has seen thousands of years of Indigenous culture omitted, too.

The prairies were populated by Ottawa offering free, fertile land to European settlers. Immigrant waves from Germany, Ukraine and elsewhere seeded communities and infrastructure on the new frontier. Significantly, Indigenous populations were displaced from their traditional lands as this new population took root.

Canada's Quonset

In the earliest decades, agriculture became these provinces' lifeblood. For rural communities, that's still true today. Almost half of Saskatchewan is agricultural, with a thousand-some rural communities comprising less than 5,000 residents, in between. While neighboring Manitoba is more urbanized, farming and livestock is economically critical. Wheat, canola, oats and barley as well as pulses, soybean and corn, ensure Canada's food security. Saskatchewan produces 71% of Canada's mustard seeds and 22% of global exports.

A Diversified Crop

Immigration defines both provinces' existence in the last half-century as much as the first. Over the last few decades, immigration has been essential with an aging pop-

Top left Swimmer, Little Manitou Lake
Bottom left Danceland dance hall

Summer on the Lake

A quaint summer resort village, just over an hour's drive southeast of Saskatoon, **Manitou Beach** is a truly magical place. The density of salt and minerals in Little Manitou Lake, comparable to the famed Dead Sea, enables effortless back floating.

The area is located on Treaty 6 territory and the traditional lands of the Cree and Saulteaux (Ojibway) Peoples; also, Dakota and Métis communities. Oral histories describe it as a place where warriors and hunters recovered both physically and spiritually. Generations after treaty-making, the lake is now popular with local farmers and other agricultural workers who come here to relieve sore muscles. The town of Manitou's population of 350 surges with summer vacationers dining at lakefront restaurants; right on the beach, locally grown Saskatoon berries and raspberries are picnic favorites.

During the summer, surrounding landscapes burst with prismatic crops – periwinkle flax (June), light purple and white lentils and yellow canola flowers (June to July), golden wheat sheaths, and wispy, green barley and oats (late July to August).

Winter's Thermal Waters

If the cool waters of the lake don't appeal, there's an indoor heated pool at the highly popular **Manitou Springs Resort & Mineral Spa**. Here, the Prairie 'Dead Sea' becomes an indulgently steamy affair consistently heated to a minimum 33°C – especially welcome during cold snaps.

Manitou's Greatest Hits

Spa Treatment Roll around in Manitou Beach's muddy shoreline – the dark, mineral-rich sludge is an all-natural, detoxifying skin treatment.

Art Stop Beat the heat by discovering **Little Manitou Art Gallery** (littlemanitouartgallery.com) and the works of 100 Saskatchewan artists.

Dance the Nights Away Spend an evening at **Danceland** (danceland.ca), a 1928-built dance hall with a one-of-a-kind horsehair floor. Or have a blast at **Manitou Music Fest** with lakeside dancing and concerts – soothe tired feet afterwards in those salty waters.

Catch a Sunset Flick Manitou's **Salty Cinema Drive-In** is one of only four left in Saskatchewan. Right next to it, the combine from *Twister* is on display.

34 Canada's DEAD SEA

SALT WATER | HOT SPRINGS | FARM SCENERY

Little Manitou Lake is a hidden gem. Tucked between grain fields in southern Saskatchewan, Manitou is one of three places in the world with 'Dead Sea' waters full of minerals and salt – meaning that you can't sink! Its therapeutic waters have a long history providing locals, from ancient Indigenous Peoples to generations of farmers, with healing and relaxation.

How to

Getting around You'll need your own wheels to get here.

When to go Summer is the best time to visit to see crops in full bloom.

Where to stay The farming town of Watrous is the main gateway to Manitou, lying 6km to the south.

Gravel roads On gravel roads, it's customary to slow down and move to the side when approaching other vehicles (a little wave is nice, too). Take out extra insurance against windshield dings.

05 Follow Lake Winnipeg's coast to **Hecla Heritage Village** and explore the Icelandic settlement by vehicle or snowshoe. The tourism center closes seasonally but historic lakefront buildings abound.

03 From **Gimli Harbor**, embark on an ice-fishing day expedition with **PrairieGal Fishing**, which offers shack rentals and learn-to-fish programs with a special focus on empowering women to try angling.

04 Discover New Iceland's 1875 origins at the **New Iceland Heritage Museum**. It's a fascinating trawl through history involving volcano eruptions, a Canadian government PR campaign, grueling overseas travel and, finally, a sovereign republic.

02 At the **Gimli Ice Festival**, explore an endless sea of cultural activities where ancestral blonds abound. Delight in horse-drawn wagon rides, tobogganing and fireside bannock and maple-syrup taffy. *Skál!*

01 Leaving Winnipeg, stop at the **Gimli Fish Market**. Find New Icelandic *hardfiskur* (wind-dried haddock), smoked trout and more fishy delicacies. As per tradition, butter your *hardfiskur*.

FROM LEFT: INTERLAKE TOURISM-COURTESY TRAVEL MANITOBA, TRAVEL MANITOBA

33 New Icelandic HORIZONS

ICE FISHING | WINTER FESTIVAL | MARITIME HISTORY

On Lake Winnipeg, a tiny fishing village is a deep-freeze of 19th-century Icelandic heritage. Every March, Gimli defrosts from hibernation during the **Gimli Ice Festival** *(pictured below; gimliicefestival.com)*. Entertainment spans thrills (lake auto-racing, fish tossing, Viking reenactments) and warming chills with *plokkfiskur* (fish stew) and cultural rituals. Ice fishing is an unforgettable experience here in the world's largest Icelandic diaspora community.

Icelandic Festival of Manitoba

August's **Icelandic Festival of Manitoba** in Gimli, attended by tens of thousands annually, tends to cast a summer shadow over the Ice Festival. **Íslendingadagurinn** *(icelandicfestival.com)* is one of North America's longest-running cultural celebrations. Spectacle highlights include Icelandic games, folk performances, and more Vikings. It's rip-roaring fun but March's Ice Festival is truly a more authentic, exclusive experience.

Trip Notes

Getting around Gimli is 1½ hours' drive north of Winnipeg on Highway 59 and Hwy 9. There's no public transportation so you'll need a vehicle with winter tires.

When to go Book accommodations well ahead. Several lodges are by the water; there are room-sharing options as well.

Top tip The drive from Winnipeg to Gimli is all highway; explore in-destination on gravel roads. Take it easy and watch out for black ice and snow drifts.

Top left A herd of plains bison
Bottom left East Block backcountry camping, Grasslands National Park

Fossils, Stargazing & Prairie Dogs

The park has two distinct sections: **East Block** and **West Block**. Both are cinematic, but dramatically different. The West Block delivers iconic prairie scenery, while the East Block is somewhat dystopian.

The West Block is the epitome of prairie landscapes – rolling hills, rugged coulees and meandering ravines. Hiking is the name of the game here. Well-marked trails go up and over the valley through native fields of purple prairie clover and cactus flower. Keep a lookout for the **stone circles** of Plains Indigenous ancestors and **free-roaming bison**. Most likely, though, are **prairie dog sightings** (Canada's only wild colonies).

Grasslands is also an official Dark-Sky Preserve. Back-road 'theaters' reveal the Milky Way, meteor showers and auroras on clear nights.

Badlands, Bison & Solitude

Dramatic coulees, hoodoos, eroded red-clay cliffs – welcome to the East Block's otherworld. It's less visited than the West – if you're seeking off-trail solitude, look no further. The **Valley of 1000 Devils** trails into Rock Creek Badlands' clay buttes. Driving the Badlands Pkwy uncovers fossil-filled vistas. Paleontological treasures are prime here. In 1874, Canada's first dinosaur remains were found in today's East Block. Countless prehistoric species have been dug up since – horned triceratops and armor-covered ankylosaurus. Of the living, be prepared for potential rattlesnakes.

Tailor Your Trip

If you're short on time, guided tours are effective adventures. **Big Muddy Tours** rolls out the **Sam Kelly Outlaw Caves** and more secrets on privately owned Badlands. Your best chance of wild bison sightings is on a self-guided **Grasslands Ecotour Scenic Drive**. Encounters are well-reported while cruising the park's designated 20km route. Untamed Grasslands, surprisingly, offers glamping. Parks Canada's **oTENTik shelters** have beds and basic furniture. Some are located in the Dark-Sky Preserve. For stays in civilization, overnight at the **Convent Inn** in Val Marie. The derelict nunnery, lovingly renovated into a charming B&B, is one of Canada's most unique homestays. One warning: paranormal activity has been reported by guests.

32 Plains of the PRAIRIES

BADLANDS | STARGAZING | BISON HERDS

Get ready for a wild time. Whether you're off-grid camping or scenic driving, visiting **Grasslands National Park** *(parkscanada.ca/grasslands)*, a four-hour drive from Regina, is always memorable. Canada's only protected mixed-grass prairie land sweeps through Saskatchewan backcountry, promising vastly different landscapes as you explore. In Grasslands, treeless hills meet endless skies – expanses can feel wild and isolating, but therein lies the charm.

How to

When to go Early summer for wildflower landscapes and mild temperatures (May and June). Warm, dry weather for hiking and stargazing season (July and August).

Getting there Val Marie (3½ hours' drive southwest of Regina) is the gateway to the park.

Top tip Unlike more crowded national parks, Grasslands allows wild camping. The **visitor center** is an invaluable resource for camping advice and other general information.

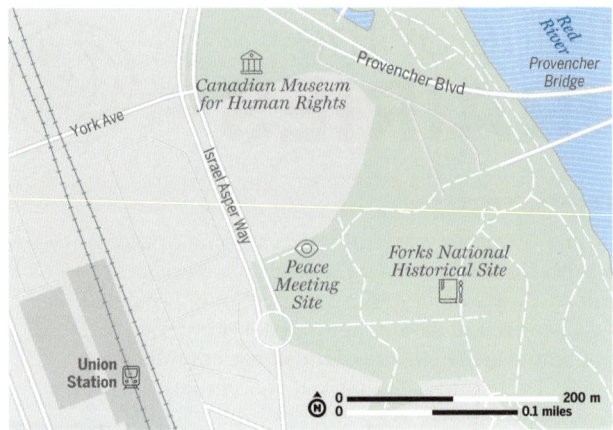

Top left Canadian Journeys gallery, Canadian Museum for Human Rights
Bottom left Canadian Museum for Human Rights, viewed from Forks

🏛 CMHR Highlights

Get up High The elevator up to the Israel Asper Tower of Hope is the museum's climax. The 100m glass spire reveals a modern panorama on ancient lands.

Hall of Hope CMHR's most photographed architectural feature is the Hall of Hope. Following the walkway, reflect on the significance of its stair-free design: open perspectives throughout represent the progress of freedom.

Garden of Contemplation This is the museum's ending point but you can come here anytime for reflection. The indoor, Zen garden–like space is made for quiet reflection.

Heroes and Leaders In the International Human Rights gallery, visit the 'Heroes and Leaders' display screens where Myanmar politician Aung San Suu Kyi, once illuminated, has been dimmed, reflecting Rohingya persecution.

Exploring Outdoors What's often eclipsed by CMHR's architectural magnificence are its outdoor surroundings – gorgeously landscaped and historically significant. CMHR is situated against **The Forks** (parks.canada.ca/lhn-nhs/mb/forks). The national historic site, located at the confluence of the Red and Assiniboine Rivers, is an Indigenous gathering site going back a millennium. Next to it, the **Peace Meeting Site** is a tranquil, urban oasis area. A traditional firepit, Manitoban flora and gigantic Adirondack chairs invite relaxation. A statue of Gandhi is at the park entrance.

Truth & Reconciliation Canada's reconciliation journey represents an overarching theme. CMHR can be an emotional experience, especially here – the **Residential School Wall** is the museum at its most visceral, displaying hundreds of victims' photographs, documents and personal belongings. Meanwhile, the Indigenous Perspectives exhibit holds a powerful art installation that weaves the past with the present. Trace by Canadian Anishinaabe (Ojibwe) artist Rebecca Belmore is a **ceramic 'blanket'**. Cascading down a gallery wall, the installation comprises over 14,000 hand-moulded beads, each crafted from Red River Valley clay by community members.

LGBTIQ+ History Canadians' struggles for LGBTIQ+ rights are explored in the **Love in a Dangerous Time: Canada's LGBT Purge** exhibition. Examining the Holocaust also highlights WWII LGBTIQ+ persecution. During **Winnipeg Pride**, special museum tours focus on queer history.

31 A Monument to HUMAN RIGHTS

WORLD-FIRST MUSEUM | HIGH-TECH EXHIBITS | INDIGENOUS ART

In Winnipeg, the **Canadian Museum for Human Rights** *(CMHR; humanrights.ca)* is the world's first museum dedicated solely to human rights. Opened in 2014, the $351 million, 24,000-sq-m-landmark spans thousands of exhibition pieces ranging from artifact to artistic and high-tech. You can easily spend an entire weekend exploring the 10 stories top-to-bottom – or focus on a few of its most fascinating features.

How to

When to go Mornings as there are lots of school groups in the afternoons. Allow at least a half-day for your visit; the museum packs in a lot of content – some exhibits are quite emotional, so you may require pauses.

What's nearby Situated against The Forks, a national historic site, there's much to explore here.

Self-guided tour Download the CMHR mobile app for a full self-guided tour; the museum has free wi-fi.

Accessibility CMHR is fully accessible; the app has features for the hearing and vision impaired.

Top left Little Brown Jug brewery
Bottom left Spirits, Capital K Distillery

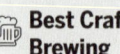

Best Craft Brewing

Taprooms are reviving warehouse districts. Hit **Bushwakker** (bush wakker.com) and **Rebellion** (rebellionbrewing.ca) in Regina. Winnipeg's Exchange District (the 'Chicago of the North'), there's **Little Brown Jug** (littlebrownjug.ca) and **Nonsuch** (nonsuch.beer). At **Crossmount Cider Company** (crossmount cidercompany.ca) near Saskatoon, enjoy a creative cider flight, while you look over apple orchards and towering pines. Signatures include Cider + Black (berries) and Vanilla Chai. Saskatchewan's largest brewery, **Great Western**, was founded by Molson employees after the local plant closed. A tour-and-taste here showcases regional grains and resilient spirit. Raise a glass to empowering diversity in the globally male-dominated brew scene. **Good Neighbour** (goodneighbourbrewing.com) in Winnipeg is Manitoba's first brewery under female-, queer-identifying ownership.

Brewing Traditions Hobby brewing has been at home on the prairies right from early on. Émigrés from Germany, Ukraine and elsewhere tapped into local grains, drawing upon homeland tradition. As towns and cities grew, large-scale production spawned the **Great Western Brewing Company** (gwbc.ca), Saskatchewan's biggest brewery, and brands such as Bohemian, a prairies-geared brand by Canada-wide Molson, drawing on Czech tradition. Respectively, their pilsner and 'Bo' lager are camping favourites. In the early 2000s, relaxed liquor laws made licensing attainable, cultivating a huge brewpub scene long before global trends. International inspiration and regional knowledge fuel a diverse, huge craft-beer scene.

Farming Legacy Short harvest seasons aren't constraints but a gateway to creativity. Local fruits, including cherries, plums, and berries, have long infused local winemaking and, especially, an iconically Canadian excellence in ice wine. Farmers (and especially their millennial offspring) have leveraged agricultural expertise, entrepreneurial spirit and harvest grains to establish distilleries renowned on home turf and beyond. Family-run businesses include Winnipeg's **Capital K Distillery** (capitalkdistillery.com), producing vodka, gin, whisky and rum using local grains, and Saskatoon's **Black Fox** (blackfoxfarmanddistillery.com) – a fifth-generation farm family distilling with their own fruit, barley and wild forest ingredients like juniper berries – showcase a thriving industry full of heart.

30 Flavors of the PRAIRIES

CRAFT BREWERIES | DISTILLERIES | WINEMAKERS

The prairies welcomed the craft beer and spirits movement with a whoop. Home brewing and wine-making on the farm has been happening over generations, and what could be a better way to pass some time when your driveway's snowed in? Abundant grain yields, can-do mentality and regional pride is breeding one of Canada's most excitingly successful craft tipple scenes.

How to

When to go Avoid driving after dark in rural areas wherever possible; fatal collisions are all too common. Almost every small town has a motel for the night.

Getting around Explore downtown brewpubs on foot; to reach on-site tours, you'll need wheels.

Driving service First Choice (*firstchoicedd.ca*) offers an affordable pickup service taking your vehicle home (and you in the backseat) to prevent drinking and driving (Regina and Saskatoon). It was started by a family who tragically lost their son.

Manitoba Brew Pass Pick up a three-day pass ($49) covering tasting flights at your choice of seven participating breweries.

EATING & DRINKING

Home brewing has deep prairie roots. Tradition infuses a vast crop of regional craft beverages (spirits, beer, wine) using prairie fruits and grains. Brewpubs are decades-old institutions.

Winnipeg boasts world-class dining, mixing up artisan cafes, experimental haute cuisine and more. Elsewhere in Manitoba, options diminish, but *bannock* (Indigenous fried bread; pictured bottom right) and smoked fish are lakeside delicacies. Regina and Saskatoon have many excellent restaurants; prairie-sourced fare is on trend. Here, and in Winnipeg, multicultural dining is endless. Stopping into small-town diners is a road-tripping highlight for peeking into rural lifestyles.

Best regional beer
Great Western Brewing

Must try craft beer Pile O' Bones Brewing, Prairie Pilsner

CONNECT & FIND YOUR WAY

Wi-fi Though improving, wi-fi in rural areas is still mostly snail-paced. Having a mobile data plan for driving is wise (gas stations do not sell SIM cards; public hotspots are rare).

Navigation Don't rely on GPS mapping in these parts; it often leads through under-serviced, winding, gravel routes that require careful navigation.

WHERE TO STAY

Across Saskatchewan, get used to staying in chain hotels; almost all little towns have at least one motel. In Manitoba, the best range of accommodations is Winnipeg; elsewhere, you're limited to mostly basic motels – or campgrounds.

Destination	Pros/Cons
Winnipeg	Wide-ranging accommodations from hotels to guesthouses; terribly pricey for downtown (where you'll want to be).
Thompson	Halfway between Churchill and Riding Mountain National Park; mostly motels ranging from passable to decent.
Regina	Plenty of hotels around town; mostly chains, though, without much (or any) special character.
Saskatoon	Excellent, independently run boutique hotels; pricey and fully booked well ahead.
Prince Albert	Budget options abound from motels to campgrounds; essentially no mid-range or top-end alternatives.

RURAL GREETING

On gravel roads, get over to the right and slow down for approaching vehicles. Even better, lift your hand casually up for a customary prairies 'hello'.

MONEY

Expect long stretches without highway services. Budget extra spending for gas and food in rural areas, and always keep emergency cash.

Practicalities

ARRIVING

Winnipeg International Airport Manitoba's main gateway; a convenient 10km west of downtown. Offers connections to cities across Canada and a few major US hubs. Regional carriers handle remote destinations, including Churchill.

Regina International Airport The main provincial entry point (though the second-biggest airport, Saskatoon, handles only slightly fewer passengers). Barely international (some US and Mexico flights); direct routes to Canadian cities including Toronto, Vancouver, Montreal and Halifax.

HOW MUCH FOR A

Bison burger $15

Star blanket $150

Bottle of fruit wine $20

GETTING AROUND

Car Getting to know the prairies is impossible without the freedom of your own wheels. Before leaving in a rental, check for working cruise control (a big help on long provincial highways). For rural explorations, a 4WD or an SUV makes for less bumpy driving, though a regular car will also do just fine.

Planes Winnipeg, Regina and Saskatoon's airports all connect with daily direct service to Toronto and Vancouver (some other destinations, too). Flight delays or cancellations during winter are common.

Train VIA Rail's Toronto to Vancouver, iconic 'Canadian' route passes through Winnipeg and smaller Saskatchewan towns such as Watrous.

WHEN TO GO

JAN-MAR
Prime time for snowy festivals and adrenaline, also aurora gazing.

APR-JUN
Blossoming wildflowers and bird migrations liven up highway driving.

JUL-SEP
Prairie crops burst towards harvest; lake life animates.

OCT-DEC
Pumpkin patches and Churchill's polar bear season.

MANITOBA & SASKATCHEWAN
Trip Builder

Don't let these rolling flatlands fool you – these prairie provinces pack in dramatic scenery and memorable, uniquely Canadian rural adventures. If Canucks are known for being friendly, prairie folks pride themselves on being the friendliest; you never know who you'll meet and what surprises are in store for you.

Float aimlessly and enjoy a DIY mud facial at **Little Manitou Lake** (p166) – North America's salty 'Dead Sea'.
🚗 2hr from Regina

Sip spirits distilled from boreal forests and prairie grain at **Black Fox Farm and Distillery** (p159).
🚗 15min from Saskatoon

Go on a stargazing expedition in **Grasslands National Park's** Dark-Sky Preserve (p162).
🚗 3½hr from Regina

Explore outlaw history amid sandstone badlands cliffs with **Big Muddy Tours** (p163).
🚗 2hr from Regina

CLOCKWISE FROM BOTTOM LEFT: SCOTT ASPINALL, TOURISM SASKATCHEWAN/CAREY SHAW PHOTOGRAPHY, INTERLAKE TOURISM-COURTESY TRAVEL MANITOBA, SALVADOR MANIQUIZ/SHUTTERSTOCK

MANITOBA & SASKATCHEWAN

RURAL SCENERY | WINTER ADVENTURES | GASTRONOMIC SURPRISES

RESEARCHED BY BARBARA WOOLSEY

▸ **Trip Builder** (p154)
▸ **Practicalities** (p156)
▸ **Flavors of the Prairies** (p158)
▸ **A Monument to Human Rights** (p160)
▸ **Plains of the Prairies** (p162)
▸ **New Icelandic Horizons** (p164)
▸ **Canada's Dead Sea** (p166)
▸ **Seeds of Community** (p168)
▸ **Listings** (p170)

Pollen Nation Farm
The Newfoundland honeybee is celebrated over cafe lunches and three-course Beestro dinners at this Indigenous Culinary Tourism Award-winning bee farm in Little Rapids, owned by chef Nathan Hornidge and Amanda Oake.

Pirate's Haven ATV Friendly RV Park, Chalets & Adventures
Take the thrilling 'Middle of Nowhere ATV Tour' with 'Pirate' Paul Gale, complete with a Newfoundland mug-up meal on an ocean beach, from this Indigenous-owned company in Robinsons.

Local Arts & Crafts

Change Islands Interpretation & Craft Centre
This interpretation center in Change Islands is chock full of mittens, cushions, quilts, crocheted blankets and other local creations, using its Facebook page to show what's available.

Fogo Island Metalworks
In Shoal Bay, Artist Marc Fiset creates artistic and functional metal pieces like puffin coat racks, salt cod hooks and cod fish book ends, as well as custom fire pits and house numbers.

Lookout Quilts & Things
Dale Payne's cozy shop in the town of Fogo is stuffed with knitted items (mitts, hats, socks) and other textile creations made from fish nets.

Durrell Museum
Tucked into the Durrell Museum in Twillingate, the Brigade Artisan Shoppe has some of the best prices in the province for gorgeous hand-knit items, jewelry and art.

Dark Tickle Co
You'll see Dark Tickle jams, jellies, sauces and vinegars sold across the province but the company headquarters in St-Lunaire-Griquet doubles as a shop and cafe. Its pickers harvest five kinds of berries.

Signal Hill National Historic Site

French Twist in St-Pierre & Miquelon

Le Musée Heritage
DIY walking tours of downtown St-Pierre should stop at this quirky museum that showcases Prohibition-era memorabilia from the time this self-governing territorial collectivity of France sold booze to US bootleggers.

Les Zigotos
Down by Pointe aux Canons Lighthouse in St-Pierre's colorful fishing shacks called Les Salines, a group called Les Zigotos builds and restores dories and offers tours in the traditional wooden boats.

Île-aux-Marins
Hop a water taxi from St-Pierre to this wee island/living museum that celebrates the cod fishing industry that lured fisherpeople here from Normandy and Brittany. Look for the *Transpacific* wreck.

Maison de la Nature et de l'Environnement
This modern nature interpretation center (partially bilingual) teaches visitors about local ecosystems and history before nudging them off on Le Cape de Miquelon trail or one of Miquelon's other hikes.

Listings

BEST OF THE REST

 Whale Tales

Cape Spear Lighthouse National Historic Site
Canada's most easterly point in St John's doubles as a popular spot to watch for migrating humpbacks, minkes and other whales. You can even rent binoculars from Parks Canada.

Trinity Eco-Tours
Based in Trinity, Skipper Bob Bartlett's passion for whales shows on ocean safaris that may luck into seeing eagles, diving seabirds and icebergs while marveling at the coastline.

St Vincent's Beach
For a brief spell in June and July, humpbacks feed on capelin in the deep water just offshore from this cobblestone beach in St Vincent's. Bring a lawn chair.

 Great Outdoors

Signal Hill National Historic Site
Located in St John's, take Canada's best urban hike from the parking lot by Cabot Tower down to the Battery. North Head Trail is short and steep with astounding views.

Mistaken Point Ecological Reserve
You can only see the world's oldest and largest collection of complex marine-life fossils on guided tours that involve a 6km hike. Meet at the Mistaken Point Interpretation Centre in Portugal Cove South.

 Heritage Highlights

Gander International Lounge
Canada's most important modernist room is an airport lounge with terrazzo floors and vintage furniture that dates back to 1959 and is now before security and open to the public in Gander.

North Atlantic Aviation Museum
One exhibit details how Gander hosted 38 diverted flights during September 11. A piece of World Trade Center steel – one of four gifted to the area – is on display.

Four Season Tours
From Cox's Cove, hop in a traditional wooden Newfoundland dory with Darren Park to explore a quiet fjord, looking for bald eagles and unique geology, and doing a little cod fishing.

French Shore Interpretation Centre
In Conche, a 227-ft-long storytelling tapestry, stitched by 12 local women, tells the story of the region's French cod fishery and unique history dating back to the Vikings.

#2 Mine Tour & Museum
Near St John's, Bell Island's iron-ore mining history is shared on tours through tunnels below the sea. Save time for the museum and nearby Theatre of the Mine performances.

Canadian Glove Museum
Visits to Canada's only glove museum are free and include a fascinating guided tour of the Superior Glove plant in Point Leamington to learn about textile innovations before crafting your own mini glove.

Indigenous Experiences

Upper Humber Settlement
Co-owner Lauralee Ledrew leads Indigenous fire-circle meditations, with DIY bannock, storytelling dinners and foraging tours. Pop in for tours/experiences or sleep at this bed-and-breakfast farmstay in Cormack.

fishers and whalers, and English, Irish and French colonizers who mixed with the Beothuk, Mi'kmaq, Innu and Inuit.

Geographic isolation helped breed and preserve dialects. We'll leave the history lesson there, except to say that everyone who isn't a Newfoundlander is now a 'come from away' or CFA.

Yes, that's also the name of the hit musical based on what happened when 38 planes were forced to land at **Gander International Airport** after the September 11 attacks and 7,000 people had to wait here for almost a week. (Spoiler alert: they loved the Rock.)

Language Lessons

'Who knit ya?' There are 120 Change Islands sayings posted on bright cards on the **Change Islands Interpretation and Craft Centre** wall. It's a conversation starter with CFAs, and a way to jog the memories of folks who might be back after years away. 'Who knit ya' is the polite way of probing someone's lineage and hometown.

> Don't be scared to ask for translations since terms can be hyperlocal or have regional nuances.

Mayor Paula Flood, who handles the center's social media is partial to 'took to'. As she explains, 'if you said something that surprised me or offended me or whatever, and I was to tell my friend, I'd say I was right took to.'

Don't be scared to ask for translations since terms can be hyperlocal or have regional nuances. Many do have one clear meaning, though, so if you're invited to a scoff and a scuff, pull out those stretchy pants and put on your dancing shoes.

Name Game

Fancy visiting **Heart's Delight**, **Heart's Desire** and **Heart's Content**? They're minutes from each other, and romantics can pass through **Cupids** if they're driving from St John's.

Is it any surprise that this language-loving province has plenty of evocative place names? **Come by Chance** is inviting. **Blow Me Down Provincial Park** is edgy. **Goobies** is fun to say and you can get gas and see the **Morris the Moose statue** at the **Goobies Big Stop Restaurant**.

And then there's **Dildo**, the origins of its name hotly debated, its much-photographed Hollywood-style sign a 2019 gift from American talk show host Jimmy Kimmel.

A Way with Words

THE STORY BEHIND NEWFOUNDLAND'S QUIRKY SAYINGS

Canada's most colorful province has a colorful secret language to match. Did it develop thanks to early settlers and geographic isolation, or because the fun-loving people who live here in their own time zone, a half an hour ahead of everyone else, just excel at creating clever words and phrases?

Left NL Sayings Bars, Newfoundland Chocolate Co **Center** Compassion Monument (in the background), Gander **Right** Dildo's town sign

It starts simply with a 'hello m'love' here and a 'whadda ya at?' there. Before long, people with delightful accents are saying 'stay where you're at til I comes where you're to' and you have no clue what they're on about. It doesn't sound like English, but the *Dictionary of Newfoundland English* says it is.

Welcome to the land of storytellers, where there's a clever saying for every occasion.

Take the Newfoundland Food Tour, for example. Sign up for one with **St John's Walking Tours** and you'd better come gut-foundered (famished). Three hours later – stuffed with moose, fish cakes, partridgeberries and toutons – you'll be stogged (too full to eat another bite) and wishing for stretchy pants.

Speaking of food, the **Newfoundland Chocolate Co** turned a cheeky Valentine's 2015 idea into NL Sayings Bars. Terms are printed on pink, white and green striped labels (the colors of the unofficial Republic of Newfoundland flag). Translations come on bookmarks or online.

'Arse on dat' (nice bum) is a fun one. So is 'yes b'y' (you can't be serious) and 'I dies at you' (you're funny).

'Our favourites are always the ones we've grown up with and use all the time,' says founder/CEO Christina Dove. 'Mine is "what odds" which is basically my attitude that anything is doable and is no problem and we can get through anything that hits us.'

Historically Speaking

So how did this unique lexicon come to be?

Long before the Dominion of Newfoundland joined Canada in 1949, this seemingly inhospitable place surrounded by enormous cod stocks attracted Viking explorers, European

Happy Hunting

There's no way to predict if – and where – icebergs might be when you visit. But **Newfoundland and Labrador Iceberg Reports**, a Facebook group, gets its members to post photos and locations in real time. The province has a map with photos at icebergfinder.com. You might luck into seeing bergs close to shore with binoculars and a zoom lens, but you will likely need to head out on a boat with tour companies like **Iceberg Quest** and **Twillingate Adventure Tours**. Sometimes they'll scoop up bergy bits and send you home with ice cubes.

Insider Intel

Icebergs must be chased. If they're two hours away, get up early and make a day of it. Be flexible with accommodations and book a few nights at various locations along Iceberg Alley. Be ready to follow advice if bergs are elsewhere. Part of the adventure is in the chase and the nooks and crannies discovered along the way. When you find your iceberg, spend time with it. As the light changes, the colors and textures are brought out. Icebergs really will take your breath away.

■ *Diane Davis, retired teacher and founder of Newfoundland and Labrador Iceberg Reports*

Above Iceberg in Newfoundland and Labrador

29 Glacial GIANTS

BOAT TRIPS | OCEAN | NATURAL WONDERS

There's really nothing as jaw-droppingly beautiful as 10,000-year-old icebergs that calve off glaciers in Greenland and Canada's Arctic and float south, melting and shape-shifting as they go. Frenzied iceberg hunters race around the province, hoping for spring and early summer sightings before it's too late. The only catch? Icebergs can't be guaranteed, which makes the chase all the more thrilling.

How to

When to go Newfoundland's season runs May to June, but can start earlier and run later. Labrador's season typically stretches March to July.

Cost Iceberg-viewing boat trips typically run $85 to $110 and last two to three hours.

Hidden dangers About 90% of an iceberg is underwater, making them unpredictable. Stay at least the length of the iceberg, or twice its height, away in case it collapses or rolls.

Welcome Guests

It's been dubbed **Iceberg Alley**. The stretch from eastern Labrador to the southeast coast of Newfoundland is where hundreds of icebergs, in shades of white and aquamarine, pass by before they melt for good. Officially, they might be domes, pinnacles, tabular, blocky or wedged. Unofficially, they might look like a toothy grin, appear so phallic they're dubbed Chilly Willy, or give off superhero vibes and be nicknamed Batberg.

Titanic Connection

Remember the iceberg that sank the *Titanic*? That happened in 1912 about 650km off Newfoundland's coast and the Marconi Wireless Station at Cape Race picked up the distress signal and helped with rescue efforts. Now the **Myrick Wireless Interpretation Centre** tells that story from the same spot by **Cape Race Lighthouse**, while the **Johnson Geo Centre** in St John's has a *Titanic* exhibit.

01 Is **Brimstone Head** really one of the four corners of the Flat Earth? Climb the short, steep trail to a viewing platform atop the rocky outcrop and decide for yourself.

04 Hike the **Great Auk Trail** that goes past **Long Studio** and along the ocean to a **bronze sculpture** of a flightless seabird that bred nearby until it was hunted to extinction.

02 Visit the **Herring Cove Art Gallery & Studio**, run by Winston and Linda Osmond, to score quilts, jams, paintings, mussel shell puffins and mats made from recycled fishing ropes.

03 Photograph the world-renowned **Fogo Island Inn** from afar, or ask about free daily tours of this architectural stunner that's run by a social enterprise. Join the waitlist for four-course dinners.

05 They say **Tilting** is more Irish than Ireland so check out the **Tilting Heritage Centre** for its craft shop, cafe and weekly kitchen party/music sessions.

FROM TOP: ZHONGYUGAN/SHUTTERSTOCK, ZHONGYUGAN/SHUTTERSTOCK

28 An Island off AN ISLAND

ARCHITECTURE | ART | HIKING

Board a ferry to Fogo Island to experience a miniature Newfoundland. Meander down hiking trails, chat with locals, museum- and gallery-hop and admire fishing stages while cruising among 11 picturesque villages. After dinner, catch a glorious sunset and maybe some live music.

DANITA DELIMONT/SHUTTERSTOCK

Trip Notes

Getting here/around A daily **ferry** (*gov.nl.ca*) runs to Fogo from Farewell – line up an hour or two in advance since there are no reservations. You'll need a car to explore Fogo.

When to go Fogo boasts 'seven seasons,' but you'll get the most out of a summer visit when everything's open.

Top tip A jar of zesty yet sweet Newfoundland mustard pickles from **Mona's Quilt & Jam Shop** is the ultimate souvenir.

Photo Safari

Caribou are like people, in that they like to eat at breakfast and suppertime. Exceptional places to photograph these majestic beasts on Fogo Island are in the bottom of Joe Batt's Arm in early March, in Shoal Bay during fall, or Tilting in May when they will have their young.

■ **Paddy Barry**, *photographer and Fogo Islander,* @paddyjbarry

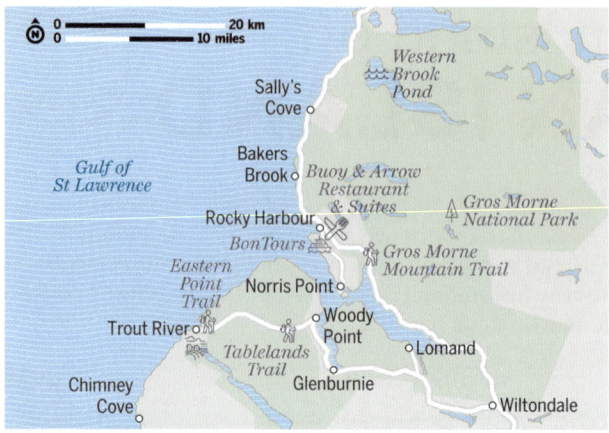

Alien Landscape

To walk the **Tablelands Trail** (4km return) is to stroll on the Earth's inner soul. You'll be surrounded by alien orange peridotite rocks that formed in the Earth's upper mantle until land masses collided half a billion years ago and pushed them to the surface. Park Canada's guided hike delves deeper into geology and plant life.

Bucket-List Hike

Flat-topped **Gros Morne Mountain** looms over the park and demands attention. Experienced hikers do the grueling 17km hike to the summit at 806m and behold the Arctic-alpine environment. Others are happy with the 9km Approach Trail through forest and past waterfalls to a viewing platform. The Summit Trail is closed in May and June to protect rock ptarmigan, caribou and Arctic hare as they give birth and care for their young.

Glacier-Carved Fjord

Western Brook Pond is Gros Morne's crown jewel, and while you can walk to the landlocked freshwater fjord and admire it, the only way to travel on it is with **BonTours**. Chatty guides bring the waterfalls, rock formations, cliffs and mountains to life.

Top left Tablelands Trail
Bottom left Western Brook Pond

☼ Seek Tranquility in Trout River

The sunsets in **Trout River** are the best I've seen. Buy mittens displayed on clotheslines in people's front yards – the original 'on-line shopping' – then find a spot to sit to the far right of the beach away from the boardwalk traffic. **Eastern Point Trail** starts between two homes and the edge of town and in 15 minutes, you'll be sitting in tall grass on a cliff listening to the wind and watching the waves of the Gulf of St Lawrence.

■ *Tara Kroes, Trout Creek resident and Transform Gros Morne founder @transformgrosmorne*

PARK
Pleasures

OCEAN | MOUNTAINS | TRAILS

There's a reason so many people stick to Western Newfoundland and devote entire trips to **Gros Morne National Park**. This UNESCO-approved wilderness has moody mountains, fascinating geology, two visitor centers and a landlocked fjord. It's a huge place – 2½ hours from end to end if you include Trout River — and since it's home to eight communities, it's full of hotels and always lively.

How To

Getting here/around Fly into Deer Lake Regional Airport and pick up a rental car. It's just 30 minutes to the park's southern boundary.

When to go Gros Morne's open year-round but gets packed in the summer. Dodge the crowds and heat during shoulder season (May/June and September/October).

Wild game Indigenous-owned **Buoy & Arrow Restaurant & Suites** in Rocky Harbour has a special license to serve moose, rabbit and sometimes bear.

Top left Puffins at the Elliston Puffin Viewing Site Bottom left Northern gannets, Cape St Mary's Ecological Reserve

Puffin Spotting from Land

The **Elliston Puffin Viewing Site** comes alive at dawn when the clumsy charmers awake. People love how it's a quick walk from the parking lot to an oceanside cliff to watch Newfoundland's provincial bird breeding on a tiny island about 30m away. Entrance is free but make a donation as you leave, peruse the nearby **Puffin Craft Shop** and consider driving 20 minutes to the **Cape Bonavista Lighthouse Provincial Historic Site** to commune with its small puffin colony.

Puffin Spotting from the Sea

Just south of St John's, the **Witless Bay Ecological Reserve** draws a staggering half million puffins to the largest colony in Newfoundland and the second largest in the world after Iceland. Tour operators like **O'Brien's**, **Gatherall's** and **Molly Bawn** handle boat trips to see these adorable flying bowling balls. **Fogo Island Boat Tours** goes by another puffin colony on visits to **Little Fogo Islands**. In **St-Pierre & Miquelon**, puffins summer on the uninhabited **Grand Colombier** island.

Puffin Saving

Drawn by light pollution, pufflings (baby puffins) sometimes wind up in danger on shore around Witless Bay. But the **Puffin & Petrel Patrol** steps in to save them and Leach's storm-petrel chicks. Volunteers register for two-hour evening patrols (puffins in August and petrels September to November) equipped with nets and crates. The lucky seabirds are released the next day on boat tours.

Seabird Bonanza

Puffins are certainly charismatic and an iconic image of Newfoundland and Labrador, but our province is home to many other enigmatic seabirds. Classy looking razorbills, guillemots and both common and thick-billed murres also breed in many of the colonies. At **Cape St Mary's Ecological Reserve**, thousands of northern gannets nest atop a giant sea stack and surrounding cliffs – certainly one of the most spectacular sights on the island as visitors hike across beautiful tundra and find themselves face-to-face with these large, majestic birds. I bring guests there many times each summer, but remain just as enthralled every time.

■ **Jared Clarke**, *founder of Bird the Rock* @birdtherocknl

26 Clowns of THE SEA

PHOTOGRAPHY | BIRDWATCHING | SOUVENIRS

About 95% of North America's puffins breed around Newfoundland and Labrador's coasts, making puffin spotting a priority for most visitors. The comical seabirds with colorful striped beaks live most of their lives at sea and return to isolated burrows every summer to breed. You can spot them from land, see them from boat tours or even help save wayward pufflings.

How to

Getting there The Witless Bay boat tours have shuttles from St John's.

Time your trip Puffins come in from the sea between May and mid-September to nest and give birth.

Be respectful Federal signs have sprung up warning puffin lovers they face a minimum $5,000 fine if they touch or approach the seabirds, their nests or their chicks. People are urged to stay behind signage.

EATING & DRINKING

Cod is king here and so when a local talks about fish, they mean cod. Eat it pan-fried, battered and deep-fried or transformed into cod au gratin. Salt cod (pictured top right) is the star of fish and brewis (traditional Newfoundland dish made from hard tack and salt cod), as well as fish cakes with a side of mustard pickles. Scallop-sized cod cheeks are a treat. Cod tongues are actually a neck muscle. This is the only Canadian province that lets restaurants serve wild moose (moose burger pictured bottom right). Other downhome delights are pea soup and toutons (baked or fried dough).

Best cod
Bangbelly Bistro, Fogo Island

Must-try moose burgers
Zimmy's, St John's

CONNECT & FIND YOUR WAY

Wi-fi There are plenty of free hotspots in hotels and restaurants. Buy SIM cards at electronics stores.

Navigation Cell service is spotty along highways outside of the cities. Go old school and get free provincial maps at visitor information centers in airports and along the highway.

WHERE TO STAY

There aren't many budget hotels left in Newfoundland, so try to choose places where parking and breakfast are included.

Destination	Pros/Cons
St John's	The busy capital. Steps away from nightlife, dining and shopping.
Twillingate	Small-town hub for iceberg hunting. Quickly gets crowded.
Fogo Island	Newfoundland in miniature. Most lodgings only have a few rooms.
Rocky Harbour/Norris Point	Central Gros Morne National Park with the most options. Major crowds.
Woody Point/Trout River	Southern Gros Morne. Near the Tablelands. Long drive to the rest of the park.
Cow Head	Northern Gros Morne. Close to Western Brook Pond. Isolated.

STRETCHING YOUR FOOD BUDGET

Most hotels have small fridges so consider supermarkets like Colemans and Foodland for fruit, yogurt, snacks or even roast chickens.

MONEY

Carry $100 cash in small bills for the odd shop or eatery that doesn't take cards. Tip housekeeping about $5 a night in hotels.

Practicalities

JENNIFER BAIN/LONELY PLANET. ARTWORK: 'FLIGHT AND ITS ALLEGORIES' BY KENNETH LOCHHEAD

ARRIVING

St John's International Airport Newfoundland's primary gateway is 15 minutes from downtown. Fixed-fare taxis to downtown hotels cost $35.

Deer Lake Regional Airport Newfoundland's smaller, west coast airport is the gateway to Gros Morne National Park.

Gander International Airport This wee airport (pictured) in the center of the province is close to Fogo Island and Twillingate. Before security, the Gander International Lounge is a modernist time capsule with exhibits about the airport's heyday.

HOW MUCH FOR A

Whale-watching trip $100

Fish and chips $20

Local craft beer $10

GETTING AROUND

Rental Cars Virtually everyone rents a vehicle, so secure yours before booking flights. Expect to pay $1000 a week in high season. Drop fees are too high to be practical, or it isn't allowed.

Taxis and Uber Taxi meter rates start at $4.50. Taxis can sometimes be hailed in cities, but it's best to order one by telephone. Uber is an option in larger centers.

Ferries Book Marine Atlantic ferries between North Sydney, Nova Scotia and either Argentia (16 hours) or Channel-Port Aux Basques (7 hours). Rates are one-way and per passenger and vehicle (based on size). Reserved seats and cabins cost extra. Ferries to Fogo Island can't be booked.

WHEN TO GO

MAY-JUN
Not everything's open but sometimes the icebergs come early

JUL-AUG
High season and the warmest weather; prime time for whales and puffins

SEP-OCT
The crowds disperse but the fall colors are gorgeous and it's perfect for hiking

NOV-APR
Time for winter sports like snowmobiling and even downhill skiing

NEWFOUNDLAND & LABRADOR
Trip Builder

Canada's youngest province is an idiosyncratic charmer with its own time zone, quirky traditions and unique dialect. Life revolves around the sea, so expect ocean adventures and salty personalities. But the Rock also has astounding geology and plenty of moose.

Take the **Western Brook Pond** cruise down a landlocked fjord (p143)
🚗 *20min from Rocky Harbour*

Walk on the Earth's mantle in the **Tablelands** (p143)
🚗 *5min from Woody Point*

Go whale watching and seabird spotting in the **Witless Bay Ecological Reserve** (p141)
🚗 *35min from St John's*

NEWFOUNDLAND & LABRADOR

ARCHITECTURE | CULTURE | ADVENTURE

RESEARCHED BY JENNIFER BAIN

- **Trip Builder** (p136)
- **Practicalities** (p138)
- **Clowns of the Sea** (p140)
- **Park Pleasures** (p142)
- **An Island off an Island** (p144)
- **Glacial Giants** (p146)
- **A Way with Words** (p148)
- **Listings** (p150)

for the June Festival of Small Halls, with concerts island-wide.

 Uniquely PEI

Prehistoric Island Tours
On these 90-minute walks through one of PEI's most significant fossil sites near Vernon Bridge, geologist Laura MacNeil tells you about ancient reptiles, fossilized trees and other geological wonders.

Maisons de Bouteilles (Bottle Houses)
The late Édouard Arsenault constructed two houses and a chapel on his seaside Cap-Egmont property, entirely made from multicolored reclaimed glass bottles – over 25,000 of them.

Beach Goats
Go paddleboarding with goats, do goat yoga on the beach, or simply come play with the animals at this beachfront farm in St Chrysostome, near Wellington.

Mysa Nordic Spa & Resort
At St Peter's Bay, alternate between thermal baths, sauna, steam, and cold plunges or showers. Then relax overlooking the water and dine in the first-rate farm-to-table restaurant.

Museums Worth a Look

Acadian Museum
Located in Miscouche, this museum's exhibits illustrate the history, foods and daily life of the French-speaking Acadians, who began arriving on PEI in the early 1700s and still influence local culture today.

Stompin' Tom Centre
Inspired by Canadian country-music icon Stompin' Tom Connors, who was raised on PEI and wrote more than 300 songs, this museum and music hall in Skinners Pond hosts free concerts.

West Point Lighthouse

International Fox Museum
With stories of fox-breeding entrepreneurs in the early 1900s, this gallery in Summerside documents how PEI became the first place to successfully raise foxes in captivity.

Creative Sleeps

West Point Lighthouse
Channel your inner lighthouse keeper with a stay in PEI's tallest lighthouse, an 1875 structure overlooking Northumberland Strait in Cedar Dunes Provincial Park.

Treetop Haven
Wake up in the forest in your TreePOD, a geodesic dome with a deck, at this nature-focused lodging located in Albany between Charlottetown and Summerside.

Nellie's Landing
Sleep in a floating wine barrel bobbing gently in the marina in Murray Harbour, with modern washrooms, an oyster bar and an outdoor kitchen nearby.

45 Steps, the Culinary Beachside Inn
At this seven-room North Shore boutique inn on St Peter's Bay, guests can join the 'Kitchen Club' for private dinners, cooking classes or other culinary events.

Listings

BEST OF THE REST

One-of-a-Kind Meals

FireWorks Feast, Inn at Bay Fortune — $$$

The island's most celebrated dining experience is this farm-to-table extravaganza near Souris, with a garden tour, 'oyster hour', sparkling wine toast and elaborate multicourse repast.

The Table Culinary Studio — $$$

Elaborate seven-course meals, served in a former Kensington church from mid-May to September, highlight local ingredients.

Acadian Dinner at Doucet House — $$$

In this historic home in Rustico, you'll help prepare a traditional Acadian meal, from chicken *fricot* to *rapûre* (a shredded potato dish), to meat pie.

 Local Eating

Charlottetown Farmers Market — $

Join residents perusing the 60-plus stalls stocked with local produce and prepared foods. The market is open Saturday year-round and Wednesday late June to early October.

Farmacy + Fermentary — $

At this downtown Charlottetown eatery, salads, bowls and sandwiches brim with fermented veggies and produce from the owners' farm. Try a tasting flight of house-made kombucha.

Gallant's & Co — $

This casual cafe-market north of Charlottetown's city center specializes in crab cakes, fried oysters and anything fresh from the sea.

Lobster Suppers — $$$

Tie on your lobster bib for crustaceans paired with chowder, mussels, salads, pies and more at New Glasgow Lobster Suppers or Fisherman's Wharf Lobster Supper in North Rustico.

Charlottetown on Foot

Secrets of Charlottetown Walking Tour

On these one-hour city walks, guides share tales of bootleggers, kidnappings and ghosts. You'll learn about heritage buildings, local characters and unsolved mysteries. It's great fun.

Heritage Players Historic Walking Tours

Costumed actors lead you through Charlottetown's history on these entertaining tours. Book online or in person at the Confederation Centre of the Arts.

The Bog Tour

Guides from Beaconsfield Historic House, a Victorian-era manor turned museum, offer 45-minute guided walks through The Bog, a historically Black neighborhood nearby.

♪♫ Toe-tapping Tunes

Ceilidh in the City

Ceilidhs are part concert and part lively kitchen party, including this one at the Jack Blanchard Centre north of downtown in Charlottetown.

Ross Family Ceilidh

This talented brother-and-sister group performs summer shows in various locations; check their website (rossfamily.ca) for details.

Trailside Music Hall

This club inside the Arts Hotel in Charlottetown programs regular concerts by local and regional musicians. It's also the headquarters

chips, baked potatoes, and many other potato creations are ubiquitous. PEI's top cheese and ice cream producer, **Cows Creamery**, even makes 'Cow Chips', chocolate-covered potato chips that give Reese's a run for their money in the sweet-salty-chocolatey sweepstakes. Yet according to the Potato Museum, both the French fry and the potato chip have origin stories linking them not to Canada, but to the United States.

> Tiny PEI grows about a third of the country's potatoes, making the province Canada's top tuber supplier.

Legend has it that Thomas Jefferson first encountered deep-fried potatoes while serving as US ambassador to France in the 1780s. After returning stateside, Jefferson had potatoes planted in his home garden and, once he became the third US president, he requested 'potatoes served in the French manner' – aka 'French fries' – at state dinners.

Another tale concerns the origin of the potato chip. An upstate New York restaurateur named Charles Crum reportedly served ultra-thin fried potato slices after a customer complained that his potatoes were too thick. The potato chip was born.

PEI Potato Experiences

To dig deeper into PEI potato lore, you can book a potato farm experience through the Canadian Potato Museum. You'll join a local farmer on their spud farm for a tour and chat about potato farming life. And if you want to know more about PEI's potato ballad, visit the **Stompin' Tom Centre** in the western PEI hamlet of Skinner's Pond. Canadian country singer Tom Connors, nicknamed Stompin' Tom, penned 'Bud the Spud' back in 1969.

Where to Eat

Nearly every restaurant on PEI serves some kind of potato. But here are a few potato specialists.

PEI Potato Country Kitchen, the cafe at the Canadian Potato Museum, serves poutine, potato soup and giant baked potatoes loaded with cheese, chili or other toppings, and more – all with a side of homemade potato chips.

The Chip Shack on Charlottetown harbor, PEI's 'Queen of Fries', sizzles up hand-cut French fries.

Dal's Potato Bar, in Charlottetown's **Founders' Food Hall**, tops PEI potatoes with Turkish-style condiments.

Oh Fudge! creates surprisingly tasty sweets from island potatoes. Find its shops at the Founders' Food Hall and in Souris.

Canada's Potato Capital

THE SCOOP ON ISLAND SPUDS

When a singer writes a song about PEI potatoes – the Canadian classic 'Bud the Spud' – you might guess that this region has a unique relationship with the tuber. In fact, Prince Edward Island is one of Canada's major potato producers. Let's get to the root of this root vegetable story.

Potatoes are big on Prince Edward Island. If you visit the **Canadian Potato Museum** in O'Leary, an enormous spud greets you at the entrance. Inside, the museum is crammed with trivia about PEI's major crop – its different varieties, its uses around the world, its diseases, even its legends.

PEI's Potato Heritage

Potatoes aren't indigenous to Canada. The first tubers likely arrived in Atlantic Canada with French settlers in the 1700s, and by the end of that century, the crop was firmly established on PEI. Newcomers who settled the region in the 1800s also brought potato plants that thrived in the island's acidic soil.

Today, China is the world's largest potato producer, and while potatoes are important to the Canadian agricultural economy, the country ranks 11th or 12th worldwide in the size of its potato crop. Tiny PEI grows about a third of the country's potatoes, making the province Canada's top tuber supplier.

Several varieties comprise most of PEI's crop. Yukon Gold, developed in Ontario in the 1960s, are sold fresh, used for boiling, baking and frying. The Atlantic variety is turned into potato chips, while the Russet Burbank is best for baking and for commercial French fry production. The Superior potato is sold fresh and used commercially for potato chips.

Tuber Tales

Nationwide, Canadians are confirmed potato eaters, consuming an average of more than 65kg of spuds per person in a typical year. Across PEI, French fries, potato

Left Flowering potato fields **Center** Canadian Potato Museum **Right** The Chip Shack

days and use buses, taxis and transportation that innkeepers provide to get to and from the trail. A growing number of accommodations welcome Island Walkers; find the services they offer – from packed lunches to trail transport – on the Island Walk website.

What to Pack Prepare for sun, rain, wind and varying temperatures, even in a single day. Bring sunscreen, insect repellent and refillable water bottles. Carry snacks and lunch, especially when you're walking the island's more rural east and west ends. It can be a long way between food stops.

> ### Island Walk Outfitters
>
> Several PEI-based outfitters can help you plan an Island Walk, recommending or booking accommodations, luggage transfer, and transportation to and from the trail. They can also suggest shorter routes if you don't want to complete the entire walk. Outfitters include **Go for a Walk: Island Walk Coordination Service** (goforawalkpei.com) and **Outer Limit Sports** (ols.ca). **MacQueen's Bicycles** (macqueens.com) provides planning services specifically for cyclists.

Left Autumn leaves on the Island Walk
Right Hikers passing Covehead Lighthouse, Stanhope

25 Walk the Island WALK

SLOW TRAVEL | WALKING | OUTDOORS

Modeled after Spain's Camino de Santiago, the **Island Walk** is a 700km walking and cycling route that circles Prince Edward Island. Starting and ending in Charlottetown, and passing PEI's sandy beaches, above its red cliffs, and through its forests, the walk is divided into 32 segments of 20km to 25km that you can tackle individually or as an extended loop.

How to

When to go June and September are the best walking months – quieter with decent weather. In busier July and August, book accommodations well in advance.

Plan your walk See the Island Walk website *(the islandwalk.ca)* and Facebook group for many useful resources. Bryson Guptill, who conceived the Island Walk, publishes a detailed route guide, available on the walk website.

Find a bathroom The 'directions' page on the walk website lists washroom locations.

Where You'll Walk Most of the Island Walk takes you along PEI's flat shorelines and gently rolling hills. Part of the route follows the Confederation Trail, a former rail line, while other sections travel dirt roads and (mostly) secondary roadways, past farms and fields of wildflowers. A few sections take you onto busier main highways.

Finding Your Way The route is designed to be walked clockwise, with signs marking turns as well as segment start and endpoints. Signposts about every 5km help ensure that you're on track. You can also map your route on the free Koomot app.

Where to Sleep Unlike Spain's Camino or other more established walking routes, the Island Walk doesn't have accommodations or other services at each segment's end. It's often easier to stay in one location for several

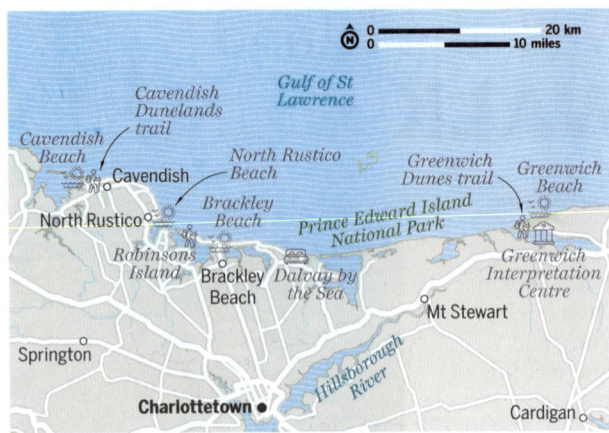

Top left Cavendish Dunelands trail
Bottom left Brackley Beach

What's Where PEI National Park has three sections, from west to east: Cavendish-North Rustico, Brackley-Dalvay and Greenwich.

Best Beaches Close to the Green Gables attractions, sandy **Cavendish Beach** tends to be crowded; walk away from the parking areas to find peaceful sands. Continuing east, **North Rustico Beach** is a short walk from the town of the same name. **Brackley Beach** is another popular dune-backed strand. **Greenwich Beach** is normally the quietest. This section of the park protects fragile coastal dunes; visit **Greenwich Interpretation Centre** to learn about the region's ecosystems and the unique parabolic dune structure.

Walking Trails Don't miss **Greenwich Dunes trail**, a moderate 4.8km path across a floating boardwalk and between the landmark dunes to the coast. Leave your car in the Brackley Beach parking area (or come by bike) and follow the flat causeway 3.5km west to **Robinsons Island**, where both walkers and mountain bikers can circle the 5km wooded loop trail, passing wildflower bushes and lookouts over the inlet. Another pretty walk is the gentle **Cavendish Dunelands trail**, which winds behind the grassy dunes near the park's west end. The trail is 2.3km each way.

Cultural Experiences Parks Canada runs interpretive programs throughout the summer, from Indigenous storytelling to nature talks. Check the park website *(parks.canada.ca)* to see what's happening when.

A Grand Manor in the Park

Alexander MacDonald, one-time president of Standard Oil Company, purchased 120 acres of land on PEI's north shore, where in 1896 he completed the construction of a grand Queen Anne Revival manor. Overlooking Dalvay Lake, stately **Dalvay by the Sea** was crafted of island sandstone and other local materials.

Today, the property is a deluxe inn and restaurant, within the boundaries of PEI National Park. Even if you don't stay in one of the classically furnished rooms or newer cottages, you can walk the grounds or sit down to a meal of seafood chowder and island-raised beef. Save room for the signature sticky date pudding.

24 PEI's National Park BEACHES

BEACHES | BICYCLING | CULTURE

With more than 65km of shorefront along the island's northern coast, **Prince Edward Island National Park** is all about the beach. Long, flat stretches of sand extend along the north shore, many backed with tall dunes or dramatic red cliffs. Whether you prefer beach-walking, leisurely cycling or swimming in the sea, head for the island's national park.

How to

Getting here and around In summer, you can take the T3 Transit bus from Charlottetown to the Cavendish-North Rustico area. Within the park, you can cycle Gulf Shore Way through the Cavendish or Brackley-Dalvay sections. Otherwise, you'll need a car.

When to go Though the park is open year-round, visitor services typically operate mid-May to mid-October.

Camp The park has two camping areas: 200-site **Cavendish Campground** and 100-site **Stanhope Campground**.

Top left Lobster Bottom left Raspberry Point Oysters

Fiddling for Your Supper Julie Chaisson and her husband, JJ, a musician and lobster fisher, run the **Fiddling Fisherman** (fiddlingfisherman.com), offering 'Lobster Lovers' excursions from Souris on their family fishing boat. After heading out to sea, you'll drop a lobster trap and 'catch' your dinner to savor on board accompanied by Chaisson's fiddle tunes.

All About Oysters For an oyster introduction, book the entertaining one-hour 'Shuck and Learn' at **Raspberry Point Oysters** (raspberrypoint.com), a large oyster farm near Cavendish. You'll learn assorted oyster trivia, before trying your hand at shucking. A traditional method of harvesting oysters is to 'tong' for them – gathering shellfish using long rake-like tongs. **Along the Edge Experiences** (alongtheedgeexperiences.com) organizes 'Oyster Tong and Shuck', where you'll collect and shuck oysters, then eat what you've harvested.

More Water Adventures The owners of **Nature Space Resort & Retreat Centre** (naturespaceresort.com) near Morell partnered with an oyster farm for an 'Oyster Lovers Kayak Experience,' where you go paddling, float through an oyster lease, and learn about oyster farming. Yes, there are samples.

Go mackerel fishing and barbecue your catch onboard with **Tranquility Cove Adventures** (tcapei.com). Tours depart from Georgetown in eastern PEI.

From Victoria on PEI's south shore, **By the Sea Kayaking** (bytheseakayaking.ca) offers a kayaking and clam-digging experience. You kayak to a sandbar, dig for clams, and enjoy fresh chowder on the beach.

Canada's Food Island

Know your bivalves How do you choose among the dozens of oyster varieties on PEI? Check out the socialshell.com, which maps the island's oyster regions and tells you about their tastes and variations.

Whet your appetite To see what's in season during your PEI visit, see the **Canada's Food Island website** (canadasfoodisland.ca) for a month-by-month guide to local foods, from berries to beans to bar clams.

■ **Crystal MacGregor,** Director of Communications and Marketing for the Food Island Partnership, a PEI-based nonprofit economic-development organization in Charlottetown. @canadasfoodisland

23 How to Catch Your DINNER

SEAFOOD | OCEAN ADVENTURES | PADDLING

You can eat lobsters, oysters, mussels and other seafood almost everywhere on Prince Edward Island. But for a unique island experience, head out to the sea or into the sand to catch or forage for your dinner. Many of these adventures set off from PEI's eastern shores, but you can experience crustacean-centered activities around the island.

How to

When to go Most ocean experiences run from July to early September. Check with each outfitter for specific schedules.

What it costs Depending on the experience and whether it includes a full meal, prices range from $89 to $159.

Bring the family While many of these activities are kid-friendly, confirm details with the outfitter before booking.

What's for dessert? Pick up creative pastries at **Maroon Pig Sweet Shop**, a bakery-gallery in Georgetown.

Far left Decorative piece using quills, Quill Work on Birch Bark Far bottom left Lennox Island Cultural Centre Left Bannock in the firepit

Meet the Lennox Island First Nation

Roughly 450 members of the Lennox Island Mi'kmaq First Nation, one of two Mi'kmaw nations on PEI, live on Lennox Island, where a causeway over Malpeque Bay connects the nation to the rest of PEI. Try one of the cultural experiences that community members have developed, where you can learn about their heritage and daily life through food, art and music.

Cook in the Sand

Learn to cook in a traditional firepit when you book the **Bannock and Clams in the Sand** experience. You'll grill local mollusks and prepare bannock (a biscuit-like bread) on a fire buried under the sand. While your meal is cooking, you can talk with your hosts about the Lennox Island community and walk through the **Lennox Island Cultural Centre**, where exhibits detail the nation's legends, heritage and cultural practices.

Learn Traditional Arts

Making jewelry or decorative pieces using the quills from a porcupine is a traditional art in many Indigenous communities. Although porcupines are not native to PEI, the Mi'kmaq developed this art around the Atlantic region. In the **Quill Work on Birch Bark** workshop, you're introduced to this craft, and you'll learn how challenging it is!

In another art-oriented experience, the **Beat of the Drum**, you make your own moose-hide drum and learn about its importance in Mi'kmaw culture. These experiences also include a tour of the cultural center.

★ PEI's Newest National Park

Canada's 48th national park, **Pituamkek National Park Reserve** will be set near Lennox Island on one of Atlantic Canada's last wild landscapes – a series of barrier islands in northwestern PEI, extending between Malpeque and Cascumpec Bays. The park is being developed in a unique partnership between Parks Canada (parks.canada.ca) and the Mi'kmaw Nation.

It's a culturally significant location for the area's Indigenous Peoples – Pituamkek means 'at the long sand dune' in the Mi'kmaw language. The new park will protect several Mi'kmaw archaeological sites, as well as a coastal dune ecosystem that's considered one of the most ecologically significant in Eastern Canada.

22 Experience Indigenous CULTURE

FOOD | ART | MUSIC

Prince Edward Island is part of the traditional territory of the Mi'kmaq; PEI's Mi'kmaw name is 'Epekwitk'. The **Lennox Island Mi'kmaq First Nation** offers experiences that introduce visitors to Mi'kmaw foods and cooking techniques, traditional art and music, and other aspects of the region's Indigenous culture, past and present.

How to

Getting here Easiest to reach with your own vehicle, Lennox Island is a 45-minute drive northwest of Summerside.

Booking and pricing See schedules and book online at **Experience Lennox Island** *(experiencelennoxisland.com)*. Prices $75 to $115 per person.

Lunch break En route from Lennox Island, enjoy afternoon tea at **Tyne Valley Teas Cafe** or try clam poutine at **Backwoods Burger**.

Learn more Indigenous PEI *(indigenouspei.ca)* provides information about the island's Indigenous heritage, culture and experiences.

01 Learn about Montgomery's life at Parks Canada–operated **Green Gables Heritage Place** (pictured far left). Then enter Anne's fictional world in her 'home' in the adjacent farmhouse.

02 Outside Green Gables, walk the trails along **Lovers Lane** (pictured above) or through the **Haunted Woods**, locations that figured in Montgomery's books.

05 Find 'Anne's Enchanted Bookcase' in the 1872 Park Corner homestead where Montgomery was married, now the **Anne of Green Gables Museum.**

04 In New London, west of Cavendish, visit the **Lucy Maud Montgomery Birthplace**, where Maud was born, to peruse the author's scrapbooks and letters.

03 Listen to tales about the author at **Lucy Maud Montgomery's Cavendish Homestead**, where Maud wrote *Anne of Green Gables* and other novels.

FROM TOP: DANITA DELIMONT/SHUTTERSTOCK, PETERSPIRO/GETTY IMAGES

21 Follow the Green GABLES STORY

LITERATURE | HISTORY | CULTURE

Anne of Green Gables, the high-spirited heroine of Lucy Maud Montgomery's 20th-century novels, may be Canada's most famous fictional character. Several sites around Cavendish, where the PEI-born author grew up, highlight landmarks from the books and from Montgomery's own life.

Trip Notes

Getting there T3 Transit runs summertime buses to Cavendish from Charlottetown or Summerside. Otherwise, it's easiest to get there by car.

Where to get lost in a book Nearby **Cavendish Beach** in PEI National Park is a scenic spot to read (or reread) the the Green Gables books.

Snack stop Fuel your literary wanderings with homemade bonbons from **Jane & Sue Chocolate**, run by two sisters in Stanley Bridge.

Anne on Stage

Continue your Anne journey in Charlottetown, where nearly every summer since 1965, the **Confederation Centre of the Arts** has staged *Anne of Green Gables – the Musical*, a family-friendly theatrical interpretation of the spunky red-haired girl's story, accompanied by a live orchestra.

Practicalities

ARRIVING

Charlottetown Airport is a 15-minute drive north of the city center. Taxis typically meet arriving flights, with a flat-rate fare to downtown.

FIND YOUR WAY

Tourism PEI (*tourismpei.com*) runs the **Charlottetown Visitor Information Centre** and has loads of useful travel information on its website.

MONEY

PEI accommodations prices are highest mid-June through mid-September; look for deals just before or after these peak months.

WHERE TO STAY

Town	Pros/Cons
Charlottetown	Centrally located. Widest selection of accommodations. Not beachfront.
Cavendish	Convenient to beaches and Green Gables sites. Very touristy.
Souris	Quiet eastern shore town. Close to ocean attractions. Fewer lodging options.
Summerside	Moderate motels. Handy for west-island experiences. Sprawls from the center.

EATING & DRINKING

Seafood is a PEI highlight, especially lobster, oysters, mussels and clams. Find 'lobster rolls' island-wide – a bun filled with lobster meat, chilled with mayonnaise or warm with butter. Ask for the day's freshest local bivalves to try raw PEI oysters.

Cook traditional Acadian cuisine
Doucet House (p132)

Best fine-dining experience
FireWorks Feast at Inn at Bay Fortune (p132)

GETTING AROUND

Car The easiest way to get around the island outside of Charlottetown.

Bus T3 Transit operates buses around Charlottetown and from the capital across the island, though rural buses run infrequently.

Bicycle Pedal the Confederation Trail, a 273km former rail line, east-west across PEI.

JUL-AUG
Peak season for beach days and water adventures.

SEP-OCT
Food festivals; best weather for walking and cycling.

NOV-APR
Most attractions close during the long, cold winters.

MAY-JUN
Island activities resume in late May.

PRINCE EDWARD ISLAND
Trip Builder

Dune-backed beaches, winding pathways for walking and cycling, adventures on the sea and at the table – plus a famous fictional red-haired girl – draw visitors to Canada's smallest province, a rural region of rolling hills, red cliffs and sandy shores.

Immerse yourself in Anne of Green Gables' world in **Cavendish** (p120)
🚗 30min from Charlottetown

Hike between the **Greenwich Dunes** (p127)
🚗 55min from Charlottetown

Feast in the garden at **Inn at Bay Fortune** (p132)
🚗 15min from Souris

Experience Indigenous culture on **Lennox Island** (p122)
🚗 45min from Summerside

Haul in a lobster with the **Fiddling Fisherman** (p125)
⛴ From Souris

FROM LEFT: TSIRIKASHVILI NODARI/SHUTTERSTOCK, CARON PALMER/SHUTTERSTOCK

PRINCE EDWARD ISLAND

BEACHES | SEAFOOD | LITERATURE

RESEARCHED BY CAROLYN B HELLER

- ▶ **Trip Builder** (p118)
- ▶ **Practicalities** (p119)
- ▶ **Follow the Green Gables Story** (p120)
- ▶ **Experience Indigenous Culture** (p122)
- ▶ **How to Catch Your Dinner** (p124)
- ▶ **PEI's National Park Beaches** (p126)
- ▶ **Walk the Island Walk** (p128)
- ▶ **Canada's Potato Capital** (p130)
- ▶ **Listings** (p132)

Vaughan Creek Covered Bridge

Their numbers might be much reduced, but new bridges are occasionally rebuilt like the one in St Martins, now the only two-lane covered bridge in the province.

Tynemouth Creek Covered Bridge

Covered bridges like this 1927 beauty were known as 'kissing bridges' because they provided cover for couples crossing rivers by horse and buggy who stopped mid-span for a moment of private intimacy.

Whale Watching from St Andrews

Fundy Tide Runners

Aboard the *Tide Runner,* a rugged Zodiac, get up close in the open air to whales the guides (who are signatories of a whale-watching code of ethics) know by name.

Cruisin' With the Whales

Gotta love the chummy name of Captain Wilcox's tour that speaks to his connection with the whales aboard *Bubs Bounty,* a converted family fishing boat.

Quoddy Link Marine

Stay warm and dry in Quoddy's powered catamaran, which can get to whales quickly with minimal disturbance and 360-degree views.

Jolly Breeze

Choose between a speedy, bumpy jet boat ride, trussed up in orange survival suits, or a leisurely sail on the small tall ship, *Jolly Breeze.*

Bites & Chocolate Boxes

Fredericton Boyce Farmers Market

The sheer variety of handhelds and takeaways makes for tough decisions among options like barbecue, samosas and salad fixings.

Adorable Chocolat

Sample delights like Atlantic Sea Salt Truffles and fill a few boxes as gifts from New Brunswick's finest chocolatiers, Adorable in Shediac.

Saint John City Market

Saint John City Market

Shop for original artwork depicting city scenes and streetscapes. Grab a few bottles of local wine. Munch on a freshly made sandwich, all while shopping for local produce.

Restaurant La Sagouine

Across a river from the French Acadian mini-theme park, Pays de la Sagouine, sample foods considered cultural touchstones like chicken *fricot*.

Magnetic Beverages

Magnetic Hill Winery

Pop in for drinks, take a tour and take home bottles from one of New Brunswick's few domestic wineries, one that proves the province's potential.

Tipsy Muse Cafe

More than great espresso drinks, Fredericton's Tipsy Muse serves up local live music and comedy along with homemade pastries and sandwiches.

Distillerie Fils du Roy

Considered by many New Brunswick's top distillers, the Roy family infuses their award-winning artisanal spirits with botanicals from their own garden.

Listings

BEST OF THE REST

 Best Fests

Harvest Music Festival
Whole streets shut down in downtown Fredericton when Harvest heats up. Outdoor concerts in small tents and on big stages fill the September air with rock, jazz and blues.

Atlantic Balloon Fiesta
Hot-air balloons float on the breeze over Sussex every September. Each evening, festival-goers are treated to a strange light show as balloons tethered to the ground glow with blasts of flame.

Sandpiper Festival
Birds make this more than just another small town festival. In mid-August, over a quarter million semipalmated sandpipers stop near Dorchester to feed in preparation for their migration to South America.

Shediac Lobster Festival
Seafood fuels Shediac's rise as a foodie destination. The world's largest lobster welcomes visitors to town, where sushi, food tours and handmade chocolates vie for attention over the July lobster festival.

 Indigenous Experiences

Metepenagiag Heritage Park
Experience two National Historic Sites dating back 3000 years in Metepenagiag, New Brunswick's oldest continuously settled community. First Nations Tourism offers tours. Stay in a teepee or lodge on park grounds.

Elsipogtog First Nation
Take the Heritage Path Tour with Mi'kmaw guides who share their traditions, including a smudging ceremony and visits to a longhouse and a sweat lodge made by a local elder.

Wabanaki Tree Spirit Tours
Cecilia Brooks and her son Anthony are trained scientists and Indigenous knowledge keepers who combine their skills to lead visitors through millennia of natural and cultural history in Fredericton.

La Belle Cabane
This rustic forest healing sanctuary with cabins is Indigenous-owned. The atmosphere builds within log palisade walls and via thermal spa experiences – dry and steam saunas, showers, cold plunge and a salt room.

Covered (Kissing) Bridges

Hartland Covered Bridge
From a high of 340, New Brunswick now has 58 covered bridges. Hartland's across the upper St John River is the longest in Canada and probably the world at 391m.

Point Wolfe Covered Bridge
The relatively new bridge, built in 1992 – it replaced one built in 1909 – spans the small river of the same name in Fundy National Park.

Hartland Covered Bridge

What's a Picaroon?

Picaroons is the original New Brunswick craft beer company. It's named for a wooden-handled hand tool with a pointed metal head used to handle logs and firewood. The tool and the beer harken back to the days when teams of lumberjacks worked the province's forests, handling logs and floating them down rivers. Craft-beer makers like Picaroons often name their brews to honor local touchstones: Timberlog Stout, Swallowtail Light and Simeon Jones are named for lumberjacking, a lighthouse on Grand Manan Island and a popular New Brunswick politician who built an early brewery in the province.

Variety is the Yeast of Life From a city with a single craft-beer brewer, Fredericton has grown in two decades to about 25 small producers, each with a distinct style. The Taproom Trail leads to nine beer taprooms (and **York County Cider**). From the big works at **Picaroons Roundhouse** in a former railway roundhouse to the nanobrewery at **The Cap**, variety is like the yeast tossed into Fredericton's lifestyle. While **Mama's Brew Pub** specializes in light, flavor-packed beers such as Cherry Blaster Kettle Sour and Blueberry Wheat Ale, Trailway Brewing is the expert in hazy, tropical brews like Dunder (a fusion of 'down under') and Seeing Citra.

Above Picaroons craft beer

20 Taproom **TRAIL**

CRAFT BEER | CITY GUIDE | WALKING

▬▬▬ Grab your Taproom Trail (*craftalcoholnb.ca*) passport and get walking. Explore New Brunswick's capital – widely considered to be Atlantic Canada's top craft-beer city – by following the route from taproom to taproom. Most are within walking distance of downtown and each other. Some are reached by crossing the St John River on the **Bill Thorpe Walking Bridge**, a former railway trestle.

How To

When to go The Taproom Trail is open year-round. In cold or wet weather, travel to those beyond downtown with a designated driver or via taxi.

Getting started Pick up your Taproom Trail passport-style map at any of the 10 participating taprooms. Collect stamps at each. Six earns a bumper sticker, eight a t-shirt.

Top Tip Some taprooms offer zero alcohol beer. Most offer other beverages and food.

Community Builders

Beer's Superpower Picaroons Brewing owner Sean Dunbar believes in the miraculous community-building power of craft beer. He says, 'Small breweries and public spaces where people can come to drink beer are vital to the life of a city and province. Bringing people together over a beer, the added sociability of alcohol encourages trust and openness and is absolutely vital to the exchange of information and ideas.'

A Bevy of Brewers Stephen Dixon of **Grimross Brewing** credits Dunbar with helping him get started by providing brewing space at a Picaroons location. Similarly, when **Graystone Brewing** was starting up, breweries like Grimross, **Maybee Brew** and **Trailway Brewing** lent them equipment, building a mutually supportive bevy of brewers.

Father of the Tintamarre

Through the 17th and 18th centuries, French settlers established communities in New Brunswick and beyond. The Indigenous Mi'kmaq helped them thrive. As tensions rose between Britain and France, British colonial forces carried out le Grand Dérangement (great deportation) of 10,000 neutral French Acadians from 1755 to 1763. Generations after returning, Acadians remained reluctant to express pride in their heritage. Monseigneur Norbert Robichaud, the Archbishop of Moncton, changed that in 1955 when he called for Acadians to take to the streets with every noisemaker they could find and make a great din, a 'tintamarre,' to mark the le Grand Dérangement bicentennial.

l'Hôtel Château Albert where you can snooze away a quiet night like it's 1907. This living museum presents the daily lives of Acadians from 1770 to 1949.

Drive the Acadian Coast

Beyond the Acadian Peninsula, New Brunswick's northeastern shore between the Quebec and Nova Scotia borders constitutes the Acadian coast. Many sites are worth a stop. The creation of **Kouchibouguac National Park** uprooted an Acadian community, acknowledged in a touching and thorough exhibit at the interpretation center. Antoinine Maillet brought to life the distinct Acadian dialect and its people in her fiction and plays. Visit **Le Pays de la Sagouine**, a mini theme park named for her most beloved character, a gossiping washerwoman.

Above Acadian Historic Village

19 Make a GREAT DIN

FESTIVAL | FOOD | FRENCH ACADIAN

Noisy, not raucous. Colorful, not garish. Proud, not haughty. These are the qualities of the annual Tintamarre (meaning 'a great din') in Acadian communities across New Brunswick and Nova Scotia. Residents and visitors march in the French *tricolor* red, white and blue while making as much noise as they can, proclaiming their persistence following their 18th-century expulsion by British colonial forces.

How to

When to go Weeks of celebration, traditional music, family reunions and gatherings lead up to the Tintamarre, held on August 15, National Acadian Day in Canada.

Getting there The small town of Caraquet is the center of Acadian celebrations, including the Tintamarre.

Top tip The population swells from about 4200 to up to 10,000 around this time, so book accommodations in or near Caraquet early.

The Heart of l'Acadie

Arrow to the Heart The arrowhead of geography that juts into the Gulf of St Lawrence is known as the Acadian Peninsula. It's the heart of l'Acadie. This is where the town of **Caraquet** holds its annual Tintamarre, the culmination of their **Festival Acadien de Caraquet** (festivalacadien.ca), in the first two weeks of August. The town fills with traditional and contemporary music, visual arts, film and dance. Attend the blessing of the fishing fleet, a moving ceremony supporting those who work at the perilous occupation. Find a noisemaker and march in the parade or watch from the sidewalk.

Celebrating 179 Years of History At the **Acadian Historic Village**, 13km from Caraquet, costumed interpreters work at their choirs in and around some 30 historical buildings, including a restaurant and

Top left Hopewell Rocks Provincial Park **Bottom left** Humpback whale, Bay of Fundy

Tides, Trails & Tea

Tides in the Bay of Fundy The tides swing 16m in six hours, making them the world's highest. It's the funnel-shaped bay that causes these surging tides, carving the shoreline and creating a rich ecosystem. **Riverfront Park** in Moncton is a gentle introduction where a small standing wave called the Tidal Bore travels 25km upstream from the bay. But it's **Hopewell Rocks Provincial Park** where the power of these tides is truly on display. Tide-carved sea stacks called flowerpot rocks for the vegetation that survives atop them, rise from the ocean bottom, walkable at low tide, kayak-accessible at high tide.

For a Longer Stay **Fundy National Park** and adjacent Alma are the perfect combination of a quiet fishing village and an activity-packed park for hiking and camping beside the bay for longer stays.

Savor the Drive The speed limit in the newly completed **Fundy Trail Parkway** is 40km, encouraging motorists to take in the cliff-top scenery and pause at the many lookouts, beaches, waterfalls and a swinging suspension bridge on the 30km route.

Shoreline Trails Take riverside walks at the **New River Beach Provincial Park** (a popular camping spot) and the corporate-owned **Irving Nature Park**.

International Park The former summer residence of US President Franklin D Roosevelt and Eleanor Roosevelt is a rarity – the **Roosevelt Campobello International Park** is jointly managed by two countries – Canada and the US. Stay to have tea as Eleanor did.

🔭 Park Champion

The creation story of the Fundy Trail Parkway features park champion Mitchell Franklin, who campaigned for years to push a coastal road through what he considered the bay's most scenic location. In 1994, he invited then New Brunswick premier Frank McKenna to the end of the gravel road at Fox Rock, today the Parkway's first stop. 'It was an absolutely glorious day,' says his daughter, Beverley Franklin. 'The bay was sparkling. McKenna said, "What I'm looking at rivals any part of the world. We're going to build the Fundy Trail Parkway." I still get emotional about it.'

18 Dynamic Coastal PARKS

OUTDOORS | ISLANDS | WHALES

National, provincial, municipal, even corporate parks dot New Brunswick's southwestern Bay of Fundy coastline. Hike, cycle, kayak, swim, camp and drive in dramatic seaside landscapes carved by the world's highest tides and preserved for their natural beauty. Wildlife thrives in and around parks. Deer, moose, beavers and over 260 bird species call the parks home. Seabirds, whales and porpoise populate the bay's rich feeding grounds.

How to

When to go Summer is peak season for hiking, kayaking and camping, but most parks are open year-round and encourage winter activities like cross-country skiing, skating and tobogganing.

Getting there Bay of Fundy parks line the coast from the US/Canada border to Moncton. Stay in or near any of these parks for quick access.

Other Most parks are accessible by car, even those on islands which are reached by a small car ferry.

17 Your Floating HOTEL

HOUSEBOATING | FAMILY | HISTORIC VILLAGE

Float in a family-sized houseboat on the St John River's deep, still waters. Spend days exploring historic sites and zipping down the slide for a cooling swim. Dream evenings away in the hot tub on the upper deck beneath a sky of stars.

Houseboat Hot (& Cool) Tips

Maps onboard point you to lesser-known trails, coves and sights. You don't have to boat far. Docked right at the marina, **Mactaquac Provincial Park** offers treetop adventures, beach volleyball courts and hiking trails. Elsewhere, take the short hike to hidden **Wheeler Falls**, accessible only from the water. Head to a small island in **McNally's Cove** for a quiet afternoon. For anglers, a fishing guide can meet you on the water. Hot tip: for a refreshing twist, turn off the hot tub heater on your houseboat and enjoy a 'cool tub' on warm days.

■ Nick Jewett, co-owner at Lakeway Houseboat Vacations
@lakewayhouseboats

📍 Trip Notes

Getting around Drive Rte 105 from downtown Fredericton to **Lakeway Houseboat Vacations** beside Mactaquac Beach. Book well in advance.

When to go July and August are prime houseboating months – everything is open and the water is warm. The season ends mid-October at peak fall color season when the water is chilly, but refreshing.

Top tip The houseboat eliminates hotel costs. The larger the group, the more affordable and fun.

Practicalities

ARRIVING

Fly into international airports in **Fredericton**, **Saint John** or **Moncton**. **VIA Rail** (viarail.ca/en) passes through several times a week from Nova Scotia and Québec, stopping at many locations.

CONNECT

Wi-fi Free wi-fi is available at most hotels, restaurants, pubs and bars. Just ask for the password.

MONEY

Credit cards are widely accepted, but carry Canadian dollars for cash-only vendors at farmers markets. Some gas outlets offer discounts for cash purchases.

WHERE TO STAY

Location	Pros/Cons
Fredericton	Attractions are walking distance downtown or cycling distance on trails.
Moncton	A central location between two coastlines and two national parks.
Saint Andrews	Affordable motels and historic inns balance the top Algonquin resort.
Miramichi	Stay at the mouth of a famous river and the heart of the French Acadian coast.

EATING & DRINKING

Poetic terms like fiddleheads (pictured top left; tips of spring ferns) and *fricot* (pictured bottom left; a rich chicken stew in French Acadian regions) pop from menus, suggesting local pride in traditional ingredients and comforting dishes with deep roots. Simultaneously, international flavors are ubiquitous and embraced in an evolving culture.

Best distillery
Distillerie Fils du Roy (p115)

Must-try fricot
Restaurant La Sagouine (p115)

GETTING AROUND

Planes, trains, automobiles... and ferries With multiple entry points by car or ferry from Québec, Maine or Nova Scotia, organize your trip around any start and end points. If you don't arrive by car, rent one.

Walking and cycling Fredericton is the most pedestrian- and cyclist-friendly city. Rent bikes at a local shop like Radical Edge or Savage's Bicycle Centre.

MAR-JUN
Maple-sugar camps serve hearty meals and the rivers are full.

JUL-AUG
Coastal waters are warm for swimming. Whales feed offshore. Festivals buzz.

SEP-NOV
Fall is for hiking and the harvest season.

DEC-FEB
Trails and hills are deep in snow for snowmobiling and skiing.

NEW BRUNSWICK
Trip Builder

Canada's only officially bilingual province has two distinct coastlines. The French Acadian region is known for warm waters and sandy beaches. In the Bay of Fundy region, the world's highest tides sculpt a dramatic shoreline, animate islands and create natural feeding grounds for whales.

March with **Tintamarre** revelers making a deafening din (p110) in Caraquet
🚗 3½hr from Fredericton

See a theme park dedicated to the gossipy washerwoman, **La Sagouine** (p111)
🚗 2hr from Fredericton

Float aboard your private **Lakeway Houseboat** (p106)
🚗 30min from Fredericton

Explore a 70-building outdoor museum at **Kings Landing** (p107)
🚗 30min from Fredericton

Cross a swinging bridge on the **Fundy Trail Parkway** (p109)
🚗 1hr from Saint John

Sip tea with Eleanor at **Roosevelt Campobello International Park** (p109)
🚗 2½hr from Saint John

GVICTORIA/SHUTTERSTOCK

NEW BRUNSWICK

HIGHEST TIDES | ACADIAN HERITAGE | CRAFT BEER

RESEARCHED BY DARCY RHYNO

- ▸ **Trip Builder** (p104)
- ▸ **Practicalities** (p105)
- ▸ **Your Floating Hotel** (p106)
- ▸ **Dynamic Coastal Parks** (p108)
- ▸ **Make a Great Din** (p110)
- ▸ **Taproom Trail** (p112)
- ▸ **Listings** (p114)

Blomidon Provincial Park (instead of Cape Split)

Spectacular Cape Split is hard to beat, but it's far less crowded on the 13.5km system of trails in Blomidon that lead to similar cliff-edge views of the Bay of Fundy.

Taylor Head Provincial Park (instead of Gaff Point)

Not overrated, but Gaff Point near Lunenburg is overused. Its mix of rugged coastline and sandy beach is found on many other trails, including the 14km peninsular trail at Taylor Head.

Seafood platter

Lobster Lessons

Halls Harbour Lobster Pound & Restaurant

Learn all about the anatomy of lobster with the hilarious interpreter (hopefully, he'll be wearing his lobster socks), then enjoy a dish made with local lobster.

Northumberland Fisheries Museum

On the Pictou waterfront, hold a live lobster (maybe even a rare blue one), see how a lobster trap works, learn about a lobster's lifecycle and check out model ships.

Fisheries Museum of the Atlantic

Learn about the traditional inshore lobster fishery. Get up close to a historical lobster boat and hear stories during the daily 'Lobster Lore' session.

Shop for Originals

Maritime Mosaic

In Amherst at the New Brunswick border, what was once the largest department store east of Montreal is now a giant arts and crafts co-op and small business incubator.

Glass Artisans Studio & Gallery

At one of many quality original shops on a small stretch of the Cabot Trail in Cape Breton, Wendy Smith makes and sells her fine-blown glass works and offers workshops.

Cabotto Chocolates

Also on the Cabot Trail, sister painters fill their walls with vibrant art and make chocolates that are just as pleasing to the eye as to the taste buds.

Laurie Swim Gallery

Lunenburg is a town bursting with art galleries where Swim's stands out for her renowned, groundbreaking quilt and fabric work, which emerges from her social and environmental interests.

Encompassing Design Rug Hooking Studio

A sense of humor permeates the high-quality hooking work covering every square inch of the walls in this studio, shop and gallery in Mahone Bay, a shopping destination.

Listings

BEST OF THE REST

Whale, Seal & Bird Tours

Petit Passage Whale Watch
From the tip of Digby Neck, head to whale feeding grounds aboard a converted fishing boat. Back on shore, grab a bite at its little cafe overlooking the Bay of Fundy.

Brier Island Whale & Seabird Cruises
On the Bay of Fundy's outermost island, choose from two Zodiacs and a former fishing boat for a whale-watching trip with an experienced, expert company.

Donelda's Puffin Boat Tours
In Cape Breton, Donelda's has built a reputation for its entertaining guides, respectful whale and seal encounters, and rewarding puffin and other seabird sightings.

Captain Cox's Whale Watch
From Nova Scotia's most northern tip, the Captain cruises the coastline to waterfalls, sea caves, shipwrecks and of course whale sightings.

Tip Top Taprooms

Tusket Falls Brewing Co $
Tusket Falls has 'Something to Say,' one of the best juicy IPAs around, served at a new taproom where its massive homemade smoker supplies the kitchen with flavorful ingredients.

Lunn's Mill Beer Company $
The atmosphere says rural, post-industrial. The outdoor patio has a laid-back, country feel where local musicians perform traditional tunes. Brickyard Red and Anvil Porter fit the vibe.

Oxford Taproom $
Halifax's loss of a beloved movie theater was mitigated by its transition into a community hub taproom with a backyard patio decorated with theater memorabilia and murals.

Route 19 Brewing $
The revitalization of this once-tired town is captured in Coal Dust Stout, Sandcastle Sour and Nineteenth Hole Ale, which honor Inverness' beachside mining past and its new life as a golfing destination.

Boatskeg Distilling $
Toast a salted caramel cocktail to the two hardworking Pubnico fishermen who renovated a family boatbuilding shed into a hip distillery with a patio overlooking a lush salt marsh.

Alternative Hikes

Fishing Cove Trail (instead of Skyline)
Overcrowded Skyline ends in a majestic view, but, nearby, the Fishing Cove Trail is a steep descent beside a stream through lush forest to a secluded cove where you can swim and camp.

Puffins

shaped pyramids out of lobster traps. Fishing is a dangerous job, especially in rough, winter weather. Strung with lights and hung with buoys bearing the names of late fishers – some lost at sea – these trees have morphed into tributes and memorials for hardworking, brave fishers. In summer, some communities hold a 'parade of lights' when crews decorate their boats and glide them along the waterfront after dark for cheering crowds to admire. One such event is held in Shelburne during their late July Dock Days festival.

> The lobster fishery dominates in Nova Scotia. Much of the activity kicks off precisely at dawn on 'dumping day.'

Living Wharves

At the Halls Harbour Lobster Pound, order lobster prepared every way imaginable right at the wharf. At the Crow's Nest Restaurant in Digby, dine on scallops next to the docked fishing fleet in the 'Scallop Capital of the World.' In Peggy's Cover, grab a **Tom's Lobster Shack** lobster roll from the food truck, then walk with it down to the wharf. Visitor interest in fishing for a living has grown to the point that Yarmouth and Acadian Shores tourism created 'Living Wharves.' At various wharves and related sites such as lighthouses, demonstrators invite visitors to hear seafaring stories, hold a lobster and try their hands at skills such as rope splicing and banding (placing an elastic band around a lobster's claw). Living Wharves is a reminder that visitors are welcome to just walk onto a wharf to see the boats up close and have a yarn with captains and crews.

⚓ History's Fastest Fishing Schooner

When the American schooner *Esperanto* won the first International Fisherman's Cup Race held off Halifax in 1920, Nova Scotia fishermen and shipbuilders responded by building the *Bluenose,* the world's fastest fishing schooner. Launched on March 26, 1921 in Lunenburg, Captain Angus Walters and the *Bluenose* crew proved themselves the most skillful at fishing the Grand Banks off Newfoundland and speeding their catch to market. Following that first fishing season, the boat reclaimed the Fisherman's Cup in October 1921 and never lost it until she retired 18 years later. Today, she graces the Canadian dime and her twin, *Bluenose II,* carries on her legacy.

Fishing for a Living

VISITOR EXPERIENCE MEETS DEMANDING, DANGEROUS OCCUPATION

The Atlantic nearly surrounds Nova Scotia, so it's not surprising that fishing is stitched into the social, cultural and economic fabric of a province famously known in song as 'the sea-bound coast.' Increasingly, there is an opening-up of authentic fishing lifestyles and community events to curious visitors.

Left Fishing boats **Center** Lobster-trap Christmas-tree display **Right** Tom's Lobster Shack lobster roll

I was born into two fishing families in a fishing community. My father harpooned swordfish and trapped lobster. His father fished and cooked for hungry crews. My other grandfather ran wholesale fish businesses. Many of my uncles and cousins fish for a living today. At home, my mother prepared seafood in countless ways – smoked haddock, pickled herring, deep fried clams, pan fried mackerel, cod tongues and cheeks, salt cod, creamed lobster, fishcakes, seafood chowder. Today, many of these dishes populate restaurant menus across the province for visitors to enjoy. Festivals, quirky celebrations and unique sites intimately tied to fishing-for-a-living welcome those same visitors.

Dumping Day

The lobster fishery dominates in Nova Scotia. Much of the activity kicks off precisely at dawn on 'dumping day.' That's the morning the entire lobster fleet of a designated district heads to sea, each boat weighed down with baited traps. In southwestern Nova Scotia, where most lobster is landed, that day is in late November. The largest catches are landed in the weeks before Christmas, each boat setting and hauling their quota of perhaps 350 traps until their holding pens are filled or bad weather forces them to port. On Dumping Day, families and friends turn out to wish the fishers fair seas, big catches and safe return.

Christmas Trees & Summer Lights

In recent years, quirky events have grown out of a collision of fishing and annual holidays. Every December, communities such as Barrington Passage build Christmas tree–

Top left Millbrook Cultural and Heritage Centre **Bottom left** Kejimkujik National Park

Cultural Journeys

Birchbark Canoe Construction Todd Labrador demonstrates on a drop-in basis how to build an authentic birchbark canoe using materials gathered in **Kejimkujik National Park**. In the same park, Indigenous crafters demonstrate decorative porcupine quill work, Indigenous games at a Mi'kmaw encampment and guided tours to a site with centuries-old petroglyphs.

Walk Into the Past **Eskasoni Cultural Journeys** (eskasoni culturaljourneys.ca) guides visitors on a 2.4km walk around Goat Island in Eskasoni 40km from Sydney to experience life among Indigenous Mi'kmaq in pre-colonial times. Step inside a traditional shelter and stop at various stations to learn about traditional hunting and foods, games, basketry and a cultural practice called smudging. Hear stories that form the foundation of Mi'kmaw culture, heritage and values.

Arts and Culture Through atrium windows, sunlight pours into the **Millbrook Cultural and Heritage Centre** (millbrook heritagecentre.ca) 6km from Truro where exhibits and artifacts on hunting, crafts and daily life – including a live-in village – show how Mi'kmaq lived in pre- and post-contact times. Two blocks away, see and buy works by the premier Mi'kmaw visual artist at **Alan Syliboy Art Studio**.

Campfire Stories At **Cape Breton Highlands National Park**, Mi'kmaw interpreters gather guests around the campfire or take them on various scenic walks to tell stories from pre-colonial times. Weekly drumming circles are an introduction to Mi'kmaw music.

🗿 Petroglyph Inspiration

On finding inspiration in the petroglyphs created by his ancestors in Kejimkujik National Park, Alan Syliboy says, 'It's a self-examination. You do it with your own life, but this is going even further back and looking where your DNA comes from. It's really important as a people because we've done ceremony for 10,000 years on this ground. They are meant to be life symbols. It's like the fern. The fern is closed up and as life goes on, it opens up. This is how your life opens up. As you gain knowledge, experience and wisdom, it unfolds.'

■ **Alan Syliboy,** *Mi'kmaw Artist* @syliboyalan

16 INDIGENOUS
Art & Culture

NATIONAL PARKS | ART | GUIDED TOURS

For hundreds of generations, Mi'kmaq have called what is now Nova Scotia home. The arrival of this Indigenous people is dated up to 13,500 years ago as the glaciers of the last ice age were retreating. Their time on these lands and waters taught them how to live in harmony with them, even while making sustainable use of their resources.

How to

When to go Peak season is July and August. In spring and fall, some experiences might be limited or unavailable.

Getting there A car is necessary to visit these sites. Fly into airports in Halifax, Sydney or Moncton and rent a car.

Powwows In Atlantic Canada, Indigenous communities hold annual powwows with music, dance and food. Visitors are welcome.

Supercontinents & Sea Stacks

Supercontinent Evidence The story of Pangea is told dramatically in the Cliffs of Fundy UNESCO Global Geopark in central Nova Scotia. About 200 million years ago, all of today's continents began to split apart from the supercontinent, Pangea. For example, coastal formations at **Five Islands Provincial Park** are made of lava that oozed to the surface as Pangea tore apart.

Older than Dinosaurs Early amphibians from over 300 million years ago pre-dated dinosaurs by over 50 million years. These Coal Age creatures left behind footprints and fossilized remains along this coastline. The **Fundy Geological Museum** (fundygeological.novascotia.ca) in Parrsboro is the best place to learn about them and their steamy, swampy habitat.

Ice Age Artifacts Indigenous artifacts found at **Mi'kmawey Debert National Historic Site** date back to the time of the last glacial period between 13,500 and 11,000 years ago, the equivalent of up to 540 generations.

Waterfalls, Sea Stacks and Coastal Cliffs Hike to these and other geological scenic sites across the park. The massive tides and the glaciers of the last ice age helped form wonders like the **Three Sisters** and **Soley Cove** sea stacks, the cliffs of **Cape d'Or** and the **Old Wife**, and the waterfalls at **Economy Falls**. For a challenging wilderness experience, hike the headlands of **Cape Chignecto Provincial Park**.

Top left Five Islands Provincial Park
Bottom left Sea stack, Soley Cove

 **Joggins**

It's just beyond the Cliffs of Fundy boundaries, but Joggins, 42km northeast of Apple River, is a vital addendum to this coastal geopark. To see why, stop at **Joggins Fossil Cliffs** for a guided tour of this important coal age, 300-million-year-old fossil deposit. Charles Darwin himself refers to it in *On the Origin of Species*.

15 The Cliffs OF FUNDY

SCENIC DRIVE | HIGHEST TIDES | FOSSILS

Officially designated the **Cliffs of Fundy UNESCO Global Geopark** in 2020, the 165km stretch of coast from Truro to Apple River is so named for its geological origins, pre-dinosaur fossils, scenic landscape and human history. The world's highest tides surge in the Bay of Fundy, carving the coastline and exposing vast stretches of ocean bottom. Millenia-deep Indigenous history and mythology blends with centuries of settler activity and heritage.

How to

When to go Peak season is July and August. In spring, waterfalls are full. Autumn colors add to the splendor. Overcrowding is never an issue.

Getting there A car or bicycle is required to complete the route. Fly into airports in Halifax or Moncton and rent a car.

Top tip From easy walks to strenuous hikes, look for the outdoor experiences that fit your ability level.

Museum (highlandvillage.novascotia.ca), an outdoor historical village on a hilltop overlooking the saltwater Bras d'Or Lake. The **Gaelic College** (gaeliccollege.edu) offers workshops and courses on traditional arts, crafts and music while providing a venue for performances year-round.

The Cabot Trail A world-class scenic drive, the Cabot Trail weaves through the ancient mountains and along the coast, through **Cape Breton Highlands National Park** and small communities. Because Celtic Colours stretches over nine days, it's easy to take the time to drive the trail and make it part of your festival itinerary.

♪♪ Celtic Colours' Magic Moments

For me Celtic Colours is anything from performing at the closing show with thousands cheering for Celtic music, or the incredible feeling of having an audience of 100 in a small church, hanging on every word as you talk about the culture you were brought up in. Or an audience that knows the music of an artist so well, five words into their song, everyone joins in. These are the magic moments of a nine-day festival that brings pure joy to a small island, its residents and visitors from all over.

■ *Wendy MacIsaac, fiddler and 2026 Artistic Co-Director @macisaacwendy*

Above Morgan Toney Trio on stage for the Pjila'si: A Wagmatcook Welcome concert during Celtic Colours 2025

14 Celtic COLOURS

MUSIC | FALL COLORS | SMALL HALLS

Against a backdrop of blazing autumn colors, nine-day **Celtic Colours International Festival** brings the world's Celtic regions together in small community halls and big stages across Cape Breton Island. From big, splashy concerts to unplugged square dances, the music is the centerpiece for a cultural celebration that includes art, storytelling, food and scenic hikes across Nova Scotia's highland island.

How to

When to go The festival takes place in mid-October.

Getting there You'll need a car to get around to performances across the island. Fly into airports in Sydney, Halifax or Moncton and rent a car. Or drive to Nova Scotia.

Top tip Build leisurely daytime drives into your itinerary to enjoy the fall colors before and after concerts.

Music of the Gaelic Diaspora

A Celtic Legacy Cape Breton Island is known for its generations of talented fiddlers, guitarists, singers and songwriters. You can draw a straight line from legendary fiddle tune composers of the past like Jerry Holland and Buddy MacMaster to the super-energized shows of contemporaries like Natalie MacMaster and Ashley MacIsaac, the likes of whom share top billing with performers of Gaelic roots music from around the world.

Gaelic History and Culture Gaelic runs deep on Cape Breton Island. While France and England battled over strongholds like the **Fortress of Louisbourg** (fortressoflouisbourg.ca) in the 18th century, Scottish settlers quietly built homes and communities across the island well into the 19th century. The story of that migration is told in reconstructions of early dwellings at the **Highland Village**

01 Walk the dyked lands of the **Grand-Pré National Historic Site** to learn about the settlement, expulsion and return of French Acadians.

02 Arrange a 'Meeting with the Governor' for a guided tour of **Port-Royal National Historic Site** (pictured left), Champlain's early 17th-century fort.

03 Duck into a 'pit house' and walk the glass floors of the **Black Loyalist Heritage Centre** to experience the lost chapter in the slavery story.

04 Cover your ears when the noon gun fires from the top of the **Halifax Citadel** and enter the fortress walls where early settler life is recreated.

05 Browse engaging exhibits at the **Millbrook Cultural and Heritage Centre** for a trip back to pre-settler, Indigenous times.

06 Spend a day (and night), dine and fire a musket at **Fortress of Louisbourg**, the largest historical reconstruction site in North America.

FROM TOP: WANGKUN JIA/SHUTTERSTOCK, MEUNIERD/SHUTTERSTOCK

13 Founders' TOUR

HISTORIC SITES | INDIGENOUS ROOTS | BLACK HISTORY

Immerse yourself in the colorful narrative of Nova Scotia's birth. Walk among Canada's second largest petroglyph collection. Visit the contemporary cultural center that tells the lost chapter of the slavery story. Watch the noon cannon fire over Nova Scotia's capital city.

Trip Notes

Getting around Because this itinerary runs the length of Nova Scotia, driving is the only way to reach all sites in one trip.

When to go In the peak season of July and August, everything is open. June and September, some sites have reduced hours. Other months, sites have reduced staff or are closed.

Top tip Crowds are rarely, if ever an issue, so feel free to travel when it's best for you.

Nova Scotia Is Over 400

Nova Scotia's creation story features a complex collision of settler French Acadians, British colonists and Black Loyalists with Indigenous people. But Nova Scotia's name, flag and coat of arms came soon after first contact in 1621 when Sir William Alexander of Scotland claimed ownership of the region and built a settlement in Annapolis Royal.

EATING & DRINKING

In the province where lobster is king, the challenge is to look past it after the compulsory lobster roll or whole steamed lobster dinner to the boatload of other local seafood. Some say they prefer Nova Scotia fish and chips to any they've had elsewhere. Oysters (pictured bottom right), mussels, scallops, haddock and halibut star on countless menus. Look further still to find specialties like the renowned Halifax donair (pictured top right), a gyro of spiced meat, vegetables and a unique sweet sauce wrapped in a pita.

Coolest distillery
Boatskeg Distilling (p100)

Must-try lobster roll
Tom's Lobster Shack (p99)

CONNECT & FIND YOUR WAY

Wi-fi Free wi-fi is available at most hotels, restaurants and bars. Just ask for the password. Alternatively, use phone data or buy an e-SIM before you leave home. Data connection is generally good, but there are dead zones in remote areas.

Navigation Use a navigation app or pick up a provincial map.

WHERE TO STAY

Halifax hotels are pricey, but there's a hostel and cheap, spare university dorm rooms. Accommodations in regional towns are more affordable. Beach and coastal cottages are great for small groups.

Location	Pros/Cons
Halifax	Most attractions are walking distance or in reach of public transit.
Lunenburg	The most choices on the South Shore, but rooms are pricey.
Annapolis Royal	Historic inns are short walks from major sites and many restaurants.
Wolfville	Historic inns are driving distance from wineries and scenic lookouts.
Amherst	Near borders with New Brunswick and PEI where two scenic drives converge.
Cape Breton	The greatest variety: suites on top golf courses, glamping domes and motels.

NOVA SCOTIA MUSEUM PASS

Purchase a **Nova Scotia Museum Pass** (adults $46.45; families $91.85) for entry into all 28 provincially operated museums.

MONEY

Credit cards are widely accepted, but carry Canadian dollars for farmers markets, where some vendors may only accept cash. Some gas outlets offer discounts for cash purchases.

Practicalities

ARRIVING

Fly into airports in Halifax or Sydney. Take a taxi (about $30) or public transit ($5 to $15) into Halifax (halifax.ca/transportation/halifax-transit) or Sydney (cbrm.ns.ca/transit). VIA Rail (viarail.ca/en) travels to New Brunswick and beyond. Ferry services connect Yarmouth with Maine (ferries.ca), Digby with New Brunswick (ferries.ca), Caribou (near Pictou) with PEI (ferries.ca) and North Sydney with Newfoundland (marineatlantic.ca). If you're crossing the border into Canada by air, water or land, carry proof of identity and citizenship.

HOW MUCH FOR A

Museum entry $8

Lobster roll $25

On-tap beer $8

GETTING AROUND

Planes, trains, automobiles and ferries With multiple entry points by car or ferry from Maine, PEI, New Brunswick and Newfoundland, you can organize your trip around many start and end points. If you arrive by plane or train, rent a car, as it's easily the best way to get around.

Bus (maritimebus.com) There are bus routes to many communities. Cities like Halifax (halifax.ca/transportation/halifax-transit) operate affordable and reliable **public transit** systems.

WHEN TO GO

MAR-JUN
The last snowfall leads into full summer by mid-June.

SEP-NOV
Celtic Colours music festival and fall colors illuminate autumn.

JUL-AUG
Whale-watching season. Beaches, hiking trails and taproom patios beckon.

DEC-FEB
The February-long Lobster Crawl festival is fun and delicious.

Walking and Cycling Cities and towns are mostly pedestrian and cyclist-friendly. Cycling and walking get you around Halifax and all the smaller communities. Rent bikes at a local shop like Lunenburg Bike Shop (lunenburgbikeshop.com) and I Heart Bikes (iheartbikeshfx.com).

- Hear millennia-old Indigenous stories around a **Cape Breton Highlands** campfire (p97)
  🚗 *1hr from Sydney*

- Square dance during **Celtic Colours** at a Cape Breton community hall (p92)
  🚗 *1hr from Sydney*

- Shop for vibrant Indigenous art by **Alan Syliboy** (p97)
  🚗 *1hr from Halifax*

CLOCKWISE FROM BOTTOM LEFT: MARC GUITARD/GETTY IMAGES, QING PAN/SHUTTERSTOCK, MR. TOBIN/SHUTTERSTOCK

NOVA SCOTIA
Trip Builder

Every Nova Scotia license plate declares the province, 'Canada's Ocean Playground'. In a place that's nearly an island with over 13,000km of coastline, that's exactly what you'll find. Whether you're on a boat tour, in a kayak or at a seafood restaurant, the Atlantic is always present.

See the **Joggins** fossils that caught Charles Darwin's attention (p95)
🚗 3½hr from Halifax

Hike to **Three Sisters** sea stacks in a UNESCO geopark (p94)
🚗 3¼hr from Halifax

Meet **Port Royal's** Governor at Champlain's early-17th-century fort (p91)
🚗 2hr from Halifax

Paddle to **Kejimkujik's** petroglyphs with an Indigenous guide (p97)
🚗 2hr from Halifax

Learn the genius Acadian technology for reclaiming land from the sea at **Grand-Pré** (p91)
🚗 1hr from Halifax

- ▶ **Trip Builder** (p86)
- ▶ **Practicalities** (p88)
- ▶ **Founders' Tour** (p90)
- ▶ **Celtic Colours** (p92)
- ▶ **The Cliffs of Fundy** (p94)
- ▶ **Indigenous Art & Culture** (p96)
- ▶ **Fishing for a Living** (p98)
- ▶ **Listings** (p100)

NOVA SCOTIA

OCEAN PLAYGROUND | CANADA FIRSTS | SEAFOOD

RESEARCHED BY DARCY RHYNO

Maison du Bootlegger $$$
An American transformed this 19th-century farmhouse north of La Malbaie into a speakeasy in the 1920s. Come for a steak dinner and tour, and stay for live music.

Fun Festivals

Carnaval de Québec
Visit Bonhomme's ice palace, watch ice canoe races and drink Caribou at Canada's oldest winter festival, Carnaval de Québec

MURAL Festival
Visit Montréal's Plateau in early June when international wall-scrawlers make their mark and Blvd St-Laurent turns into an arty block party.

Festival International de Jazz de Montréal
World's largest jazz fest, with around 3000 musicians giving 500 performances across 10 days between late June and early July in Montréal. Around 350 of those concerts are free.

Festival d'Été de Québec
In July, 11-day music festival on Québec City's Plaines d'Abraham, featuring global and local artists on stages across the city.

Pow Wow International
See traditional dancing, garments and crafts and taste a range of foods in this important meeting point for members of the Huron-Wendat diaspora in Wendake.

Le Festif!
Every July, 50,000 people come to Baie-St-Paul to attend 135 concerts at 30 different sites across town. You might see a show on someone's balcony or splish-splash at a concert in the river.

Outdoor Adventures

Parc Marin du Saguenay–St-Laurent
Spot as many as 13 species of cetaceans, including beluga, minke, humpback, fin, harbor porpoises and blue whales between May and October from this Parks Canada national marine park.

La Route des Vins
Cycle or drive to Québec's finest wineries and gourmet food producers in the Eastern Townships (Cantons de l'Est).

Les Cultures du Large
Go on a two-hour sea excursion in Les Îles-de-la-Madeleine to learn about oysters and try the freshest shucks of your life.

Parc National des Hautes-Gorges-de-la-Rivière-Malbaie
Hike up l'Acropole-des-Draveurs, a difficult 5.6km trail with an 800m vertical rise to an altitude of 1048m at this Sépaq park in Charlevoix.

Special Mentions

Espace Pour La Vie
Four museums, a leaning tower from the 1976 Olympics and glorious green spaces linking them all: no one's getting bored at Montréal's science and cultural oasis.

Bota Bota
Melt above the mighty St Lawrence in Montréal at this floating Finnish spa originally built as a ferry in the 1950s with saunas, steamrooms, heated pools, cold plunges and meditation rooms.

AstroLab
The largest research telescope in Canada and the first Dark-Sky Preserve outside the US hosts stargazing evenings throughout the year at Parc National du Mont-Mégantic.

Chute Montmorency
It's hard to convey the sheer magnitude of these Québec City cascades, which drop 83m into a nimbus of froth and mist next to vertical walls of sandstone and shale on either side.

Listings

BEST OF THE REST

Perfect Poutine

Ma Poule Mouillée $

Montréal favorite next to Parc La Fontaine where poutine meets the Azores, with tangy São Jorge cheese, chicken and chorizo, all glazed in a special garlicky sauce.

Le Chic Shack $$

Gourmet poutine with hand-smashed potatoes is the name of the game at this Québec City favorite. Try La Forestière and a boozy milkshake.

Cantine des Navigateurs $

Go all-out with a seafood poutine, featuring huge chunks of local lobster, from this seaside fry shack in Ste-Flavie, Gaspésie.

Café de la Grave $$

Acadian-style restaurant of 40-plus years on Les Îles-de-la-Madeleine, serving comfort food like clam chowder and loup-marin (seal) poutine, with frequent live music.

Destination Dining

Vin Mon Lapin $$$

At this classic French bistro with a modern Montréal makeover, wines are funky, veggies are fresh and plates are shareable. Reservations mandatory.

Damas $$$

Whether opting for a tasting menu or meze plates, don't overdo it on the made-to-order pita: you'll want room for more Syrian specialties at this Montréal restaurant.

Maison de Soma $$$

Seasonal ingredients from its 2.4 sq km farm in Les Laurentides, served in a modern dining room.

La Bûche $$

Urban sugar shack in Québec City serving *pâté chinois* (Québécois shepherd's pie), deer tartare and smoked trout.

Speakeasies & Cocktail Bars

Coldroom $$$

Enter this underground lounge in Old Montréal by ringing the doorbell reading 'Patience' – which you may need while waiting for a seat.

Bar George $$$

Tycoon Sir George Stephen's Victorian mansion in Downtown Montréal turned gentlemen's club now houses a wood-paneled restaurant and bar, ideal for sipping smoky scotches.

Big in Japan $$$

A bow-tied waiter takes orders behind the labyrinthine bar, swirling like a dragon's tail in this sexy, unmarked speakeasy beside Patati Patata in Montréal's Plateau.

JJacques $$$

Named one of the 50 best bars in Canada, this Québec City speakeasy has succulent seafood towers and delicious cocktails.

Bonhomme's ice palace, Carnaval de Québec

there's no language barrier when it comes to physical comedy and juggling. Arrive 20 to 30 minutes before curtain to enjoy the full experience.

Or head north to **TOHU** (tohu.ca), a one-of-a-kind 360-degree structure purpose-built for circus performances. The structure is also a remarkable example of green architecture, using methane from a former landfill to power the complex. Come seven days a week for the free L'art... du cirque exhibition that explains the history of circus.

> Performances combine death-defying stunts with passionate storytelling that's unlike anything else.

Feel like being more than just a spectator? Learn trapeze, aerial silks, dance and much more at the **Académie de Cirque de Montréal** (academiedecirque.com).

July Festival

The best time to visit Montréal if you're into circus (and if you want the best weather) is in July for the **Montréal Complètement Cirque** (montrealcompletementcirque.com) festival. For 10 days, pedestrian-only Rue St Denis in the Latin Quarter is taken over by trapeze artists flipping overhead, contortionists on top of shipping containers, stilt walkers and clowns pranking passersby. Free performances extend across the city – a recent feature was Les 3 Géants, three 50-foot-high arches in the shape of giants that circus performers used for acrobatics. Le Monastère and other venues also have performances during the festival.

Toast to TOHU

Montréal is recognized around the world as the circus capital of North America, a place where creativity, innovation and cultural diversity come together. Since Cirque du Soleil burst onto the scene in the 1980s, the city has become a hub for circus, launching companies onto the international stage. There's nowhere else like Montréal, a city that offers a unique environment where local and international artists can meet, explore, and exchange ideas – supported by institutions like the National Circus School and La TOHU, North America's only circus-specific presenter and venue.

■ **Aaron Marquise,** *Deputy Director of Circus Arts Programming and Development at TOHU* @la_tohu

Circus City

QUÉBEC-BORN CIRQUE DU SOLEIL CAME FROM A PROUD TRADITION

In Montréal's Plateau neighborhood, it's not uncommon to see someone whizzing by on a unicycle – even if it's snowing. Indeed, Montréal isn't shy about its passion for circus, and this wacky and jaw-dropping performance style is as entrenched in Québec culture as poutine and musical wooden spoons.

Cirque du Soleil's Roots

Circus as we know it might've started in the 18th century with a British squire, but its roots in Québec date to the early 1980s when a group led by Gilles Ste-Croix and Guy Laliberté called Les Échassiers de Baie-St-Paul (The Stiltwalkers of Baie-St-Paul) wowed the Québec village northeast of the capital with their non-traditional circus performances. Instead of focusing on animals or magic tricks, they did juggling, dancing, fire-breathing and composed their own music. Audiences couldn't get enough. In 1984, Ste-Croix and Laliberté took their show on the road across the province and later the US, calling it Cirque du Soleil.

Head to the Big Top tent in Montréal's Old Port to be wowed by **Cirque du Soleil** *(cirquedusoleil.com)*, one of Québec's most famous exports. Performances combine death-defying stunts with passionate storytelling that's unlike anything else – as the hundreds of thousands worldwide who've seen them can attest. Unfortunately, Cirque du Soleil only performs in Montréal between spring and summer, taking its show on the road the rest of the year.

Circus High & Low

Cirque du Soleil is far from the only act in Montréal. At nonprofit **Le Monastère** *(le-monastere.ca)* see circus cabaret performances in a stunning 19th-century neo-Gothic church – it's downright sacrilegious. Shows are set up like theater-in-the-round, with performers on a central stage ascending heaven-high on everything from silks and straps to trapeze and stacked chairs. The cabaret's comedic relief usually performs in French, but don't worry:

Left Cirque du Soleil site in Montréal
Center Acrobats, Montréal Complètement Cirque **Right** Performer, TOHU clown show

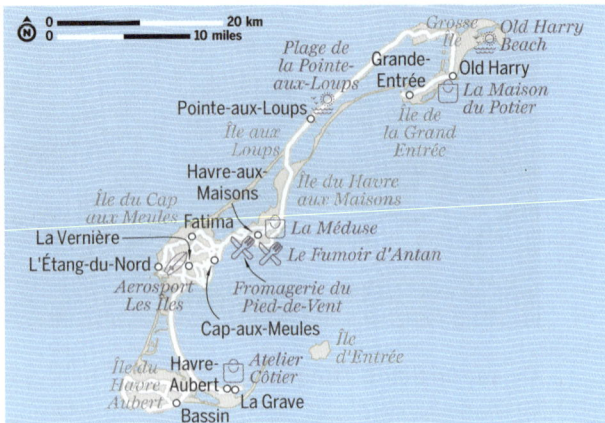

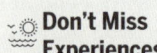

Top left Plage de la Pointe-aux-Loups
Bottom left Glass jellyfish creation by La Méduse

Go Beaching Les Îles-de-la-Madeleine are a cluster of eight major islands, six of which are connected by a 200km highway. Drive around to visit its many vistas and sandy beaches, including: **Plage de la Pointe-aux-Loups**, a long beach strip with soft dunes, turquoise waves and plenty of space for picnicking, and **Old Harry Beach**, 8.5km of gentle sand and a surfable riptide. Hold your hat, as the islands have 250 windy days a year. Or hold a kite, as Les Îles are a top kitesurfing destination. **Aérosport Les Îles** (aerosportlesiles.ca) rents equipment and offers lessons.

Procure the Perfect Picnic On your way, stop at over two dozen food producers to make the ultimate picnic. On Havre-aux-Maisons, **Le Fumoir d'Antan** (fumoirdantan.com), produces smoked herring, scallops, salmon, mackerel and halibut kippered under white birch and maple logs. Nearby, **Fromagerie du Pied-de-Vent** (fromageriedupieddevent.com) makes delicious cheeses made with milk from Canadienne cows.

Meet the Artisans The striking landscapes on Les Îles-de-la-Madeleine have long attracted artists and artisans who draw inspiration – and often their materials – from the place where they live. On Havre-aux-Maisons, Sophie Bourgeois and Catherine Chevrier-Turbide blow delicate jellyfish and other sea creatures out of glass fired at 1160°C at **La Méduse** (lameduseim.com). On Grande-Entrée, expert ceramicists at **La Maison du Potier** (poteriedesiles.com) make pottery with ingredients like local brown clay. And on Havre-Aubert, **Atelier Côtier** (ateliercotier.com) artisans make objects like clocks and lamps from sand.

☼ Don't Miss Experiences

Phare du Borgot (Cape Lighthouse) offers the craziest sunset you can see on the Islands.

La Shed Surf Bar at L'Anse aux Baleiniers is amazing for a beer in the afternoon and at night for great parties around the fire.

Cave exploring at La Salicorne is the best activity to do on the Islands.

Les Pas Perdus has Monday jams where locals play their instruments and anyone can just jump in and play along with everything.

■ **Charles Bégin,** who comes to the Islands every summer from Québec City to sell cheesy pies at Pizza d'la Pointe @pizzadlapointe

12 ESCAPE TO Les Îles-de-la-Madeleine

BEACHES | KITESURFING | GOURMET

Psst...want to know a secret? There's an archipelago in Québec lined with sandy beaches, iron-rich red cliffs, gourmet food, fantastic artisans and cute maritime houses painted from a kaleidoscopic palette – and few outside the province know about it. Fly or ferry to Les Îles-de-la-Madeleine (the Magdalen Islands) to experience the magic.

How to

Getting there Most visitors travel to Les Îles-de-la-Madeleine via the CTMA *(traversierctma.ca)* car ferry, which travels between Souris, Prince Edward Island and Cap-aux-Meules. Alternatively, fly from Gaspé or Bonaventure with connections to Québec City and Montréal.

When to go Most businesses are shut outside peak season (June to September).

Book ahead Many Québécois book their Îles-de-la-Madeleine summer vacation a year or two in advance – plan accordingly.

01 In **Ste-Flavie**, see stone figures leading out to the water at **Centre d'Art Marcel Gagnon** and 3000 tropical plants and art installations at **Jardins de Métis** (pictured above).

03 **Gaspé** is the 'Birthplace of Canada', with a cute shopping strip and two worthwhile museums: **Musée de la Gaspésie** and **Site d'Interprétation Micmac de Gespeg**.

02 **Forillon National Park** is a mix of ancient geology, dense high-altitude forests, wind-smacked beaches and military history; German U-boats sank some 20 warships and merchant vessels off this coast between 1942 and 1944.

05 The **Battle of the Restigouche National Historic Site** displays the huge hulls and other recovered artifacts from French warships sunk by the Brits in 1760 during the Seven Years' War.

04 **Percé** features the drive's postcard: **Rocher Percé** (pictured left), an 88m limestone stack jutting up from the gulf. And take a boat tour to see **Île Bonaventure**'s thousands of northern gannets dive-bombing for fish.

FROM TOP: JOEL BALSAM/LONELY PLANET, KRISTI BLOKHIN/SHUTTERSTOCK

11 Road Trip
GASPÉSIE

MARITIME QUÉBEC | LIGHTHOUSES | CANADA'S BIRTHPLACE

A road trip through Québec's southeastern boot is a rite of passage and one of Canada's most scenic drives. The windy northern coast is lined with cute towns and lobster poutine shacks, while the Anglo-influenced southern Baie-des-Chaleurs coast has calmer, warmer water for swimming.

Trip Notes

Getting around Rte 132, Québec's longest highway, hugs the coastline, with endless views (look for whales) and glacier-patterned cliffs with waterfalls gushing from above.

When to go Gaspésie is always windy, but it's particularly chilly outside of peak season: late June to mid-September.

Top tip Detour inland to **Parc National de la Gaspésie** for your best chance in southern Québec of seeing caribou and moose in the wild.

See the Light

Keep an eye out for the peninsula's 14 historic lighthouses, including **Pointe-à-la-Renommée** (pictured left), built in 1880 to prevent (frequent) St Lawrence River shipwrecks. Unfortunately, the lighthouse did little to stop the *RMS Empress of Ireland* from colliding with a Norwegian former icebreaker, sinking the 1580-passenger luxury cruise liner in 1914. Learn more at **Musée Empress of Ireland** (shmp.qc.ca).

Top left Mont Tremblant Resort
Bottom left Cycling in Les Laurentides

Memorable Mont-Tremblant Founded in 1938 and home to Canada's first chairlift, **Mont Tremblant Resort** *(tremblant.ca)* has 100 or so runs and 14 lifts leading from its luxurious (and kitschy) Alps-style resort town. Disembarking from the gondola above the clouds and gliding past evergreens sagging in marshmallow-white blankets is unforgettable. From June to October, ride the gondola to the top to see **Tonga Lumina** *(tongalumina.tremblant.ca)*, an immersive journey through sound and light that shares Polynesian legends with a pro-conservation message.

Outdoor Sports Region Outside of ski season, bicycles replace skis as the premier way to whizz around these scenic hills. Ride the 234km **Le P'tit Train du Nord** *(ptittraindunord.com)* multi-use path to experience Les Laurentides in one fell swoop. Or get out on Les Laurentides' 9000 lakes and rivers by combining an easy 7km paddle on La Rivière du Nord with a 4km cycle via **À l'Abordage** *(alabordage.ca)* in Val-David. Longer paddling trips are idyllic in **Parc National du Mont-Tremblant** *(sepaq.com/pq/mot)*, Québec's oldest provincial park, and **Parc National de la Mauricie** *(pc.gc.ca/eng/pn-np/qc/mauricie)*. Les Laurentides' newest attraction can be found 40m above the town of Mont-Blanc, nestled between the trees and squirrels at **Sentier des Cimes** *(treetop-walks.com/laurentides)*. It's a 2.7km round-trip wooden footbridge and 40m wooden tower with a mesh hammock on top for some high-altitude chilling.

Magic in the Mountains

This region is full of magic: sparkling lakes, vast forests, and mountains that invite both peace and adventure. Each season transforms the landscape into something breathtaking. The air is crisp, the people are welcoming, and time slows down. The Laurentians are more than a destination – they're a place where the soul feels rooted, inspired, and fully alive. For outdoor lovers, it's a dream come true – every path leads to wonder and every moment reconnects you with nature.

Lori Anne Jones, *artist, baker and manager at Café Boréal, located beside Sentier des Cimes @kingston_1977*

Outdoors Les
LAURENTIDES

10

SKIING | CYCLING | TREETOP ADVENTURES

Kick back and relish Québec's pristine scenery in Les Laurentides (Laurentians), one of the world's oldest mountain ranges. There are rolling hills, thousands of freshwater lakes, cuter-than-cute villages, cozy log-cabin chalets and Mont-Tremblant, eastern Canada's most popular ski resort, which rises to a peak of 932m.

How To

Getting there Mont-Tremblant Ski Resort (tremblant.ca) offers free shuttle buses between the resort and parking lots, as well as a coach service from Montréal's Trudeau airport.

When to go September to November is peak season for leafing. Ski season stretches from late November to mid-April.

Find a chalet Use a local platform to find accommodations, including WeChalet (wechalet.com), Maisons & Chalets à Louer (maisonsetchalets alouer.com), Origine Hotels (originehotels.com) and Camping Québec (campingquebec.com).

06 Beluga whale
Belugas, along with blue, fin and minke whales, are easily spotted from the northern shore of the St Lawrence River near Tadoussac.

07 Québec flag
See thousands wave Québec's blue and white national flag, the *fleur-de-lisé*, on St-Jean-Baptiste Day (June 24).

08 Bonhomme
This jolly snowman is the ambassador of **Carnaval de Québec**, the world's largest snowy winter carnival.

09 Biosphere
The geodesic dome on Montréal's Parc Jean-Drapeau remains a memory of when the city hosted the World Expo in 1967.

10 Wooden spoons
Spoons slapped on a thigh, preferably in a bar, are key instruments in Québecois folk songs called *chansons à répondre*.

01 BONCHAN/SHUTTERSTOCK. 02 STEPH COUVRETTE/SHUTTERSTOCK. 03 MARC BRUXELLE/SHUTTERSTOCK. 04 ELENA ELISSEEVA/SHUTTERSTOCK. 05 FOODGRAPHY39/SHUTTERSTOCK. 06 DAVID MERRON PHOTOGRAPHY/GETTY IMAGES. 07 MOSTOCK27/SHUTTERSTOCK. 08 ADRIEN LE TOUX/SHUTTERSTOCK. 09 SHAWN.CCF/SHUTTERSTOCK. 10 STUDIO LIGHT AND SHADE/SHUTTERSTOCK

Québec
SYMBOLS

01 Poutine
Born in the 1950s, Québec's most renowned dish is poutine: fries topped with fresh squeaky cheese curds and smothered with hot brown gravy.

02 Smoked meat
Romanian-Jewish immigrant Reuben Schwartz opened **Schwartz's** in 1928, and his cured and smoked beef sandwich is still a Montréal must.

03 Maple taffy
Québec produces roughly 72% of the world's maple syrup. Try the sweet stuff rolled in snow at a *cabane à sucre* (sugar shack).

04 Bagels
Who makes Montréal's best fire-baked dough ring: **Fairmount Bagel** or **St-Viateur Bagel**? Try both Mile End institutions and decide for yourself.

05 Tourtière
Meat pie, likely originating from British sailors, is one of Québec's most traditional dishes. Find it in the Saguenay–Lac-St-Jean region.

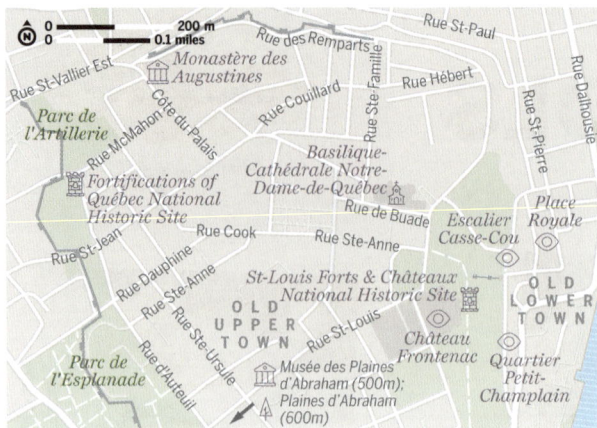

Top left Basilique-Cathédrale Notre-Dame-de-Québec **Bottom left** Place Royale

Fortified City Under constant threat from the British between 1690 and 1759, the French built stone **Fortifications of Québec National Historic Site** (parks.canada.ca/lhn-nhs/qc/fortifications) that continue to wall off Old Québec. Wander within the stone walls and visit the ruins of the **St-Louis Forts & Châteaux National Historic Site** (parks.canada.ca/lhn-nhs/qc/saintlouisforts) beneath **Terrasse Dufferin**, once home to the French governors who monitored the river and planned battles.

Uptown & Lowtown The settlement of Kebec started in Basse-Ville (Lower Town), where **Place Royale** stands today. The neighborhood surrounding the church became a busy wharf and warehouse district, with workers living in **Quartier Petit-Champlain** – now an artisan boutique strip. Up the **Escalier Casse-Cou** (1635; Breakneck Steps) to Haute-Ville, see the holy door and single-domed tower at **Basilique-Cathédrale Notre-Dame-de-Québec** (1759–1843), iconic Fairmont **Château Frontenac** hotel and **Monastère des Augustines** (monastere.ca) the first permanent hospital in North America in 1644.

Battle for Canada Southwest of Old Québec is the historic **Plaines d'Abraham** (plainesdabraham.ca), where, on September 13, 1759, a surprise attack by British General James Wolfe defeated Marquis de Montcalm's French soldiers and Indigenous allies, leading to the Treaty of Paris (1763), which laid out the boundaries for British North America (including Québec). On July 1, 1867, British North America would become known as Canada. The **Musée des Plaines d'Abraham** chronicles this history and offers 45-minute guided bus tours ($4.25).

Québec City Black History

Olivier Le Jeune, the first Black person to live permanently in Canada, arrived as an enslaved person in 1629. There's a plaque in the square of the Seminaire recognizing him as a person of historical importance in Québec and Canada. In a quiet corner, I talk about segregation, African American and Afro-Caribbean history and how slavery in those places and here are interconnected and different. In the 20th century, Château Frontenac turned down a lot of Black people because it wanted to cater to the Southern states of the US. Hôtel Clarendon was a safe space for Black visitors.

 ■ **Webster,** (@webster_ls), rapper, historian and tour guide. qchistoryxtours.ca

09 HISTORIC
Québec City

FRANCOPHONE CULTURE | ARCHITECTURE | BATTLEGROUNDS

Skip the transatlantic flight to Europe with a trip to Québec City, where 400 years of history and culture whisper through every crevice. You'll meet French-speaking locals, wander through fascinating museums and snap photos of postcard-worthy sites, including where British and French soldiers fought for the prize of Canada.

How To

Getting around Old Québec is walkable, though there are RTC buses and bikes available to rent at **Cyclo Services** *(cycloservices.net)*.

When to go In autumn, trees in Québec City light up in a rainbow of colors. Winter is lovely in Québec City, as the stone walls and snow make for romantic acoustics.

Best view See Old Québec from the water on the 15-minute **Lévis Ferry** *(traversiers.com; $3.45)*.

TV screens. Lamotte is a cunning bilinguist, serving as impresario at her intimate venue – and following in the high heels of local drag legend Armand Larrivée Monroe, who paved the way by opening the city's first dedicated drag bar in 1972.

The Show Goes On

Mado isn't the only drag show in town. Lip-sync assassins slay stages at **Le Cocktail** (*@barlecocktail mtl*) and **Complexe Sky** (*@complexeskymontreal*). Wigged wonders sometimes strut across the 2nd floor of **Café Cleopatre** (*@cafecleo*), which also hosts public striptease karaoke nights, **Bareoke** (*@bareoke*), the first and third Saturday of the month.

🏃 Out in the Village

Stereo Best of melodic house and transcendental techno flood the speakers of this all-hours dance floor, revered for its exceptional sound system.

Club Unity This club is the definition of 'bi' – two dance floors with two different styles of music and an all-are-welcome rooftop with LGBTIQ+ flavor.

Renard This 'Fox' has a split personality: weeknights he's a *5 à 7* cocktail-with-dinner gentleman; weekends he's a dance-till-dawn diva.

Saloon This queer-centric alternative to dance dens serves dinner until 8pm before doubling down on cocktails.

Above Fierté Montréal

08 LGBTIQ+
Montréal

PRIDE | DRAG | DANCE ALL NIGHT

When it comes to queer life, Montréal is tops. The city's annual Pride parade – **Fierté Montréal** (*fiertemontreal.com*) – is the largest LGBTIQ+ gathering in the francophone world. The rest of the year, come to the city's Gay Village, aka the Village, for a taste of this shimmering culture.

How to

Getting around Walk along Rue Ste-Catherine in the Village – it's Montréal's only year-round pedestrian zone. The Village is accessed via the Beaudry and Papineau metro stops, or you can walk east from Berri-UQAM.

When to go Montréal's Pride is in early August.

Top (no) tip Save your bills: though tipping is normal at most drag shows, you're not expected to toss loonies and toonies at the talent at Cabaret Mado.

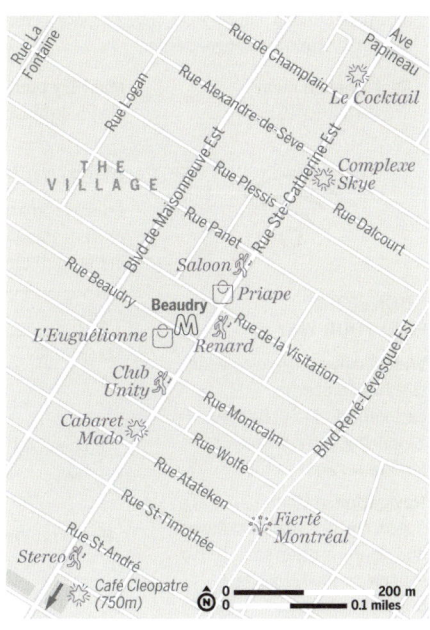

Go Shopping

Walk along Rue Ste-Catherine for a taste of Montréal's proud LGBTIQ+ culture in the Village. Stop in **Priape** (*priape.com*), a gay-centric shop opened in 1974 that's now a three-level emporium specializing in handcrafted leather fetish gear and adult toys. **L'Euguélionne** (*librairieleuguelionne.com*) is a queer feminist bookstore stocked with French and English literature. Pick up a pamphlet by a contemporary artist to uncover the city's latest LGBTIQ+ stories, hot off the presses.

Dare to Drag

Hairline-high eyebrows, puckered lips and a wardrobe screaming 'clown chic' is what to expect when Montréal drag pioneer Mado Lamotte takes the stage at her eponymous Rue Ste-Catherine **Cabaret Mado** (*mado.qc.ca; tickets from $34*). Mado – who goes by Luc Provost offstage – started treading the boards in 1987, long before *Canada's Drag Race* sashayed onto

EATING & DRINKING

Québec is the birthplace of Canada's most recognizable dish: *poutine* (pictured top right; browned fresh fries and squeaky cheese curds bathed in gravy), best eaten at a roadside *casse-croûte* (snack shack), *cantine* in Gaspésie or ski lodge. And Montréal is a battleground for the best place to eat its most proud foods: bagels, smoked meat and piri piri chicken. Drinks-wise, whisper the secret password to sip maple whiskey (pictured bottom right) in a Montréal speakeasy, and look out for Québec-made natural wine, *cidre de glace* (ice cider), gin and craft beer made from local ingredients.

Best smoked meat
Schwartz's (p72)

Must-try poutine
Ma Poule Mouillée (p82)

CONNECT & FIND YOUR WAY

Wi-fi Widely available. Consult ville.montreal.qc.ca/cartemtlwifi (Montréal) or zapquebec.org (Québec City) for free service.

Navigation In Montréal, what's called 'north' is really northwest and 'south' is often east. This is because the French laid out their settlement's street grid along the St Lawrence River, which swerves northward around Montréal, making the street directions off-kilter.

WHERE TO STAY

Québec is massive – almost three times the size of Texas. Fortunately, most destinations and activities are found along the St Lawrence River in the southern part of the province.

City	Pros/Cons
Montréal	Artistic, cosmopolitan city and transport hub. Busy and less access to nature.
Québec City	Historic, walkable provincial capital. Less happening than Montréal and cooler.
Mont-Tremblant	Ski resort and access to thousands of lakes. Pricey.

DISCOUNTS

Passeport MTL (mtl.org/en/passeport-mtl) offers museum discounts: buy admission for three to five major tourist attractions and save around 35% on ticket prices.

MONEY

Debit and credit card payments are most popular – you'll rarely need cash. Québec has a 9.975% sales tax, which is added onto the 5% federal tax. Tipping at least 15% is expected in restaurants and bars.

Practicalities

ARRIVING

Montréal-Pierre Elliott Trudeau International Airport Most visitors arrive in Québec via this airport. Take STM Bus 747 (45 mins, $11) to reach the Lionel-Groulx metro station or Gare D'Autocars intercity bus terminal downtown. A ticket for the airport bus includes public transport in the city for 24 hours.

Québec City Jean Lesage International Airport Best for accessing the provincial capital or for touring eastern Québec destinations like Gaspésie. RTC Bus 80 (55 mins, $3.75) gets you into town.

HOW MUCH FOR A

Plate of poutine $10

Museum ticket free–$30

Pint of beer $5–10

WHEN TO GO

DEC-MAR
Temperatures chill to -30°C; cozy up in a wooden chalet.

APR-MAY
Unpredictable weather can bring rain, heatwaves and slush.

JUN-AUG
Festival season as Québec celebrates its short summer.

SEP-NOV
Leafing season as trees transform into a kaleidoscope of color.

GETTING AROUND

Metro and bus Montréal's underground metro system races over one million daily riders to 68 stations and its STM bus system has over 200 routes. The RTC bus system is Québec City's primary public transport option, connecting downtown to the suburbs.

Bike Montréal is one of North America's best cycling cities and has BIXI, a year-round bike-sharing program. Québec City's cycling infrastructure is best for leisure cruises along the St Lawrence River. **La Route Verte** is a 5400km network of trails around the province.

Car You'll want a car to travel beyond the major cities, as intercity buses with companies like Orléans Express and Intercar are infrequent and only stop in hubs.

QUÉBEC
Trip Builder

Québec truly feels like a nation within a nation – an island of Francophone linguistic and cultural identity in Anglophone-dominated Canada. Come taste its unique cuisine, party at a Montréal festival and road trip its coastline – we guarantee you'll see why Québec is so proud.

Sip drinks at Prohibition-era speakeasy **Maison du Bootlegger** (p83)
🚗 2hr from Québec City

Ski **Mont Tremblant Resort** (p75)
🚆 1¾hr from Montréal

Sing with drag queens in Montréal's **Gay Village** (p68)
🚆 3hr from Québec City

See where Canada was won on the **Plaines d'Abraham** (p71)
🚆 3hr from Montréal

QUÉBEC

FRENCH-CANADIAN IDENTITY | MAPLE SYRUP | OUTDOOR ADVENTURES

RESEARCHED BY JOEL BALSAM

- **Trip Builder** (p64)
- **Practicalities** (p66)
- **LGBTIQ+ Montréal** (p68)
- **Historic Québec City** (p70)
- **Québec Symbols** (p72)
- **Outdoors Les Laurentides** (p74)
- **Road Trip Gaspésie** (p76)
- **Escape to Les Îles-de-la-Madeleine** (p78)
- **Circus City** (p80)
- **Listings** (p82)

Found Coffee $

Aussie-style specialty coffee, delicious brunch bites and a sweet terrace just steps from Trinity Bellwoods Park, in Toronto's trendy West End.

Little Victories Coffee Roasters $

Refuel with ethically sourced specialty brews at this indie Ottawa roaster with several branches, including a cozy downtown spot in a red-brick building.

Morning Parade Coffee Bar $

Arty third-wave spot on Dundas West, where you can join a cool Toronto crowd for locally roasted coffee, delicious baked goods and neighborhood vibes.

Kingston Global Eats

Sally's Roti Shop $

Home-style Caribbean cooking and a wonderfully warm owner welcome draw people in for deliciously spiced roti wraps and curry plates, including shrimp, squash and jerk chicken.

Wok-In $

Flavors from across Cambodia, Thailand and Vietnam fill fresh, spice-laden dishes like crispy banh xeo pancakes, coconut-shrimp curry and steaming noodles.

Mad for Markets

St Lawrence Market Complex

Old Toronto's 1902 red-brick building is a feast of Ontarian produce and market-counter meals. Go early on Saturdays for the hugely popular farmers market held in the bold new northern building.

Toronto Cocktail Scene

Bar Pompette $$

Bringing a splash of Parisian flavor to Little Italy, this chic drinking den is known for its house-made ingredients, creative cocktails and lively buzz.

St Lawrence Market Complex

Evangeline $$

Stylish year-round rooftop lounge with downtown views and a lovely terrace at the design-forward Ace Hotel, perfect for inventive cocktails. We also love the lobby bar.

Small Plates & Wine Bars

Paradise Grapevine $$

The Bloor St branch of this understated Toronto wine bar does snacky bites like cheese boards to go with natural drops. Also has an urban West End winery.

Grape Witches $$

Wander through a stylish natural-wine store on Toronto's Dundas West strip to sip by the glass on the hidden-away back patio and snack on season-inspired bites.

Arlo $$$

Dinner-party vibes paired with natural wines, original cocktails and zippy seasonal small-plate menus (such as scallop tartare with black garlic), in downtown Ottawa.

Grey Gardens $$$

Bistro-feel restaurant in Toronto's Kensington Market, where you can dine at the bar overlooking the open-plan kitchen. Creative seasonal sharing plates, perfect wines.

Listings

BEST OF THE REST

Tours for Food Lovers

Culinary Adventure Co
Dive into Toronto's diverse neighborhoods through their fabulous food scenes, from dosas in Little India to dim sum in Chinatown. Also runs early-access visits to St Lawrence Market.

Kingston Food Tours
Discover why Canada's first capital is a foodie city to watch, on a small-group route that involves strolling through the monument-rich downtown between bites.

Chopsticks & Forks
It's all about the multicultural flavors of Toronto's buzzing Chinatown and Kensington Market districts on this standout culinary adventure led by engaging local guides.

Must-See Art Galleries

Art Gallery of Ontario
Brightly colored works by Anishnaabe artist Norval Morisseau, bold landscapes from the Group of Seven and dreamlike Frank Gehry design dazzle at Toronto's top art hub.

National Gallery of Canada
Ottawa's finest art collection awaits within a spectacular granite-and-glass building created by architect Moshe Safdie, with landmark outdoor sculptures and landscaped gardens.

McMichael Canadian Art Collection
A standout stop for anyone heading north from Toronto, with Canadian-focused galleries on 100 acres of trail-threaded conservation land. Highlights include the shack where landscape painter Tom Thomson lived.

Out in the Wild

Thousand Islands National Park
Paddle out by kayak, hop on a cruise or camp overnight to explore some of the 21 islands that make up this 1904-founded reserve on the St Lawrence River.

Pinery Provincial Park
On Lake Huron, this protected space has a rare oak savanna landscape, forested campsites, and some of Ontario's loveliest beaches, with dunes and turquoise water.

Sandbanks Provincial Park
Beloved protected park on Lake Ontario, best known for its sandy beaches with enormous dunes. Escape some of the crowds by heading to quieter Lakeshore Beach.

Diner Vibes

White Lily Diner $$
Arrive early or join the waitlist for scrumptious all-day, diner-inspired breakfasts using own-farm ingredients, which have bagged this East Toronto fave a Michelin Green star.

Corner Peach $$
Seasonal produce fuels the menus at this stylish diner-bistro in Ottawa's Chinatown, where sourdough is freshly baked and zingy plates might include whipped ricotta with beets.

Coffee Culture

Rooster Coffee House $
Drink in views of Toronto's skyline over a flat white and a fresh scone on the lively patio at this much-loved East End spot. Also in the Old Town.

It is arguably while venturing along the meandering waterways themselves that Ontario's canoeing backstory is felt most powerfully. Following the decline of the fur trade from the 19th century onwards, recreational paddling emerged with the dawn of contemporary tourism in Canada in the early 20th century. Today, across Ontario's many pristine nature reserves and protected parks, getting out on the water for a paddle remains a major attraction for visitors. Algonquin Provincial Park, for example, is known for its adventurous backcountry canoe trips, which involve portaging between inky lakes, often following routes that have existed in one shape or another for thousands of years. Killarney Provincial Park is another beloved canoeing destination, taking in both inland waterways and Georgian Bay's lakeshore, and nearby Point Grondine Park has canoe routes managed by the Wiikwemkoong First Nation. Flowing westwards into Lake Huron, the Saugeen River also beckons paddlers.

> Ontario traces its canoe culture back to the river routes and portage paths used for millennia by Indigenous Peoples in the region

While most contemporary-style canoes are now made from durable materials like carbon fibre, traditional canoe-making techniques still live on, sharing their creators' stories, skills and knowledge. And when out exploring Ontario's endless waterways, every paddle stroke evokes a rich heritage spanning millennia.

Canadian Canoe Museum

Located on the Trent-Severn Waterway in Peterborough, the **Canadian Canoe Museum** (canoemuseum.ca) holds the world's largest collection of canoes, kayaks and other paddled watercraft, with around 650 pieces. Relaunched in 2024 following a complete redesign and relocation, in collaboration with experts from six Indigenous communities, the innovative space is much more than a multimedia gallery. Along with standout pieces like Kokomis Tchiman (an 8m-long birchbark canoe created by Métis elder Marcel Labelle), it also offers the chance to experience Ontario's canoe culture through a raft of activities, including paddle-carving workshops and guided trips on voyageur canoes launching from the attached dock.

ONTARIO ESSAY

Canoe Culture

THE WORLD OF THE CANOE IN ONTARIO'S HISTORY

In the grand Exhibition Hall at the Canadian Canoe Museum in Peterborough, Ontario, an entrancing installation of suspended full-size canoes swirls towards the ceiling like a school of giant fish. It is a fitting, evocative tribute to a lake-laced land that has been intimately connected with paddled watercraft for thousands of years.

Left Canoes line the shelves of the Collection Hall, Canadian Canoe Museum **Center** The 'Living Traditions' exhibit, Canadian Canoe Museum **Right** Canoeists, Killarney Provincial Park

Defined by a landscape of more than 250,000 lakes and bordered by four of the five Great Lakes, Ontario traces its canoe culture back to the river routes and portage paths used for millennia by Indigenous Peoples in the region. Inscriptions and rock paintings of canoes believed to date from over 1000 years ago have been found in both northern Ontario and in the Peterborough area between Toronto and Ottawa. Traditionally crafted from white birch bark by Indigenous master builders and constructed from the outside in, the light and speedy watercraft was used for hunting, fishing, transport, day-to-day activities and even war.

With the arrival of European colonization, early settlers and fur traders sought canoes and guides from Indigenous communities, before eventually starting to build their own vessels. At its peak, the main fur-trade canoe route ran westwards from Montréal to the Great Lakes and beyond. The French, Mattawa, Ottawa and St Lawrence Rivers were all key. As a result, many modern-day towns across Ontario have strong links to the region's canoe history. These include Peterborough, where an important canoe-building industry thrived from the mid-19th century until the 1960s. The remains of one of the world's oldest birch bark canoes – a 6m-long creation dating from the late 1700s – are now in the care of Peterborough's Canadian Canoe Museum. The Thunder Bay area in northern Ontario at the mouth of the Kaministiquia River on Lake Superior, was once a major fur-trade hub. Traditional canoe-building has recently been revived here as part of a youth outreach initiative on Fort William First Nation, just outside the City of Thunder Bay.

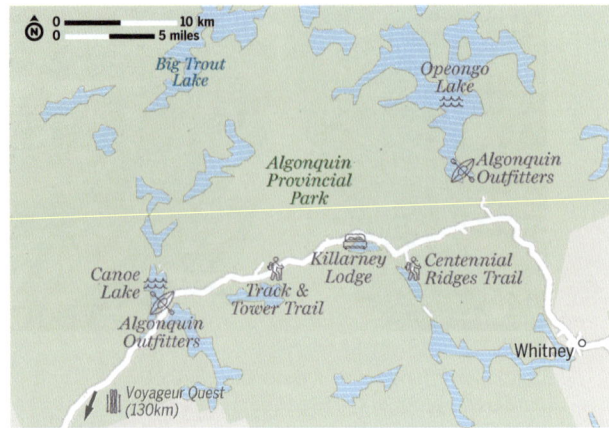

Top left Bull moose, Algonquin Provincial Park Bottom left Canoeists, Algonquin Provincial Park

Paddling Out Algonquin is at its most spectacular when you're out on the water, hearing the swish of a paddle as it dips into the deep-blue water and breathing in the scents of surrounding pines, cedar and firs. With stores on both Canoe Lake and Opeongo Lake, **Algonquin Outfitters** (algonquinoutfitters.com) is the go-to for renting canoes (including multi-day packages) and also runs expert-guided day trips.

Other Outdoor Thrills The park might be best known for its waterways, but there are some terrific hiking routes threading through its vast expanses. The challenging, 10.4km **Centennial Ridges Trail** is a standout for sprawling views, while the also superb 7.5km **Track & Tower Trail** partly follows disused railway tracks. As the park morphs into a silent, frosty winter wonderland, adventurous souls head here for snowshoeing, backcountry skiing and even dogsledding, with reputable guiding companies including **Voyageur Quest** (voyageurquest.com). You might even find a steaming sauna waiting at the end of the day.

Sleep Under the Stars Don't miss the chance to experience Ontario camping culture by staying a few nights at one of the park's lakeside campsites, where options include secluded canoe-in sites on the water as well as more easily reached spots with car access (advance bookings essential; ontarioparks.ca). Alternatively, a handful of country-charm resorts offer highly memorable stays within Algonquin's wilds, including waterfront **Killarney Lodge** (killarneylodge.com).

Wild Creatures

A distinctive sound often heard out on Algonquin's sparkling lakes is the haunting call of Ontario's provincial bird: the red-eyed, black-and-white-feathered loon. Also a beloved symbol of Algonquin, the loon shares its home with over 270 other bird species, many of them seasonal. The park is renowned, too, for being one of the finest places in Canada to spy moose (best months May/June, ideally around dawn). Other famous, though much more elusive, local residents include black bears and eastern wolves. Easier to spot are beavers and otters frolicking in the many lakes, rivers and ponds.

07 All-Seasons ALGONQUIN

CANOEING | WILDERNESS | ADVENTURE

Extending around 280km north of Toronto, the wonderfully wild 7630-sq-km **Algonquin Provincial Park** holds a special place in Ontario's heart as Canada's first provincial park. The beauty of its quiet forests, gently rippling lakes and secluded backcountry famously inspired Tom Thomson and the Group of Seven painters. Now people head here to get lost in the landscapes on active explorations, with pulse-racing adventures awaiting at any time of year.

How to

Getting here/around Most visitors arrive with their own vehicle. **Parkbus** (*parkbus.ca*) offers a few seasonal excursions from Toronto.

When to go The best months weather-wise are July to mid-September; these are also the busiest. September/October is the time for fall colors. Accommodations options are reduced in winter.

Permits A day-use vehicle permit ($21) is required for all visitors to Algonquin, except those who have overnight campground reservations. Book ahead (*ontarioparks.ca*). The main visitor center is near the East Gate.

and accessible by water taxi. The First Peoples Hall dives into the history of Indigenous Peoples across Canada, without shying away from complex chapters, while the canoe-shaped Grand Hall has a collection of monumental poles crafted by Indigenous artisans.

Cultured Kingston

A strategic location where the St Lawrence River meets Lake Ontario made Kingston the first capital of the then United Province of Canada from 1841 until 1844, hence its impressive stash of brick and limestone buildings. The neoclassical **City Hall** *(cityofkingston.ca)*, built from limestone in the mid-19th century, is the most distinctive structure. On Tuesdays, Thursdays and Saturdays, don't miss **Kingston Public Market**, going since 1801.

Indigenous Ottawa

A hidden gem I often recommend is **Âjagemô**, an indoor public art gallery that consistently features top-notch Indigenous art. It's a welcoming space for visitors to experience contemporary creativity and living culture in the heart of downtown Ottawa. I usually end tours at the Aboriginal War Veterans Memorial. It's a powerful place to reflect on the contributions of Indigenous veterans and how, as protectors and warriors, they formed part of a sacred circle of protection. Colonialism punctured that circle, disrupting the balance across generations, yet the memorial also shows the resilience and strength of communities when those circles remain strong

■ **Jaime Morse,** founder of *Indigenous Walks in Ottawa.*
@indigenouswalks

Above Gothic revival buildings, Parliament Hill

06 Capital CULTURE

HISTORY | MUSEUMS | ARCHITECTURE

▬▬ Pair the elegantly attractive national capital with a riverside student city that was once modern Canada's first capital, on a culture-packed jaunt around the historic sites of Ottawa and Kingston. Impeccably preserved heritage buildings and some of the country's finest museums set the tone in enjoyably strollable downtowns, while fabulous food scenes sing with international flavors in both cities.

How to

Getting here/around Both cities are pleasantly walkable and have good cycling. **VIA Rail** *(viarail.ca)* trains connect them in two hours.

When to go May to October have the best weather and vibes, with patios and festivals in full swing. Cold winters offer ice-skating opportunities.

Free tours Guided free walks of several Parliament Hill buildings and Kingston's City Hall are great for peeking behind the scenes. Check timings ahead.

The Canadian Capital

There is more to bilingual Ottawa than its grand role as the nation's capital since 1857, but the imposing Gothic Revival buildings of **Parliament Hill** *(visit.parl.ca)* undoubtedly dominate downtown, looming over the Ottawa River. Gaze up as you stroll past green-copper turrets, pointed archways and landscaped gardens while taking in the House of Commons, Senate and East Block (the Centre Block is closed for renovations until 2032). In July/August, catch the Changing of the Guard ceremony at 10am daily. A National Historic Site of a different kind draws people to the UNESCO-listed **Rideau Canal**, which morphs into one of the globe's largest ice-skating rinks each winter.

Admire Parliament Hill's spires from a whole new perspective at the **Canadian Museum of History** *(history museum.ca)*, a standout, sensitively conceived museum just across the river in Gatineau (on the Québec side)

03 Extending across 2766 sq km, **Manitoulin Island** is the traditional territory of six First Nations. Join **Wiikwemkoong Tours** (wikytours.com) to forage for wild ingredients and hike with Indigenous guides, or attend a powwow in summer months.

04 Northern Ontario's 645-sq-km **Killarney Provincial Park** lures outdoors lovers with wilderness hiking trails, dramatic white cliffs, starry nights, glassy lakes for paddling across, and the chance to camp out near the water.

05 With scenic hiking and mountain-biking trails, **Beausoleil Island** is the main hub for **Georgian Bay Islands National Park**. Boat-based day trips depart from Honey Harbour, or join a cruise from Midland or Penetanguishene.

02 Hit the wild hiking trails in **Bruce Peninsula National Park**, where forest-fringed cliffs cascade into turquoise waters. Then hop on a boat trip around **Fathom Five National Marine Park** (pictured below) or stroll past coastal dunes at beautiful **Singing Sands Beach**.

01 Charming, bayside **Collingwood** tempts visitors with its fired-up food scene, adventure activities and laid-back beaches. Dive into this region's Black heritage at the nearby, family-run **Sheffield Park Black History & Cultural Museum** (sheffieldparkblackhistory.com).

FROM TOP: NELZTABCHARANI316/SHUTTERSTOCK, ESKYSTUDIO/SHUTTERSTOCK

05 Georgian Bay ADVENTURE

LANDSCAPES | INDIGENOUS CULTURE | ACTIVITIES

The coastline of Georgian Bay – which is actually part of Lake Huron – takes in some of Ontario's most spectacular landscapes, from plunging quartzite cliffs to waters in endless shades of blue. From Toronto, head north to Collingwood; otherwise, jump into this 1300km-long route at any point.

Trip Notes

Getting here/around The two-hour *MS Chi-Cheemaun* ferry ride links Tobermory (Bruce Peninsula) with Manitoulin Island from mid-May to mid-October (*ontarioferries.com*).

When to go June to mid-October, when services and transport are fully open and weather is best. If possible, avoid summer weekends in the parks, which get busy. September/October is fall-color season.

Practicalities Reserve tours, ferries, campsites and park parking permits ahead (*parks.canada.ca*). Georgian Bay's waters can have dangerous conditions; follow local guidance.

Top Hikes

Many hiking trails through Bruce Peninsula National Park take in sections of the long-distance **Bruce Trail**. **Halfway Log Dump** and the **Grotto** (pictured left) are popular, easy-to-reach viewpoints, also linked by a challenging 7.7km stretch of the Bruce Trail. Over in Killarney Provincial Park, standout hikes include the 6km-long **The Crack** route, which involves clambering past boulders.

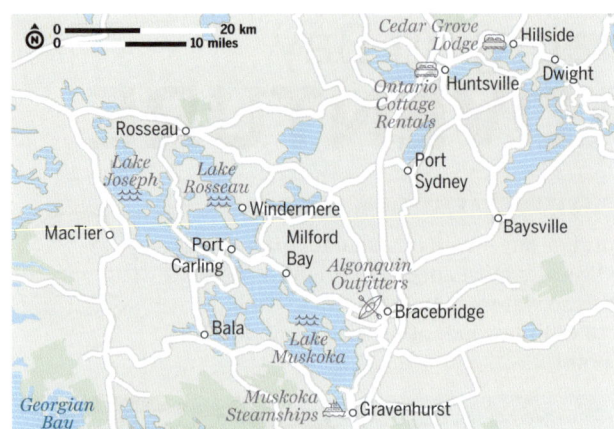

Top left Steamship cruise on Lake Muskoka **Bottom left** Wooden dock, Lake Muskoka

Out on the Water On the traditional territories of the Anishnaabe people, Muskoka's dazzling landscapes encompass more than 1500 forest-lined lakes, sprinkled near Lake Muskoka, Lake Rosseau and Lake Joseph, around two hours' drive north of Toronto. Even simply sitting out on the dock with a coffee listening to the rustling sounds of forest life or spending the evening grilling up goodies on the barbecue is a treat. But it is no surprise that water-based activities are a key part of any cottage-country adventure, from swimming to kayaking to wakeboarding. The first modern-day tourists arrived in Muskoka in the late 19th century, crisscrossing the lakes by steamboat. From the peaceful wharf in pretty Gravenhurst, **Muskoka Steamships** (realmuskoka.com) evokes this era with classic steamship cruises out on Lake Muskoka. Better yet, get a taste of the lakes' immense natural beauty by paddling out independently into the vast blues to soak up the tranquility. **Algonquin Outfitters** (algonquinoutfitters.com) rents canoes, kayaks and paddle boards from its base in lively Bracebridge.

Cottage Stays Ask anyone locally and they'll say the best place to stay in Muskoka is at a friend's cottage. Happily, a wave of private rentals provides visitors with their own cozy cottages; book through the usual platforms or a regional operator such as **Ontario Cottage Rentals** (ontariocottagerentals.com) and **Jayne's Luxury Rentals** (jaynescottages.com). Alternatively, take advantage of charming lakefront cottage resorts like **Cedar Grove Lodge** (cedargrove.on.ca), just outside Huntsville.

Market Time

There is no buzzier time to dip into Muskoka's lake towns than on a summer market day, when farmers and producers set up stalls selling everything from freshly baked butter tarts to locally grown berries and Ontario-made honey. From around May to October, each lake town – Gravenhurst, Bracebridge, Huntsville, Bala – throws its own farmers market, pulling in a mixed crowd of local residents and vacationing cottagers. In summer, this means delicious Ontario-grown fruits like peaches. As fall looms, hearty produce like squash arrives alongside cranberries grown in Bala, which even hosts a popular cranberry festival every October.

04 Life on THE LAKES

NATURE | WATER SPORTS | COTTAGES

Ontario's thousands of glittering lakes provide a serene escape, especially in summer when the endless greens of dense forests reflect off their cerulean waters, or in the fall as the landscapes turn a million shades of flaming orange, yellow and red. An escape to Ontario's beloved Cottage Country is an essential local experience, and the beautiful Muskoka region is a top pick. As the T-shirts say, life is indeed better at the lake.

How to

Getting here/around Best to have your own wheels. **Ontario Northland** *(ontarionorthland.ca)* buses connect Huntsville, Bracebridge and Gravenhurst with Toronto.

When to go Some accommodations operate only from May to October, but a growing number of places are now staying open year-round for all-season adventures. Book well ahead.

Bring layers While it can be warm in the day, temperatures typically drop overnight, even in summer (when you'll also need insect repellent).

Top left Vineyard, Niagara Peninsula
Bottom left Icewine bottles in ice sculpture, Peller Estates

Niagara Peninsula

Niagara's cool microclimates yield around 85% of the province's grapes, with vineyards sprawling around historical Niagara-on-the-Lake and beyond. Many local wineries offer the chance to savor the region's deliciously rich signature tipple: icewine. At long-established **Peller Estates** (peller.com), you can sip while kicking back in a stylish sub-zero icewine lounge (winterproof coat provided). **Inniskillin** (inniskillin.com) and **Reif Estate Winery** (reifwinery.com), both founded in the 1970s, are pioneers of Niagara icewine.

Today, a crop of contemporary vineyards is making waves in sustainable, organic and vegan-friendly wine production. Highlights are **Stratus** (stratuswines.com), housed within Canada's first LEED-certified winery building; **Two Sisters Vineyards** (twosistersvineyards.com), with an excellent restaurant; **Southbrook Vineyards** (southbrook.com), also awarded LEED certification; and **Tawse Winery** (tawsewinery.ca) in the Benchlands area. Other leading lights include **Thirty Bench** (thirtybench.com) and **13th St** (13thstreetwinery.com), which doubles as an art gallery.

Beyond Niagara

Hop between relaxed vineyards in pretty Prince Edward County, fronting Lake Ontario around 2½ hours' drive from Toronto or Ottawa. Local favorites include early arrival **Closson Chase** (clossonchase.com) and low-intervention-focused **Trail Estate** (trailestate.com). On Lake Huron's beachy shores, small-scale family-owned vineyards are emerging, such as **Dark Horse Estate Winery** (darkhorseestatewinery.com) and **Maelström Winery** (maelstromwinery.ca).

Ontario Grapes

Sweet icewine is the most prized drop in Canada's largest wine-producing region. Grapes – mostly Vidal and Riesling – are hand-harvested before sunrise at temperatures below -8°C and pressed while still frozen. But Niagara now flaunts over 40 different types of cool-climate grapes, each vineyard influenced by its own microclimate. Popular red picks include Cabernet Franc, Pinot Noir and Merlot, while favored white-wine grapes range from Sauvignon Blanc to Chardonnay and Riesling. Over in Prince Edward County, Pinot Noir, Cabernet Franc and Chardonnay steal the show. Natural, low-intervention wines are on the rise too, creating funkier bottles often based on these same grape varietals.

03 From Grape TO GLASS

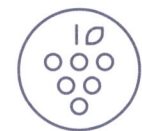

WINE | COUNTRYSIDE | HISTORY

Home to one of Canada's leading wine industries, Ontario has been growing grapes since the 1970s. Queen of Ontario's wine scene is the prestigious icewine-making Niagara Peninsula, north of Niagara Falls, but it isn't the only region raising a glass. Other wineries across the province are also busy paving their own way on the scene, often offering a more intimate experience for visitors. Cheers!

How to

Getting here/around It's best to drive, or hire bikes from Niagara's **Zoom Leisure Bikes** (zoomleisure.com) or Prince Edward County's **Closson Rd Cycles** (clossonroadcycles.com). Niagara-based **Cellar Door Wine Experience** (cellardoortours.ca) and **County VIP Tours** (countyviptours.com) in Prince Edward County offer expert-led winery-hopping tours.

When to go Summer is a great time, with vines blooming. September is grape-harvest season.

Bookings needed? Most larger wineries offer drop-in tastings. Book ahead for in-depth tours, especially at smaller vineyards.

Top left Pride Parade
Bottom left Church St street sign

Out and Proud in Church-Wellesley Village Often simply known as the Village, the downtown area around Church St between Gerrard and Charles Sts has been Toronto's LGBTIQ+ hub since the 1980s. You'll know you've arrived from the rainbow crosswalks and cheeky stores like **Out on the Street** (outonthestreet.ca). This is the heart of June's Pride Toronto celebrations, with stalls, parties, workshops and events, as well as a sparkling Pride Parade down Yonge St, a Trans Rally and March and a Dyke March. **O'Grady's on Church** (instagram.com/ogradysonchurch) has drag shows and a sweet outdoor patio. Later on, go dancing at **Woody's** (instagram.com/woodysonchurch) or **Crews & Tangos** (instagram.com/crewsandtangos), both with fab drag shows.

Beyond the Village There's a more low-key scene along Queen West, where you'll spot colorful 'Queer West' signs in windows. **Sweaty Betty's** (sweatybettysbar.com) on Ossington and Parkdale's **Tammy's Wine Bar** (instagram.com/tammyswinequeen) and **Three Dollar Bill** (threedollarbill.ca) are popular spots. Also here is **Glad Day** (gladday.ca), the world's oldest surviving LGBTIQ+ bookshop. Heading east, LGBTIQ-owned **Buvette Pacey** (buvettepacey.com) is a Corktown cafe-bar with a Montréal vibe.

Beach Time On sunny days, people from all over the city head to the gorgeous **Toronto Islands**, where clothing-optional, dune-fringed **Hanlan's Point Beach** has been a hub for the LGBTIQ+ community for decades. Canada's first-ever Pride gathering was held here in 1971 as the Gay Day Picnic. There's often a buzzy party atmosphere. Bring snacks and join the fun.

LGBTIQ+ Events

Many of Toronto's most fun offerings for the LGBTIQ+ community happen as inclusive pop-up events, so it's well worth checking ahead about what's on whenever you happen to be in town. **Yohomo** (yohomo.ca) curates switched-on roundups of cultural, arts and nightlife recommendations, from party nights to sober-friendly events. Held every May for over three decades, **Inside Out** (insideout.ca) is Canada's largest LGBTIQ+ film festival and hosts various other occasional events too. Toronto-based digital mag and community platform **Xtra** (xtramagazine.com) helps visitors engage with queer culture in the city and beyond.

02 Join the LGBTIQ+ PARTY

NIGHTLIFE | LGBTIQ+ CULTURE | BEACHES

Host of one of the globe's most dazzling Pride celebrations, Toronto welcomes all with rainbow flags and a fabulously good time. When Pride sashays into town each June, three million people head out to play. But it doesn't matter when you're here: from community beaches and bookshops to club nights and drag bingo in Church-Wellesley Village, there's always something happening on the LGBTIQ+ calendar.

How to

Getting here/around Take subway line 1 to Wellesley or College for the Village *(ttc.ca)*. Streetcar 501 runs along Queen St. Regular 10-minute ferries head to Hanlan's Point from downtown's **Jack Layton Ferry Terminal** *(toronto.ca)*.

When to go Late June is Pride time, though the Village and other LGBTIQ+ venues around town buzz year-round, especially on weekends.

On stage Catch a show at **Buddies in Bad Times Theatre** *(buddiesinbadtimes.com)*, the world's oldest LGBTIQ+ theater company.

(juicydumpling.shop), 24 hours a day on Friday and Saturday (until midnight otherwise). On Spadina since 1983, mural-filled **Anh Dao** (anhdaorestaurant.ca) is the spot for herby rice-paper rolls and fragrant house pho (until 11pm on weekends).

A Creative Touch Down a fluorescent-lit hallway in neighboring Kensington Market, speakeasy-vibe **Sunnys Chinese** (sunnyschinese.com) has put itself on Toronto's contemporary food map with its inventive flavors from across China (open until midnight on weekends). Try the cilantro-packed tiger salad or the zingy Sichuan-style noodles. Just steps away, **El Rey Mezcal** (elreybar.com) does a mean margarita to pair with Baja-fish tacos, until midnight.

> **Must-Try Bites**
>
> Chinatown comes to life with the glow of flicking signs at noodle shops, bars and restaurants that welcome the city's hungry nightgoers. Chinatown and neighboring Kensington Market have always been a safe landing pad for new flavors and immigrant restaurants. Nighttime in Chinatown is calmer, but with more characters. My absolute go-to favorite is the shiu mai from Rol San. The steaming yellow-lined baskets are filled with fresh, plump hot dumplings made to order each and every time. Perfect anytime, especially with a touch of their scorching chili oil. 
>
> ■ **Kevin Durkee,** *Owner and Big Cheese of Culinary Adventure Co in Toronto.* @culinaryadvco

01 Toronto's Late-Night DINING

FOOD | CULTURE | NEIGHBORHOODS

Late-night eats are something of a specialty in food-loving Toronto. Busy Chinatown – in the thick of downtown – is renowned locally for its offerings. Whether you're rolling out of an evening theater performance or refueling after a night at the clubs, join the after-hours crowd around Spadina Ave for a delectable, down-to-earth bite of the city's famously diverse food scene.

How to

Getting here/around The 501, 505 and 506 streetcars run east-west along Queen St, Dundas St and College St respectively *(ttc.ca)*. The 510 streetcar travels north-south along Spadina Ave.

When to go May to October are the best months weather-wise, especially July and August when evenings are warmer. Winter is *cold*, though a steaming bowl of noodles warms up any night.

Practical tips Some old-school restaurants don't accept card payments. The best days for late meals are Friday and Saturday.

Neighborhood History With its family-owned restaurants and bright-neon signs centered on Spadina Ave between Queen St W and College St, Toronto's main Chinatown emerged from the 1950s onwards, after residents were displaced west along Dundas St from the original Chinatown.

Digging into the Classics A third-generation Spadina staple, **Rol San** *(instagram.com/rolsan.to)* sees queues for its handmade dumplings, house sauces and steaming buns, served at plastic-cloth tables. Going until 3am on weekends, it has been dishing out all-day dim sum since the 1990s. On Dundas St, **House of Gourmet** *(instagram.com/houseofgourmet.to)* does Hong Kong–style congee, BBQ and noodles until 1am or 2am. Local faves **Mother's Dumplings** and **Yummy Yummy Dumplings** might close by 10pm, but you'll find Shanghainese pockets of goodness at nearby **Juicy Dumpling**

EATING & DRINKING

Ontario's fabulous food scene reflects its richly multicultural identity, and dining out in the big cities is a highlight. You'll find flavors from all over the world here, from French to Caribbean to Vietnamese, and there is a particularly strong line-up of Asian cuisines. As a major farming region, Ontario produces delectable cheeses and summer fruits (peaches, berries), on show at its thriving farmers markets. Beloved Ontarian staples include butter tarts (pictured top right) and peameal bacon sandwiches. Wines from Niagara (including icewines) and Prince Edward County are a treat, while Ontario-grown apples (pictured bottom right) fuel the cider scene.

Best creative Asian cuisine
Sunnys Chinese (p45)

Must-try winery
Two Sisters Vineyards (p49)

CONNECT & FIND YOUR WAY

Wi-fi Free wi-fi is readily available at hotels, restaurants, cafes and shops. That said, having your own data (ideally an e-sim) is best, particularly for navigating the big cities or road-tripping across Ontario.

Navigation Note that phone signal can be patchy (or non-existent) in some remote natural spaces, so it's best to download maps in advance for national parks and the like.

WHERE TO STAY

Place	Pros/cons
Toronto	Wide array of accommodations, but generally high prices. Big transit hub. Wonderful food, arts and culture scenes.
Niagara Wine Region	Charming B&Bs and historic hotels in Niagara-on-the-Lake. Chance of winery stays. Scenic landscapes. Limited public transport.
Ottawa	Impressive choice of accommodations for most budgets, from B&Bs to boutique hotels. Walkable and well-connected.
Kingston	Delightful, compact downtown. Access to cruises and Thousand Islands. Accommodations lean higher-end. Good transport.
Muskoka	Lake and forest scenery/tranquility. Few formal options. Some cute B&Bs and private cottage rentals.
Algonquin Provincial Park	Perfect for campers, nature lovers and wildlife-spotting. Pricey in-park resorts. Good, varied options on park's fringes.

FREE ENTRY

Most major museums and galleries offer free entry at dedicated times each week or month; check schedules ahead. Many attractions also run free guided tours.

MONEY

Once here, accommodation is likely to be your biggest cost. Book well ahead to bag the best deals and consider visiting outside the peak summer months to help the budget.

Practicalities

ARRIVING

Toronto Pearson International Airport Most travelers arrive into Toronto's main airport, from where the **UP Express** (upexpress.com) train zips to/from downtown's Union Station in 25 minutes. Some flights use the small Billy Bishop Toronto City Airport on the Toronto Islands, linked to downtown by a pedestrian tunnel or short ferry.

Ottawa Macdonald–Cartier International Airport The **OCTranspo** (octranspo.com) transit system has buses and O-Train light rail services to/from the airport.

HOW MUCH FOR A

Canoe rental from $30

Craft beer $10

Poutine $15

WHEN TO GO

JAN-MAR
The coldest, quietest time of year brings winter activities (ice skating, snowshoeing...)

APR-JUN
Spring blossoms, outdoor-dining patios open up, warmer days, Pride celebrations

JUL-SEP
Best weather for city wandering, outdoor activities and nature escapes

OCT-DEC
Fall colors in October give way to festive markets and cooler weather

GETTING AROUND

Car Renting your own wheels is the most efficient way to explore Ontario beyond its major cities, especially the national and provincial parks.

Train & subway The **VIA Rail** (via rail.ca) train network connects Toronto with Niagara Falls, Kingston, Ottawa and Montréal (among others), in addition to long-distance services traveling to/from the Canadian Rockies and Vancouver. **GO Transit** (gotransit.com) trains travel from Toronto to Niagara Falls plus several other southern-Ontario destinations. **Toronto Transit Commission** (TTC; ttc.ca) runs the city's expansive subway, streetcar and bus services. **OCTranspo** (octranspo.com) runs an extensive bus network and developing O-Train light rail that takes you across Ottawa.

Bus Services fan out across Ontario from hubs like Toronto and Ottawa. Main operators include **Flixbus** (flixbus.ca), **Megabus** (megabus.com) and **Orléans Express** (orleans express.com).

ONTARIO
Trip Builder

Learn about Indigenous cultures and art on **Manitoulin Island** (p53)
🚢 2hr from Tobermory (Bruce Peninsula)

Hike along clifftop trails in beautiful **Bruce Peninsula National Park** (p53)
🚗 4hr from Toronto

Go dancing or join the Pride fun in the **Village** (p46), Toronto's LGBTIQ+ hub
🚇 10min from Union Station

Famously multicultural Toronto (the Ontarian capital) and Canada's elegant capital city, Ottawa, anchor the most populous province in the country. Beyond the thrilling urban arts scenes, culinary cultures and dynamic neighborhoods, plunge into Ontario's vast forests, sparkling lakes and star-studded wine regions.

- ▸ **Trip Builder** (p40)
- ▸ **Practicalities** (p42)
- ▸ **Toronto's Late-Night Dining** (p44)
- ▸ **Join the LGBTIQ+ Party** (p46)
- ▸ **From Grape to Glass** (p48)
- ▸ **Life on the Lake** (p50)
- ▸ **Georgian Bay Adventure** (p52)
- ▸ **Capital Culture** (p54)
- ▸ **All-Seasons Algonquin** (p56)
- ▸ **Canoe Culture** (p58)
- ▸ **Listings** (p60)

ONTARIO

MULTICULTURAL CITIES | OUTDOORS | WINERIES

WRITTEN BY ISABELLA NOBLE; CONTRIBUTIONS BY JOEL BALSAM

WATCH

Double Happiness (Mina Shum; 1994) Sandra Oh stars in this Cantonese Canadian domestic drama.

Monsieur Lazhar (Philippe Falardeau; 2011; pictured top right) An Algerian teacher seeking asylum in Québec deals with tragedy.

Stories We Tell (Sarah Polley; 2012) A documentary of family stories by a noted Canadian director.

Schitt's Creek (Dan Levy, Eugene Levy; 2015-2020; pictured bottom right) A wealthy clan moves to a Canadian village. Comedy ensues.

North of North (Stacey Aglok MacDonald, Alethea Arnaquq-Baril; 2025) A contemporary Inuk woman's life in Canada's Arctic.

FOLLOW

Miss 604 (miss604.com) Guide featuring things to do around Vancouver.

Destination Indigenous (destinationindigenous.ca) Resources for Indigenous experiences.

Hike, Bike, Travel (hikebiketravel.com) Details for planning outdoor activities nationwide.

Traveling Canucks (travelingcanucks.com) Adventures of a traveling Canadian family.

Gurdeep Pandher (@gurdeeppandher) Yukon-based Bhangra artist dancing across the north.

Sate your Canadian dreaming with a virtual vacation

Read, Listen, Watch & Follow

 READ

Brother (David Chariandy; 2017) Sons of Trinidadian immigrants confront prejudice in metro Toronto.

The Jade Peony (Wayson Choy; 1995) A family saga set in Depression-era Vancouver Chinatown.

Five Little Indians (Michelle Good; 2020) Indigenous residential school survivors try to overcome the past.

Bone & Bread (Saleema Nawaz; 2013) Sisters, psychiatric illness, and death in Montreal's Mile End neighborhood.

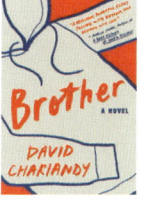

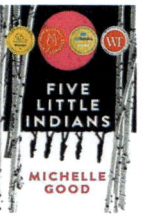
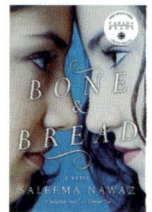

 LISTEN

Shadowland (kd lang; 1988) Debut solo album by the legendary queer Alberta-born country singer-songwriter.

Unreserved (CBC Radio; ongoing) This podcast highlights Indigenous voices across the country.

Here & There (Canadian Geographic; ongoing) A podcast sharing human stories of Canadian culture and heritage.

Fully Completely (The Tragically Hip; 1992) A classic album from this band with Kingston, Ontario roots.

Night Train (Oscar Peterson Trio; 1963; pictured above) The king of jazz piano plays standards including 'Hymn to Freedom,' which became a civil rights anthem.

5 Where to Say *Bonjour*

English and French have been Canada's two official languages since 1969. Both are taught in schools, required on product packaging, and used in anything that the federal government oversees, from airports to national parks. More than 20% of Canadians are native French speakers. French is the primary language in Québec; both New Brunswick and Ontario have significant Francophone communities.

▶ For some French lingo, see p250

6 Multiculturalism in Canada

Immigration has brought people to Canada from across the globe. Toronto, the nation's capital, is frequently considered the most multicultural city in the world. While the country has two official languages – English and French – in many places you'll be more likely to hear Mandarin, Cantonese, Punjabi, Tagalog, Vietnamese, Arabic, Spanish, or other tongues.

Unlike the US idea of a 'melting pot,' where newcomers are expected to assimilate into the American mainstream, Canadians talk about the 'mosaic,' where you can bring your own cultures and traditions into the diverse Canadian society. Canada became the first country in the world to codify its multiculturalism policy, when the nation's parliament passed the Canadian Multiculturalism Act in 1988. While prejudices and discrimination still exist, the act made it official that the country would recognize and preserve its residents' varied backgrounds and work to ensure that all receive equal treatment under the law.

7 Canadian Food Is Local Food

In such a big country with varied climate zones, ask for what grows locally and what's in season during your travels. Find out when different fish or shellfish are caught. Look for meats raised in the region, cheeses made nearby, and wines from local fruit.

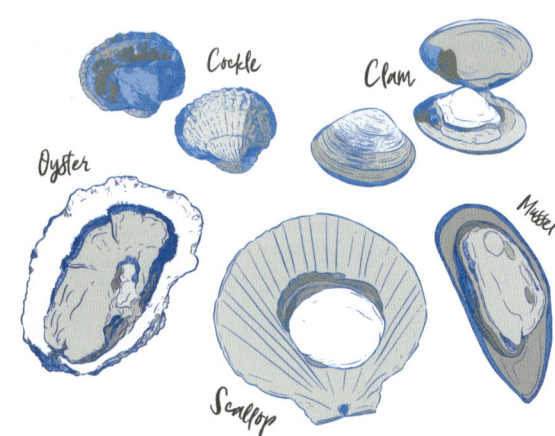

7 Things to Know About CANADA

INSIDER TIPS TO HIT THE GROUND RUNNING

1 Indigenous Cultures Are Diverse

Canada's constitution officially recognizes three Indigenous groups: First Nations, Inuit and Métis. The traditional territories of the 630 First Nations span present-day Canada, while the homelands of the Inuit, the Indigenous people of the Arctic, encompass parts of Yukon, Northwest Territories, Nunavut, Labrador and Northern Québec. Concentrated in the prairies, the Métis have a mixed Indigenous-European heritage. While communities may have similar customs or foods, their varied backgrounds have created unique cultures.

2 It's an Enormous Country

Don't expect to hop from the Pacific to the Arctic to the Atlantic in a week. The world's second largest nation covers more than 9 million sq km. If your time is short, focus on one or two regions. But with more flexibility, you can plan an epic road or rail adventure through Canada's disparate landscapes, bustling cities and small communities.

3 Sorry!

Be courteous. Canadians have a well-deserved reputation for politeness. Even if you've bumped into someone or stepped on their foot, they'll likely say 'sorry!'

4 Canada's Three Bears

Canada's most common ursine species, black bears, are found across the country. Grizzlies live in BC, Alberta and the north, while 90% of Canada's polar bears reside in Nunavut or the Northwest Territories.

1 PANJI DWI CAHYA/SHUTTERSTOCK, 2 RESERVOIR DOT/SHUTTERSTOCK, 4 GALEXS/SHUTTERSTOCK,
5 ADRESIASTOCK/SHUTTERSTOCK, 6 PENSEE SAUVAGE/SHUTTERSTOCK, 7 KIRPMUN/SHUTTERSTOCK

Iqaluit
Get acquainted with Inuit culture and with the vast region of Nunavut in its territorial capital. Visit local cultural centers, then hike across arctic tundra in Sylvia Grinnell Territorial Park.
✈ 3½hr from Ottawa

Dempster Highway
Drive this rugged roadway 740km across the Arctic Circle, navigating the remote landscapes from just east of Dawson City north to Inuvik in the Northwest Territories.

Yellowknife
See the city that gold and diamonds built, tracing its complex mining history. Rent an e-bike and pedal the 70km Ingraham Trail. Stay up late to see the northern lights.
✈ 2hr from Whitehorse

THE FAR NORTH
Trip Builder

TAKE YOUR PICK OF MUST-SEES AND HIDDEN GEMS

Why travel to Canada's far north? Journeying through the Yukon, Northwest Territories and Nunavut offers intrepid travelers Indigenous cultures, Gold Rush history, remote landscapes, and the opportunity to understand the people who live where no roads go.

Trip Notes

Hub towns Whitehorse, Yellowknife, Iqaluit

How long Allow 3 weeks

Getting around No roads connect most communities in the territories; expect to fly in. In the Yukon, the Alaska and Klondike Highways link Whitehorse, Dawson City and Haines Junction.

Tips Canada's territories offer a front-row seat for the aurora borealis. While it's easiest to see the northern lights in winter, September's lengthening nights offer a less frigid alternative.

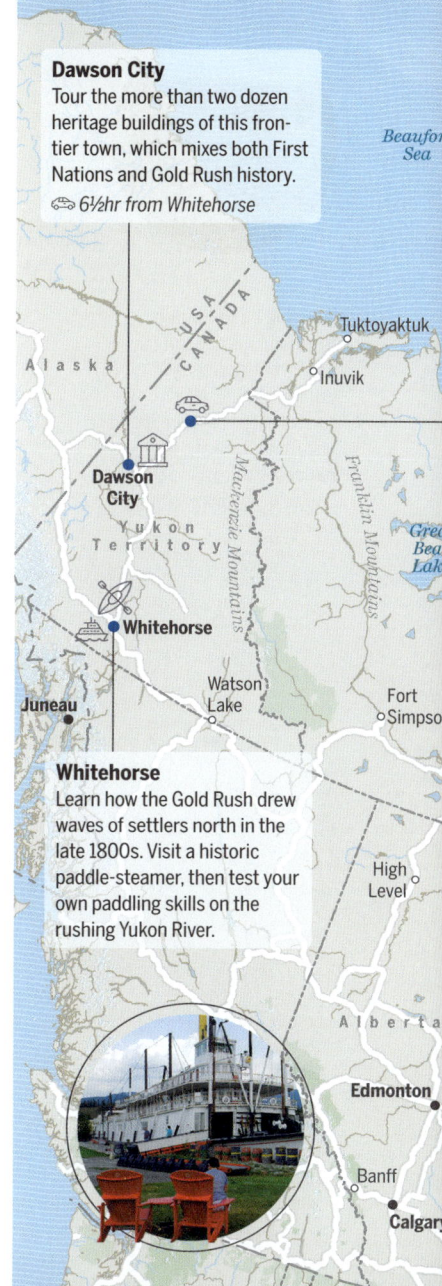

Dawson City
Tour the more than two dozen heritage buildings of this frontier town, which mixes both First Nations and Gold Rush history.
🚗 6½hr from Whitehorse

Whitehorse
Learn how the Gold Rush drew waves of settlers north in the late 1800s. Visit a historic paddle-steamer, then test your own paddling skills on the rushing Yukon River.

CLOCKWISE FROM BOTTOM LEFT: PASCAL RATEAU/SHUTTERSTOCK, SAFFRON BLAZE/GETTY IMAGES, SERGE SKIBA/SHUTTERSTOCK

Edmonton
Add an urban edge to your Rockies adventures in Alberta's capital, with its cool contemporary art gallery, excellent natural history museum, and North America's longest-running fringe theater festival.

🚗 4hr from Jasper

Banff & Lake Louise
Base yourself in Banff for hiking, hot springs, and other mountain adventures. Museums share the history of Canada's first national park, while Lake Louise is gorgeous in any season.

🚗 1½hr from Calgary

Calgary
If you're a music fan, visit Studio Bell, Canada's National Music Centre, in Calgary, the gateway to the Canadian Rockies. The annual Calgary Stampede is the city's biggest party.

Dinosaur Provincial Park
Day-trip east from Calgary to see one of the world's largest deposits of dinosaur fossils and assist scientists on a guided excavation.

🚗 2½hr from Calgary

CANADIAN ROCKIES
Trip Builder

TAKE YOUR PICK OF MUST-SEES AND HIDDEN GEMS

Turquoise lakes, glacier-topped peaks and scenic drives make the Canadian Rockies a magnet for outdoor adventurers. Beyond the don't-miss destinations of Banff, Lake Louise and Jasper, national parks like Yoho offer equally dramatic landscapes, while throughout the region, First Nations- or Métis-led experiences introduce you to Indigenous traditions.

Trip Notes

Hub towns Calgary, Banff, Edmonton
How long Allow 10 to 12 days
Getting around Calgary is the Rockies' main air hub, closest to Banff National Park. Edmonton's airport is nearest to Jasper. Having your own vehicle is most convenient, but shuttles offer car-free transport options.

Tips Reserve accommodations well in advance in Banff, which is busy year-round. Some Banff-area roads are closed to private vehicles; get transport tips from Parks Canada.

FROM LEFT: TRPHOTOS/SHUTTERSTOCK,
CAVAN IMAGES/GETTY IMAGES, AMBER BRACKEN/LONELY PLANET

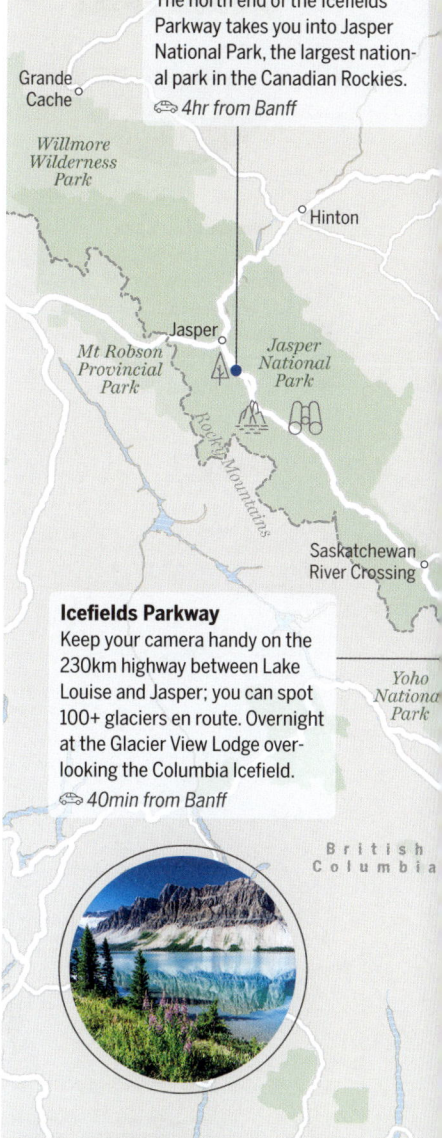

Jasper National Park
The north end of the Icefields Parkway takes you into Jasper National Park, the largest national park in the Canadian Rockies.
🚗 4hr from Banff

Icefields Parkway
Keep your camera handy on the 230km highway between Lake Louise and Jasper; you can spot 100+ glaciers en route. Overnight at the Glacier View Lodge overlooking the Columbia Icefield.
🚗 40min from Banff

Little Manitou Lake
Soak in the therapeutic, mineral-laden waters of Saskatchewan's Little Manitou Lake, where its Dead Sea–like properties keep you afloat.
🚗 1½hr from Saskatoon

Gimli
Dip into Icelandic heritage – and sample fermented shark – in this lakeside town that settlers who first arrived from Iceland in the 1870s and their descendants have long called home.
🚗 1hr from Winnipeg

Winnipeg
Visit the world's first human-rights museum for its thought-provoking exhibits, serene contemplation garden, and dramatic Tower of Hope (pictured left), then discuss the exhibitions over craft beer in the Exchange District.

PRAIRIE PROVINCES
Trip Builder

TAKE YOUR PICK OF MUST-SEES AND HIDDEN GEMS

Manitoba and Saskatchewan are Canada's heartland, pairing prairie scenery with distinctive regional experiences. Roam through expansive national parks, learn about unusual local histories, and spot bison and other wildlife.

Trip Notes

Hub towns Winnipeg, Regina, Saskatoon
How long Allow 8 to 10 days
Getting around A car is essential here.
Tips Bundle up: January through March are the best months for snowy festivals and for catching the aurora borealis.

Saskatoon
Sample the spirits at family-run Black Fox Distillery, try a flight at Crossmount Cider Company, or sip the suds at Great Western, Saskatchewan's largest brewery.
🚗 *3hr from Regina*

Grasslands National Park
Gaze at the dark skies over the prairies, wander among the wildflowers that bloom in late spring, and wonder at the hoodoos and fossils of its surreal badlands.
🚗 *3½hr from Regina*

CLOCKWISE FROM TOP LEFT: DOUGALL_PHOTOGRAPHY/GETTY IMAGES, JACOB BOOMSMA/SHUTTERSTOCK, JP MEDIA WORKS-COURTESY OF TRAVEL MANITOBA

Whistler
Ski, snowboard, snowshoe, hike, zip-line, mountain bike, ride the gondola, cross a swaying suspension bridge, or simply stroll the village in this mountain adventure hub.

🚌 2hr from Vancouver

Kelowna
Sip your way through BC's wine country, where you can also paddle the lakes and cycle among the vineyards.

🚗 4½hr from Vancouver

Vancouver
Cycle the seawall or hike the rainforest trails in Stanley Park, before hopping on the ferry to Granville Island to graze through the public market.

Osoyoos
At the Okanagan's southern end, explore British Columbia's desert and visit Canada's first Indigenous-owned winery.

🚗 4½hr from Vancouver

BRITISH COLUMBIA OUTDOORS
Trip Builder

TAKE YOUR PICK OF MUST-SEES AND HIDDEN GEMS

Learn to surf. Go hiking or mountain biking. Kayak with an Indigenous guide. Cycle through the vineyards. On the sandy Pacific beaches, the peaks of the coast mountains, the desert-like wine country, or the remote islands of Haida Gwaii, British Columbia offers all kinds of outdoor adventures.

Trip Notes

Hub town Vancouver

How long Allow 3 weeks

Getting around Buses run from Vancouver to Whistler. You can reach Tofino by bus and ferry, but having a car gives you freedom to explore. You'll want a car in the Okanagan Valley. Fly from Vancouver to Haida Gwaii, or take a ferry from Prince Rupert.

Tips Continue east from the Okanagan to Banff to extend this trip to the Canadian Rockies.

Haida Gwaii
Kayak these remote northern islands and learn about the culture of the Indigenous people who've lived here for thousands of years.
2hr from Vancouver

Tofino
On Vancouver Island's west coast, Canada's surfing capital has sandy beaches, trails through the rainforest, and excellent eateries to enjoy when you come in from the surf.
6hr from Vancouver

FROM LEFT: ELENA_ALEX_FERNS/SHUTTERSTOCK, COURTESY TOURISM WHISTLER, MICHAEL WHEATLEY/GETTY IMAGES

Twillingate
Hunt for dramatic ice formations along Newfoundland's 'Iceberg Alley.' Book a boat tour for the best viewing options.
🚢 5hr from St John's

Gros Morne National Park
Allow plenty of time to explore the fjords, unusual landscapes and hiking trails of this vast park in Western Newfoundland.
✈ 1hr from St John's

Cape Breton Island
Drive the Cabot Trail, tour North America's largest historical reconstruction site, and tap your toes to the Celtic tunes.
🚗 4hr from Halifax

St John's
Go puffin spotting outside of Newfoundland's capital. You'll find the largest colony of birds south of the city at the Witless Bay Ecological Reserve.
✈ 2hr from Halifax

Halifax
Start in Nova Scotia's capital, strolling the waterfront and checking out its historic attractions. Then drive north to Grand-Pré National Historic Site to consider the sobering Acadian heritage.

ATLANTIC CANADA
Trip Builder

TAKE YOUR PICK OF MUST-SEES AND HIDDEN GEMS

Journey to Canada's eastern reaches for dramatic tides, sandy beaches and gentle walking trails. Learn about the region's Indigenous traditions and about cultures drawing from Acadian, British and Gaelic influences. Savor the seafood, including lobster rolls and fresh oysters, and sample only-in-Newfoundland dishes.

Trip Notes

Hub towns Halifax, St John's

How long Allow 3 weeks

Getting around Halifax is Atlantic Canada's main transport hub. You can reach New Brunswick or PEI from here, then catch the ferry from North Sydney, Nova Scotia, to explore Newfoundland. You need your own vehicle to get around the Atlantic region.

Tips Reserve a rental car as early as possible. Remember: Newfoundland time is 30 minutes ahead of the Maritime provinces.

Acadian Coast
Explore the culture of the francophone communities along New Brunswick's Acadian Coast. Try to schedule your trip during the Festival Acadien de Caraquet and join the revelry.
🚗 *3hr from Moncton*

Prince Edward Island
Follow Anne of Green Gables' legacy around Cavendish, participate in a cooking or craft workshop with the Lennox Island First Nation, and catch lobster or tong for oysters near Souris.
🚗 *3½hr from Halifax*

Bay of Fundy
Marvel at the world's highest tides at Hopewell Rocks Provincial Park in New Brunswick.
🚗 *3hr from Halifax*

FROM LEFT: CHIYACAT/SHUTTERSTOCK, J DUQUETTE/SHUTTERSTOCK, WINDCOAST/SHUTTERSTOCK

Ottawa
Tour the parliament buildings in Canada's national capital, then visit the country's grand museums. Don't miss the National Gallery of Canada, in a spectacular granite-and-glass building overlooking the Ottawa River.
🚗🚆 4½hr from Toronto

Montréal
Creative cuisine and buzzy bars, including a lively LGBTIQ+ scene, are highlights in this mod francophone metropolis, where festival after festival enlivens daily life.
🚗🚆 2hr from Ottawa

Québec City
Travel to the 1600s in Québec City, as you wander beneath the stone walls of the once-fortified city and learn about the British-French battles important to Canada's early history.
🚗🚆 3hr from Montréal

Kingston
Stroll among the limestone buildings of Canada's first capital and visit the bustling Public Market in this university town on the St Lawrence River.
🚗🚆 3hr from Toronto

Prince Edward County
Cycle among the vineyards and savor fine contemporary cuisine in Prince Edward County, one of Ontario's main wine-making regions.
🚗 2½hr from Toronto

ONTARIO & QUÉBEC
Trip Builder

TAKE YOUR PICK OF MUST-SEES AND HIDDEN GEMS

Immerse in Canadian heritage and urban life in Ontario and Québec, the country's most populous provinces. Travel back in time in historic Québec City, tour the capital of Ottawa, and dive into the modern era in sophisticated Montréal and diverse Toronto, with lush vineyards and canoe culture along the way.

Trip Notes

Hub towns Toronto, Ottawa, Montréal

How long Allow 10 to 12 days

Getting around Trains and buses connect major cities in Ontario and Québec, while urban transit systems let you travel car-free. For smaller towns, a car is more convenient.

Tips From Toronto, it's an easy day-trip to Niagara Falls and to the wineries of Niagara-on-the-Lake. Have more time? From Québec City, rent a car and road trip the scenic Gaspé Peninsula.

Toronto
Wander the varied neighborhoods, ponder the museums of art and culture, and chill on the beach on the offshore islands around Canada's largest city.

Peterborough
Visit the Canadian Canoe Museum, which houses the world's largest collection of canoes, kayaks and paddled watercraft. Its exhibits illustrate these boats' importance in both Indigenous and settler cultures.
🚗🚆 *2hr from Toronto*

FROM LEFT: BENEDEK/GETTY IMAGES, JOSEPH S L TAN MATT/SHUTTERSTOCK, ADELE HEIDENREICH/SHUTTERSTOCK

Don't Bug Me

Mosquitoes and black flies can swarm in northern Ontario, Québec and Labrador. Bring a bug net for spring outdoor activities.

FROM LEFT: JSA PHOTO/SHUTTERSTOCK, SIMONAKOZ/SHUTTERSTOCK, SEBASTIEN MARIE/SHUTTERSTOCK, PUGALENTHI INIABARATHI/SHUTTERSTOCK, NIKITA BURDENKOV/SHUTTERSTOCK
BACKGROUND: GARY A CORCORAN ARTS/SHUTTERSTOCK

↘ Beach Days Ahead

Kicking off summer, seasonal attractions begin to open around the Victoria Day holiday, unofficially known as 'May Long Weekend.'

↖ Tulip Time

Did you know tulips thrive in Canada? Ottawa welcomes spring at the Canadian Tulip Festival, the world's largest tulip fête.

↖ Iceberg Spotting

Late spring is the season to go iceberg spotting along the coasts of Newfoundland and Labrador.

MAY

Average daytime max: 11°C
Days of rainfall or snow: 12

Average daytime max: 18°C
Days of rainfall: 13

Be prepared for snow in the Rockies and other mountain regions as late as May or June, especially at higher elevations.

🧳 Packing Notes

Bring layers for changeable weather, especially in the mountains, where snow can linger.

CANADA PLAN BY SEASON

→ Spring Blossoms

Spring comes early on the British Columbia coast, with flowers blooming across Vancouver and Victoria beginning in March.

↖ Maple Syrup Season

Sample fresh syrup and maple treats during maple sugaring season at the 'sugar shacks' in Québec and Ontario.

Spring in Nunavut

Iqaluit's Toonik Tyme Festival in April marks the sun's springtime return with Inuit cultural celebrations and traditional games.

MARCH

Average daytime max: 5°C
Days of rainfall or snow: 11

APRIL

Canada in SPRING

Westcoasters don't let winter showers keep them indoors; don good rain gear, carry an umbrella and get outside.

↓ Art, Culture & Food
Theater, music and other events, including Dine Out Vancouver, Canada's biggest food and drink fest, keep cities lively in winter.

Prepare for Snow
Driving through the mountains? Make sure you have winter tires October to March and that you're comfortable in snowy conditions.

↖ Illuminating Winter
Laugh at the cold in Québec, where Montréal en Lumière is one of the world's largest winter festivals.

Average daytime max: -1°C
Days of rainfall or snow: 9

FEBRUARY

Average daytime max: -1°C
Days of rainfall or snow: 9

Many attractions in coastal Atlantic Canada and in the north close during the cold winter months, from November through April.

Packing Notes
Stay warm: insulated jackets, snow pants, hats, mittens, boots. Bring raingear for the Pacific coast.

Ski and snowboard resorts open in November or December, with the season in some locations extending into April.

↓ **Northern Lights**
Travel to the far north to marvel at the aurora borealis, which is occasionally visible further south.

↗ **Bargain Hunting**
The day after Christmas, Boxing Day is a popular shopping day, with many stores offering sales.

DECEMBER

Average daytime max: 2°C
Days of rainfall or snow: 10

JANUARY

Canada in WINTER

↓ Look Skyward

Stargazers head to Jasper, a designated Dark Sky Preserve, for the October Dark Sky Festival.

On the Pacific coast, winter rains begin by November, when cold and snow sweep in elsewhere.

↖ East Coast in Autumn

Popular Atlantic Canada events include Cape Breton's Celtic Colours International Festival and PEI's Fall Flavours Festival.

📍 Cape Breton Island
▶ celtic-colours.com; p92

NOVEMBER

Average daytime max: 15°C
Days of rainfall: 12

Average daytime max: 8°C
Days of rainfall or snow: 10

Trees take on brilliant colors, especially in Ontario and Québec, and the larches glow golden in the Canadian Rockies.

Packing Notes

Dress for crisp days and cool nights. By November, you'll need cold weather gear.

Though summer is Canada's peak season, many Canadians will tell you the weather is best in September and early October.

↓ When Toronto Glitters

Celebrities shine during the annual Toronto International Film Festival (TIFF) in September, featuring the year's newest movies.

↖ 'Orange Shirt Day'

National Day for Truth and Reconciliation (September 30) honors Indigenous children who survived residential schools and remembers those who didn't.

↘ Give Thanks

Canadians celebrate Thanksgiving in October with turkey, pie and family time, with less hoopla than the United States' November holiday.

SEPTEMBER — Average daytime max: 22°C / Days of rainfall: 10 — **OCTOBER**

Canada in AUTUMN

↓ Top Summer Festivals

Summer highlights include the Montréal International Jazz Festival, Toronto Caribbean Carnival (pictured below), Winnipeg's Folklorama, Calgary Stampede and Vancouver Folk Music Festival.

Should You Celebrate?

On Canada Day, many Indigenous people and their allies acknowledge the harm that settlers caused to the original inhabitants.

↑ Canadian Pride

Celebrating the LGBTIQ+ community, Canada's largest Pride fests take place in Toronto (June), Vancouver (July/August), and Montréal (July/August; pictured above).

AUGUST

Average daytime max: 27°C
Days of rainfall: 11

Average daytime max: 26°C
Days of rainfall: 10

Demand for accommodations peaks in summer. View tours and overnight adventures in advance at lonelyplanet.com.

Packing Notes

Pack sunscreen, lightweight rain gear, insect repellent for the forests, prairies, mountains and eastern coasts.

July and August are the busiest months across the country. Costs are highest, but weather is warm to hot everywhere.

↑ Francophone Fests
Saint-Jean-Baptiste Day (June) celebrates French culture in Québec, while Acadians party in New Brunswick during August's Festival Acadien de Caraquet.

↘ Indigenous Cultural Events
National Indigenous Peoples Day, held on the summer solstice, recognizes the contributions of the First Nations, Métis and Inuit Peoples.

↑ Canada Day
The nation marks its 'birth' on Canada Day (July 1), with Ottawa hosting the country's biggest party.

JUNE   Average daytime max: 24°C   **JULY**
Days of rainfall: 11

Canada in SUMMER

ISLAND ADVENTURES

Canada may not have palm trees and Caribbean waters, but the country does have thousands of islands that you can explore. Some, like Vancouver Island on the Pacific or PEI in the east, are known for their sandy beaches, while others offer outdoor adventures or unique cultural experiences.

Best Island Experiences

▶ Ride the waves in Tofino, Canada's surfing capital. (p200)

▶ Escape to Les Îles-de-la-Madeleine, Québec's remote island getaway. (p78)

▶ Hike and bike on Beausoleil Island in Ontario's Georgian Bay Islands National Park. (p53)

▶ Dive into the fictional world of *Anne of Green Gables* on Prince Edward Island. (p120)

▶ Explore an island off an island – Newfoundland's Fogo Island. (p144)

↙ CANADA'S LARGEST ISLAND

Measuring more than 500,000 sq km, Nunavut's remote Baffin Island is the country's biggest island and the fifth largest island in the world.

DID YOU KNOW...?
The Thousand Islands dot the St Lawrence River between Ontario and the US border, but further north, Georgian Bay has more than 30,000 islands.

Above Surfer, Tofino (p200)
Left Marshy landscape along the Akshayuk Pass Route (p234), Baffin Island

INDIGENOUS PEOPLES

About 1.8 million Indigenous people live in Canada, comprising about 5% of the total population.

First Nations, Métis and Inuit Peoples speak roughly 70 different languages.

More than 150,000 Indigenous children were forced to attend government-sanctioned residential schools.

Best Indigenous Experiences

▶ Absorb Haida heritage as you kayak the islands of Haida Gwaii. (p206)

▶ Learn about Métis culture at Indigenous-run Métis Crossing. (p189)

▶ Hike Manitoulin Island, the traditional territory of six First Nations. (p53)

▶ Watch Mi'kmaq birchbark canoe construction in Kejimkujik National Park. (p97)

▶ Visit Iqaluit for an introduction to modern Inuit life. (pictured above; p230)

INDIGENOUS CULTURES

Indigenous Peoples have lived in present-day Canada for more than 10,000 years, establishing distinct and still-thriving cultures. A growing number of experiences highlight Indigenous foods, traditions and practices of the northern Inuit communities, the Métis of the prairies, and the more than 600 First Nations across the land. Acknowledge whose land you're visiting and take time to learn more.

EYEEM MOBILE GMBH/GETTY IMAGES

DINING & DRINKING

An array of regional specialties reflects Canada's cultural makeup, from Indigenous food traditions to the cuisines of the many settlers – British, French, Chinese, Ukrainian, Syrian, Haitian and others – who call this country home. Poutine in Québec, salmon on the west coast, or moose burgers in Newfoundland – it's all deliciously Canadian.

DRINK LIKE A CANUCK
Try Québec's *cidre de glace* (ice cider). Sip spirits brewed from Saskatchewan's harvests. Down a Caesar where it was created, in Calgary.

Best Eating & Drinking

▶ Shop for local cheese, artisanal charcuterie, and baked goods at Vancouver's Granville Island Public Market. (p202)

▶ Sample the wineries of BC's Okanagan Valley or Ontario's Niagara region. (p208 & p48)

▶ Graze through Toronto's Chinatown or join a food tour to explore the city's delectable diversity. (p44)

▶ Seek out Montréal's best poutine and smoked meat. (p82)

▶ Catch your dinner at sea or in the sand on Prince Edward Island. (p124)

↙ ONLY IN...
In Newfoundland, breakfast on *toutons* – fried dough with molasses. In New Brunswick, sample Acadian specialties. In the north, try *muktuk* bites (whale blubber).

Above Poutine **Left** *Muktuk* bites (whale blubber)

SNOW FACTS

British Columbia's Whistler-Blackcomb is Canada's largest ski area.

Opened in 1926, Banff's Mt Norquay was the first ski resort in the Canadian Rockies.

The northern lights are visible in the Northwest Territories an average of 240 nights per year.

SNOW SEASON

▬▬ Bundle up! From Québec's Laurentian Mountains to the Canadian Rockies to Whistler in the west, winter in Canada means playing in the snow. Whether you're snowboarding down a steep mountain trail, exploring the woods on snowshoes or cross-country skis, or marveling as the northern lights sweep across the sky, Canada's coldest months offer plenty of adventures.

Best Snow Experiences

▶ **Get oriented to Whistler's trails with a guided snowshoeing experience.** (pictured above; p204)

▶ **Dance in the snow at festive Carnaval de Québec.** (p83)

▶ **Soak in Banff's soothing hot springs as the snow falls.** (p183)

▶ **Go dogsledding with reputable guiding companies in Ontario.** (p57)

MARINA POUSHKINA/SHUTTERSTOCK

→ ON THE FRINGE

While Edmonton hosts North America's longest-running fringe fest, you'll find these contemporary theater festivals in cities nationwide, including Toronto, Vancouver, Winnipeg, Ottawa and Halifax.

▶ More on the Edmonton International Fringe Theatre Festival on p180

Left Cycling along Vancouver's seawall **Right** Winnipeg Fringe Theatre Festival **Below** 2010 Winter Olympics, Whistler (p204)

TORONTO'S CHINATOWNS

Toronto's Chinatown was established downtown in 1878. The city now has several more 'Chinatowns' – in East Toronto and in suburban Markham, Richmond Hill and Scarborough.

▶ Explore Toronto's Chinatown on p44

↑ SPORTY LOCALES

Canada hosted the Olympic Games three times: the 1976 Summer Games in Montréal, 1988 Winter Games in Calgary, and 2010 Winter Olympics, held jointly in Vancouver and Whistler.

▶ For more on Whistler, see p204

Best Urban Experiences

▶ See what's on stage at the eclectic Edmonton International Fringe Theatre Festival. (p180)

▶ Visit the Canadian Museum for Human Rights in Winnipeg, the first of its kind in the world. (p160)

▶ Let Québec-born Cirque du Soleil wow you under the Big Top in Montréal. (p80)

▶ Celebrate the LGBTIQ+ community at the dazzling Toronto Pride celebrations. (p46)

▶ Follow the Taproom Trail in Fredericton, New Brunswick's craft-beer capital. (p112)

CITY STATS

In multicultural Toronto, the racialized population accounts for more than 50% of the city's residents.

Montréal's annual Pride parade is the largest LGBTIQ+ gathering in the francophone world.

Vancouver's seawall is the world's longest uninterrupted waterfront path.

URBAN
CANADA

Canada's three largest cities – multicultural Toronto, chic Montréal and outdoorsy Vancouver – couldn't feel more different, yet together, they reflect the diversity of Canadian metropolitan life. You can embrace cowboy traditions in Calgary, wander the European-style streets of historic Québec City, or snap photos of St John's colorful Jellybean Row. Museums, theatre, vibrant cultural communities – Canada's cities have all that and more, with a specifically Canadian perspective.

→ GO THE DISTANCE

Want an epic adventure? Consider long-distance hiking routes like BC's Sunshine Coast Trail, Ontario's Bruce Trail or Newfoundland's East Coast Trail.

Left Banff National Park (p182)
Right Bruce Trail (p52) **Below** Moose

BE PREPARED

Wear sturdy hiking shoes or boots. Carry water, snacks, sun protection and insect repellent. Pack a trail map; some areas don't have cell service.

Best Hiking

▶ Choose among the 1600km of hiking trails in the mountains of Banff National Park. (p182)

▶ Trek through the wilderness amid dramatic white cliffs in Ontario's Killarney Provincial Park. (p53)

▶ Tromp across the network of gorgeous alpine hiking paths at Whistler. (p204)

▶ Circle coastal PEI on the Island Walk, a 700km walking and cycling route. (p128)

▶ Challenge the trails through the Arctic-alpine environment of Newfoundland's Gros Morne Mountain. (p143)

↑ WHAT ABOUT WILDLIFE?

Bears, cougars, moose and other animals are found across Canada. Research what lives where you're hiking and what to do if you encounter wildlife.

THE GREAT TRAIL
Dubbed 'the Great Trail', the Trans Canada Trail currently extends more than 27,000km through every province and territory. It's the longest multi-use trail system in the world.

ON THE TRAILS

Canada's hiking trails are as varied as its geography, from gentle coastal meanders to steep mountain treks. With their snow-topped peaks and glacial lakes, the Canadian Rockies rank among the country's premier hiking destinations. You can also hike through Ontario's forests, explore unusual landscapes in Newfoundland, circle an entire island on PEI, or tackle numerous pathways through the national, provincial and territorial parks.

Columbia Icefield Skywalk (p185)

Built on Gold & Diamonds	226
Journey into the Arctic	228
A Taste of Nunavut	230
Listings	234

Practicalities	236
Arriving	238
Getting Around	240
Safe Travel	242
Money	243
Responsible Travel	244
Accommodations	246
Essentials	248
Language	250

ESSAYS

Canoe Culture	58
Circus City	80
Fishing for a Living	98
Canada's Potato Capital	130
A Way with Words	148
Seeds of Community	168
Indigenous Culture in Alberta	188
Exploring BC Responsibly	210
Indigenous Culture in the Territories	232

VISUAL GUIDES

Québec Symbols	72
Alberta Giants of the Prairies	190
Wildlife Roundup	212

Land Acknowledgement

Lonely Planet respectfully acknowledges that Canada is the traditional territory of more than 630 First Nations communities as well as Inuit and Métis communities. We offer gratitude to the Indigenous Peoples for their care for, and teachings about, this land.

Contents

Best Experiences 6
Calendar 14
Trip Builder 22
7 Things to Know
About Canada 34
Read, Listen, Watch
& Follow 36

Ontario 38
Toronto's Late-Night
Dining................................ 44
Join the
LGBTIQ+ Party 46
From Grape to Glass 48
Life on the Lakes 50
Georgian Bay
Adventure 52
Capital Culture 54
All-Seasons
Algonquin 56
Listings 60

Québec 62
LGBTIQ+ Montréal............ 68
Historic Québec City........ 70
Outdoors
Les Laurentides................74
Road Trip Gaspésie 76
Escape to Les Îles-de-
la-Madeleine.....................78
Listings 82

Nova Scotia 84
Founders' Tour.................. 90
Celtic Colours 92
The Cliffs of Fundy 94

Indigenous
Art & Culture 96
Listings 100

New Brunswick 102
Your Floating Hotel 106
Dynamic
Coastal Parks 108
Make a Great Din............. 110
Taproom Trail................... 112
Listings 114

Prince Edward Island 116
Follow the
Green Gables Story 120
Experience Indigenous
Culture 122
How to
Catch Your Dinner 124
PEI's National Park
Beaches...........................126
Walk the Island Walk 128
Listings 132

Newfoundland & Labrador 134
Clowns of the Sea 140
Park Pleasures 142
An Island off an Island 144
Glacial Giants 146
Listings 150

Manitoba & Saskatchewan 152
Flavors of the
Prairies.............................158

A Monument to
Human Rights 160
Plains of the Prairies.......162
New Icelandic
Horizons..........................164
Canada's Dead Sea.........166
Listings 170

Alberta 172
Celebrate Calgary
Stampede........................178
Fringe Theatre
Festival............................ 180
Canada's Oldest
National Park...................182
The World's Most
Scenic Road.....................184
Dinosaur Provincial
Park..................................186
Listings 192

British Columbia 194
Catch Tofino Waves.........200
Granville Island
Like a Local 202
Wintery Whistler 204
Indigenous Shores
of Haida Gwaii 206
Sip Through the
Okanagan 208
Listings 214

The Territories 216
Whitehorse
& the Yukon River 222
Dawson's
Gold Rush History...........224

Puffins, Witless Bay Ecological Reserve (p141)

CANADA MEET OUR WRITERS

Kelsey Olsen
@kelseyolsen

Visiting Tonquin Beach (p201) feels like escaping to a private cove. As you venture through the towering old-growth forest, the sound of waves crashing against the shore grows louder and louder. Wooden boardwalks offer glimpses of the sandy shoreline until you reach a clearing that opens onto the golden sand. It's the perfect place to linger, watch shorebirds, beachcomb, and enjoy the fading sunset alongside locals.

Darcy Rhyno
@rhynopics

Darcy's lifetime living in Nova Scotia and exploring Atlantic Canada makes it difficult to choose a favourite experience, but houseboating on the St John River (p106) is among his top picks. 'Floating about with half a dozen friends, making up the itinerary of stops as you soak in the rooftop hot tub feels both liberating and decadent.'

Brendan Sainsbury
X @sainsburyb

Brendan has long nurtured a fascination with Jack London and the Klondike gold rush, and he never tires of visiting Dawson City. Small and attractive while, at the same time, hardnosed and authentic, its historical core has been masterfully preserved for posterity by Parks Canada. You can almost feel the ghostly presence of London and his stampeding sidekicks roaming the streets.

Barbara Woolsey
@xo.babxi

Visiting the Canadian Museum for Human Rights (p160) in Winnipeg, Barbara felt proud to be a Canadian – and even more so, to come from the Prairies. Western Canada often gets overshadowed within such a vast country. Seeing progressive values being championed in the heartland is incredible.

PREVIOUS SPREAD: SENTIER DES CIMES (P75), VINCENT JIANG/SHUTTERSTOCK